Psychoanalytic Concepts of Depression

Psychoanalytic Concepts of Depression

Second Edition

Myer Mendelson, M.D.

The University of Pennsylvania
and The Institute of the Pennsylvania Hospital
Philadelphia, Pennsylvania

S P Books Division of
SPECTRUM PUBLICATIONS, INC.
Flushing, New York

Distributed by Halsted Press
A Division of John Wiley & Sons
New York   Toronto   London   Sydney

To

Peggy
and
Sarah

Spectrum Publications, Inc.
75-31 192 Street, Flushing, N.Y. 11366

Distributed solely by the Halsted Press division of John Wiley & Sons, Inc., New York

Printed in the United States of America

Library of Congress Cataloging in Publication Data

Mendelson, Myer.
  Psychoanalytic concepts of depression.

  Bibliography: p.
  1. Depression, Mental. 2. Melancholia.
3. Psychoanalysis. I. Title. [DNLM: 1. Depression.
2. Psychoanalytic interpretation. WM207 M539p]
RC537.M46 1974 616.8'528 74-17332
ISBN 0-470-59355-5

Preface To Second Edition

ONE CANNOT BE HUMAN without having experienced depression at some point in life. All people have had occasion to experience, in their own idiosyncratic, subjective ways, the subtle nuances of depressed feelings and moods. Grief, sadness, pessimism, unhappiness, loneliness, emptiness and a host of other such terms are the labels with which men and women try to convey the flavor of their depressed feelings. But there has been an increasing awareness of the differences between depressed feelings, moods or symptoms and the depressive states or illnesses which are the subject of this volume.

With Gallic expressiveness, Nacht and Racamier (1960) refer to the study of depression as leading "to the centre of the fundamental drama that troubles the heart of man." This is quite true in the sense that one cannot study or treat the depressive disorders without confronting the themes of love and hate, normal dependency and devouring neediness and the fundamental aspirations, the fulfillment of which represent the foundations of self-esteem and psychic well-being. The study of depressed states introduces the clinician into some of the most powerful emotions and the most searing agonies that characterize the human condition.

The first edition of this work was submitted for publication fifteen years ago. In its concluding section I wrote: "This book represents the summary of an era. This era was chiefly characterized by boldly speculative theoretical formulations and by insightful clinical studies. It was a richly productive era in which sensitive and intuitive observers mapped out whole continents of the mind that had previously been unexplored. It was an era of large-scale conceptualizations and generalizations."

I predicted at the time that the coming years would see an increasing number of clinical and biological investigations. I believe that this prediction has been borne out.

In the first chapter I have carried my story forward to include the clinical and statistical psychiatric studies that have poured in an ever-increasing flood from the hospitals, clinics and the university departments of psychiatry. I have briefly referred to the psychopharmacological and neurophysiological advances in the first and last chapters of this revised edition. I believe that at some point during the last fifteen years, psychiatry advanced from a prescientific to a scientific stage in its evolution.

The psychoanalytic edifice that was so brilliantly and painstakingly constructed through the years since Abraham and Freud turned their thoughts to the problem of melancholia still stands. The psychoanalytic additions to the theory of depression during the last decade and a half have, with the exceptions noted below, been relatively minor. They mainly represent clinical confirmation of what one or another of the great theorists had sketched out in their broadly conceived formulations.

There have, however, been some major contributions in the form of long series of publications written by Sandler and his collaborators, by Beck and by Bowlby. Each of these have approached their subjects via an empirically motivated rethinking of classic psychoanalytic themes. Sandler and his colleagues, by the very nature of their well-known attempt to index the clinical material at the Hampstead Child Therapy Clinic in London, have had to analyze and reformulate many of the clinical and metapsychological concepts that confronted them in their indexing task. I have in this revised version given their work the attention that I believe it deserves.

Beck, as a consequence of clinical studies of very broad scope, has drawn attention to a largely neglected area of clinical observation, namely, the cognitive distortions that are found in this group of illnesses which have traditionally been referred to as the affective disorders, with the noncognitive implications inherent in this term.

Bowlby has concerned himself with a thoroughgoing study of attachment, separation and mourning behavior in children temporarily removed from their homes. In the process, he has recast some classical psychoanalytic theories in a manner derived from

ethological studies, though there have been psychoanalytic prece-
dents for some of his views. His study of mourning behavior in
children then led me to review and evaluate the literature on
mourning and depression in childhood, a topic that was omitted
from the previous version of this book.

As I noted in the first edition, psychoanalytic theory on depression has kept pace through the years with the general body of
psychoanalytic theory. The last fifteen years have been characterized by an accelerating volume of criticism of certain traditional
concepts in psychoanalytic theory. It has been a period of careful
conceptual analysis of a variety of constructs which long passed as
legitimate currency in a too uncritical and careless fashion. This
body of criticism was intended to reexamine and reformulate
these concepts in a more precise and acceptable fashion.

I have attempted, in a rather metapsychological chapter, to
subject psychoanalytic theory on depression to a searching analysis from the perspective of these critiques that have appeared so
abundantly in the psychoanalytic journals. This metapsychological
chapter, as Smith (1971) wryly noted in a different connection, "is
the sort of thing which interests people who are interested in that
sort of thing." Since this task of conceptual analysis of psychoanalytic theories of depression had not been attempted before, I
felt that it was appropriate to do so in this critical review of depression.

And, finally, in a tentative, speculative way, I have cautiously
suggested an approach that might serve as a first step in an inter-
weaving of the psychoanalytic and biological concepts of depression.

I wish to express my appreciation to Dr. Sydney Pulver and to
Dr. Allan B. Wells for giving generously of their time in reading
parts of this book. Their advice and criticisms were most helpful.
Needless to say, they bear no responsibility for whatever defects
undoubtedly remain.

I wish to express my loving indebtedness to my wife and to my
daughter who have accepted so tolerantly my absorption in this
time consuming task of revision.

I am especially grateful to Mrs. June Strickland, the medical
librarian of the Institute of the Pennsylvania Hospital, who has
provided so generously of her time and her interest.

A final note of appreciation is due to the superb psychiatric
library of the Institute of the Pennsylvania Hospital, the quality

of which owes so much to Mrs. Strickland and to her predecessors.

Wynnewood, Pennsylvania
May 1974   M.M.

Preface To First Edition*

DESPITE SEVERAL HISTORICAL REVIEWS of depression, there has as yet been no survey of this subject comprehensive enough to place recent developments in theory in their proper perspective. Zilboorg (1941a) devoted comparatively little space to depression in his history. Aubrey Lewis' (1934a) scholarly study of the concept of melancholia up to 1930 did not neglect psychoanalytic contributions, but his summary of them was relatively cursory as was his treatment of Adolf Meyer's views and influence. Lewin (1950) included a brief literary and historical survey of depression in his book *The Psychoanalysis of Elation,* but his interest was of course primarily in the euphoric and excited pole of the manic-depressive dichotomy. Bellak's (1952) summary of the psychoanalytic contributions to the theory of manic-depressive psychosis was also relatively brief. Perhaps Garma's (1947) was the most detailed psychoanalytic review of a historical type, whereas Fenichel's (1945) chapter on the subject in his textbook remains the most comprehensive and authoritative exposition of the Freudian concepts of depression up to the time of his survey. But none of these reviews has attempted to study in any meaningfully critical way the pattern of the historical development that has led to the present still imperfect understanding of this problem.

This is the task that I have set myself in this study. I have not undertaken to propose any new theory of depression. I have instead confined myself to the critical examination of the concept of depression as it has evolved and as it prevails today.

To help the reader follow my treatment of this theme I believe

*Mendelson, Myer, *Psychoanalytic Concepts of Depression.* Springfield, Ill.: Charles C. Thomas, 1960.

a brief preliminary sketch would be helpful. Although this book is primarily devoted to a consideration of psychoanalytic concepts of depression, there is an introductory chapter relating these psycho-dynamic theories to the broader field of clinical psychiatry. In this chapter, after reference is made to the pre-Kraepelinian thought on the subject of depression, the Kraepelinian contribution is dealt with together with subsequent European and American developments.

In the next two chapters I have presented the theoretical models of the psychoanalytic workers who have contributed most to the theory on depression. These writers are Abraham, Freud, Rado, Gero, Melanie Klein, Bibring, Edith Jacobson and Mabel Blake Cohen and her colleagues, as well as authors whose contributions have been of lesser importance. I have presented the views of these writers in roughly chronological order and have tried to show how at every point their theories were rooted in what had been developed previously and at the same time were subtly shaped by contemporary psychoanalytic theory.

In the next chapter* attention is focused on specific themes in the development of this body of theory. The perspective here is cross-sectional rather than longitudinal as in the preceding two chapters. The themes considered are constitutional and psychological factors predisposing to depression, the question of whether there is a central anxiety situation in human development and its relation to depression and the role that obsessional elements, aggression, orality and introjective mechanisms play in depression.

This chapter is followed by one on diagnostic considerations in which relatively neglected aspects of this subject are considered. In this chapter an attempt is made to emphasize the variety of depressive reactions, and to stress the implications of this in any theory of depression.

The next chapter** is one in which the psychoanalytic literature on treatment of depression is carefully and critically reviewed.

A concluding chapter then follows in which I reflect on the scientific workmanship of this body of psychoanalytic literature from the point of view both of its accomplishments and of its failings. I finally attempt to distill the most convincingly documented facts and ideas from the theoretical and empirical literature which I have reviewed.

*Chapter V of this edition.
**Chapter VIII of this edition.

Acknowledgments
for First Edition

I WISH TO EXPRESS my gratitude and indebtedness to a number of teachers, colleagues and friends whose encouragement, advice and interest were very important to me in connection with this book: Dr. John C. Whitehorn, professor of psychiatry at Johns Hopkins, whose kindly and generous encouragement prompted the expansion of what was a brief paper into a full-length study; Dr. Kenneth E. Appel, professor of psychiatry at the University of Pennsylvania, who provided the impetus and the enthusiasm which eventually led to the publication of this manuscript.

I am especially grateful to Dr. Albert J. Stunkard of the University of Pennsylvania for his continuing interest and for his generously given encouragement, help and advice. His sensitive and thoughtful suggestions in matters of style, content and philosophy were invaluable to me.

I am also indebted to Dr. John Imboden of Johns Hopkins and to Dr. Frederick Ziegler, now of La Jolla, California, for their interest in reading large sections of the manuscript prior to its publication.

I wish to acknowledge a special debt to three friends who have helped to shape my thinking in psychiatry and whose influence is consequently woven into the structure of this book: Dr. Robert O. Jones of Dalhousie University, Halifax, Nova Scotia, who taught me an orientation to psychiatry that is, in its essentials, unchanged to this day; Dr. Eugene Meyer of Johns Hopkins with whom, for several years, there has been a continuing and stimulating exchange of ideas; Dr. Solomon Hirsch of Dalhousie University, with whom I have had so many long, exciting discussions about psychiatry and about life.

Finally, I am deeply grateful to Mrs. Betty Brewer for her patient and careful preparation of this manuscript. Her interest, forbearance and good humor were beyond the call of duty.

Acknowledgment is due to the editors of *The Bulletin of the Maritime Psychological Association* and *The British Journal of Medical Psychology* for material previously published and reutilized in this book.

M.M.

Contents

Psychoanalytic Concepts of Depression

Chapter I

INTRODUCTION

THIS PRESENT STUDY begins in the decade around the turn of the century. It was in this period that Kraepelin, Meyer and Freud began to develop the theories that in one way or another were destined to influence psychiatric thinking so decisively. Now, over seventy years since these workers first began to apply their integrative and intuitive genius to the understanding of human behavior, we are beginning to gain some insight into the reverberating depths of this complex subject.

One question that has always engrossed the attention of those who have studied the depressed states has been how the various kinds of depression are related to one another. It was Kraepelin's attempt to solve this riddle that ushered in the modern period of psychiatric thought. It was this enigma that preoccupied the German students of the problem for the first twenty-five years of this century, and the English clinical psychiatrists for the next twenty-five years. And it does not now fail to engage the attention of the present writer.

To appreciate the intellectual atmosphere in the psychiatric world of the 1890's, the time when this study begins, it is worthwhile to take note of the subjects which drew forth comment from Adolf Meyer, who was to do so much to revolutionize and humanize American psychiatry. In 1895, in *A Review of the Signs of Degeneration and of Methods of Registration*, although protesting against the psychiatric overemphasis on what were known as the stigmata of degeneration, Meyer nevertheless conceded that the "alienist" could not dispense with such a study, and provided detailed suggestions for the observation and measurement of

1

these signs. For example, he advised that "for the study of facial asymmetries the following oblique measures should be taken: Distance from the external angle of the eye to the angle of the mouth-right; left . . . etc." He listed twenty-two ear anomalies and included a method of analysis of the parts of the ear which contained thirty-four questions on each ear.

The climate of general psychiatric thought as late as 1916 is suggested by the fact that in a discussion of the data on heredity, Meyer pointed out that the concept of morbid taint, which had come to preoccupy the psychiatric world, had become closely associated, in the profession's mind, with the concept of degeneration. A morbid taint was considered by many workers to be fully established when there was a "history of gout, rheumatism, diabetes, gravel, phthisis, migraine, epilepsy, asthma, or of peculiarity of character, criminal record, or nervous or mental disorders in one or more persons of the family." In opposition to this loose thinking, he contended that no statements about heredity could be admitted except "where the corpus delicti, the inherited feature, has a sufficient relation to the disturbance of health which brings the person under consideration."

In England in the 1890's so strongly did the psychiatric profession believe in the etiological role of heredity and degeneracy in mental illness that Henry Maudsley, the founder of the famed London psychiatric teaching and research hospital, could imply (1895) that it was useless to think about prognosis in terms of the usual course of any particular clinical entity since the real determining factor was the inexorable unfolding of each individual's illness in accordance with his particular inherited constitution.

In Germany probably the two outstanding writers other than Kraepelin were Wernicke and Ziehen. Wernicke, besides presenting a mass of acutely observed empirical data, and influenced by his brilliant demonstration of sensory aphasia, attempted to correlate psychopathology and brain pathology far beyond where the facts would allow—the kind of attempt that Meyer was to decry so vehemently a little later. Ziehen was so interested in the derangements of psychological elements such as sensations, memories, intellectual tones of feeling, etc., that this influenced his classification of mental disorders. For example, Meyer (1904a) pointed out in his chapter on paranoia that Ziehen placed "side by side the chronic incurable states of delusions of persecution and grandeur, lasting the entire life, and the acute curable exhaustive puerperal psychoses, delirium tremens, periodic and circular disorders, and even the transitory deliria of epileptics." As Kraepelin (1894) remarked, " 'We evidently stand here on the ground of hot and cold fevers, as they were spoken of before the days of stethoscope, thermometer, and pure culture.' "

KRAEPELIN AND MEYER

It was in 1896, in this era of conflicting emphases on grossly misunderstood hereditary factors, isolated psychological components and overextended neuropathological speculations, as well as of magnificent advances in the study of disease entities facilitated by "the stethoscope, thermometer and pure culture," that Kraepelin published the revolutionary fifth edition of his textbook. In an effort to define disease entities in psychiatry on the model of general paresis of the insane, with an etiology, a course and an outcome, he broke away from contemporary thinking and gathered together from the four corners of the psychiatric world a number of heretofore separately designated symptom-complexes into two main divisions: the episodic nondeteriorating manic-depressive insanity and the progressive deteriorating dementia praecox.

Under the concept of manic-depressive insanity, Kraepelin included numerous disorders variously named and with previously ascribed very diverse outcomes, e.g., simple melancholia, melancholia with delusions, melancholia activa, periodic psychosis, simple mania, etc. In his words (quoted in Meyer, 1904b), "manic-depressive insanity comprehends on the one hand, the entire domain of so-called periodic and circular insanity, and on the other, simple mania usually distinguished from the above. In the course of years I have become more and more convinced that all the pictures mentioned are merely forms of one single disease process. . . . It is, as far as I can see, quite impossible to find any definite boundaries between the single disease pictures which have been kept apart so far. From 'simple' mania, the numerous cases with two, three, four attacks in a lifetime lead over quite gradually to periodic forms, and from these we reach circular insanity, through those cases in which a more and more marked initial or terminal stage of depression gradually complicates the pure picture of mania, or in which the long series of maniacal attacks is unexpectedly interrupted by a state of depression. . . .

Manic-depressive insanity, as its name indicates, takes its course in single attacks, which either present the signs of so-called manic excitement (flight of ideas, exaltation, and over-activity), or those of a peculiar psychic depression with psycho-motor inhibition, or a mixture of the two states."

Thus its course. As for its outcome, Kraepelin observed no essential deterioration (unlike dementia praecox) no matter how severe the individual attacks. With regard to etiological factors he was uncertain. He (1902) postulated that "defective heredity is the most prominent, occurring in from seventy to eighty per cent of cases. . . . Physical stigmata may also be present. . . . Of external causes, besides gestation, alcoholic excesses are perhaps the most prominent; others are mental shock, deprivation, and acute diseases."

The term "disease process" was used by Kraepelin to describe a precise condition. He meant an illness with a definite neuropathology but with the diversification of symptomatology mentioned above. What this anatomical pathology might be, he had no idea; that it existed, he had no doubt. Bleuler, although Freudian in some ways, was in this respect essentially Kraepelinian. What he said of schizophrenia (quoted in Meyer, 1908) he may well have said of manic-depressive insanity: "The real disease or disease process is still wholly unknown. It may be an auto-intoxication or an infection or anything whatsoever." And Nissl (1902), another follower of Kraepelin, dogmatized as follows: " 'In almost all the functional psychoses it is possible to demonstrate anatomical findings in the cortex. As soon as we agree to see in all mental derangements the clinical expression of definite disease processes of the cortex, we remove the obstacle which today makes impossible all agreement among alienists.' "

Kraepelin's bold hypothesis gave rise to two major controversies that raged in German psychiatry for many years. From his original concept of manic-depressive insanity he had excluded the melancholia of the involutional period which he considered a separate clinical entity with variable prognosis. In this entity he included all the morbid anxious depressions of the later years that did not represent phases of other psychoses. This exclusion engendered considerable controversy until Dreyfus (1907), following a study of a series of melancholics at the Heidelberg Clinic, demonstrated their almost universal eventual recovery except where dementia intervened. Thus, by using Kraepelin's own criterion of prognosis, he contended that this syndrome belonged in the general category of manic-depressive insanity. This evidence caused Kraepelin to concede the point, and in the eighth edition of his text he accepted the orphan child of involutional melancholia into the all-embracing entity of manic-depressive insanity. But this concession merely provided more ammunition for a withering attack on the whole concept of "disease entity"—clinically distinguishable *"Krankheitseinheiten"*—by such men as Hoche (1910), who trenchantly pointed to the Kraepelinians as giving " 'the impression of a great number of diligent workmen, most energetically engaged in clarifying a turbid fluid by pouring it busily from one vessel to another.' " It was, he said, as if " 'a kind of thought compulsion, a logical and aesthetic necessity, insists that we seek for well-defined, self-contained disease-entities, but here as elsewhere, unfortunately, our subjective need is no proof of the reality of that which we desire, no proof that these pure types do, in point of fact, actually occur.' "

And indeed the matter was not as simple as some of the systematizers had made it appear. Kraepelin taught that a sufficiently careful scrutiny of the symptomatology of any patient should provide the basis for a valid prognosis of whether he would or would not deteriorate, i.e., whether he belonged in the manic-depressive or the dementia praecox category. It sounded too good to be true. And so it was. Even in Kraepelin's hands, in his own clinic, it proved to be impossible only too often to prognosticate correctly. Too many patients diagnosed as manic-depressive became chronic and too many cases with apparent deterioration surprisingly seemed to recover. And there were many patients who defied classification in either group. By 1920 even Kraepelin was forced to concede that " 'we are thus obliged to limit to the utmost the assumption that this or that disorder is characteristic of a definite disease-process.' "

In the United States, Adolf Meyer gave Kraepelin's classification a very appreciative reception. In 1896 he introduced Kraepelin's scheme of diagnosis into the Worcester Hospital, probably one of the first institutions outside of Kraepelin's own clinic in Heidelberg to make use of it. He felt that Kraepelin's new alignment of clinical pictures brought order into what had been a hopelessly confused situation. And Kraepelin's emphasis on outcome appealed to Meyer's essentially human outlook. But by 1905 Meyer was warning against the overextension of the terms "manic-depressive" and "dementia praecox" lest a new kind of arbitrary confusion be set up. He stressed the fact, for example, that there were many depressions that had neither the characteristics of manic-depressive depression nor those of the involutional melancholic depression. And later on he (1921) was to protest even more vigorously that "safer clinical methods should be used than the largely prognostic considerations of Kraepelin, and that dynamic formulations come closer to the needs of both physician and patient than the formal and peremptory dichotomy claimed by those who see but one of two fates, either manic-depressive disorder or dementia praecox." But by this time he had already formulated his psychobiological theory of reaction types—biological reactions of the mental type—and had definitely discarded the concept of disease entities, a concept of which, indeed, he had been suspicious from the very beginning.

By 1908 he had already become impatient with his colleagues' hypnotic preoccupation with undiscovered lesions in the cortex. "To try and explain a hysterical fit or a delusion system out of hypothetical cell alterations which we cannot reach or prove is at the present stage of histophysiology a gratuitous performance. To realize that such a reaction is a faulty response or substitution of an insufficient or protective or evasive or mutilated attempt at adjustment opens ways of inquiry in the direction of modifiable determining factors and all of a sudden we find ourselves in a live field, in harmony with our instincts of action, of prevention, of modification, and of an understanding doing justice to a desire for directness instead of neurologizing tautology. The conditions which we meet in psychopathology are more or less abnormal reaction types, which we want to learn to distinguish from one another, trace to the situation or condition under which they arise, and study for their modifiability. . . . Steering clear of useless puzzles liberates a mass of new energy."

It is interesting to speculate how much this awareness of and interest in the reactive aspects of depression and other psychopathological formations was stimulated by Freud's early work in this field. Meyer was writing review articles on analytic theories as early as 1905. However, his interest in psychopathology took a significantly different form, manifesting itself in an investigation of the faulty reactions to life and of attempts at their modification, rather than in the study of complexes and the unconscious.

Despite his previous prophetic observation ("any attempt at inventing too many new names meets a prompt revenge, as the fate of the books of Kahlbaum and Arndt have shown"), Meyer (1904b) devised an entirely new Greek terminology based on the root word "ergasia," implying activity of the individual as a person. The affective reactions became known as the "thymergasias" and included the manic-depressive group of Kraepelin's together with the agitated depressions of the involutional period.

What was accomplished in these hectic and fruitful years around the turn of the century? Not only new theories but actually new dimensions were introduced into the study of behavior. By adding the dimension of time with his interest in the outcome, Kraepelin was able to discern two main clinical pictures in the utterly confused mass of nineteenth-century psychiatric functional disorders —clinical pictures which he boldly labeled "disease processes." In the United States, this concept met first with appreciation and then with impatience, and finally in his pragmatic way Adolf Meyer became surfeited with the pointless devotion to an undemonstrated brain pathology; encouraged by the Freudian stirrings across the water, he helped add another new dimension to psychiatry: the dimension of depth. Psychiatrists, under the influence of Meyer and Freud, were no longer to stand at a distance content to describe what they saw but were to inquire into what lay beneath the surface manifestations of psychopathology, i.e., to explore with increasing interest the depths of human personality. Psychiatry ceased to be a psychology of surfaces and became a psychology of depths. And this new interest in depth was to extend the interest in time from its exclusively forward glance backwards to the beginnings of habit deterioration and the crystallization of character structure. Thus, from its long history as a classificatory and descriptive science, was psychiatry humanized in these few decades.

Yet after all these years one must agree with Lewin (1950) that despite the fact that Kraepelin's concepts were stripped of their universal usefulness, his careful subdivisions nullified and the implications of an organic disease process not validated, "it must be something more than respect for authority that has kept us Kraepelinians tacitly, when we speak in psychiatric terms."

HOCH, KIRBY AND OTHERS

During particularly the second decade of this century, a series of thoughtful studies was published by a group of workers centered around the New York State Psychiatric Institute. Under the leadership of August Hoch, Kirby and MacCurdy drew inspiration from three sources: Meyer's emphasis that psychiatric syndromes were biological types of reactions, Freud's observations on the unconscious and on infantile sexuality, and Kraepelin's interest in the outcome of disorders. Under the influence of Meyer and Freud, they studied and corroborated the importance of psychological factors in the depressive reaction types. Their work seemed to promise much but actually accomplished little in the direction of a psychodynamic and psychogenetic understanding of depression. What was accomplished, however, as Lewin (1950) has pointed out, was that they helped to make American psychiatrists interested in the psychological aspects of depression and thus more receptive to psychoanalytic thought on this subject.

Sharing Kraepelin's interest in deterioration and recovery, they delineated several groups out of the amorphous mass of dementia praecox which they considered to have a good prognosis. These included a carefully described group of stupors (Hoch, 1921), which they called "benign stupors," and perplexed states (Hoch and Kirby, 1919), which, because of their favorable prognoses, they labeled "benign psychoses" allied to or included in the manic-depressive group. Hoch attempted to prove that depression and elation were not the only two affect anomalies in this group, but that apathy, agitation and distressed perplexity also belonged there. "In other words," as MacCurdy (1921) commented, " 'anxiety-apathy Insanity' would be as appropriate, theoretically, as Kraepelin's term."

In 1909 Kirby reviewed Dreyfus' monograph on involutional melancholia and refused to accept his contention that this condition was really a subgroup of manic-depressive psychosis. His rejection of Dreyfus' views was based mostly on what he considered the inadequate diagnostic criteria which Dreyfus had employed for these two disorders. And in a challenging paper Hoch and MacCurdy (1922) took issue with Dreyfus' contention that melancholics almost always got better. They demonstrated that in their series there were cases which did improve (which they labeled "benign psychoses of manic-depressive variety") and cases which did not improve ("malignant psychoses clinically related to dementia praecox"). Thus on the basis of Kraepelin's criterion of prognosis, they disputed the unity of the involutional melancholic syndrome. In these days of improved therapeutic techniques we do not often observe the uninfluenced course of this disorder, so it might be of interest to note that they considered a patient hopeless only if he failed to show improvement after four years. Their malignant cases were characterized by restriction of interest or affect (instead of, for example, the frank fear reactions in the benign cases), attention to the body either of a severe hypochondriacal nature or of an autoerotic type and by irritability or peevishness.

BLEULER AND THE EFFECTS OF HIS THEORY

It will have been observed that all this classification and study were based mostly on the criterion of recoverability. If the patient recovered, the illness was a benign psychosis and was most probably allied to manic-depressive insanity; if not, dementia praecox claimed him.

Though productive of much sound work and valuable observation, this obsessive preoccupation with prognosis was just about outliving its usefulness when Bleuler struck the blow that was destined—not immediately, it is true, but inexorably—to bring that phase of psychiatry to a close. In 1911 he published his descriptive and theoretical tour de force on schizophrenia and declared the problem of prognosis deceptive. It was his belief that the accepted standards for recovery were altogether too gross, and he implied that many syndromes were said to have a good prognosis when actually some deterioration had taken place. He contended therefore that the diagnosis of a disorder be made by clinical symptomatology and specifically, as far as the so-called functional psychoses were concerned, by the presence or absence of certain characteristic primary symptoms.

He devised the term "schizophrenia," by which he designated "a group of psychoses whose course is at times chronic, at times marked by intermittent attacks, and which can stop or retrograde at any stage, but does not permit a full restitutio ad integrum. The disease is characterized by a specific type of alteration of thinking, feeling, and relation to the external world which appears nowhere else in this particular fashion." And it was this "specific type of alteration," of which he gave numerous examples, that he considered diagnostic, not the outcome which was so difficult to estimate. He felt that the degree of failure to reach full recovery was sometimes so slight that to detect it taxed the observational powers of a skilled psychiatrist, but that it existed he considered implicit in his conception of the disease.

The "outcome" in the Kraepelinian sense was dethroned. The result of this new outlook, as far as the entity of manic-depressive psychosis was concerned, was that those cases of affective disorder which demonstrated contaminating schizophrenic signs were stripped away from it. Bleuler's criteria of diagnosis, if not his concept of the schizophrenic disease process, gradually met with acceptance throughout the American psychiatric world. The perplexed states began to be considered unquestionably schizophrenic. And Rachlin, in a follow-up study of Hoch's benign stupor cases (1935) and in a later statistical study of this syndrome in five New York State hospitals (1937), considered the schizophrenic nature of this so-called benign psychosis. So far did the criterion of deterioration appear irrelevant for the diagnosis of schizophrenia that the concept now includes what is variously termed "ambulatory schizophrenia" (Zilboorg, 1941), "pseudoneurotic" forms of schizophrenia (Hoch and Polatin, 1949) and "borderline states" (Knight, 1953).

The disputable entity of involutional melancholia had been originally excluded by Kraepelin from his manic-depressive category on the basis of its poor prognosis. It had later gained entrance to this grouping after Dreyfus had defended its ultimately favorable outcome. Hoch had then shown it to have a variable prognosis and had therefore split it up into a benign and a malignant form. Now that prognosis had been discarded as a differentiating feature, it was reestablished as an independent diagnostic entity, primarily as the result of a series of papers the most significant of which were those of Titley (1936), Palmer and Sherman (1938) and Malamud, Sands and Malamud (1941). These papers, all based on the comparative study of involutional melancholic patients with manic-depressives (in Titley's paper, also with normal subjects), can be summarized as arguing that involutional melancholia is an entity or syndrome different from manic-depressive psychosis in at least two areas: prepsychotic personality and symptomatology.

Prepsychotic manic-depressives were described by Henderson and Gillespie (1950) as having "frank, open personalities. They are either bright, talkative, optimistic, aggressive people, who make light of the ordinary affairs of life, or else they take a gloomy outlook, bewail the past, make mountains out of mole-hills; or there is a combination of the above moods, rendering the person emotionally unstable and variable." While differing in some details, this description, so reminiscent of similar descriptions by earlier writers, also characterized the prepsychotic personalities of the manic-depressive patients whom Titley and Palmer and Sherman studied.

Contrasted with this picture was Noyes' (1948) impression of the prepsychotic personalities of involutional melancholics: "A review of the patient's previous personality and temperament often shows that he has been an inhibited type of individual with a tendency to be quiet, unobtrusive, serious, chronically worrisome, intolerant, reticent, sensitive, scrupulously honest, frugal, even penurious, stubborn, of stern unbending moral code, lacking in humor, overconscientious and given to self-punishment. . . . often his interests have been narrow, his habits stereotyped, he has cared little for recreation, has avoided pleasure and has had but few close friends."

Titley's description was in the same vein. "Narrow range of interests, difficulty in adjusting to change, limited capacity for sociability and friendship, rigid adherence to a high ethical code, marked proclivity for saving, reserve that becomes positive reticence so far as intimate matters are concerned, an ever present anxious tone, profound stubbornness, overwhelming conscientiousness and strained meticulosity as to person and vocation are constant concomitants of the group." All of these writers were quite agreed that the involutional melancholics and the manic-depressives whom they studied differed markedly in their prepsychotic personalities.

As for the differences in clinical symptomatology, Henderson and Gillespie's observations also reflected the empirical findings of this group. They described the manic-depressive as being characterized by "difficulty in thinking, depression and psychomotor retardation," whereas in involutional melancholia there was "depression without retardation, anxiety, a feeling of unreality and hypochondriacal or nihilistic delusions." Palmer and Sherman stressed the agitation and the restlessness that they found in this type of patient and observed that in only three or four of their series of fifty involutional melancholics did they see definite psychomotor retardation.

It was also pointed out that while manic-depressives suffer many episodes of psychosis, the involutional patients fail to show a history of previous attacks of psychotic depression. Furthermore, it was argued that, unlike manic-depressives, involutional melancholics never have an episode of elation following their depression.

As a result of this preponderance of evidence and opinion, involutional melancholia came to be considered a type of reaction which was essentially independent and different from manic-depressive psychosis, a point of view exemplified, for instance, in most textbooks of the time and in the *Diagnostic Manual of the American Psychiatric Association* (1952), where it was termed "Involutional psychotic reaction." Although its designation is somewhat different in the new edition of the *Diagnostic Manual,* the same point of view relative to its separate identity has been maintained.

Nevertheless, during the 1950's and 1960's the idea of the existence of involutional melancholia as a distinct entity was regarded with mounting skepticism. Roth (1959), Stenback (1963), Lehmann (1959) and Redlich and Freedman (1966), with varying degrees of conviction, asserted that the concept of a special involutional pattern of endogenous depression was no longer tenable—although the distinctiveness of this entity continued to have its supporters, especially among the writers of textbooks, e.g., Mayer-Gross et al. (1960), Henderson and Batchelor (1962), Noyes and Kolb (1963) and English and Finch (1964).

Rosenthal (1968), in a systematic survey of the controversy surrounding this syndrome, reviewed the correlation of involutional melancholia with endocrinological factors, the menopause and hormonal treatment. He described the initial enthusiasm concerning various endocrine preparations during the 1920's and the subsequent disillusionment in the following three decades. The prevailing feeling at the present time is that although vasomotor symptoms related to the menopause are significantly improved with estrogens, the depressive symptoms are not improved (Rogers, 1956).

Rosenthal (1968) also reviewed the factor analytic studies that had been carried out in the sixties and that I will be considering later in this chapter. When Rosenthal and Gudeman (1967) analyzed one hundred female patients by age groups, the patients "between the ages of 40 and 59 had average scores substantially the same as patients between 25 and 39 and patients aged 60 and above on such traits as agitation, hypochondriasis, retardation, guilt, severity of depressed mood, anxiety, somatic delusions, and obsessional personality."

As Rosenthal (1968) commented, the failure of his and others' "correlational techniques to demonstrate the classical involutional pattern is not conclusive evidence that it does not exist, but that in the depressive populations studied it is not common enough to be demonstrated by these methods."

THE GREAT DEBATE

The concept of neurotic depression has so far not come up for consideration. Kraepelin vaguely recognized such a condition, including it under the term "congenital neurasthenia" and listing it under the category "constitutional psychopathic states." He also recognized that some depressive psychoses seemed to be precipitated by environmental factors. His pupils made similar observations, all characterized by a high degree of indefiniteness.

In the British literature, the controversy over whether there was any difference between neurotic and psychotic depressions was set off by a highly provocative and challenging paper in 1926 by Mapother, the head of the Maudsley Hospital. His paper started off a debate that continued for years and led to an extensive clinical and theoretical study of the question. He asserted that "the distinction between what are termed neuroses and psychoses has really grown out of practical differences, particularly as regards certification and asylum treatment. . . . I can find no other basis for the distinction; neither insight, nor cooperation in treatment, nor susceptibility to psychotherapy will serve. . . . To assume that an enduring physical basis for habitually abnormal behaviour is probably non-existent because at present its exact nature is not demonstrable, seems to me a flat defiance of all relevant experience in medicine. . . . It is at least conceivable that some of the primary modes of abnormal mental reaction correspond to fairly definite bodily changes, perhaps to particular systems of neurons which we shall some day be able to identify." The heated controversy that followed, in addition to directing attention to the actual clinical study of depressed patients, threw a good deal of light on the state of thinking in English psychiatric circles two decades after Meyer had propounded his views on psychological reactions.

Mapother's observations met with a resolute and sometimes

acrimonious rebuttal. In order to prove that there was a difference between neurotic and psychotic depressions, appeals were made to differences in prognosis, heredity, body build, psychological and physical symptoms, dependence on or independence of external stimuli, metabolic factors and insight. Dissenting voices declared that manic-depressive psychosis "was an unalterable congenital component of the patient's entire being" (Strauss, 1930), whereas "reactive depression" was not endogenous and constitutional. There were some prepared to compromise, e.g., Reynell (1930), who felt that "complex entities cannot be classified into 'either-or,' they are usually both and sometimes neither."

Impressed by the overabundance of views and paucity of facts, a number of observers turned to a scrutiny of their case material to determine whether they could delineate categories within the depressive group. Gillespie (1930) studied and was able to subdivide a group of twenty-five patients on the basis of their "reactivity." He did not use this term to refer to the psychological precipitation of the depression, for he found that precipitating causes of a similar kind were almost universally present in his patients. By "reactivity" he meant "how [their] condition varied from day to day under the various external stimuli of general environment and treatment and the internal stimuli of their topics of pre-occupation."

In a comprehensive classical study of sixty-one depressed patients, Lewis (1934b) came to conclusions that directly contraverted the claims of the separatist school. He attempted to apply Gillespie's criterion of "reactivity" to each of his patients, and after a detailed discussion of the difficulties in applying this measuring rod concluded that the concept was so vague as to defy utilization. In order to come to some decision on the question of the role of environmental factors, Lewis made an attempt "to decide with regard to each case whether there was a definite situational factor responsible for the precipitating or the maintenance of the symptoms. The criteria were the previous good health of the patient before this situation arose, the temporal relationship between the situation and the beginning of the illness, and the apparent adequacy of the situation from a 'commonsense' point of view. . . . But the more one knew about the patient the harder this became. . . . [Except for ten patients] all the others were understandable examples of the interaction of organism and environment; it was impossible to say which of the factors was decidedly preponderant." As for the ten in whom there was apparent absence of psychogenesis or environmental influence, he concluded that the explanation may have been "our inability or disinclination to probe deeply into the total previous experience and reactions of the sick man." He observed that the better one knew a man's past, the more definitely did prodromal features become evident, and, with reference to the precipitating factor, acknowledged that "one does not call the last straw the cause of the camel's broken back, at any rate if one is talking in scientific language." And thus, after his comprehensive and scholarly study, Lewis came to a conclusion that surprised no one who had properly understood the teachings of Meyer and Freud—namely, that even in so-called endogenous psychoses environmental factors and lifelong patterns of reactions could be observed.

With regard to precipitating factors, Bellak (1952) summed the matter up as well as anyone. "In a differential consideration of reactive versus endogenous depression, one could actually speak of a continuum that extends from a minimum of an external precipitating factor to a maximum of such a factor. All other factors being equal, it can probably be said that the prognosis is better as the importance of external precipitating factors increases. What this very simply implies is that the patient who needed quite a realistic blow to react with a depression has a more stable premorbid personality than the one who reacted to a minimal situation; the first one would by the same token recover more quickly and more completely."

In 1940, Rogerson reexamined the problem of categorization. He rejected the criterion of environmental influence as a precipitating factor, which had over and over again been shown to be demonstrable in every type of depressive illness, and settled on a differentiation "concerned only with the patient's relationship to reality in a broad sense." Rogerson failed to work out the implications of this observation but nevertheless in his emphasis on the patient's clinical symptomatology, rather than on reactivity or prognosis, reformulated the problem in a manner that sharpened the issues.

In summarizing this prolonged controversy, up to this point we see that on the one hand a group of writers, the outstanding ones among them being Mapother and Lewis, contended that there was no essential difference between "neurotic" and "psychotic" depressions, terms that were shown to be not synonymous with "reactive" and "endogenous" depressions. In support of their views, they pointed to similarities in precipitating factors and difficulties in clinical differentiation, and even speculated about a common physical basis for these disorders. This anti-separatist school gained a new exponent in 1952, when Ascher also questioned the value of the concept of neurotic depression, stating that in his opinion "neither the course of the illness nor the therapeutic success of various procedures, nor the danger of suicide are consistently dependent on [this differentiation in diagnostic terms] to justify their continued use."

On the other hand a group of workers, numbering among them Gillespie and Rogerson, maintained that there was an essential and pertinent difference between neurotic and psychotic depressions. The difficulty in distinguishing between these two clinical pictures was variously assessed by members of this school.

A third point of view was best expressed in the literature by Tredgold (1941) and Bellak (1952). This maintained that there was a continuum, or graded series or spectrum, at either end of which the clinical pictures could be clearly and indisputably distinguished as neurotic or psychotic on the basis of symptomatology (including the "relation to reality") but which contained a large number of borderline cases admittedly difficult to classify.

Bellak tried to explain why one depressed patient is neurotic and another psychotic by invoking the concept of "ego strength." By this term he designated a "factor which by and large, determines the form which the content assumes, how the content expresses itself—as in a dream, a neurotic symptom, a delusion, or a hallucination." He believed "that the . . . content may be hypothetically the same in two patients, but that with a difference in ego strength, one patient may be a neurotic (with neurotic symptoms) and the other may be a psychotic (expressing the same content in delusions and hallucinations), while a third individual —a 'normal'—may express the same content in dreams and in some character formations." However, he was forced to admit that there were no reliable indicators of ego strength.

CONTINUATION OF THE CONTROVERSY

When specific treatments for depression were introduced, they were used to provide ammunition for this continuing controversy.

Some writers (e.g., Kalinowsky, 1959; Rose, 1963; Carney, Roth and Garside, 1965; Mendels, 1965a, b, c) noted that patients with the characteristics of an endogenous depression responded very significantly better to ECT than did neurotic depressives. Other workers (e.g., Kuhn, 1958; Kiloh and Ball, 1961; Kiloh et al., 1962) reported that depressed patients who were classified as endogenous responded significantly better to imipramine than reactive depressives did. The adjectives "neurotic" and "reactive" had gradually come to be used interchangeably.

Kiloh and Garside (1965) expressed the dualistic position quite unequivocally: "The group of depressive states consists of two separate entities conforming with those conditions known for so long as 'endogenous' depression and 'neurotic or reactive' depression."

However, Rose's sample of patients contained some labeled as "doubtful endogenous" and "doubtful reactive" which somewhat marred the symmetry of this general classification. Similarly, Mendels found so much overlap of symptoms among his patients that he labeled the majority of the patients as "endoreactive." Thus the sharp distinction of Kiloh, Carney and their respective colleagues was found to be considerably more hazy by Rose and Mendels, although Garside and Kay (1968) in a more modest formulation argue that "some, at least, of depressed patients can usefully be diagnosed as either endogenous or neurotic."

Hamilton and White (1959) had by statistical techniques differentiated endogenous and reactive patients on the basis of severity. Rose (1963), controlling for this, conceptualized the distinction between these two groups as qualitative, not quantitative. Kiloh and Garside (1965) also distinguished between the two groups not on the basis of severity but on a qualitative basis.

A retrospective case-record study by Rosenthal and Klerman (1965) supported the existence of a consistent pattern of symptoms which they referred to as the "endogenous depressive pattern." They felt that this pattern, "originally derived from different populations, with different sex ratios, indeed in different countries," replicated the findings of Hamilton and White (1959) and Kiloh and Garside (1963).

This chorus of agreement based on studies carried out with the use of sophisticated statistical techniques was interrupted by two dissenting publications. McConaghy et al. (1967), who carried out a replication of Kiloh and Garside's (1963) study, failed to support their conclusions. They were unable to demonstrate patterns of symptom clusters that characterized the commonly accepted clinical pictures of endogenous and neurotic depression.

In an impressive monograph, Kendell (1968) applied statistical methods to a study of 700 unselected, consecutive patients at the Maudsley Hospital. This is, of course, the hospital with which both Mapother and Lewis, the chief "unifiers," were associated. As Kendell put it, the ongoing argument had to do with the question of "whether psychotic or neurotic depressions are clinically distinct, if overlapping, conditions or whether they are the two ends of a single continuum . . . an argument about whether the blacks and the whites (the 'pure' forms) are more or less common than the greys (the 'mixed' forms)." He pointed out that some of the studies involved patients who were clearly diagnosed as neurotic or endogenous, and were thus preselected, and that other studies (e.g., Ball and Kiloh, 1959; Kiloh et al., 1962; Kiloh and Garside, 1963) did not indicate whether or not the patients consisted of a consecutive series. "It is self-evident that if the greys are omitted from the original material, blacks and whites will predominate at the end. Unless the starting material is unselected, bimodal distribution curves, for whatever parameters, prove nothing" (p. 14).

His study of 700 consecutive depressed patients supported the hypothesis of a continuum, at either end of which patients were clearly neurotically or endogenously depressed but with a gray overlapping intermediate area, and of a continuum reflecting a unimodal distribution rather than the bimodal distribution of previous investigators.

In the meantime, however, Carney and Roth (1965), with methods similar to Kendall's, had arrived at a diametrically opposite finding, namely, that neurotic and endogenous types of depression formed distinct populations. As Kendell conceded, "the distribution was unequivocally bimodal" (p. 66). He advanced various possible criticisms of Carney and Roth's work but noted that Sandifer et al. (1966) in a similar study had reported a similar distribution of diagnostic scores.

Kendell's own work was subjected to extended statistical critiques by Hope (1969) and Eysenck (1970). Furthermore, Mowbray (1969) replicated Kendell's work on a smaller sample (seventy-three depressed patients) but using the same statistical techniques. His findings did not support Kendell's continuum model but were more consistent with bimodality or the two-illness viewpoint.

Kendell, together with Gourlay (1970a), then replicated his own study using "more reliable data obtained by standardized interviewing procedures and a wider range of clinical variables." This study, while still not demonstrating a "bimodal distribution of patient scores," nevertheless found a reduced overlap, compared with his previous study, between the psychotic and neurotic groups.

His zeal in demonstrating the unity of psychiatric illness is indicated in the very next paper in the same journal (Kendell and Gourlay, 1970b) in which the authors tried to determine whether the affective psychoses and schizophrenia were distinct entities or mixed states. They concluded that their analysis "did not lend support to the view that schizophrenia and affective psychoses were distinct entities."

After a review of these statistical efforts to resolve the issue of whether there is a difference between endogenous-psychotic and reactive-neurotic depressions, Mowbray (1973) concludes that the application of statistical techniques to settle this issue "resulted in an impasse as insoluble as that which had previously been reached when the argument was based on clinical impression alone."

Yet there had been a drawing closer of the views of the leading exponents of the unitary and binary hypotheses. Everett, Gourlay and Kendell (1971), in a new attempt to validate traditional syndromes by cluster analysis, failed—as had other investigators (e.g., Pilowsky et al., 1969; Paykel, 1971)—to obtain a "discrete cluster of neurotic depressives." Their findings led them to conclude that "psychotic depression is a more firmly based concept than its neurotic counterpart." Still unwilling to abandon the unitary point of view, they now tend to regard all depressives as psychotic although sometimes contaminated by "elements of a variety of other psychiatric disorders."

Kiloh et al. (1972), after further studies, "now believe that the support provided by factor analytic techniques for the existence of neurotic depression as a distinct syndrome is an artifact." Their revised view is that "neurotic depression is a diagnosis made by exclusion of the features of endogenous depression and that it is likely to be heterogeneous." Thus there has been a growing agreement about the vagueness of neurotic depression as a distinct entity. Kiloh et al. refer to a statement of Everett et al.: ". . . 'if a more limited concept were employed it might be possible to demonstrate a valid boundary between it [psychotic depression] and other forms of depression.' " Kiloh et al. add, "The only difference between us now is that we believe this has already been achieved." All of the above is a far cry from the earlier adamant positions of both Kiloh and Kendell.

A number of other attempts have been made to delineate clinical groupings by means of factor analysis (e.g., Grinker et al., 1961; Overall, 1963; Friedman et al., 1963).

There are large areas of congruence among these various studies, but, since they are not directly relevant to this extended debate on the endogenous-exogenous problem, I will refrain from commenting further on them other than to note one factor pattern that both Grinker's and Friedman's groups found that resembled a group of depressed patients that has been described by Lazare and Klerman (1968). The latter reported a depressive pattern occurring in hysterical personalities and characterized by "less intense feelings of depression, hopelessness and worthlessness, less retardation, and fewer paranoid and obsessional symptoms." They were also "more hypochondriacal and showed a greater number of hysterical symptoms than the non-hysterical group."

The hysterical personality was defined by Lazare and Klerman as "egocentric, exhibitionistic, and overdramatic, sometimes to the point of lying. Affect is labile as she goes through the motions of feeling. Although there is provocative sexual behavior, there is fear of sex. She is immature sexually and otherwise. The typical hysteric is usually suggestible and is often demanding and dependent." This is, of course, the stereotyped picture of the hysterical personality that is so familiar in the literature. The authors' suggestion that when hysterics become depressed, their depressions appear different from those of non-hysterical patients—i.e., that they respond less well to ECT—is in accord with the findings of Grinker et al. and Friedman et al. It is a finding that deserves more examination and study. The position of this group of depressed patients vis-à-vis the neurotic versus endogenous controversy has not yet been clearly outlined, although it would appear that they belong within the neurotic group or at the neurotic end of the continuum depending on whose schema is used.

This controversy concerning neurotic and endogenous depressions also included some work of a physiological nature which deserves mention at this point. Strongin and Hinsie (1939) found that parotid gland secretions were markedly decreased in endogenous but in no other types of depression. This was later confirmed by Busfield et al. (1961). And Shagass and his co-workers (1956) found that the sedation threshold ("an objective determination based upon the EEG and speech changes induced by intravenous amobarbital sodium") was markedly different in patients with neurotic and psychotic depressions. According to Kiloh and Garside (1963), Boudreau (1958) and Nymgaard (1959) reached the same conclusion, although others, especially Ackner and Pampiglione (1959) but also Roberts (1959) and Martin and Davies (1962), were unable to replicate this and similar work of Shagass and his collaborators (1958a, 1958b).

TERMINOLOGICAL CONSIDERATIONS

After so much discussion about the separateness of a clinical syndrome called "endogenous depression," I would like to examine the origin and usage of this widely misunderstood term. Five reviews of this concept have been particularly useful in my survey of the background and current usage of this term (Heron, 1965; Rosenthal and Klerman, 1965; Mendels and Cochrane, 1968; Klerman, 1971; Carroll, 1971).

As Heron indicates in a thoughtful study of the concept "endogenous-exogenous," the current use of these terms stems from Kraepelin (1913). The words "endogenous" and "exogenous" seem to have been originally used in 1813 by a Swiss botanist, de Candolle, and derive from the word *genesthai*, which means "to be born" or "to produce." "Endogenous," therefore, implies being produced from within and "exogenous" from outside the organism. This dichotomy, according to Heron, was introduced into German psychiatry by Moebius (1894), who in turn was influenced by Morel's (1857) theory that all pathological deviations in human behavior were caused by degeneration of the germ plasm. Moebius, however, also believed that bacterial, chemical and other "exogenous" toxins could produce morbid changes in human behavior. He did not take psychological or emotional factors into consideration in his discussion of exogenous factors. Nor did Kraepelin when he adopted this dichotomy. Heron quotes Kraepelin: "The principal demarcation in aetiology is above all between internal and external causes. The two major groups of diseases, exogenous and endogenous, are thus naturally divided" (Kraepelin, 1913, p. 15). The word "endogenous" as here used clearly has an etiological and not merely a descriptive significance. Kraepelin, of course, assumed that both dementia praecox and manic-depressive psychosis were endogenous in origin—a conclusion, as Heron points out, that is merely deductive, not inductive. On theoretical rather than on empirical grounds, he ruled out an environmental origin for these illnesses, for, as Heron notes, "by definition an endogenous illness cannot be at the same time an exogenous illness."

Again according to Heron, Kraepelin's pupil Lange (1928) directed attention to those depressions which developed in response to life stresses. He referred to this group of psychogenic melancholias as "reaktive." This term was adopted by Gillespie (1930) but with a descriptive not an etiological meaning. He used the word "reactivity" to refer to the capacity to respond or react to intercurrent circumstances *during* the course of a depressive illness. According to Gillespie, the feature that most characterized endogenous depressions was the absence of reactivity of this kind.

In the course of the debate reviewed in the previous section, the dichotomy endogenous-exogenous became quite generally replaced by the dichotomy endogenous-reactive (psychogenic) or neurotic.

The term "reactive" has thus come to be used in two different ways: (1) Gillespie's usage, in which the word refers to the patient's responsivity to the daily flow of events, a characteristic which he believed the endogenous depressive lacked, and (2) the usage that has turned out to be the commonest, in which the word "reactive" is synonymous with "psychogenic."

Instead of using Kraepelin's designation "manic-depressive psychosis," the literature for a long time tended to refer to "endogenous depressions"—a syndrome, according to Heron, that was "responsive to electroconvulsive therapy, characterized by early morning waking, diurnal variation, anorexia, sustained depressive mood, etc., occurring in a wide variety of personality types, often with a history of deprivation or loss . . . and clustering mainly in the second half of life."

Rosenthal and Klerman (1965), in the course of a thoughtful analysis of the concept of endogenous depression, pointed out that the term had come to imply a relationship between three facets of the depressive picture:

1. A particular configuration of signs and symptoms was expected to be present.

2. The patient was expected to have a relatively stable and nonneurotic premorbid personality.

3. The illness was less likely to be precipitated by life stresses, and the patient was expected to reveal less reactivity to his environment during the course of his illness.

They indicated that "in a secondary usage" of the term—one that was less useful—the criterion of absence of obvious precipitant was more stringently applied with no regard for the symptom picture "and with the implication of aetiological certainty."

Outlining the typical traditional configuration of signs and symptoms in an endogenous depression, they listed the following elements: lack of reactivity; severity; feelings of guilt, remorse and unworthiness; sleep disturbance, especially middle-of-the-night insomnia and early-morning awakening; diurnal variation of symptoms; psychomotor retardation; agitation; visceral symptoms; decreased libido; weight loss; loss of interest.

They performed a factor analysis of fifty consecutive depressed patients and compared their findings with those of Hamilton (1960) and of Kiloh and Garside (1963). Most of the above items "loaded highly" (i.e., were distinctive to the endogenous pattern) not only in their own sample but also in the other two studies. There were a few discrepancies: for example, although Rosenthal and Klerman found that diurnal variation of mood was found among patients with and without this pattern of endogenous depression, Kiloh and Garside found diurnal variation to be more specific to the endogenous syndrome.

It is important to note that only a small percentage of Rosenthal and Klerman's patients were psychotic; that they did not use the terms "endogenous" and "psychotic" synonymously; and that in their opinion "psychosis is not one of the necessary criteria of the endogenous depressive pattern."

With respect to premorbid personality, many authors (e.g., Gillespie, 1930; Astrup et al., 1959; Roth, 1959) had referred to the well-adjusted, well-integrated, cheerful premorbid personality of endogenous depressives in contrast to the high degree of neuroticism and personality defects in the premorbid neurotic depressives. Rosenthal and Klerman found nothing more definitive than an absence of "hysterical personalities" in patients with the endogenous pattern. In a later study, however, Rosenthal and Gudeman (1967) found that obsessiveness and chronic depression correlated significantly and that "oral, cyclothymic and schizoid traits correlated positively but not significantly" with the pattern of endogenous depression.

With respect to precipitants, as Rosenthal and Klerman (1966) summarized the situation, some writers (e.g., Gillespie, 1930; Riddoch, 1930) acknowledged that a precipitant may be found; Astrup et al. (1959) reported that although the first attack may be precipitated, it was less possible to find precipitants for subsequent depressions; Roth (1959), acknowledging that precipitants may occur, nevertheless felt that the resulting depression was out of proportion to the precipitant; Mayer-Gross et al. (1960) believed that the apparent "causes" might actually be symptoms of the illness. At the other extreme, American writers such as Ewalt and Farnsworth (1963) and Noyes et al. (1963) postulated psychological precipitants in every endogenously depressed patient. On the other hand, Thomson and Hendrie (1972) could not find environmental stress prior to disease onset in either endogenous or neurotic depression. Rosenthal and Klerman's findings supported the clinical observation that there was a lack of apparent precipitants in depressions with the endogenous cluster of symptoms. However, they observed that the "absence of a precipitant, while more likely, is *not* a prerequisite for the endogenous pattern."

Not every author agreed that "endogenous" was the best term for the symptom pattern that went by that name. Gillespie (1930) preferred "autonomous depression" since once the depression began, it went its own autonomous way regardless of external circumstances. Rosenthal and Gudeman (1967) also prefer this adjective. Heron (1965) thought that "primary depression" was a less controversial designation. In Europe, according to Mendels and Cochrane (1968), the term "vital depression" is widely used as a descriptive equivalent to the syndrome known as "endogenous depression" in England and on this continent. The misleading etiological implications of the word "endogenous" are thus avoided. Kay et al. (1969), for similar reasons, prefer the designation "retarded depression" since "the use of a purely descriptive term would also have the great merit of avoiding the question-begging 'endogenous-neurotic' or 'endogenous-reactive' dichotomies."

NEW CATEGORIES

Although some authors still believe it to be the most useful designation available (e.g., Hollister, 1973, p. 75), this absorbed preoccupation with the concept of endogenous depression finally waned. As more and more biochemical and neurophysiological research became possible in the general area of the affective disorders, a need began to be felt for homogeneous populations that could be studied. It was becoming obvious that research on heterogeneous populations of affectively ill patients could only be misleading. As Klerman (1971) pointed out in a very thoughtful review of clinical research in depression: "The validity of most clinical research depends on the nature of the sample of depressed patients selected by the investigator." The growing literature on the subject reflected no absolute consensus about its clinical characteristics (e.g., Rosenthal and Klerman, 1965; Kiloh and Garside, 1963) although there actually was considerable agreement about its clinical features. More specifically, some studies (Detre et al., 1972; Kupfer et al., 1972) have demonstrated hypersomnia rather than insomnia as an important symptom in some manic-depressive patients, a feature which certainly blurs the clear outline of the traditional picture with its middle-of-the-night insomnia and early-morning awakening.

The term "endogenous depression," whether it represented one end of a continuum or a separate disease entity, was in no sense homogeneous. It included manic-depressive disorders with and without mania, patients who were labeled psychotic depressive reaction and involutional depressive reaction in the *Diagnostic Manual* as well as patients who were also alcoholics.

It was time then to shrug aside the mesmerized obsession with endogenous depression and to attempt to delineate more and more homogeneous groupings. In a sense this might seem like a backward step since it would undo the work of that great synthesizer, Kraepelin. His work, however, had accomplished its purpose —that of achieving a unified perspective in the midst of hopeless and useless diversity. There was now a need for distinct homogeneous groupings if meaningful research was to be carried on.

Leonhard (1957) and his colleagues took the—in retrospect— obvious step of separating the manic-depressive group into two categories: one ("bipolar") which contained both depressive and manic episodes and another ("monopolar") in which the patients experienced only recurrent depressions. Fish (1964) introduced Leonhard's concept of bipolarity to the English-speaking psychiatric world.

Perris (1966) demonstrated the usefulness of this categorization in a study of 138 bipolar and 139 "unipolar" (his substitute for the

term "monopolar"—a change that has been accepted generally in
the literature) patients that revealed a genetic difference between
these two groupings, a finding that had been obscured previously,
and one that has been since confirmed by Angst (1966). Whybrow
and Mendels (1969) suggested a triangular rather than a bipolar
model of manic-depressive illness, and Court (1968, 1972) introduced a continuum model in which depression is visualized as an
intermediate stage in a continuum that goes from normality to
mania. Neither model has as yet received much notice nor won
acceptance among workers in this field.

Winokur and his collaborators, concluding that it was not possible to separate out specific diseases by the use of clinical pictures
or predisposing psychological features, adopted a different
method of accomplishing this type of differentiation. He and Clayton (1967), using medical analogies, felt that "the fact that certain
symptoms tend to hang together clearly appears to be a math-
ematical certainty" but that this did not necessarily have any biological meaning. They also regarded categorization on the basis of
response to treatment as being of questionable value. Another
classification method, that of utilizing the presence or absence of
psychological precipitants, was also discarded (Winokur and Pitts,
1965). In a continuing series of publications, they have approached
the subject through family histories, genetic studies and attention
to sex and age. Others have adopted similar methods. An attempt
to be comprehensive would be inappropriate in a book such as
this, so I will omit any discussion of the work of investigators such
as Hopkinson (1964) and others, and I will refrain from describing
in detail such work that I will survey. My main purpose is to
indicate the direction, the thrust and the types of findings uncov-
ered by such an approach. Winokur (1973), however, has provided
a succinct summary of his findings based on clinical, familial and
genetic factors as well as differences related to sex and age of
onset.

Winokur and his colleagues, for purposes of research, have
adopted the division of affective disorders into primary and secondary groups. Woodruff et al. (1967) defined these groups as follows:

> *Primary affective disorder* is a current affective syndrome occur-
> ring in a patient whose previous history may be characterized in one
> of three ways: (1) he has been psychiatrically well, (2) he has had a
> previous episode of depression or mania which is diagnosable as such

in retrospect, (3) he has had previous psychiatric symptoms none of which was inconsistent with depression or mania, but which did not form a full picture of depression or mania. These symptoms may or may not have been episodic. (Anxiety symptoms are included here if they do not form a complete picture of anxiety neurosis.)

Secondary affective disorder is defined as a current affective syndrome occurring in a patient who has had a pre-existing diagnosable, non-affective, psychiatric illness. . . . The symptoms of the previous, non-affective psychiatric illness may or may not merge temporally with those of the current depression.

Since I will not be concerned further with the secondary affective disorders, I might add here that Winokur (e.g., in Winokur and Clayton, 1967) categorizes the non-primary affective disorders under three main headings:

1. Secondary depression, associated with psychiatric illness
2. Depression related to physical illness:
   a. Depressions associated with physical illness
   b. Depressions caused by physical illness
3. Reactive depression, usually a short-lived response to psychological factors

In one study of reactive depression, Winokur and Pitts (1964) concluded that no reliable criteria existed currently for definitely diagnosing depressions as reactive according to their classification. Bereavement and defeat were subsequently added as usable criteria. Also looking at the influence of life events, Hudgens et al. (1967) were unable to find any support for the effect of life stresses on the onset of primary affective disorders.

Leonhard (1957, 1966) had reported that bipolar patients had more psychotic relatives than did unipolar patients, a finding that was confirmed by Perris (1966), among others. Angst (1966) found that the morbid risk for depression in brothers of unipolar patients was significantly lower than for their sisters, whereas the risk for illness in brothers and sisters of bipolar patients was equal.

By means of family studies (which included the personal interviewing of very large numbers of first-degree relatives of index patients) and with attention to the parameters of age and sex, Winokur and his collaborators have attempted to classify the primary affective disorders into homogeneous groups. These include the following:

1. Primary affective disorder, manic-depressive disease. This group corresponds to Leonhard's and Perris' bipolar manic-

depressive group. The patients in this group have all had episodes of mania as well as depressions, and their relatives have a significantly higher incidence of mania than do the patients in the next group of primary affective disorders (Winokur and Clayton, 1967).

2. Primary affective disorder, depressive disease. This group corresponds roughly to Leonhard's monopolar and Perris' unipolar types of manic-depressive illness. The patients in this group have had no episodes of mania and the incidence of mania among their first-degree relatives is significantly lower than among the relatives of patients with manic-depressive disease (Winokur and Clayton, 1967). This group has been divided into two subgroups:

a. Pure depressive disease. This disease is especially found in late-onset (after forty years of age) male patients with depressive disease (Baker et al., 1971). It occurs with equal frequency among both male and female first-degree relatives of index patients (Cadoret et al., 1970). Patients with this disease tend to be more constipated and agitated and have more weight loss and fewer psychological symptoms than do the patients in the next subgroup (Baker et al., 1971). The members of this group seem to make up many of the patients traditionally referred to as involutional melancholic.

b. Depressive spectrum disease. This disease is especially found in early-onset (before forty years of age) female patients with depressive disease. The female relatives of these patients have more depression than do the male relatives. The latter compensate statistically for the disparity in depression by alcoholism and sociopathy. The patients in this group felt more guilt and were more tearful, worrisome and irritable than the patients in the late-onset male group (Baker et al., 1971; Winokur et al., 1971).

Winokur and his collaborators call the type of depressive illness seen in early-onset female patients with their alcoholic and sociopathic relatives "depressive spectrum illness," since the manifestations of this illness seem not only to be limited to depression but include alcoholism and sociopathy in the first-degree relatives of the patients. In contrast, they now call the late-onset depressive illness "pure depressive illness," since the relatives of these patients do not seem to display any other clinical picture. Although they have reported these findings using familial, sex and age parameters, the investigators are aware that they have not absolutely proven that a genetic factor is involved in either group.

They also recognize that this classification does not account for late-onset females and early-onset males, who may represent mixed types.

Examining this issue from another angle, Winokur et al. (1970) reported on 507 personally interviewed first-degree relatives of 259 alcoholic patients. They were found to have alcoholism and depression more frequently than one would expect by chance alone. As Winokur (1972) put it: "The modal illness for female relatives was depression; the modal illness for male relatives was alcoholism. The alcoholic female patients themselves had a primary diagnosis of depression in a quarter of the cases."

In still another study published by Winokur and his collaborators (Baker et al., 1972), in which the authors discuss a possible mode of genetic transmission of depressive disease and depression spectrum disease, they very appropriately caution that their "findings may well be an artifact produced by not knowing how to define a homogeneous group of probands." They acknowledge that "it may be impossible to do this until laboratory or biochemical findings specific to the various subtypes of depression are available." It will have been noted that the major criterion in the distinction between primary and secondary affective reactions is chronology. A primary affective disorder is one which has not been preceded by any other psychiatric condition. Recognizing the unlikelihood of acquiring, in the near future, laboratory or biochemical tests for differentiating depressions, Lehmann (1972) welcomed Robins' et al. (1972) vigorous advocacy of this "radical, simple, and effective method of distinguishing between primary and secondary depressions."

Mendlewicz et al. (1972), using a method advocated by Winokur, identified two subgroups within the category of manic-depressive illness (bipolar). "In patients with a positive family history (for manic-depressive illness) there is an earlier onset, with more psychotic symptoms occurring in the manic phase. Alcoholism, if present, is of an episodic pattern. In patients with a negative family history, there is a later onset, with psychotic symptoms occurring in the depressive phase. Alcoholism, when present, tends to be chronic."

CONCLUSION

The story seems to have come full circle. It began in the last quarter of the nineteenth century with some preliminary mutterings about heredity and morbid taints and with a search for the pathological lesions of the numerous entities of the pre-Kraepelinian era. It went on to describe the grand illuminating synthesis that Kraepelin accomplished so brilliantly and that brief moment in time when the psychiatric stage was swept bare of its many players to leave standing only those two grand protagonists, manic-depressive psychosis and dementia praecox.

The moment could not last. And our story went on to describe the debates that raged about manic-depressive insanity. Was or was not involutional melancholia included within its scope? Were or were not neurotic depressions different from manic-depressive psychosis? At about this point the chorus of arguments changed its language from German to English.

Appeals were heard on clinical and historical grounds for both the unity and the diversity of what was beginning to be called depression. Lewis published his magisterial studies and judgments. The battles took on stereotyped styles: Endogenous versus Reactive. A new campaign was fought with the advent of every new treatment.

Gradually, new weapons were introduced into the fray. Computers made complex types of statistical analyses possible and the same battles raged with more sophisticated artillery. But each temporary victory for one side was met by equally convincing statistics from the other.

Finally, weary of the inconclusiveness of the Great Debate, investigators began to approach depressive illness from a different perspective. Using techniques involving life histories, family studies, genetics and considerations of age and sex, they began to carve up the body of depressive illnesses into different shaped components: unipolar and bipolar manic-depressive illness, primary and secondary affective disorders. The group of primary affective disorders was subdivided into manic-depressive disease and depressive disease. Depressive disease was further subdivided into genetically more homogeneous subgroups. And at the end of the story Mendlewicz et al. subdivided manic-depressive disease into two further subgroups. The morbid traits of the early clinical observers were replaced by the morbid risks of the clinical statisticians. Hereditary traits were giving place to genetics.

Are these subgroups we now read about real or artifacts? As Winokur acknowledges, it is too early to tell. But the Kraepelinian simplicity is gone. The psychiatric stage—now converted into a research laboratory—is once again populated by numerous players. Yet there is still a Kraepelinian flavor to it. His confident assumption of pathologic lesions has been replaced by a sophisticated search for biochemical lesions. Since the Klinik has been replaced by the laboratory, we hear discussions about neurophysiology, biochemistry and endocrinology, about catecholamines and indoleamines.

Let us return to the beginning, but to a different beginning that takes place neither in a psychiatric hospital nor in a laboratory; let us open the story with the consulting rooms of the early psychoanalysts.

Chapter II

ABRAHAM

Disregarding some early tentative ideas of Freud's (1896), one might say that the psychoanalytical contributions to the subject of depression began with a paper by Abraham (1911). In this he declared that neurotic depression occurs when a person "has to give up his sexual aim without having obtained gratification. He feels himself unloved and incapable of loving, and therefore he despairs of his life and his future." He differentiated this from the mechanism in psychotic depression which he had studied in six cases of manic-depressive psychosis.

Freud (1909) had observed that in the obsessional neurotic, hatred and love were always interfering with one another. Abraham was struck by the presence of this ambivalent imbalance in the depressed patient too: "The tendency such a person has to adopt a hostile attitude to the external world is so great that his capacity for love is reduced to a minimum." In every one of his cases of psychotic depression, he concluded that the condition resulted from an attitude of hatred which was paralyzing the patient's capacity to love. Abraham's focus on ambivalence in depression has, to a considerable extent, determined the shape of psychoanalytic thinking on this subject up to the present time.

In a formula reminiscent of Freud's (1911) formulation for paranoia, Abraham explained the depression of such patients in terms of their use of the projective mechanism: " 'I cannot love people; I have to hate them.' " The content of this perception is repressed and projected externally: " 'People hate me . . . because of my inborn defects. Therefore I am unhappy and depressed.' " Abraham felt that this repressed hostility revealed itself in dreams and symptomatic acts and particularly in a tendency to annoy other people and in violent desires for revenge.

He found that the more violent the patient's unconscious hostility, the more marked was his tendency to form delusional ideas of guilt; that is to say, the patient would feel just as guilty about his repressed impulses as if he had actually carried out his destructive and revengeful fantasies. And in this "omnipotence of thought," as Freud had called it, he also resembled the obsessional neurotic. Another symptom that Abraham explained on the basis of the strength of the hostile impulses in the depressive was the delusion of poverty which he so often observed. This feeling of impoverishment, he felt, sprang from a repressed perception by the patient of his own inability to love, i.e., of his own emotional impoverishment. He also commented on the hidden pleasure the depressive seems to derive from his own suffering and from continually thinking about himself.

Abraham's next contribution to this problem was greatly influenced by Freud's views on infantile sexuality. In 1905, the latter had described several developmental stages or phases of sexual behavior prior to the genital stage. The phases were postulated on the basis of erogenous zones which were described as portions of skin or mucous membrane, the stimulation of which produced feelings of pleasure of a definite quality. In Freud's view the oral, or, as he sometimes rather dramatically called it, the cannibalistic stage was the first pregenital phase of sexual organization. It was one in which the primary mode of sexual pleasure was the gratification of the oral erogenous zone, the mucous membrane of the mouth, by the act of sucking. Thus, sexual gratification was combined with the gratification of the need for nourishment. Freud postulated that later on in life the desire for sexual pleasure is usually separated from the desire for taking nourishment. One step on the way to this emancipation is the sucking of objects, e.g., the thumb, which though giving gratification to the oral zone does not satisfy the need for nourishment. The association of sexual pleasure with the lips and mouth is of course never completely broken but is integrated into normal sexual behavior as foreplay, for example, in the act of kissing.

In 1916 Abraham wrote a paper to corroborate and to supply clinical evidence for Freud's hypothesis of an oral pregenital stage of sexual life. It was mostly an empirical paper in which, from his clinical material, he recorded many examples of patients whose method of obtaining sexual pleasure had not achieved independence from the nutritive act.

First he mentioned the resistance that some children display to the act of weaning, and cited two examples: a girl of nine who could be induced to leave her bed in the morning only by being brought a bottle of warm milk and a boy of thirteen who had not yet been weaned from the bottle. He then described three adult patients who did not indulge in ordinary heterosexual activity but who did derive great pleasure from eating sweets. One of these patients, a female, in periods of abstinence from masturbation often experienced a violent longing for sweets. She bought and ate these sweets with great secrecy and with intense feelings of pleasure and gratification.

He repeated his earlier theory that lack of their accustomed sexual gratification leads to depression in many neurotics and went on to say that autoeroticism in neurotics has two uses: to prevent a depression of spirits when it is threatened and to remove it when it has occurred. He included the various kinds of gratification of the oral zone among the autoerotic methods used to dispel depression. As an example he cites a young female patient of his who used to relieve her depression by eating. Another patient of his, a male, lay in bed one day overcome with depression. His mother happened to bring him a cup of milk. "As he put the cup to his mouth and his lips came in contact with the fluid, he had, as he expressed it, 'a mingled sensation of warmth, softness, and sweetness.' This sensation surprised him, and yet seemed to be something known to him in the distant past; and at the same time it had an inexplicably soothing effect on him." Psychoanalysis and information from his parents revealed that he had had a very extended nursing period and an openly expressed desire for the breast lasting over several years. The cup of milk had presumably reactivated very early pleasurable memories and had served to alleviate his depression temporarily. Abraham also made passing reference to the frequently favorable effect on depressed neurotics of swallowing medicines, even when they had no pharmacological effect. He believed that in addition to the effect of suggestion, a bottle of medicine was useful in this way because of the accompanying gratification of the oral zone which awakened early pleasurable memories.

Abraham went on to consider two symptoms which were related to food and which appeared frequently in depressed patients, especially psychotic ones: the refusal to take food and the fear of dying of starvation. He had observed earlier that depressed patients mourn for their lost capacity to love. They then, he believed, regress to an earlier phase of sexual development in which gratification is obtained by oral means. In addition to, or instead of, the overt expressions of such a regression as were described above, Abraham postulated that in his unconscious the melancholically depressed patient directs upon his sexual object the wish to incorporate it. This incorporation is colored by the depressive's repressed hostility, so that really in the depth of his unconscious mind such a patient wishes to devour and demolish his object,* to destroy it by eating it up. He referred to the very revealing self-accusations of this type that one observes in such patients, and quoted an example from Kraepelin: " 'According to himself the patient had plunged the whole world into misfortune, had eaten his children and drunk up the springs of grace.' " In a later paper, he provided clinical examples from fantasies and dreams of the depressive's wish or tendency to incorporate and devour the beloved object. Abraham felt that only by keeping these unconscious cannibalistic wishes of the patient in mind could one understand his refusal to take food. "He behaves as though complete abstention from food could alone keep him from carrying out his repressed impulses. At the same time he threatens himself with that punishment which is alone fitting for his unconscious cannibalistic drives—death by starvation."

Thus Abraham in these two papers stressed the importance of hostility and orality in depression. But he made this explicit reservation: "I have attempted only to explain the wish-content of certain depressive delusional ideas and the unconscious strivings that underlie certain characteristics in the conduct of the melancholic and not the causes of melancholic depression in general."

*It is relevant at this point to refer to a reply made at a much later date by Fairbairn (1955) to a critic who complained that the term "object" was too impersonal and inappropriate a word to denote a person with whom a subject establishes a relationship. Fairbairn defended the usefulness of this comprehensive though clumsy term by pointing out that "whilst it is fundamentally with persons that the individual seeks to establish relations, the vicissitudes of emotional life . . . lead to [relationships with] innumerable other objects which are not persons, and which may be either animate or inanimate. . . . Apart from teddy-bears and the like (to which children become attached) . . . there are also such concrete objects as totem-poles and such abstract objects as the State. It seems necessary, therefore, to have some comprehensive term to cover all these objects. . . ."

FREUD

In the following year there appeared Freud's classic paper *Mourning and Melancholia* (1917) in which he compared and contrasted melancholia with the normal emotion of grief. He cautioned that the various clinical forms which this disorder assumes, some of them appearing more somatic than psychogenic, do not seem to warrant reduction to a unity. He nevertheless ventured to define this state as follows: "The distinguishing mental features of melancholia are a profoundly painful dejection, abrogation of interest in the outside world, loss of capacity to love, inhibition of all activity, and a lowering of the self-regarding feelings to a degree that finds utterance in self-reproaches and self-revilings, and culminates in a delusional expectation of punishment." This description is essentially that of a psychotic depressive reaction. But from it we have no way of knowing whether he was referring, as Abraham explicitly was, to a manic-depressive psychosis or to the nonrecurring depression of later life that clinical psychiatry calls involutional melancholia. From internal evidence in the rest of his paper, however, it seems quite clear that, like Abraham, he was describing a manic-depressive melancholia.

Freud considered that melancholia resembled mourning in occurring after the "loss of a loved person or the loss of some abstraction which has taken the place of one, such as fatherland, liberty, an ideal, and so on," but he felt that, unlike mourning, melancholia occurred only in specially predisposed people. The melancholic need not have lost his loved object in reality but may have lost it intrapsychically; that is to say, his emotional attachment to it may have been broken off unconsciously because of a hurt or disappointment. Also the patient may not be consciously aware of *what* it is that he has lost in the loved object, even when he can consciously perceive that a loss has occurred, and when he knows whom he has lost.

The normal person in mourning, Freud postulated, gradually and painfully withdrew his emotional attachment (his libidinal cathexis) from the loved object, i.e., from the intrapsychic representation of the loved person. To the grieving person, the world becomes poorer, whereas "the disturbance of self-regard is absent in mourning." But Freud noted that in melancholia it is the ego that becomes poor. It is his own ego that the melancholic vilifies and reproaches and hates. He does not complain of the loss of a loved object, but abases himself and laments his crimes and inadequacies.

It was this self-directed rather than external reality-directed vilification that Freud found so puzzling. In pondering its meaning, he conceded that the patient "was really as lacking in interest, as incapable of love" as he claimed; and that indeed there might be some truth hidden in his excesses of self-criticism. But "there can be no doubt that whoever holds and expresses to others such an opinion of himself. . . . that man is ill, whether he speaks the truth or is more or less unfair to himself." To understand this perplexing phenomenon Freud searched for an explanation beyond Abraham's view that the melancholic's self-reproaches were based on the projection of his lovelessness and hate.

Freud found such an explanation. "If one listens patiently to the many and varied self-accusations of the melancholic," he wrote, "one cannot in the end avoid the impression that often the most violent of them are hardly at all applicable to the patient himself, but that with insignificant modifications, they do fit someone else, some person whom the patient loves, has loved or ought to love. . . . so we get the key to the clinical picture—by perceiving that the self-reproaches are reproaches against a loved object which have been shifted onto the patient's own ego. The woman who loudly pities her husband for being bound to such a poor creature as herself is really accusing her husband of being a poor creature in some sense or other." That is to say, instead of complaining, a patient is really accusing—and not actually himself but the person who was loved. "This kind of substitution of identification for object-love" represented for Freud "a regression from one type of object-choice to the primal narcissism . . . a regression from object cathexis to the still narcissistic oral phase of the libido." In Freud's developmental scheme the "oral" is, as we have seen, the earliest libidinal phase. In this phase the infant is presumed to be at first not able to distinguish himself from the world of objects. This lack of differentiation between the world and himself is referred to by Freud as "identification." The phase in which identification of this kind is said to exist is also referred to as "narcissistic" since it is presumed to be a period when all the libido remains invested in the ego and is not yet directed toward objects. The infant's mode of relating to the world at this time is alleged to consist largely of placing objects into his mouth and into himself, as it were. This operation—"oral incorporation" or "oral introjection"—serves to enhance his presumed sense of identity with the object world around him.

It is in accordance with this developmental model that Freud considers melancholia to be a regression from object-choice to the earliest way of relating to objects, namely narcissistic identification, a type of relationship in which the object is not distinguished from the ego and in which all the libido is withdrawn from objects and invested again, as in the earliest phase of development, in the ego. The process by which this identification takes place is called, according to the infantile model, "introjection." Fenichel (1945) later referred to this as the "pathognomonic introjection," since the development of melancholia depended upon its having taken place. This concept of introjection as the important mechanism in melancholia was at variance with Abraham's view that it was projection that gave rise to depressive disorders, and one does not again encounter this latter view in the literature.

Freud felt that this psychic introjection could only occur in that type of person whose object-choice was of a narcissistic kind. He thought that only an individual who loved persons who were very much like himself could so easily abandon his love-object and so readily confuse that object with himself. His feeling that only such people could develop melancholia was still, he very properly admitted, unconfirmed by investigation. Furthermore, Freud, like Abraham, stressed the importance of ambivalence in the predisposition to melancholia: "Melancholia contains something more than normal mourning. In melancholia, the relation to the object is no simple one; it is complicated by the conflict due to ambivalence." In another instance, he lists ambivalence as one of the preconditions of melancholia.

Freud postulated that after the loss of the object and its introjection, the hostile part of the ambivalence which had been felt toward the object manifested itself in the hatred and sadism which was directed at the ego (and its introjected object), in self-reproaches and self-vilification. In considering how the melancholia finally comes to an end, Freud theorized that "each single conflict of ambivalence, by disparaging the object, denigrating it, even as it were by slaying it, loosens the fixation of the libido to it."

As we have seen, in attempting to explain how the ego introjects the objects, Freud postulated that it uses the method of oral incorporation, i.e., that it devours its object, and agreed with Abraham's explanation for the melancholic's refusal of nourishment. It seems to the writer pertinent at this point to quote a very significant warning of Blanco's (1941)—a warning that was to be repeated later in similar terms by Glover (1945)—that "it is very important to distinguish between a fantasy and a mechanism." This warning came much later in analytical history when the confusion between these two concepts had muddied English analytical thought to an extraordinary extent. Although still referring to the oral "method" of introjection, Lewin (1950) refers to various kinds of fantasies other than oral that accompany the psychic process of introjection. He mentions cases in which introjection is conceived "as an intro-duction through the anus (Van Ophuijsen, 1920), as a smearing of feces into the skin (Lewin, 1930), as an inhalation (Fenichel, 1931), possibly as a 'taking in' by the eyes (Fenichel, 1937)." And Green-acre (1951) has also described a case of respiratory incorporation. Brierley (1941), in a very intelligent appeal for an awareness of the distinction between subjective and scientific descriptions of psy-chological events, also protested against mixing the language of fantasy with that of abstract terminology. She pointed out that "introjection" is the scientific term for a psychic mechanism, whereas "incorporation" is a term which belongs to the realm of patients' fantasies.

It will have been noted that Freud did not concern himself with that aspect of the depressive's orality which manifests itself as the gratification of sexual needs by eating, drinking or sucking but that his emphasis was on the unconscious cannibalistic introjection of the loved object. Describing what followed this psychic introjec-tion, Freud referred to "the conflict between one part of the ego, and its self-criticizing faculty." In this, and in a similar remark in an earlier paper (1914), we have the germ of the idea that was to develop later into the concept of the superego.

Thus, from case material of psychotically depressed patients, Freud gave us these valuable, ingenious, intuitive formulations about the meanings of the melancholic's self-abasement and self-reproach. But as he himself was quick to protest, "Any claim to general validity for our conclusions shall be foregone at the out-set."

One indication that Freud did not consider his explanation for melancholia to be applicable for all types of what we now call depressive illness is his comment on "obsessional depression." He felt that when an obsessional person undergoes mourning, the conflict due to ambivalence forces the mourner to reproach *him-self* "for the loss of the loved object, i.e. that he has willed it." He went on to say that, unlike the situation in melancholia, "these obsessional states of depression following upon the death of a loved person show us that the conflict due to ambivalence can achieve by itself when there is no regressive drawing-in of libido as well." He thus clearly distinguishes melancholia from other types of depressive disorder and indicates that his formulation for melancholia need not apply to other kinds of depression.

One factor that caused him to refrain from generalizing too widely from his observations was his uncertainty about the extent of the constitutional or somatic component in melancholia. This reservation expressed itself several times in his paper. He made reference to the various clinical forms of melancholia, "some of them suggesting somatic rather than psychogenic affections." He referred to the frequent improvement in the melancholic condition toward evening as being "probably due to a somatic factor." He considered that the marked ambivalence of the melancholic was "either constitutional" or a product of early experience. In his reluctance to indulge in premature generalization, he raised the question "whether a loss in the ego apart from any object (a purely narcissistic wound to the ego) would suffice to produce the clinical picture of melancholia and whether an impoverishment of ego-libido directly due to toxins would not result in certain forms of disease."

It is of historical interest that, independently of Freud, an English worker, Alfred Carver (1921), made some very similar observations in his comments on the analysis of a case of melancholia. He came to the conclusion that it was after the loss of a beloved person that his patient lost her interest in the environment. Moreover, he felt that she unconsciously harbored a grudge against her husband for having died and left her. "The mental mechanism in the . . . case seems to be a displacement of the reproach from the environment, including the husband, to the self; analysis showing the abuse which the patient heaped so lavishly upon herself was really intended for the former." He further spoke of "an identification of the self with a beloved person who is blamed for having caused the deprivation." He identified the mental mechanism in this case as introjection, and held that it was diametrically opposed to that of projection, "which is characteristic of the paranoiac."

In a footnote Carver remarked that since writing his paper, early in 1920, it had come to his attention that Freud, during the war, had also written on the subject of melancholia. From a review of this paper, he judged that his own findings were not at variance with Freud's "unmeasurably though they must fall below them."

ABRAHAM

In his next contribution to the subject, Abraham (1924) pre-sented interesting clinical data to corroborate and amplify Freud's observations. On the basis of the psychoanalysis of two manic-depressive patients and of brief glimpses into the structure of this illness in other patients, Abraham discussed further the relation-ship between obsessional neurosis and manic-depressive psycho-sis, leaning heavily on evidence obtained from his patients' libidi-nal and aggressive fantasies. He reiterated his observation that, like the obsessional neurotic, the manic-depressive is ambivalent to his love-object, even in "free intervals" of relative health. He also observed that in his free interval the manic-depressive resem-bles the obsessional patient in his character structure, e.g., in his attitude to cleanliness and order, in his obstinacy and defiance and in his feelings about money and possessions. He concluded that both these conditions are related to one and the same phase of psychosexual development. But, he pointed out, these conditions are nevertheless not one and the same illness and he proceeded to outline his conception of the difference between them.

He stated that he did not know why sadistic impulses exhibited a special affinity for anal erotism, but that they did so appeared clear to him. He observed from empirical data that both anal erotism and sadistic impulses contain two opposite tendencies. Anal erotic gratification could be obtained in two ways: by the pleasurable excitation of the anal zone that accompanies either expulsion of feces or by the reverse process, its retention. Analogously, sadistic impulses contained two opposite tenden-cies: the tendency to destroy the object and the tendency to con-trol it.

He postulated that in the anal stage of psychosexual develop-ment, an individual "regards the person who is the object of his desire as something over which he exercises ownership, and that he consequently treats that person in the same way as he does his earliest piece of private property, i.e., the contents of his body, his faeces." Thus a loss of an object is equated in the unconscious of such a person with the "expulsion of that object in the sense of a physical expulsion of faeces." Abraham drew attention to the "anal way" in which some neurotics react to every loss, i.e., with either constipation or diarrhea, depending on whether in their uncon-scious they are denying or affirming the loss. He also cited the primitive ritual, described by Roheim, in which the deceased man's relatives perform the defecatory act on his newly made grave. And he provided fascinating linguistic examples of the close unconscious connection between losing and destroying, between the anal expulsive tendency and the sadistic destructive tendency; that is, he showed that a loss may be unconsciously equated with either an expulsion or a destruction of the object. Similarly, he illustrated how the tendencies to retain and to control the object combine and reinforce one another.

He felt that the more archaic and primitive of these two sets of tendencies are those that aim at the destruction and expulsion of the object, and that when the melancholic and obsessional are compared it can be seen that the former has broken off his object relationship while the latter clings to his. This Abraham saw as the crucial difference between these two conditions. As soon as a threat to their possession of the object takes place, both types of patients react violently. But the melancholic regresses to the anal expulsive-destructive phase and unconsciously destroys and rejects his object and becomes depressed. The retentive tendencies come to the aid of the obsessional and he maintains contact with his object. Once the object has been given up, Abraham believed that the melancholic may regress even beyond the earlier phases of the anal sadistic level to the oral phase, e.g., in his cannibalistic fantasies. And when he recovers, Abraham postulated that he progresses to the retentive controlling level of the anal phase at which he may be able to function fairly well, like the obsessional neurotic.

Abraham presented case material to corroborate Freud's essentially intuitive grasp of introjection. For example, he cited the case of the daughter of a thief who repeatedly accused herself of being a thief. He also described several cases of mourning in which certain of the physical and psychological characteristics of the deceased loved person were taken on by the mourner, but he stressed the important differences between this process in mourning and in melancholia. The mourner has had a real loss, a death, and is endeavoring to compensate for his loss, of which moreover he is quite conscious. The melancholic is depressed over an unconscious psychic loss and in his ambivalence is overwhelmed by feelings of hostility which he has to deflect onto himself.

Abraham observed that in mourning affectionate feelings for the loved object easily displace hostile ones but that in the melancholic ambivalence is so marked that love and hate are always in conflict. "A 'frustration,' a disappointment from the side of the loved object, may at any time let loose a mighty wave of hatred which will sweep away his all too weakly-rooted feelings of love. Such a removal of the positive libidinal cathexes will have a most profound effect: it will lead to the giving up of the object." Melancholia will then ensue. The abandonment of the loved object is followed in an ever-expanding manner by a detachment of interest from every human being, from his profession, from his former interests, from the whole world. But unlike the schizophrenic who may appear indifferent to a similar withdrawal from reality, the melancholic complains of his loss.

In considering the problem of the method of introjection, Abraham described one patient who, in his desire to repossess the loved object which he had rejected in the typical melancholic way, had a compulsive fantasy of eating excrement. By means of this and other examples from his patients, Abraham provided what he considered clinical corroboration of Freud's hypothesis that introjection takes place by an oral mechanism.

Abraham reported numerous clinical observations of cravings, fantasies, symptoms and perversions that centered around the mouth and which he took to be evidence that patients who had lost their objects and had regressed to the anal sadistic level of libidinal development continued to regress even beyond that stage, to the oral level. Fantasies of biting the breasts, penis, arm or other parts of the loved object, of cannibalism and necrophagia or reaction formations against these impulses, such as refusal to take nourishment or resistance against chewing, he interpreted as evidence of regression to an oral sadistic level, whereas he took fantasies of suckling or the relief of depressive feelings by the drinking of warm milk as signs of regression to an early oral sucking stage.

Abraham agreed with Freud's shrewd observation that far from acting with the humility that he professes, the melancholic gives trouble to everyone, takes offense readily and generally behaves as if he had been treated with great injustice. He pointed out that the melancholic's so-called delusions of inferiority, besides being reproachfully directed against the introjected love-object, may actually represent him to be a very powerful and omnipotent monster of wickedness. He drew attention to the contempt and condescension that many of these patients display. And he discerningly noted the latent grandiosity that in so many manic-depressives awaits the manic state to manifest itself.

Abraham found all of the following factors to be essential in the psychogenesis of melancholia. Each one by itself, he felt, might have contributed to the formation of some other psychological disorder:

1. Rather than admitting a direct tendency to inherit manic-depressive psychosis, Abraham postulated a constitutional and inherited overaccentuation of oral erotism. By this he meant an increased potentiality for experiencing pleasure in the oral zone.

2. A special fixation of psychosexual development at the oral level, as a result of the constitutional intensification of oral erotism, leading to excessive needs and consequently excessive frustrations connected with the acts of sucking, drinking, eating, kissing, etc.

3. Early and repeated childhood disappointments in love, as when a child shatteringly discovers that he is not his mother's favorite, or even worse, that he is not really loved by her at all.

4. The occurrence of a child's first important disappointment at an age before his oedipal wishes are resolved, i.e., while his desires for his mother's love and his rivalry with his father have not yet reached a compromise. Abraham postulated that in such a case there may occur a permanent association of his libidinal feelings with the hostile destructive wishes that hold sway over him at this time.

5. The repetition of the primary disappointment in later life.*

Thus the study of an admittedly small number of manic-depressives led to the following conclusions: that melancholia occurs in an individual with an inherited overaccentuation of oral erotism and with a consequent fixation at the oral stage of psychosexual development who has suffered early disappointments in his love relationships and who has a subsequent repetition of these disappointments. These first disappointments were believed to be par-

*Abraham believed that since all the melancholic's "subsequent disappointments derive their importance from being representations of his original one, the whole sum of his anger is ultimately directed against one single person—against the person, that is, whom he had been most fond of as a child and who had then ceased to occupy this position in his life." He went on to postulate that the melancholic's self-reproaches and self-criticisms were aimed not only at his abandoned love-object but were also directed "against that former object." He found that the melancholic's hostility toward his mother was, as a result of the early disappointment he had suffered at her hands, even greater and more pronounced than his hatred and jealousy of his father, a state of affairs which he considered quite different from that found in other conditions.

ticularly pathogenic if they occurred before the oedipal conflicts were resolved, the person thereafter being even more likely to relate to his love-objects in a highly ambivalent way. Such an individual on the occasion of a subsequent disappointment finds his love so overwhelmed by an upsurge of hate that he abandons the object as if it were feces and then introjects it into his own ego and becomes narcissistically identified with it. He then heaps reproaches upon himself, i.e., upon his introjected object, until finally a second expulsion takes place and he is free again. After reviewing this process, Blanco (1941) ingeniously remarked, "Judging from his description, it looks as though [Abraham] had the idea that melancholia was a kind of mental indigestion." And considering Abraham's preoccupation with the unconscious libidinal and aggressive activities of the gastrointestinal tract, this does not seem like an irrelevant observation. He himself refers to the love-object going through "a process of psychological metabolism within the patient." He seems to have thought of the melancholic's love-object primarily as something to gratify the excessive pleasure needs of the oral zone, i.e., as something to be sucked perpetually and unprotestingly and to be retained and controlled in an anal way. If it failed to fulfill this role, he thought of it as being cannibalistically incorporated and then sadistically battered and assaulted until, having lost its attraction as a love-object, it was disdainfully excreted and rejected.

RADO

In the meantime Freud had moved on from his interest in instinctual development to a consideration of the structure of the mind. In 1923, he published *The Ego and the Id*, in which he set up his scheme of the mental apparatus. In this scheme, by an animistic conceit, the superego became the repository of ego ideals, the precipitate of parental standards and the embodiment of one's introjected or internalized objects, the parents. It was in the framework of these structural concepts that Rado (1928) made the next important theoretical contribution to the study of depression. He traveled further along the trail that had been blazed by Freud and Abraham, although one misses in his paper the abundance of clinical illustrations that the earlier two writers had used to document their conclusions.

As we have seen, Abraham emphasized what he thought of as the melancholic's constitutional intensification of oral erotism leading to excessive frustrations. Rado conceptualized all of this in a more psychological fashion, describing what he termed the depressive's "intensely strong craving for narcissistic gratification" and his tremendous "narcissistic intolerance." He discerned that the depressive is like a young child whose self-esteem is overwhelmingly dependent on the love, approval, regard and recognition of others. The healthier human being, as he grows up, is able to derive self-esteem from his own achievements and activity. But Rado saw the depressive as too greatly dependent for self-esteem on love and approval from without, on what has been called external narcissistic supplies, and with a correspondingly high intolerance for narcissistic deprivation, i.e., for trivial offenses and disappointments that other more secure individuals can shrug off.

Because of this disproportionate dependence on love and affection, the person prone to depressive states vigorously seeks evidence of regard for himself from his friends and love-objects. As Rado succinctly commented, he is "most happy when living in an atmosphere permeated with libido." However, Rado felt that once the depressive has won a love-object, he treats such a person as a possession, domineeringly and autocratically. If the love-object then withdraws his love, the patient reacts with hostile bitterness and with angry vehemence. This constitutes the rebellion that Rado postulated occurs before every depression and that he believed helps to explain the far from humble touchiness and troublemaking of the melancholic.

It is only when this rebellion fails, Rado believed, that recourse is taken to "a fresh weapon (the last weapon)" to win back love. The ego punishes itself, is full of remorse and begs for forgiveness. Rado described melancholia as "a great despairing cry for love." But the stage on which this love scene is taking place is no longer the real world. It is no longer the lost love-object that is being courted. The ego has moved from reality to the psychic plane. And it is this move from reality that constitutes the psychosis.

The love-object whom the patient has lost may be considered the latest representative of the objects whose love he has been seeking all his life, the original prototypes of which were his parents. When a child does wrong and angers his parents, penance and punishment restore their love to him. Soon, deeds which could incur the parents' disapproval are being atoned for by the child himself with a feeling of guilt, without the intervention of parental punishment; that is to say, the reparation takes place on the psychic plane and his self-esteem is again raised, just as it would have been if his parents had bestowed their love upon him after a period of estrangement. He has, as it were, won the love of his parents, his internalized parents or his superego by the punishment that was intrapsychically administered, i.e., by his guilt. His ego becomes the object of aggression or punishment by his superego which is, at one and the same time, the internalization of both his judging and his loving parents. After the punishment, the ego is again reconciled to the superego. In slightly less animistic language, the guilt serves the purpose of gradually decreasing the tension between the ego and the superego. Thus the sequence: guilt, atonement and forgiveness.

It was Rado's thesis that the melancholic goes through the same sequence. But why the guilt? "He feels guilty because by his aggressive attitude he has himself to blame for the loss of the object." But how can this explanation be reconciled with Freud's dictum that it was the introjected object that was being attacked? Rado integrated this into his theory by observing that despite his guilt, the melancholic cannot entirely absolve the object from blame either; that is to say, despite his repentance and remorse he unconsciously feels that the love-object is to blame for having provoked the quarrel by "caprice, unreliability and spite." So, part of the aggression vented by the superego upon the ego is, as Freud observed, directed at the introjected object. But it must be noted that the object is not all bad, for the depressive has once had a relation of love with it. Rado postulated that in the supplication of the superego, the ego is trying to win back the love not only of the archetypical love-objects but also of the latest love-object, whose good qualities have been introjected into this source and origin of all love and affection. In Rado's words, "The 'good object' whose love the ego desires is introjected and incorporated in the superego. There, in accordance with the principle which . . . governs the formation of this institution, it is endowed with the prescriptive right . . . to be angry with the ego—indeed very angry. The 'bad object' has been split off from the object as a whole, to act, as it were, as 'whipping-boy.' It is incorporated in the ego and becomes the victim of the sadistic tendency now emanating from the superego."

As a result of this sequence of hatred, guilt, self-reproach and

to disappointment with hate and wild sadistic impulses which she attempted to ward off with her rigid self-control. The resulting stiffness and self-consciousness kept people at a distance and thus frustrated her even further. Gero obtained ample evidence of oral and anal sadistic fantasies, e.g., fantasies of savage feasting on bloody meat and defecating on the analyst's grave. The lack of fulfillment of her immoderate and urgent needs kept her continuously depressed. She had identified herself with her lost love-object and had erected this object, her father, within herself; she had taken over his obsessional character structure, his taciturnity and reserve. Gero reported that "she said herself that her father was so much within her, his self so much absorbed by the identification, that she could scarcely imagine him as an independent personality." It is interesting that despite this identification she did not heap reproaches upon herself and her introject in the characteristic melancholic way that Freud had described. Her sadism was controlled by her obsessional character structure. Gero's formula for her depression was "Nobody loves me whatever I do, nobody understands me, I am lonely and forsaken—as I was in my childhood"—a statement of grief rather than a reproach or an atonement or any other restitutive measure.

The study of his second patient is also interesting and instructive. Although very complex, it too revealed a person with infantile narcissistic longings for attention, friendliness and love, whose overwhelming needs were hidden by a façade of self-sacrifice, consideration of others and extremely high ego ideals. He was a man in his thirties who had had periodic severe depressions since the age of fourteen, when his father had died, relieved by slightly manic phases and by free intervals during which he was frightened, inhibited and excitable. This patient exhibited very clearly Rado's double introjection of the object into the superego and ego. His high ego ideal and his immoderate demands upon himself (which screened his covetousness and infantile greed) were the result of a strong identification with his father, and his endless self-accusations were directed against both his parents. Although exceptionally strong, healthy and robust, he complained that he felt old, weak, forgetful and sick like his remembered elderly and decrepit father. His self-torment too was used aggressively against his mother, to whom he repeatedly complained that nobody could help him. His tremendous hatred and hostility were also manifested openly in violent scenes between himself and his mother and in outbursts of rage against the analyst. In this patient Gero was particularly able to observe the voluptuous pleasure in self-accusations and the sadistic intention behind this masochistic manifestation. There were also numerous examples of oral fantasies and at the depths of his depression the patient would feel a ravenous hunger.

Thus in these two patients Gero was able to demonstrate clearly the underlying infantile narcissistic hunger, the intolerance of frustration and the introjection of the love-objects. In the one patient, due to the use of the obsessive character defense, this identification did not lead to self-accusations nor was the aggression directed in a masochistic fashion at others. In the second patient the ego ideals supplied fuel for the self-torment which was used to bludgeon those around him. This patient was not obsessive and Gero disagreed with his predecessors about the universality of the obsessional character structure in depression.

In addition to supplying the literature with his detailed study of these two cases, which contained much interesting material besides that specifically mentioned above, Gero contributed a broadened interpretation of the concept of "orality." Rado had postulated that the pleasurable stimulation that the infant experienced during feeding was not confined to the oral zone but culminated during the period of satiation in an "alimentary orgasm," a questionably useful term obviously employed to underscore the libidinal aspect of the whole nutritive process. With fuller understanding of the significance of object relationships, Gero was able to point out that the importance of the "oral" experience in infancy had infinitely less to do with the satisfaction of the erotism of the oral or alimentary zones than with the wider and more comprehensive aspects of the mother-child relationship. "The essentially oral pleasure is only one factor in the experience satisfying the infant's need for warmth, touch, love and care." This, of course, conforms to the fairly general current usage of the term "orality" in this symbolic sense, as the longing for "shelter and love and for the warmth of the mother's protecting body" rather than, or in some cases in addition to, the desire for pleasurable stimulation of the oral zone. It was in this very symbolic sense that Gero agreed with Rado and indirectly with his predecessors when he said that "oral erotism is the favorite fixation point in the depressive."

Gero asked why it was that the depressive persisted in his infantile demands for love and why he could not develop more ego-syntonic and mature ways of acquiring narcissistic supplies. This happened, he felt, "because the way to genital love-activity is barred. In a genital love-relationship the infantile wishes for warmth and tenderness may also be fulfilled. Such a love-relationship is the only possibility for the adult to safeguard the inheritance of infancy. People for whom this path is not open—and they are the neurotics—suffer from an insoluble contradiction; for they long for something unattainable, being grown up they want to be loved like children. In other words the anxieties overshadowing the genital sexuality press the libido back into the pregenital positions. Thus these demands gain an uncanny force."

And from where do these genital anxieties arise? Gero, in the classical tradition, affirmed that they originate in the oedipal period. At that time, because of excessively traumatic experiences, genitality and sexual fantasies become colored by aggression and guilt. "The neurosis ends when one has succeeded in mastering the genital anxieties, the feeling of guilt oppressing the genital impulses, and when the capacity of experiencing genital life and object-relations to the full, and without ambivalence, is re-established." Gero was able to show how genitality had been repressed in each of his patients because of its admixture with aggression and suffering and guilt. And he was able to demonstrate that after the specific character defenses of the patients had been loosened sufficiently for the analysis and the solution of the pregenital fixations to take place, the genital impulses with their accompanying anxieties could then be experienced by the patients and eventually, with the help of the analyst, mastered.

It is worth noting that Gero's very detailed case studies provided no clinical confirmation of Rado's theory of intrapsychic propitiation in depression. Although he quoted Rado extensively, he made no specific mention of this concept and one is forced to conclude that he did not find it demonstrated in his patients.

MELANIE KLEIN

The authors considered above regarded depression as one of the psychopathological disorders, a little more common than some others, perhaps, but essentially of no more central importance than, say, the phobic states. It remained for the English writers to reexamine the implications of this complex of depressive feelings and anxieties and to discern and to emphasize its broader theoretical importance. They, as a consequence of their increased interest in this subject, provided the literature with perceptive appraisals and sensitive word-pictures of the depressive and allied conditions. They isolated theoretically and described clinically the painful torment of the state which they called the "depressive position."

Melanie Klein (1932, 1948) was the founder of the so-called "English school" and remains its most influential member. It was her contribution to psychoanalysis to push the area of analytical interest back to the infant's first year of life and to examine the effects of the processes of introjection and projection on his psychic development. It will be remembered that Freud, in his paper on melancholia, described the process of introjection as one of the essential features in the melancholic process. To judge by the examples that he and Abraham gave, this term implied the taking-on by the patient of some attribute of the lost love-object, either psychological or physical. Freud at first felt that this process occurred only when the object choice was of a narcissistic type. He later became aware that this process had wider significance than he had originally attributed to it. By the time he wrote *The Ego and the Id* (1923), he had come to see that introjection, the exact nature of which, he admitted, was still unknown to him, "has a great share in determining the form taken on by the ego and that it contributes materially towards building up what is called its 'character.' " He felt that whenever an object is given up, it is reinstated psychologically within the ego and thus becomes part of the person. He even speculated about whether this identification might be the sole condition under which love-objects can be given up. At any rate, he felt that in the early phases of development this process is a very frequent one. In a classic dictum, he maintained that "the character of the ego is a precipitate of abandoned object-cathexes and that it contains a record of past object-choices." Thus introjection was conceived as occurring not only in melancholia but also whenever an object is lost, preeminently when the oedipal love-objects are given up, in which case the resulting introjection gives rise to the formation of the superego.

Klein conceived of the process of introjection as occurring even in the first months of life. To present her views intelligibly in a concise form is always a difficult undertaking. Her theories often appear to be written in a strange dialect of the psychoanalytical tongue which has to be translated into the more standard speech in order to be understood. Her views have met with strong opposition on theoretical and clinical grounds and even her sympathizers (e.g., Blanco, 1941) have been driven to protest against "a certain number of developments in the Melanie Klein school, reminiscent of the casuistry of the Middle Ages. The introjected object has become something so concrete, so well delimited or sharply defined, that when one hears of people introjecting either the whole or part object, and then projecting it on to the outside world, introjecting it again, cutting it to pieces, blowing it up, putting the pieces together again—when one hears all this one cannot help recalling the animistic conceptions of children and primitive people." Nevertheless, despite what most American and many English writers consider her theoretical excesses and unjustified retroactive application of observable data, her observations on depressives are worthy of consideration and are helpful in the understanding of these patients.

In her use of Freud's and Abraham's concepts of oral, urethral, anal and other types of sadism, Klein (1932) examined these phenomena under the magnifying glass of her interpretive technique and transformed these sufficiently cruel-sounding concepts into phases of incredible savagery and hatred that are presumed to take place during the first year of life. She made her observations of the infant's sadism mostly from "derivatives of its phantasies . . . for normally we only get comparatively faint indications of the small child's impulses to destroy its object." She pointed out, moreover, that "the extravagant phantasies which arise in a very early stage of its development never become conscious at all."

Her pictures of the sadistic fantasies during the first year, whether oral in type, in which the child gets possession of the mother's breast and the inside of her body by sucking, scooping, biting and devouring it, or urethral in nature with "phantasies of flooding, drowning, soaking, burning and poisoning by means of enormous quantities of urine," leave no doubt regarding her feelings about the vividness and imagery and strength of the aggressive drive during the first year.

Klein maintained that an infant reacts to frustration and to lack of gratification with rage and sadistic fantasies corresponding to his phase of development. When suffused with anger, an adult may feel several different anxieties as a consequence of his rage. He may feel anxiety about the very force of his anger, perhaps about the potential physiological harm to himself as a result of it. He may experience anxiety about the weakening of the emotional ties during the attack of rage, with the resulting feeling of being bereft of a loved object. He may also be anxious about retaliation and revenge from the object. An infant feels these same anxieties in the situation of rage even more intensely, according to Klein. She believed that the weakness of the infantile ego gives rise to a feeling of helplessness in the face of these immense tensions and to a state of fear of being exterminated by these powerful impulses; i.e., his rage constitutes an internal instinctual danger. In this danger situation, mechanisms of defense are mobilized and some of this rage is projected outward to the object which, in the first few months, is a part-object, e.g., a breast. The danger, which is now felt to emanate from external persecutors as well as internal instinctual forces, influences the fantasied defensive sadistic attack on the mother's body.

These external persecutors are now introjected; that is to say, the child has fears of the external objects even when they are not present, and distorts the danger when they are present. This is the famous persecutory or paranoid position that is so important in Klein's theories: a phase of development in which the child is beset by anxieties about its own dangerous aggressive impulses and by anxieties about "bad objects" outside.

These nameless and formless fears may a little later assume more definite shape. Klein remarked that "in analyzing some quite young children I have found that when they are alone, especially at night, the feeling they had of being surrounded by all sorts of persecutors like sorcerers, witches, devils, phantastic forms and animals and their anxiety in regard to these had a paranoid character." Later, these fears may be even further objectified in the form of animal phobias, according to Klein.

But to go on with how all this affected her views on depression (1934, 1940), she believed that it is not only feelings of hostility that the infant entertains toward his parent. Warmer emotional ties also exist when his needs are satisfied and when he is looked after. Gradually a feeling of being loved takes form and tempers the savagery and force of the early sadism; that is, in Klein's language, "good objects" are also being introjected. Another way of saying this is that the "good" loving *aspects* of the mother are introjected. These are experienced in the unconscious as "good *objects.*" However, she maintained that until the infant can become confident of love despite his rage, every frustration, every removal of the breast, every absence of the mother is interpreted by him as a loss of a good object, a loss which is due to his own destructive fantasies and which is accompanied by feelings of sadness, guilt and regret. She believed that this feeling of loss and sorrow can occur only when the warmth of a relationship with a loving "whole" person has once been experienced, and that this cannot happen as long as the relationship is purely on the level of need and satisfaction of that need by a "part-object," the breast. "Not until the object is loved *as a whole* can its loss be felt as a whole." This is presumed to occur when "the ego becomes more fully organized."

Klein maintained that every infant regularly experiences these feelings until he becomes more fully assured of his mother's love for him, i.e., until he has firmly established his good objects within himself. Those children who are so unfortunate as not to meet with sufficient love for this to happen or whose reality testing is insufficiently developed to disprove these anxieties, who have never succeeded in securely installing their good objects within themselves and who consequently never feel sufficiently loved, are presumed by her to be always predisposed to return to the depressive position, to feelings of loss and sorrow and guilt and lack of self-esteem. In other words, they are particularly liable to depressive episodes.

The sorrow and desolation over the loss of the good objects (i.e., over the loss of all love, goodness and security) which she believes that every infant experiences periodically until his good objects are secured within himself (until, under the influences of his parents' love, he feels secure even when they are absent) is considered by her to be so overwhelmingly painful that it is accorded the rank of the central anxiety situation in human development, "the deepest source of the painful conflicts . . . in the child's relation to people in general."

She called this anxiety situation "the depressive position" and included in it two sets of feelings: on the one hand, persecutory fears stemming from the dangers of internal aggressive drives, and on the other, "feelings of sorrow for the loved objects, the fear of losing them and the longing to regain them."

Klein considered that while the infant is still in the depressive position he cannot be certain that his good object has not been destroyed and lost to him forever when it becomes rejecting or denying. He still has not enough confidence in his own goodness and in the trustworthiness of the object to be sure that when this object denies him something this rejection is only temporary or that when the object leaves him it will return. His awareness therefore that his good object can unaccountably turn bad and his fear that it might at any time become lost to him—perhaps forever —are considered by Klein to be sources of pain and suffering to the infant. This liability to depressive anxiety and suffering is presumed by her to continue until his love for his real and internalized objects and his trust in them become securely established. Until this happens Klein believed that he has to resort to various defensive techniques in order to reduce his suffering and pain.

One of these defensive mechanisms is to deny his anxiety-creating awareness of the complexity of the love-object. It becomes for him at any given time either all good or all bad. When it is bad his depressive anxieties are confirmed. But by means of this defense he need no longer be aware that his good object can turn into a hateful and denying one.

As Mabel Blake Cohen and her colleagues (1954) were to emphasize later, this tendency to see objects as bad or good, black or white, remains a striking characteristic of the adult manic-depressive who has presumably never successfully passed through the depressive position and who therefore has to resort to this and other defensive techniques to control his depressive anxieties.

It is also worthwhile interjecting here that much later Joffe and Sandler (1965) observed that what Melanie Klein saw as a "position" seemed to them to be a very much oversimplified condensation of a series of developmental processes which extend over considerably varying periods of time. Winnicott (1954), as these authors pointed out, regards the "depressive position" not as a phase but as an achievement. The earlier it occurs, the better it is for the child. Winnicott views this "achievement" as one in which the infant relates to the whole mother with an ambivalence which includes "concern for the object."

Joan Riviere (1936) drew a vivid and almost poetic picture of what she presumed the underlying fantasy content of the depressive position to be: "the situation in which all one's loved ones *within* are dead and destroyed, all goodness is dispersed, lost, in fragments, wasted and scattered to the winds; nothing is left *within* but utter desolation. Love brings sorrow and sorrow brings guilt; the intolerable tension mounts, there is no escape, one is utterly alone, there is no one to share or help. Love must die because love is dead. Besides there would be no one to feed one, and no one whom one could feed, and no food in the world. And more, there would still be magic power in the underlying persecutors who can never be exterminated—the ghosts. Death would instantly ensue—and one would choose to die by one's own hand before such a position could be realized."

Although Melanie Klein (1934) spoke of little children passing through anxiety situations, "the content of which is comparable to that of the psychoses of adults," it must not be thought, and she specifically disclaimed this implication, that infantile psychotic states or phases are postulated. In differentiating what takes place in the child from what occurs in the psychoses of adults, she referred to the fact that in the child these psychotic anxieties never solely predominate but are quickly followed by and alternate with normal attitudes. There are, however, children in whom this quick changeover does not take place and in whom the depressive picture persists. René Spitz (1946) has graphically described "anaclitic depressions" in infancy following upon the loss of the mother. But it would appear that he is attacking a straw man when he denies that such depressed states are the lot of every infant. What Klein described are not persisting clinical states of depression but the transient anxieties and the presumed content of the fantasies, essentially unconscious, of all infants.

It will be useful at this point to compare the views of the general analytic writers with those of Melanie Klein. As a general statement it might be said that the former occupied themselves with the concept of depression as a reparative mechanism, as a restitutive measure designed to overcome the psychic injury resulting from the loss of the object. Freud saw melancholia as a continuing period of torment during which the introjected object is punished for its badness until it is sufficiently devalued for the affective wounds resulting from its loss to disappear. Abraham described this process in greater theoretical detail but essentially from the same point of view. Rado expanded the concept of restitution and conceived not only of the introjected object being punished but on another plane of the patient repeating the archetypical pattern of suffering punishment himself in order to win back the love of his internalized love-objects.

Klein, by way of contrast, became interested not primarily in the mechanism of reparation but in the factors that predisposed to depression and in the feelings and fantasy content of the depressive state. Not that the other analysts had neglected this topic: Freud and Abraham had also speculated about the predisposition to depression. But it was Melanie Klein who first elaborated the theory that this predisposition depends not necessarily on one or a series of traumatic incidents or disappointments but rather on the quality of the mother-child relationship in the first year of life. If this is of a type which does not promote in the child a feeling that he is secure and good and beloved, he is, according to Klein, never able to overcome his pronounced ambivalence toward his love-objects and is forever prone to depressive breakdowns. The predisposition to depression, then, is not necessarily characterized by specific traumatic events or overwhelming disappointments but is simply the result of the child's failure to overcome his early depressive fears and anxieties and his lack of success in establishing an optimal level of self-esteem. This outcome, according to Klein, depends in part on the prevailing attitude of the mother toward the child which is so important in determining how he comes to terms with his own ambivalence and with his guilty fears and sorrowful anxieties. Thus, despite her numerous questionable premises, Melanie Klein's basic contribution to the theory of depression consists in the concept of the "depressive position," a developmental phase during which the child has to learn how to modify his ambivalence and to retain his self-esteem despite periodic losses of the "good mother."

COHEN

The report from Chestnut Lodge entitled *An Intensive Study of Twelve Cases of Manic-Depressive Psychosis* is worthy of review for the very pertinent observations and conclusions it contains. Mabel Blake Cohen and a group of co-workers (1954) have written what is essentially an empirical study of a small group of manic-depressive patients. This study is very far removed, on the face of it, from the type of metapsychological speculation so characteristic of Jacobson's work. The language employed in this paper is basically Sullivanian and even words like "superego" are assiduously avoided. Yet the concepts are visibly related to those of Rado, Gero, Klein and others. The similarity of many of this group's observations to those of Jacobson, whose views I will discuss in the next chapter, will be especially apparent in a later chapter when their respective views on the treatment of manic-depressive psychosis will be considered. In view of the terminological differences, it is interesting to note that Cohen and her colleagues considered that the approach of Melanie Klein was closest to their own thinking.

The authors' intention in this study was to discover those experiences with significant people which made it necessary for the future manic-depressive to develop his characteristic patterns of interaction. They stressed not single traumatic events but "the interpersonal environment from birth on," which, interacting with the constitutional endowment, produces the manic-depressive.

The authors reported certain similarities in the family backgrounds of their patients. Each family was in some way "different" from others in the community, either because it belonged to a minority group, because it was in worse (or in one case much superior) economic circumstances or because one parent was alcoholic or psychotic. The families were keenly aware of this difference and reacted to it by striving to conform to the neighbors' standards or to augment their prestige by accomplishments of one kind or another. The children were used in this struggle for prestige and were expected to conform to the strict and conventional code of good behavior attributed to "them," the envied neighbors. The parents' approval of the children was contingent on what they accomplished, whether in the form of grades, medals or teachers' praise. The child destined to be a manic-depressive was often selected as the family's standard-bearer in this battle for prestige because of his superior gifts or beauty or because of his position in the family.

The mother was prone to depreciate her husband and was usually ambitious and aggressive and the stronger and more determined and stable parent. The fathers of these manic-depressive patients were usually unsuccessful, weak men who complained of their wives' contempt and coldness. Paradoxically, the patients loved their fathers much more warmly than their mothers and tended to defend and justify them. Thus the unreliable contemptible parent was also the loved one, whereas the reliable, strong parent was the disliked one.

This study is valuable in that it is the only psychoanalytic one that has specifically examined the family backgrounds of manic-depressive patients. The authors, however, were cautious about generalizing too widely from their relatively small group. They felt that a statistical study of the problem was needed to confirm or refute their findings. One must agree that this would be desirable. One's own clinical experience and a review of the case histories in the literature would tend to arouse doubts as to the universality of just this particular type of family background in the lives of all manic-depressive patients.

Melanie Klein (1948) had earlier suggested that every child in the course of normal development has to come to terms with his increasing awareness that his mother could sometimes be "good" and satisfying and at other times "bad" and denying. She argued that this awareness that his "good object" could at any time become "bad" is so troublesome to the child and so productive of depressive anxieties that he has to resort to various defensive techniques to hide this from himself until such time as he has firmly internalized his good object and has acquired the necessary confidence that his good object will return even if it does leave him temporarily or becomes for a time denying or frustrating.

One of the most important of these techniques is the regressive splitting of the mother into a "good mother"—always bountiful and satisfying—and a "bad mother" who is rejecting and unsatisfying and who can be hated unreservedly. That the satisfying and the rejecting aspects of the mother are really different facets of the same person are thus denied. The mother at any given time is by the use of this technique either all black or all white and the child is defended against the anxieties of having to view her as a complex multifaceted individual.

Mabel Blake Cohen and her group believed that this denial of the complexity of people, this insistence on seeing them as either all black or all white, persists in the adult manic-depressive and is a distinguishing characteristic of his interpersonal relationships. They felt that the persistence of this defense can be attributed to the greater-than-average difficulty that these patients as children had in integrating the different aspects of their mothers into a unified picture.

The research group noted that the mothers of these patients found their children more acceptable when they were infants and presumably more dependent than when they began to assert themselves with increasing rebelliousness and independence. The children found their hitherto tender, loving mothers abruptly changing into harsh, punitive figures at about the end of their first year. It appeared to the writers that these attitudes were more strikingly different from one another than in the lives of other, more fortunate children and were correspondingly more difficult to integrate into one picture of a whole human being, sometimes affectionate and sometimes punitive, sometimes "good" and sometimes "bad." The patients as children learned to think of their parents as tyrannical punitive figures from whom good things could be expected only if they were not displeased by unconventional or unconforming behavior. The parents were powerful entities who had to be continually placated by good behavior.

These workers found that their patients, as children, felt keenly the responsibility of increasing the prestige of the family by personal accomplishments. This role tended to give them a considerably different picture of the significant members of the family from the ones their siblings had. The patients were extremely lonely people, often unconsciously so, despite the frequently clannish nature of the family. Their strangely preeminent positions in the family made them unconsciously afraid of the envy of their siblings, and many of them developed a defensive pattern of underselling themselves in order to hide the full extent of their superiority. Another device used by these patients who were so sensitive to envy and competition was to be exceptionally helpful to their brothers and sisters and later on to other people. The fee they unconsciously demanded from their siblings and the successors of these siblings was complete acceptance and preference by them.

These cyclothymic patients, during their healthy periods, are described as being superficially well-adjusted (despite perhaps some mild mood disturbances), conventional, hard-working, conscientious individuals who have a considerable degree of social facility and often numerous but shallow relationships with people. They are, however, characteristically involved in one or a few relationships of extreme dependency. They are usually unconscious of this dependency even though their inner feeling may be one of emptiness and need. Demands are made for approval, love and service not necessarily in return for having met the reciprocal needs of their love-objects but because of what they consider to be their own sacrifices. These sacrifices seem to consist of the underselling of the self which appears to be unconsciously designed to avert the love-object's envy and to indicate their own need.

The authors stressed the manic-depressive patient's incapacity for emotional give-and-take, and his insensitivity to interpersonal phenomena to the point where he is not even aware of the extent to which he may be irritating or annoying to the person from whom he has been trying to extort narcissistic supplies. He does not see other people as human beings who have their own individual reactions, responses and idiosyncrasies. Instead he tends to see them as stereotypes. His interpersonal activities seem to consist of maneuvers designed to ensure the other's goodness and approval.

Cohen and her co-workers, like Bibring (1953) but unlike Melanie Klein (1934, 1940) and Jacobson (1953), felt that the manic-depressive's hostility has been considerably overstressed as a dynamic factor in his illness. They saw hostile feelings in this condition as a secondary formation arising from the frustration of the patient's needs. Moreover, much of the hostility that has been attributed to the manic-depressive was considered by them to be the result of the annoyance he arouses in others by his demanding behavior, rather than a reflection of a primary wish to harm others.

The group's conception of the psychotic attack conforms in most of its essentials to formulations with which we are already familiar. It can be either a loss or a success that precipitates the attack, because the important thing is that the event, whatever it is, is appraised by the patient as removing him from a position of relatively stable dependency. The patient then resorts to depressive techniques. He whines and complains and tries to elicit the gratifications he requires. These efforts fail because of their offensiveness but the attempt is renewed with redoubled energy. This continues until "he loses hope and enters into the psychotic state when the pattern of emptiness and need is repeated over and over again in the absence of any specific object. . . . The appeal may be mute, acted out by his despair, sleeplessness and inability to eat, or it may be highly vociferous and addressed verbally to all who come in contact with him, in the form of statements about his bowels being blocked up, his insides being empty, his family having been bankrupted or killed, and so on."

These authors felt that the manic-depressive does not suffer genuine guilt. They believed that he does not experience genuine feelings of regret and that he does not make any effort to modify his behavior. He sees the love-object as an authority figure who has certain expectations of him and who has to be placated. Guilt for such a patient is merely a means to an end. He makes no attempt to change the nature of his relationships. He merely depends on "the magic of uttering guilty cries to placate authority." Thus guilt and self-reproach are viewed by these writers as exploitative techniques and not as the result of a regressive identification with or introjection of the abandoned love-object.

To sum up, Mabel Blake Cohen and her colleagues reported an empirical study of a small group of manic-depressives in the course of whose treatment they were able to delineate a typical family situation, a typical kind of parent-child relationship, a typical role performed for their families by these patients and, finally, a typical kind of personality structure with its characteristic pattern of interpersonal relationships. Most of these factors have not previously been formally described as determinants of the manic-depressive personality, but the cyclothymic personality structure as outlined by these writers has been, in most of its essentials, confirmed numerous times in the literature both in its descriptive (e.g., Titley, 1938; Palmer and Sherman, 1938) and dynamic aspects, although Gregory (1968, p. 419) cites evidence to suggest that at least one-third of manic-depressive patients had been found in one study (Kohn and Clausen, 1955) to have been partially or more socially isolated at thirteen or fourteen years of age.

While adopting many concepts about early development from previous writers, concepts which inevitably involved a certain amount of theorizing, Cohen et al. nevertheless manifested a disinclination to engage in speculation. They preferred to concern themselves with the "interpersonal" aspects of their patients' illnesses and as a result appeared not to find very useful the standard formulations about the introjection of the bad object. They preferred to see the guilty self-accusations as coercive maneuvers to obtain gratification of their dependency needs, a point of view which Rado also emphasized, particularly in his later work (1951). It is in the study of the transference and countertransference aspects of the treatment of these patients that this group's work is most valuable, and this will be discussed in a later chapter.

Chapter III

INTRODUCTION

SEVERAL OF THE most important recent contributions have been concerned with the question of whether or not all depressive conditions have similar origins and similar mechanisms. Before discussing these issues it will be necessary to take up again for a moment the wearisome controversy concerning the difference between neurotic and psychotic and between "reactive" and "endogenous" depressions. It may be a bit surprising in view of the intensity of the controversy in the clinical psychiatric literature that there was very little debate on this issue among psychoanalytic writers. Practically every writer on this subject from Abraham and Freud onwards has explicitly or implicitly acknowledged a distinction between neurotic and psychotic depressive reactions. The criteria that have been used have been based neither on outcome nor on psychogenesis but rather on clinical grounds, that is to say, on symptomatology, on the extent to which the patient has withdrawn from or broken with reality.

It must not be thought, however, that analytic writers saw this "turning away from reality" as a sharp end point or as an unequivocally recognizable element serving to distinguish, as it were, the neurotic sheep from the psychotic goats. Rado (1928), for example, felt that neurotic depressions also involve a turning away from reality, with the love-object being replaced by psychic institutions and with the attempts to win back this love-object taking place partly on the intrapsychic plane rather than in the external world. The word "partly" defines his view of the neurotic depression. The object is not really abandoned and the relation to reality is, despite everything, preserved: "It is only that the patient's hold on it is loosened and the weakly ego has begun to give up the struggle with the world. Thus, neurotic depression is a kind of partial melancholia of the [neurotic] ego; the further the depressive process extends within that ego at the cost of its relations to the object and to reality, the more does the condition of narcissistic neurosis approximate to melancholia."

In the same vein Fenichel (1945) wrote: "The difference between a neurotic and a psychotic depression . . . is determined by the depth of the narcissistic regression," by which he meant the extent to which "object relationships are replaced by relations within the personality." The difference is thus defined in quantitative rather than qualitative terms, a point of view with which Jacobson was later to take issue, as we shall see.

It should be noted that it was Fenichel who first indicated quite explicitly what was certainly implicitly contained in Freud's and Rado's formulations but which had not previously been outlined so clearly. This was that in depression there were really two regressive processes taking place, an "instinctual" regression and a regression of the ego, processes which had previously somehow been telescoped together and thought of practically synonymously as an "oral narcissistic regression." Fenichel postulated that there was a regression to the oral phase of libidinal development in both the neurotic and the psychotic depression but that the latter was also characterized by the regression of the ego to the state before the successful establishment of a separate ego. He, like Rado, believed that all depressions represented struggles to reestablish self-esteem, but he felt that in a psychotic depression there was a regression of the ego to a period before it could be aware of objects as separate from the self. He did not wish to be understood as implying that the depressive psychosis was identical with this archaic ego state: "All psychoses contain elements that do not represent the repetition of infantile factors but remainders of the prepsychotic adult personality." Nevertheless he did mean that in a psychotic depression, the patient was unable to distinguish the object from himself.

This is what Freud (1917) had referred to when he described the "regression from object-cathexis to the still narcissistic oral phase of the libido." It was in this sense but with his refinement of conceptualization that Fenichel defined the difference between a neurotic and a psychotic depression as "determined by the depth of the narcissistic regression," by which he meant the extent to which the object is given up and confused with the self, for he believed that in all depressions, neurotic or otherwise, identification *to some extent* takes the place of object relationships. And it is also in this sense and by the symptomatology that characterizes this regressive process that modern psychoanalytic writers distinguish neurotic from psychotic depressions.

As for the distinction between "reactive" and "endogenous" depression, it was Fenichel also who met this issue most squarely. He refused to be impressed by the seeming absence of precipitating factors in many a case of depression, believing that this argument overlooked the existence of the unconscious. He held that one does not distinguish between "endogenous" and "reactive" hysterical seizures on the basis of the absence or presence of immediate precipitating events because it is assumed that the apparently spontaneous attacks have unconscious precipitating causes. The same, he believed, holds true for depressions. He felt that every depression is to some extent reactive even though the provocation may not be demonstrable: "A person predisposed to illness by oral and early ego fixation may fall ill as a result of mild precipitating circumstances that are not readily observable; however, even one with relatively little predisposition may fall ill if severe and obvious circumstances appear."

Having observed that analytic writers did recognize a distinction between neurotic and psychotic types of depression, it might well be asked what the clinical basis was for the various assumptions regarding the specificity or universality of depressive mechanisms and depressive etiology. And it might be asked whether there is any evidence that these conclusions were based on clearly differentiated clinical material, and whether there is any consensus in the literature concerning the various aspects of depression. A glance at the literature is instructive.

It will be remembered that from the study of a small series of patients with manic-depressive psychosis, the correct diagnosis of which he took pains to establish, Abraham (1911, 1916, 1924) drew certain conclusions about the oral and anal fixations and fantasies found in this condition, made certain observations about the importance of ambivalence in the predisposition to this psychosis and introduced the important concept of a "primal depression" in the infancy of patients with this disorder.

It will also be recalled that Freud (1917), after a careful study of the self-accusatory reproaches and delusions of manic-depressive patients, formulated his theory about the introjection of abandoned loved objects in melancholia, protesting, however, that "any claim to general validity for our conclusions shall be foregone at the outset." So far from claiming general validity for his theory was he that he speculated "whether a loss in the ego apart from any object (a purely narcissistic wound to the ego) would suffice to produce the clinical picture of melancholia and whether an impoverishment of ego-libido directly due to toxins would not result in certain forms of the disease."

Rado (1928), as was seen above, on the basis of his experience but without producing any clinical documentation of his thesis, postulated that there was only a quantitative difference between the neurotic and the psychotic depression and attributed general validity to the conclusions that Abraham and Freud had drawn so painstakingly from the study of fantasies, delusions and self-accusations in manic-depressive patients.

Later, Helene Deutsch (1932) was to be more reserved about the universality of the features and mechanisms which had previously been described. Speaking of the process of introjection, she admitted that "whether this is true for all cases of melancholic depression one cannot say with complete certainty. . . . There are without a doubt cases of melancholic depression in which an unusual severity on the part of the superego is alone enough to cause it to rage sporadically and even periodically against the ego." And Gero in 1936 disagreed with previous writers about the universality of the obsessional character structure in depressed patients.

By 1951 Rado had sufficiently lost his earlier certainty about the general validity of the classical psychodynamic formulation to remark, "We encounter depressions in drug-dependent patients, neurotics, schizophrenics, general paretics, patients afflicted with severe physical illness, etc. The question arises whether or not significant psychodynamic differences exist between depressive spells that occur in different pathogenic contexts. Further psychoanalytic investigation may provide an answer to this question."

Indeed, it was a very pertinent question. Whether the formulations chiefly derived from the study of a small group of manic-depressive patients are as applicable to the wildly agitated depressive psychoses of the involutional period, the empty, lonely depressed conditions found in young schizophrenics and the listless apathetic post-viral depressions as they are to the deeply retarded periodic melancholias of the manic-depressive type is a very pertinent inquiry. It was a question which many workers had tended to ignore or to answer with misplaced and unwarranted confidence.

Gero (1953) addressed himself to this same question. He uttered a warning about the dangers inherent in not clearly recognizing the nature of the clinical material forming the basis of any particular theory. He pointed out that "we do not always realize that we are talking about different phenomena and arrive at theories which contradict each other." Not only did he believe that all depressed patients do not necessarily belong to the same clinical groups that Freud and Abraham studied, but he also felt that even "in the same type of depression different aspects of the symptomatology necessitate different explanations." He described a case of anorexia which showed many of the essential features of chronic depression but which nevertheless exhibited certain differences in symptomatology which he believed were indicative of different mechanisms at work in the patient. He felt "that such an approach reflects the general state of psychoanalytic thinking in our days. We are much less apt to reach easy generalizations, but much more able to develop concepts and correlations which are descriptive of the unending varieties of the phenomena presented to us by our patients."

BIBRING

Two writers, Bibring and Edith Jacobson, attempted to modify the theory of depression to take into consideration these challenging facts and observations. Of the two, Bibring's view (1953), though more simply written and more easily presented in a review like this, departed more radically, in certain respects, from the classical theory.

Bibring allied himself with those writers who see the depressive reaction as essentially an affective state characterized by a lack of self-esteem. Rado and Fenichel in particular had emphasized the loss of self-esteem in depression. Bibring agreed with them that the predisposition to depression is a result of traumatic experiences which occur in early childhood and which bring about a fixation to the state of helplessness and powerlessness.

But from here on Bibring struck out in a new direction. Previous writers had emphasized the "oral fixation" of the depressive. Fenichel (1945), for example, speaking of traumata in early childhood, stated that "the narcissistic injury may create a depressive predisposition because it occurs early enough to be met by an orally oriented ego." This meant that a failure to obtain love at a period in childhood when one's "lovability" and worth and self-esteem had not yet been decisively established left one chronically hungry for affection and filled with needs and demands for love, warmth and appreciation and with a proneness to react with depression to the frustration of these aspirations. Bibring described the narcissistic aspirations associated with the oral level as "the need to get affection, to be loved, to be taken care of, to get the 'supplies,' or by the opposite defensive need: to be independent, self-supporting."

While acknowledging the great frequency of oral fixations in the predisposition to depression and of the orally dependent type among those so predisposed, he appealed to clinical experience to substantiate his thesis that self-esteem may be decreased in ways other than by the frustration of the need for affection and love. He outlined how self-esteem can be lowered and depression brought about by the frustration of other narcissistic aspirations, e.g., of "the wish to be good, not to be resentful, hostile, defiant, but to be loving, not to be dirty, but to be clean, etc.," which he associated not with the oral but with the anal phase. Depression over the lack of fulfillment of these aspirations will be colored by feelings of lack of control and weakness, i.e., by feelings of being too weak to control the libidinal and aggressive impulses or of guilt at this lack of control.

He described still another set of narcissistic aspirations which he believed were associated with the phallic phase. He characterized these as "the wish to be strong, superior, great, secure, not to be weak and insecure." The depression and the loss of self-esteem resulting from the frustration of these wishes will be colored by feelings of inadequacy and inferiority.

He believed that the frustration of any of these wishes will lead to a feeling of helplessness and a decrease of self-esteem. Since the infant of the oral phase is so realistically helpless, he considered it understandable that so many incidents predisposing to depression arise in this phase. He argued, however, that "any severe frustration of the little child's vital needs in and beyond the oral phase" will achieve the same result, except that the situations precipitating depressions in later life will have different characteristics.

Another major deviation of Bibring's was his concept of depression as an ego phenomenon. It had been customary to think that depression was brought about by an intersystemic conflict, for example, by a conflict between the ego and the superego. Bibring, on the other hand, conceptualized depression as stemming from conflict or tension within the ego itself. Just as Freud (e.g., 1936) came to think of the ego as the site of anxiety, so did Bibring also consider depression to be an affective state which is, like anxiety, a "state of the ego." He defined it as "the emotional expression (indication) of a state of helplessness and powerlessness of the ego, irrespective of what may have caused the breakdown of the mechanisms which established [the] self-esteem."

Rado in his earlier paper (1928) and Fenichel (1945) were the two chief defenders of the thesis that all depressive processes were carried out according to the same mechanism. This mechanism can be described as the loss of self-esteem and the resulting struggle to win back narcissistic supplies. Fenichel stated that "the whole depressive process appears as an attempt at reparation, intended to restore the self-esteem that has been damaged." This formula was broad enough to cover both neurotic and psychotic types of depression. The distinction between the two lay in the observation that the object from which the neurotic was trying to wrest narcissistic supplies was still an external object, one in the outer world. In the case of the melancholic, however, the "pathognomonic introjection" had taken place. It will be noted that it was the two components of loss of self-esteem and propitiation of the love-object that characterized the alleged similarity of all depressions. It was merely the extent of the turning away from reality that determined their difference.

Bibring, as indicated above, also saw all depressions as having a common basic structure. This common "core of normal, neurotic and probably also psychotic depression" is the loss of self-esteem, the ego's painful awareness of its helplessness to achieve its aspirations. But unlike Rado and Fenichel, he did not see all depressions as attempts at reparation. Instead, he saw these reparative attempts as reactions to the depression, i.e., to the loss of self-esteem.

He assumed that the various clinical depressive syndromes represent "complications" of the basic type of depression. He acknowledged that depression is frequently accompanied by self-accusations and self-reproaches, but he disagreed with the deduction from this that all depressive reactions are therefore a redirection of object-directed aggression against the self. He did not question the validity of the classical theories of the role which aggression or oral strivings play in certain types of depression, but he did challenge the universality of these phenomena.

He felt that his formulation about the basic mechanism in depression was broad enough to include grief and the exhaustion type of depression. In the former he believed that the depression derives from the fact that the ego is confronted with an inescapable situation, one in which it does not have the power to undo; in the latter also he argued that the ego is faced with a situation of powerlessness which it is unable to solve.

In summary, Bibring reduced the multiplicity of depressive conditions to what he considered their lowest common denominator, a loss of self-esteem, designating all other manifestations of depression as secondary "complicating" phenomena. He thus succeeded in indicating that all depressive reactions have something in common without at the same time denying that depressed states exhibit a complexity and multiplicity of forms.

He gave explicit recognition to the several ways in which depressives experience their unhappiness, and with this insight he found himself forced to deny the universality of oral fixations in depressed conditions.

His conceptualization of depression as an ego phenomenon or experience leads directly to one of the most complex and least understood problems in psychoanalytic theory, one that will be discussed in more detail in a later chapter.

JACOBSON
[1]

With the consideration of Edith Jacobson's (1943; 1946; 1953; 1954a, b, c; 1957a, b; 1964; 1971; 1973) contributions to the subject of depression a new level of discourse is reached, a level both complex and subtle in presentation and content, although Searles (1965) complains that her "many creative insights are expressed through a Procrustean bed of technical jargon." She constructs a comprehensive and elaborate formulation which is offered as a key to the understanding of states of mind as seemingly diverse as normal self-regard, depressive moods and psychotic states. Her papers are too numerous and lengthy to permit any but the briefest and sketchiest of outlines. Her theoretical model is a very

closely knit and interlocking construction. It is based on a painstaking exposition of the development of the self, ego identifications, the ego ideal and the superego. In order to make her theory
of depression comprehensible, it will be necessary to review this
development as she visualizes it. It is not entirely novel, being
solidly based on classical analytic theories (many of them previously outlined in the pages of this review), but her model is no
mere recapitulation of previous conceptions of psychological development. She tries particularly to eradicate terminological imprecisions and to give body and detail to previously more sketchy
expositions of ego identifications, ego-ideal formation and other
concepts.

Although the purpose here is to review her theories only insofar
as they throw light on the subject of depression, they nevertheless
provide the opportunity to view the depressive states in useful
perspective against the background of normal development. Her
theory concerns itself with the pathology of self-esteem, but it is
first necessary to study the development and the anatomy of this
self-esteem as she presents it.

She makes use of and incorporates earlier ideas about depression in a manner that illustrates the organic growth of these theories, so related are her concepts to what had been thought before
and so natural a development are they from the earlier formulations. While she disagrees with Bibring on several crucial points,
her observations have convinced her too of the great number of
sources from which depressed states may arise. She too is
impressed, as was hinted above, with the central importance
of the loss of self-esteem in depression. And she too acknowledges a difference between neurotic and psychotic depressions.

She examines this whole subject using the concepts, greatly
elaborated, of the new psychoanalytic ego psychology about
which a few words are in order at this point. In his remarks on the
psychoanalytic theory of the ego, Hartmann (1950) took care to
distinguish more carefully than had been done previously between the meanings of the words "ego" and "self." The former is
an abstraction used to refer to one particular psychic system in
contradistinction to the other personality substructures, the id and
the superego. The word "self" refers to one's own person as distinguished from other persons or things, or, to use the rather clumsy
terminology, other person- or thing-objects. Hartmann also made

use of the term "self-representation," which Jacobson has also extensively adopted. This term refers to the "endopsychic representations of our bodily and mental self in the system ego," the self-image. An analogous term is "object-representation." These self- and object-representations are cathected by libidinal or aggressive energy, according to this conceptual model. If, for example, the self-representation is highly cathected with libidinal energy, one's self-esteem is said to be high, since self-esteem is in large measure considered to be a reflection of the type of cathexis, whether libidinal or aggressive, of the self-image.*

Our self-image is said to derive essentially from two sources: first, from the direct perception and awareness of our inner feelings, experiences, sensations and thoughts; secondly, from a more detached and introspective perception of our bodies, thoughts and emotions as objects. The latter is, of course, much more "intellectual" than directly felt and is proportionately secondary in importance in our conception of ourself which tends to fluctuate more in accordance with our emotional experience.

According to Jacobson (1954b, 1964), our self-image is at first not a firm unit. It is derived from sensations which are scarcely distinguished in infancy from perceptions of the gratifying part-object (the breast) and it is therefore at first fused and confused with object-images. Rather than being an enduring concept, it is made up of an incessantly changing series of self-images derived from the continual fluctuations of the primitive mental state.

She postulates that some of the most fundamental goals of development are the integration, organization and unification of these images into a firm and consistent self-image, the establishment of stable and enduring boundaries between the self- and object-representations and the optimal cathexis of these representations

---

*The reader should be warned that following on Hartmann and Jacobson's attempts at terminological precision, other writers have also attempted the same task. The state of affairs at the present time is that many terms such as self-image and self-representation are used somewhat differently by different writers (e.g., Spiegel, 1959; Sandler and Rosenblatt, 1962; Lichtenstein, 1965; Schafer, 1968). In this volume, since Jacobson's writings bear most directly on depression, her usage of these terms has been followed. However, since there is as yet no generally accepted convention about how these words are to be defined, it may eventually turn out that her usage of these terms will be superseded.

with libidinal energy. In other words, these goals include the firm establishment of one's own identity, the clear differentiation of one's self from others, the development and maintenance of an optimal level of self-esteem and the capacity to form satisfactory object-relationships.

These goals can best be reached in an atmosphere of parental care and affection in which tolerable frustrations are experienced in manageable doses. There are dangers from two directions. Overgratification with undue prolongation of the mother-child unit will delay the establishment of firm boundaries between self- and object-images and will retard the development of independence and the formation of a realistic view of the outer world. Excessive frustrations, beyond the capacity of the developing ego to master them, will result in an immoderately aggressive cathexis of object- and self-images with unsatisfying interpersonal attitudes and feelings of inferiority and self-disparagement.

Jacobson (1954b, 1964) outlines in considerable detail her theory of the development of ego identifications. Although it is not in every respect original (which indeed it is not claimed to be), it is nevertheless characterized by a noteworthy thoroughness of conceptualization. She considers that ego identifications develop through essentially three stages: (1) the fusion of the child's self-image with the image of his mother; (2) the child's imitation of his love-objects; (3) his real modification of himself to become like his parents.

She considers participation in the mother-child unit to be the earliest stage in infancy. The child, she believes, can discriminate between himself and his mother only after the function of perception develops, and it is frustration particularly that makes the infant aware of the distinction between himself and the object. Frustration, deprivation and separation from the mother cause the infant to become aware of himself as a separate entity from his mother. Theoretically these also lead to wishful fantasies of reunion. When the infant nurses or is close to his mother, these wishful fantasies are gratified and the images of the self and the mother are presumed to merge again. "Thus the hungry infant's longing for oral gratification is the origin of the first, primitive type of identification, an identification achieved by refusion of self- and object-images and founded on wishful fantasies of oral incorporation of the love-object. This refusion of self- and object-images will be accompanied by a temporary weakening of the perceptive functions and hence by a return from the level of beginning ego formation to an earlier, less differentiated state."*

The next phase in the development of ego identification is said to consist of the child's increasing attempts to imitate his love-objects. Identification is now sought by imitation. The child begins early to notice, respond to and emulate the gestures, actions and emotions of the mother. His maturing speech and motor facility, his ability to talk and move around—in short, his developing ego activities—are all used in the service of being "like" his mother. There are magic illusory components to this type of imitation. They "indicate how much the child wants to maintain the mother as a part of himself and to adhere to the primitive aims of identification: the merging of maternal and self-images without distinction of and regard for the external and his own, inner reality."

It is during this period that the infant is considered to be learning to tolerate his ambivalence. This learning process is characterized by "constant cathectic shifts and changes" in which libido and aggression are continuously turned from the self to the love-object and back again, or from one object to another. Frequent fusions and separations of the self- and object-images occur in this phase. Sometimes one image is cathected only with libido, while all the aggression is directed to another one. This will go on until ambivalence can be tolerated and distinct images can be cathected with mixtures of both love and hate. During this period of marked cathectic changes, "the child will display submissive clinging attitudes or behavior alternating with temporary grandiose ideas showing his 'magic participation' in the parents' omnipotence. There will be erratic vacillations between attitudes of passive, helpless dependency on the omnipotent mother and active, aggressive strivings for self-sufficient independence or for a powerful control over the love-objects."

It is worth repeating that it is the child's still not fully developed ability to distinguish between internal and external reality—his poor reality testing, in other words—that is said to be so important in maintaining the haziness and weakness of the endopsychic boundaries between the self- and object-images. And it is this haziness that is thought to facilitate the exaggerated cathectic shifts between them. It is this same developmental immaturity that is believed to allow the child to distort the images of his

---

*Therese Benedek (1956) describes the nursing process in a similar way: "The mother becomes with each nursing and feeding, part of the self again."

love-objects until they conform to his own wishful fantasies, to project onto them those undesirable features of himself that he wishes to disown, or to aggrandize his own self-image with their admired attributes. All this is presumed to derive from the lack of adequate distinction between the child's images of himself and his parents and from his incomplete ability to discriminate between his images of objects and the objects themselves. The world of the pre-oedipal child is a magical world characterized by fantasies that he is part of his parents or that he becomes identified with them by imitating them or pretending to be them. It is this period of the child's life that is most marked by belief in the omnipotence of thought and in the magic of words.

This pre-oedipal magic world is not necessarily entirely relinquished. Remnants of it survive in the attitudes and fantasies of adults and it is to this stage that the psychotic ego is thought to regress. Whether or not the metapsychological explanations and theoretical reconstructions of this developmental stage are accepted, the magical world itself, the omnipotent fantasies and the hazy boundaries between the concepts of the self and of objects, have all been extensively observed and documented in the voluminous literature on child psychology and clinical psychiatry. Werner (1940) in particular is worth mentioning for his valuable comparative study of the thinking of the child, the primitive and the psychotic.

In the later stages of ego identification the child does not strive for complete unity with his parents, nor are his efforts necessarily directed toward the imitation of his love-objects. Instead, he utilizes a more mature form of identification. His efforts are now directed toward becoming *like* his parents by a real modification of the self and the self-image as he takes over many of their attitudes and interests and ways of behaving. Before he can do this, of course, there must be a more or less firm boundary between his self- and object-representations. And he must have reached a point where he is able to have a distinct conception of his parents' mental and bodily characteristics. Jacobson also discusses the vicissitudes of the sexual identifications with the oedipal rival in this eventful period.

Not only are ego identifications now established but the parental standards, prohibitions and demands are also gradually internalized and comprise the basis of superego identifications and self-critical superego functions. The precursors of the superego system in the pre-oedipal stage are said to be the first reaction formations. Parental attitudes cause revisions in the attitude of the child toward himself and the world of objects. If successful, these reaction formations permeate all mental areas. "Thus the reaction formations acquired during bowel training will show, first, in ideas that feces are dirty and belong in the toilet and children who soil are bad; second, in feelings of disgust at the bowels, of shame at loss of bowel control, of pride in achieving cleanliness and of pleasure in clean, neat, and beautiful things; and third, in active efforts to move the bowels punctually on the toilet, to keep clean and to accept the meaning of time, the routine of life and schedules in general. Additionally and secondarily, aesthetic interests and the urge for artistic creation may develop, indicative of a beginning sublimation of anal drives." It should be mentioned that Jacobson recognizes other roots than bowel training in the development of the above-mentioned reaction formations.

One type of reaction that plays an important role during this period of bowel training is also considered by Jacobson to have wider significance. This is the reaction of devaluation or depreciation. As the child suffers frustrating and disappointing experiences at the hands of his love-objects, he entertains at first perhaps fleeting but later more persistent conscious and unconscious derogatory and hostile feelings, thoughts and impulses toward them. If too pronounced or too early, they endanger the establishment of his self-esteem, which is so dependent on his respect and affection for his love-objects. But this type of disillusionment in his parents, if not too extreme, plays a beneficial role in the development of his sense of reality and in the giving up by the child of his magical fantasies about his parents and himself.

However, besides devaluation, there is another tendency at work during this developmental period, one which aids the child in his struggle with these feelings of hostility. This is the tendency to idealize his love-objects. The remnants of the magic belief in their omnipotence and value become split off from the more realistic appraisal of their worth and powers and become molded into the ego ideal.

It is postulated that in the pre-oedipal child there are close connections between the self- and object-images and that the devaluation of the parent has a tendency to increase self-devaluation, just as has the painfully dawning awareness of the lack of one's personal omnipotence. In a similar way, and counteracting all this, the self-image shares in this process of idealization and thus the "narcissistic wounds" are helped to heal. "Forever close to the id and yet indispensable for the ego, the ego ideal is eventually molded from . . . idealized object- and self-images and set up as part of the superego system, as a pilot and guide for the ego."

The ego ideal is composed of more than the idealized parents, however. The establishment of the ego ideal is saved from becoming merely a survival of magic fantasies and images by the advancing maturation of the ego functions of discrimination and judgment. These allow the distinction to be maintained between the "real" parents and the idealized images, and they permit this idealization to be extended to "abstract values in general, to ideas, ideals and ideal pursuits." Compromises are made between irrational yearnings and rational necessities. The magical, idealized self- and object-images survive in part of the ego as abstract models of what we would like to become even though these goals may never be achieved. This longing to become like the ego ideal stimulates ego development so that in counteracting self-devaluation it is next in importance to parental love, "which is of course the best guarantee for a sound development of object-relations and self-esteem."

Jacobson considers that self-esteem, the emotional expression of self-evaluation, represents the degree of discrepancy or harmony between the self-representations and the wished-for concept of the self. This way of looking at self-esteem bears a resemblance to that of Bibring (1953), who spoke of self-esteem as "the tension between . . . highly charged narcissistic aspirations on the one hand, and the ego's acute awareness of its (real and imaginary) helplessness and incapacity to live up to them on the other hand."

Jacobson's description, however, of the factors involved in self-esteem seems much more encompassing and comprehensive. She considers the variables involved to be as follows:

1. *The superego.* By virtue of the experience of guilt which is the expression of superego fear, the superego exercises an enormous influence over our feelings, thoughts and actions. Any discrepancy between these and the ego ideal brings about an increased aggressive cathexis of the self-representations since the superego is considered to be endowed with both libidinal and aggressive energy.

2. *The self-critical ego functions.* With the maturation of the ego and the increasing ability to discriminate between the reasonable and the unreasonable, our concepts of value and our actions are considerably modified. The more mature the self-critical ego functions are, the more tempered and realistic will be our idealism and

expectations and goals. The less unattainable our ideal, the less vulnerable is our self-esteem.

3. *The ego ideal.* The more within reach this is, the more prone it is to stimulate ego activity to live up to it and thus to enhance self-esteem. But, according to Annie Reich (1953), who has paid particular attention to the study of the ego ideal, "An over-grandiose ego ideal—combined as it not infrequently is, with inadequate talents and insufficient ego strength—leads to intolerable inner conflicts and feelings of insufficiency."

4. *The ego functions.* It is clear that the degree of success in measuring up to the demands of the ego ideal has a considerable influence on the level of self-esteem.

5. *The self-representations.* Pathological development of the self-representations, for any reason, will, of course, have an important effect on the self-esteem. As an example of this, one might point to the effect of a devalued or distorted body-image on self-esteem (e.g., Stunkard and Mendelson, 1961; Mendelson, 1964; Mendelson and Stunkard, 1964; Peto, 1972).

Jacobson indicates the broad base of her concept of self-esteem by her comment, "Increase or decrease of libidinous or aggressive discharge, inhibition or stimulation of ego functions, libidinous impoverishment or enrichment of the self caused by external or internal factors, from somatic, psychosomatic, or psychological sources, may induce or enhance the libidinous or aggressive cathexis of the self-representations and lead to fluctuations of self-esteem." In other words, success or failure, good or bad health, affection and love or neglect and dislike from the earliest or the most current love-objects all have an effect on the libidinous or aggressive cathexis of the self-image, i.e., on the self-esteem.

It is worthwhile considering one of these determinants of self-esteem, the ego ideal, in a little more detail. As will be remembered, idealization is considered to be a very important process which serves to protect the child against the feelings of depreciation that he entertains toward his parents and toward himself. Annie Reich (1953) considers that the ego ideal "is based upon the desire to cling in some form or another to a denial of the ego's as well as the parent's limitations and to regain infantile omnipotence by identifying with the idealized parent."

In an interesting paper (1954), she studies a few cases in which the ego ideals were unattainable either because they were too grandiose and too omnipotent or else because the ability to translate these goals into goal-directed activity was lacking. In these patients she describes fluctuations in self-esteem which occurred because on the one hand there was an awareness of the failure to reach the goal and on the other hand there was an intermittent blurring of reality testing sufficient to allow the patient to feel that he had actually attained his goal.

In another study of pathological identifications, Rochlin (1953a) also describes a group of patients with fluctuations of mood. These fluctuations were of sufficient magnitude for him to refer to the condition as "the disorder of depression and elation." His cases, though he does not describe them as doing so, confirm several aspects of Bibring's and Jacobson's theories. For one thing the patients he describes complain not of being unloved or of being guilty, but of being weak and inadequate. This is a result of what Rochlin describes as conflicts on the phallic level of development, although elements of previous phases are also incorporated into their psychopathology. In each of his four cases he shows that the self-devaluation sprang from an identification with a devalued mother and a wish to be like the idealized father who is conceived in very phallic terms. His cases illustrate Jacobson's formulation of the determinants of self-esteem, though Rochlin makes no reference to her theory nor does he use her terminology. There is present in his patients a grandiose and unattainable ego ideal, a severely critical superego, an impairment of the self-critical functions and an inability by ego functions or ego activity alone to attain to the ego ideal, all resulting in an immoderately aggressive cathexis of the self-image, in other words, in loss of self-esteem and depression. Like Annie Reich's cases, his patients had episodes when their ability to differentiate their ideal from themselves became impaired and in which they became elated because of the magical fusion of their ego ideals with their self-representations.

[2]

Having digressed in order to consider in more detail one of the determinants of self-esteem, namely the ego ideal, and the part that it plays in fluctuations of mood, let us now return to Jacobson's (1953, 1954, 1971) views on self-esteem and depression. As was indicated previously, she considers these two states to be intimately related. She believes that loss of self-esteem (or, in other words, feelings of inferiority, weakness, impoverishment and helplessness) represents "the central psychological problem in depression." All the factors that can be included among the determinants of self-esteem, then, can also be considered as having important relevance for depression.

Jacobson distinguishes between neurotic and psychotic depressive reactions. She considers that the self-esteem is diminished in both but that psychotic patients sustain in addition "a severe regressive process in the whole personality organization." She agrees with Freud (1917) that psychotic depressions have somatic components which cannot be explained on a psychological basis alone. She feels that psychotics are predisposed to their severe regressions by a defective ego and superego development which remains fixated at an immature pre-oedipal level. This impaired development is considered to be a result both of their inherited constitutions and of their early infantile emotional deprivations and frustrations. It will be remembered that Jacobson postulates that solid ego and superego identifications can only develop in an atmosphere of parental love and care. In such an atmosphere, the self- and object-images become sharply separated and the magical, idealized, primitive qualities of the self and the love-objects are depersonified and retained in an ego ideal distinct and separate from these self- and object-images. The parental commands and standards are also depersonified and integrated into a superego system.

Severe disappointments in the first years of life bring about a premature devaluation of the love-objects. This interferes with the normal establishment of self-esteem by virtue of the identification with the love-object that exists at this stage. In other words, the self-image shares in the aggressive cathexis of the object-representations because of their incomplete separation and their tendency to fuse and coalesce. If the parent is prematurely devaluated, the child "must get involved in the collapse of the magic world . . . [and he] may swing from an optimistic to a pessimistic illusion which again distorts reality." Jacobson believes that this premature and excessive disappointment in the parents with the accompanying devaluation of them—and the self—occurs in the early life of depressive patients and helps to explain the fixation of their ego and superego identifications at pre-oedipal levels.

The prepsychotic personality has many of the characteristics of this pre-oedipal magic stage of personality development. "The self- and object-representations and the ego ideal will not be sharply separated; they will retain attributes of early infantile object- and self-images. . . . The superego will not be a firmly integrated system. It will be personified, unstable in its functions, and will tend either to assume excessive control of the ego or to disintegrate, dissolve, and merge with object- and self-representations. It will be easily reprojected on the outside world." The superego, object- and self-representations will be prone, in times of stress, to lose their distinctness and boundaries, such as they are. They will tend to fuse together regressively until they are indistinguishable from one another or else to split into even more primitive early images. The prepsychotic person will tend to handle his conflicts with methods characteristic of the pre-oedipal phase such as massive withdrawals and shifts of aggressive and libidinal cathexis from object to self or from object to object.

Jacobson emphasizes the unusual degree of dependency which these cyclothymic patients display. Their objects need not necessarily be persons since they are just as capable of establishing intense emotional ties to causes or organizations of a political, scientific or religious nature. These persons or causes become ideal powerful love-objects upon which they become very dependent for love or moral support. As was mentioned previously, the cyclothymic patient's object-representations are insufficiently separated from the parental component of the ego ideal and are therefore correspondingly and unrealistically idealized. It is this overevaluation which permits these patients who feel themselves to be so helpless and weak to become so dependent on their love-objects for strength and support.

This type of exaggerated dependency is closely linked to what Jacobson regards as a "specific ego weakness" in these patients, namely, their extreme intolerance to hurt, frustration or disappointment. Failings in the love-object or in the self are both prone to precipitate depressive states. In either case the patient tends to feel hurt and disappointed and to put blame on the love-object.

And since the object is so excessively idealized it is inevitable that it will eventually fail to live up to the patient's expectations. This intolerance to hurt and disappointment represents an important and particularly characteristic vulnerability in this type of person. One defense against this tendency to be disappointed in the love-object is the mechanism of denial, the denial of weakness or inadequacy in the love-object. And this same mechanism serves in another way to keep the patient in a dependent position since it conceals from him his own intrinsic worth and promotes his tendency to see himself as a weak and helpless person.

This presentation of Jacobson's concept of depression has necessitated the consideration of several different aspects of this rather complex subject. It might be helpful at this point to pull these different theoretical strands together by glancing back briefly over the material that has been reviewed thus far. Her version of the way in which ego and superego identifications develop has been discussed. An outline has been given of her description of the maturation of the self- and object-representations. This, as will be remembered, involves a development through passive and active pre-oedipal magical phases into the period of stable, enduring self- and object-images. These images, as Jacobson thinks of them, are sharply separated from one another and from the ego ideal and superego systems which represent the depersonified and abstract remnants of the early omnipotent and magic images of the parents and the self. The relationship of these metapsychological concepts to her understanding of the development and maintenance of self-esteem has been described. Attention has also been drawn to her observations on the constitutional and developmental predisposition to psychotic depression, on the specific vulnerability of the prepsychotic manic-depressive to feelings of hurt and disappointment and on the characteristic defense of denial which this type of patient employs to master his narcissistic injuries.

To return to the cyclothymic patient's reaction to loss and disappointment, Jacobson observes that the denial mechanism may be so augmented that the patient will lose touch with reality and go into a manic state. She believes that this manic phase represents "a state of lasting participation of the self in the imagined omnipotence of the love-object," a view of elation which corresponds to the conceptions of Annie Reich (1953, 1954, 1960) and Rochlin (1953a).

If on the other hand the denial mechanism breaks down and this phase does not occur, the patient may try to undo his narcissistic injury by drastic cathectic changes. He will shift all the aggressive cathexis to the object-image while transferring the whole libidinal cathexis to the self-image; i.e., he will assert himself by renouncing and derogating the love-object. This self-inflation, in contrast to that described in the previous paragraph, is associated with a devaluation of the love-object rather than with a participation in its omnipotence. This is an untenable position for the manic-depressive. He "cannot bear a self-assertion through derogation of his love-object. . . . He is so afraid of a lasting self-inflation at the expense of the love-object, because it might lead to a complete libidinous withdrawal and a letting loose of all his severe hostility on this one object."

He will therefore become hyperaware of any defects in himself or in his achievements and there will be a rapid reversal of the previous situation with a reflux of aggression from the object- to the self-image. All this, of course, is reflected in marked vacillations of mood. However, it may happen that he is no longer fully able to recathect the object. All that is left for him in that case is an aggressive devaluation of both himself and the love-object. This phase of depression Jacobson refers to as "the primary depressive disturbance," and it consists of a pessimistic, disillusioned, uninterested attitude to life and to the self which makes everything seem empty, worthless and without pleasure.

Jacobson has observed that some patients will now make use of what she refers to as secondary attempts at defense and restitution. The patient, in order to replenish his depleted libidinal resources, may turn for narcissistic supplies to some object other than his former love-object. He will attach to him his ideal object-images and will hope to function through the magic love that he expects to obtain from this person. He will desperately gather all of his available libido and pour it on this individual in an attitude of clinging submission. He will, in effect, "try to blackmail him into a continuous show of omnipotent love, value, and power." If he happens to be a patient in treatment, he may, at this point, direct his massive demands toward the therapist.

If this attempt does not succeed, the depressive may then go one step further. In his desperate need he may give up his hope for an infinitely loving object and may attempt to settle for a love-object that is at least strong and powerful. "The patient may now attempt to hold on at least to the reanimated image of an omnipotent, not loving, but primitive sadistic object. This will manifest itself in the patient's increasing masochistic provocations of the analyst's anger, to a show of aggression, which may bring temporary relief but will actually promote the pathological process."

If this maneuver also fails, the patient may then resort to his last restitutive attempt, to his last line of defense, the final retreat from the object world. In her description of this mechanism Jacobson follows closely upon Rado's (1928) conception of the last weapon to win back love and regain self-esteem, except that she rephrases it in the more detailed and precise language that is characteristic of her formulations. It will be remembered that Freud (1917) recognized the self-accusations of the melancholic to be essentially accusations against the abandoned love-object, now identified with the self. Rado, however, felt that the self-condemnation of the depressive also represented an act of contrition to win back the love of the archetypical love-object, the superego who has now replaced the abandoned love-object. As Rado put it, "The melancholic has transferred the scene of his struggle for the love of his object to a different stage. He has withdrawn in narcissistic fashion to the inner world of his own mind and now, instead of procuring the pardon and love of his object, he tries to secure those of his superego."

Rado felt that in the appeasement of the superego, the ego tries to win back the love not only of the original love-object but also of the latest love-object, the good aspects of which have been introjected into the superego, the internalized fount and source of all goodness and love. Thus he conceived the abandoned love-object to have been split into two parts. Its "bad" aspect, "the bad object," has been introjected into the ego and punished, while its "good" aspect, that aspect of it which was formerly loved, has been introjected into the superego and supplicated.

Jacobson restates much of this but with greater terminological precision. She emphasizes the continuity of this restitutive process with the earlier methods of maintaining self-esteem. It will be recalled that one of the secondary attempts at restitution involved the setting up of a powerful, primitive object-representation in the ego and the desperate effort to force the real object to conform to this picture. Jacobson (1953) postulates that in the melancholic psychotic phase "this reanimated, inflated image will now be dissolved as a representation in the system ego and will be absorbed by the superego, whereas the deflated worthless object-image merges with the self-representations."

In her theory it is not the object which is split up but the object-image. The deflated worthless object-image merges not with the ego, as was previously thought, but with the self-representations. The powerful but primitive object-image merges with the superego. These fusions are facilitated, in Jacobson's view, by the inadequate initial separation of the self- and object-images from one another and from the superego. In other words, Jacobson considers the melancholic psychotic process to consist of a regressive dissolution of the identifications which had been precariously built up in the prepsychotic manic-depressive, a dissolution which results in fusions of bad or good love-object images with the self-image and with the superego and which leads to a very pathological conflict between the self and the superego.

Freud (1917) had referred to the melancholic process as one of "narcissistic identification." Jacobson, as we see, prefers to think of what happens not as an identification of ego with the object but as a partial or total fusion of the self- and object-images in the system ego. In this type of identification the ego does not assume the characteristics of the love-object. Instead, the self is experienced or treated as though it actually were the love-object. In her own terminology it would perhaps be more proper to speak merely of an introjection rather than an identification since no actual transformation of the ego, characteristic of identification, takes place. What happens, rather, is that the self-representations take on the characteristics of the object-images by a process of fusion.

Jacobson, believing that this regressive process represents but a continuation of previous attempts at restitution and defense, points out that in the manic-depressive's retreat from the object world and in his internalization of the conflict, he is still trying to reconstitute a powerful love-object but now in the superego rather than in the external world. She conceives of the self in this intrapsychic continuation of the struggle with the love-object as being as helpless and powerless as a small child who is dependent upon and being punished by a cruel, primitive parent. She also draws attention to the fact that this inner feeling of helplessness and inadequacy is augmented by the actual inhibition of ego functions that the melancholic experiences.

To review Jacobson's contribution to the theory of depression, what she has done is in essence as follows: She has asserted that the loss of self-esteem is the central psychological problem in depression and has examined the determinants of this self-esteem. She has moreover described the mechanisms which the pre-psychotic manic-depressive uses to maintain his precarious self-esteem and has outlined some of the restitutive maneuvers he employs to regain it once it is lost. It is in this theoretical scheme that she has fitted the manic-depressive's last restitutive maneuver, the final withdrawal from reality with its characteristic intro-jection of the love-object, a mechanism which previous authors had studied so intensively and sometimes so exclusively. She has furthermore suggested that the manic-depressive's ability to re-sort to this psychotic restitutive maneuver is dependent not sim-ply on early traumata but more specifically on an incomplete and pathological development of ego and superego identifications.

She believes that it is insufficient to say that there is a libidinal regression to the oral phase. Moreover, to say simply that there is also an ego regression in psychotic depression is for her also insuffi-ciently informative and precise. It is therefore her particular con-tribution to have ventured beyond this formula and to have at-tempted to clarify the nature of this ego regression. Her theory that what happens is, in the first place, an insufficient maturation and separation of self- and object-images and ego ideal and su-perego systems, and, in the second place, a regressive dissolution of these identifications, represents a provocative attempt to offer a sophisticated and imaginative conception of an important depressive mechanism. Zetzel (1960), while in the main in agree-ment with Jacobson on this point, nevertheless sounds a caution-ary note which has application to what, at times, gives the appear-ance of being a too ambitious act of model building on Jacobson's part. "The relation," Zetzel noted, between ego regression "and the original process of development and maturation remains an area of considerable obscurity and controversy."

Other writers too feel much more tentative about the details of the developmental process that Jacobson so confidently outlines. Searles (1965), for example, in an appreciative review of her book *The Self and the Object World* (1964), notes uneasily that "it grad-ually dawns upon the reader that there seems to be nothing which leaves [Jacobson] mystified, as though her theories encompassed everything, accounted for everything, and left no matters for con-tention, for debate, and, above all, for further investigation."

BECK

For the last fifteen years, Beck has been contributing exten-sively to the understanding of depression. He has undoubtedly performed more empirical studies than any other investigator of this topic. His psychoanalytic interest in depression dates back at

least to the late fifties (Beck and Hurvich, 1959). He has contributed a valuable and widely used Depression Inventory (Beck
et al., 1961), and has also been continuously engaged in a series of
psychological, clinical and therapeutic studies of depression (1961,
1963, 1967, 1970, 1971, 1972, 1973, 1974). Besides publishing a valuable, detailed book-length overview of the general subject of
depression (1967), he has interested himself especially in one aspect of this subject that has consistently preoccupied psychoanalytic theorists almost from the beginning: namely, the depressed person's perspective on himself. He has, however, been
doing so in a more focused phenomenological way that suggests
that it is only one aspect of a more comprehensive constellation
of related symptoms. He has approached his subject matter from
a variety of perspectives.

He underlines with special emphasis the well-established point
(see Grinker et al., 1961; Sandler and Joffe, 1965) that depression is
more than just an affective disorder. He notes that physiologic and
behavioral disturbances are nearly always present in abundance in
depressive illness. But his major contribution has been to focus
attention on the cognitive distortions in depression.

He examines these distortions under his clinical microscope and
presents us with probably the most comprehensive and detailed
phenomenological picture of these distortions in the literature. He
reminds us of the general conception of schizophrenia as a
thought disorder, but, as he puts it, "it has not generally been
acknowledged that misconstructions of reality may also be a characteristic feature of other psychiatric disorders" (p. 238). Nor
should this be surprising, since reality testing is not an all-or-none
phenomenon that is either present or absent in human beings. As
I have observed elsewhere (1967), reality testing is "an ego function with varying degrees of impairment. Even the average normal human being develops a subtly individual perspective on reality that is a consequence of his unique life experiences. There are,
furthermore, no objectively calibrated models of reality by which
to measure precisely the accuracy of someone's reality testing."

Noting that "a thinking disorder may be common to all types of
psychopathology" (p. 239), Beck observed and catalogued the cognitive distortions that he found in depression. He identified three
major cognitive patterns that force the patient to see himself, his
world and his future in an idiosyncratic way, referring to these
patterns of distortion as "the cognitive triad."

The patient's negative interpretation of his own experience constitutes the first component of this triad. He sees himself especially prone to defeat and failure ("I'll never be able to do this") and consistently tends to underestimate his own performance. He experiences relatively trivial events as constituting deprivation. He may feel that he is losing valuable time or companionship, others' interest or approval of him, or, more materially, money or possessions. He may see himself as criticized or denigrated, a bore to others, the subject of unfavorable comment which he feels to be deserved. He may perceive the most innocent or innocuous comment or behavior of others as evidence of their low opinion of him.

The second element of this cognitive triad in depression is the patient's own devaluation of himself. The patient may see himself as wicked, inadequate, ineffective or unattractive. He may generalize from a particular act, disappointment or misfortune and see himself as fundamentally and essentially characterized by an undesirable quality. A business reverse may be experienced as "I'm stupid" or "I never win." A romantic disappointment may be seen as "I must be repulsive." Beck makes an important and interesting distinction between the patient's negative interpretation of experience and his negative view of himself by comparing the paranoid with the depressed patient: "Like the depressed patient, the paranoid person may see others as thwarting or neglecting him, but unlike the depressed patient, the paranoid maintains a positive concept of himself" (1967, p. 259).

The third component of Beck's cognitive triad is the patient's negative view of the future. "He seems to be unable to view his current state as having any time limits or to consider the possibility of any improvements" (p. 260). A patient of my own, a very knowledgeable psychiatrist, aware of the cognitive distortions that occur in depression, reported that when he was depressed he would review in his mind a variety of future activities, including professional and academic possibilities, but could visualize no possible future situation in which he would experience satisfaction or gratification. (See Sarwer-Foner, 1966, on this theme.)

Thus the affective components that are ordinarily included in the concept of low self-esteem and of depression are considered by Beck to be the consequences of the cognitive distortions that he has described so well. As he puts it: "The affective state can be regarded as the consequence of the way the individual views himself or his environment. . . . The way in which an individual structures his experiences determines his mood" (p. 261). At another point he observes that "in my clinical studies I noted that changes in the intensity of the depressed feeling followed changes in the patient's cognitions" (p. 262). In brief, Beck gives etiological primacy in depression to the disturbed cognitions, which then, he feels, gives rise to depressed affect.

Although he early (1963) drew attention to the interlocking cognitive, affective and motivational aspects of depression, he has recently (1972) drawn renewed attention to the observation that affects as well as cognitions have stimulus properties. "Irrespective of its origin, the aroused affect becomes part of the stimulus field," giving use to cognitive processes in ways comparable to external stimuli: dysphoria itself can give rise to cognitive distortions. "The patient thinks, 'I'm feeling bad, so things must be bad.'" This sequence he refers to as the affect-cognition chain. He postulates not only that cognitions lead to affective changes but that affective experiences influence the cognitions in a "downward spiralling phenomenon of depression." He has coined the designation "continuous cognition-affect cycle" to refer to this sequence of events.

Beck examines the question of how an individual develops the concepts that predispose him to depression. Like many other writers on the subject, he explains this on the basis of the individual's early life experiences and the reflected appraisal of others. He visualizes self-concepts or self-images as "clusters of favorable and unfavorable attitudes derived from his personal experiences, from his identification with significant others, and from the attitudes of others towards him." Subjective experience tends to be filtered through the self-concepts or schemas so formed. If these self-concepts are negative, subsequent negative experiences or judgments tend to reinforce the critical attitude to the self. These negative self-concepts or schemas may be latent or repressed and may become conscious on being activated by particular kinds of circumstances, possibly leading to a clinical depressive illness. Also like other writers he observes that situations that may affect a person's self-concept, such as failing an examination or losing a job, are frequent precipitants of depression. He thus visualizes the vulnerability to depression as being due to latent negative self-concepts.

It will have been noted that Beck prefers terms such as "self-concept" or "schema" to the more traditional "self-esteem." This is not surprising since "self-esteem" carries both cognitive and affective connotations and since it has been Beck's intention to dissect out, distinguish and establish the relationship between the cognitive and the affective elements in depression. As we have seen, it is his thesis that the cognitive distortions have etiological primacy in the various types of depression, "including those that might be classified as neurotic or psychotic, endogenous or reactive, involutional or manic-depressive" (1967, p. 255).

He (pp. 230–37) goes on to classify and categorize these cognitive distortions in terms of their thematic contents, typology and formal characteristics (e.g., inferences, overgeneralizations, etc.), but I believe that I have sufficiently indicated the thoroughness of his analysis of cognitive distortions in depression.

As we have seen, Beck has emphasized that depressive illness is a multifaceted disorder of which the affective component is only one and, in his eyes, not the most important of a number of elements. He has, furthermore, explicitly proposed that "the typical depressive affects are evoked by erroneous conceptualizations" (p. 239), that is, that cognitive distortions give rise to depressive affects.

He is more reserved, however, in his formulations concerning the physical and vegetative symptoms of depression in the framework of his cognitive model. He does attempt (p. 266) to offer psychological explanations for phenomena such as retardation ("passive resignation"), agitation ("He desperately seeks some way to ease his distress . . . 'I've got to do something' ") and stupor ("the patient may believe that he is dead"). However, he feels that the patients' verbal productions provide data altogether too scanty to establish meaningful relationships between their cognitive distortions and such psychophysiological signs and symptoms as early-morning awakening, diurnal variations of mood, etc.—the type of symtomatology which, it will be recalled, Freud (1917) believed to have no psychological explanation.

Arieti (1962) views the slowing of the thought processes and depressive stupor as psychological mechanisms designed to decrease the quantity of thoughts in the depressive in order to decrease the amount of mental pain and suffering. This, like Beck's formulation, is an inference derived from clinical data. It does illustrate how the same clinical phenomena can give rise to quite different inferences which, in turn, may give rise to or support broader formulations at a still greater remove from the data.

In summary, then, Beck has drawn explicit attention to the

cognitive elements in depressive disorders. He has examined and classified these cognitive distortions and has proposed that they are etiologically responsible for depressive illness, although he has made room in his model for a "continous cognition-affect cycle" to indicate the way that even dysphoric affect can give rise to distorted cognitions which in turn produce depressed affects. This has all been a major contribution indeed.

He, like most other writers whom I have reviewed, has, however, not given particular attention to those instances of depressive illness (statistically rare, no doubt, but seen often enough by the author) in which negative self-concepts do not seem to play any role in the depression, where the patient experiences his illness as a physical disease with no implications regarding his worth or effectiveness; nor to depressive illnesses which clear up, with or without medication, without any resolution of negative self-concepts that are not so much latent as ever-present; nor to those depressions which come and go suddenly, which Jacobson has described* and which I have seen, without any identifiable cognitive preliminaries. Nor has he attempted to explain those unusual instances of manic-depressive illness which cycle through twenty-four hours of depression and twenty-four hours of mania year after year without stopping; nor are his explanations for retardation, agitation and stupor really satisfying; nor does he offer any explanation at all for a variety of vegetative and psychophysiological symptoms. But one should not carp at what this theory does not yet explain and be appreciative for what additional or new light it does throw on depressive illness.

Furthermore, Beck goes beyond the minimal obeisance paid to "constitutional factors" by most of the other writers I have reviewed in the last two chapters. However, his tendency is to note and carefully to review nonpsychological determinants of depression such as drugs (e.g., reserpine), genetic factors and central nervous system biochemistry, rather than to take them into consideration in an explicitly inclusive way in his model of the etiology of depressive illness.

Finally, it must be said that despite the importance that he has

---

*"Manic-depressive patients whose depressions worsen gradually may nevertheless remember precisely the day when their depression began and often also the day when it was over, when they 'woke up' and suddenly 'felt different, healthy again' " (Jacobson, 1957; 1971, p. 105).

attached to cognitive distortions in depression, the existence of which is confirmed every day in clinical practice, Beck's theory of their etiological primacy in all (rather than in some) varieties of depressive illness has so far failed to win general acceptance. Nevertheless, he has more than gratified the hope, expressed in the last page of the first edition of this book, that empirical research might someday supplement the psychoanalytic theories reviewed in that volume.

SANDLER AND COLLEAGUES

Sandler and his colleagues provide additional insight into many facets of depression in the course of a provocative reevaluation of the concept of self-esteem. Self-esteem has held a central position in much of the psychoanalytic literature on depression. In *Mourning and Melancholia,* Freud (1917) referred to "the lowering of the self-regarding feelings" as an important symptom of melancholia. It was Rado (1928) who first designated the outstanding feature in melancholia as a "fall in self-esteem and in self-evaluation." He observed that those subjects who were predisposed to depression were almost completely dependent on others for the maintenance of their self-esteem. He was particularly struck by their remarkably strong vulnerability or intolerance to even trivial disappointments or offenses to which they would react with a fall in self-esteem. There was a correspondingly strong need or craving for narcissistic gratification. As he put it, "They have a sense of security and comfort only when they feel themselves loved, esteemed, supported and encouraged." Their self-evaluation is largely dependent on whether they receive these external supplies of esteem.

Fenichel (1945) too conceptualized depression as a breakdown in self-esteem. He visualized the person who is predisposed to depression as one whose self-esteem is regulated by external narcissistic supplies. "He goes through this world in a condition of perpetual greediness. If his narcissistic needs are not satisfied, his self-esteem diminishes to a danger point" (p. 108). He referred to such people as "love addicts" desperately needing these supplies of affection or regard no matter from whom or from where. This dependence on external supplies he termed an "archaic type of regulation of self-esteem" (p. 110) analogous to the infant's need for love. He felt that depressions were precipitated by a loss of self-esteem or by a loss of the supplies that maintain self-esteem. He believed that in normal development the superego eventually takes over the inner regulation of self-esteem. This means that simply being loved no longer determined the level of one's well-being. What then determines it, in Fenichel's language, is living up to the expectations of one's superego.

I have already reviewed in some detail Bibring's emphasis on the importance of self-esteem in depression. As will be recalled, he felt that depressions represent the emotional correlate of the collapse of self-esteem, engendered by the individual's failure to live up to his aspirations. He went beyond Rado and Fenichel's exclusive emphasis on external narcissistic supplies as the important determiners of self-esteem in those predisposed to depression. He conceptualized the determinants of self-esteem to include factors having to do with success or failure in achieving aspirations to be good, worthy, effective and adequate, as well as loved.

Jacobson too, as we have seen, subscribed both to the importance of self-esteem in depressive illness and to a broadened understanding of the determinants of self-esteem in both normal individuals and in those predisposed to depression.

The next sustained attempt to conceptualize the affective state referred to by so many writers as self-esteem was that of Sandler and his colleagues. In an early paper, Sandler (1960a) approached this subject in a consideration of what he called a "feeling of safety." To convey the content of this feeling, he referred to it as the "background of our everyday experience"; as "more than a simple absence of discomfort or anxiety but a very definite quality within the ego"; "a simple background feeling which can be compared to a level of tonus in a resting muscle"; "a sort of constant affective background to all our experience." As a foretaste of later formulations, he even made reference to a *safety-principle* which, he felt, reflects the fact that "the ego makes every effort to maintain a minimum level of safety-feeling, of what I have called ego-tone. . . ."

In another paper published the same year, Sandler (1960b) referred to an "affective state of well-being" which he correlated, in terms of energy, with the libidinal or narcissistic cathexis of the self and which encompasses feelings of self-esteem and the normal background feelings of safety that he had referred to in his previous paper. He designated to this *central affective state,* the state of well-being, as "perhaps the most powerful motive for ego development."

In a later paper (Sandler, Holder and Meers, 1963), the authors still used the classic terms "narcissism" and "self-esteem" as well as their own term, "well-being," interchangeably.

It was not until 1965 that Sandler, along with his colleagues Joffe, explicitly articulated his ideas about the relations between self-esteem, well-being and depression. They described a clinical picture which they referred to as a depressive reaction in the children studied at the Hampstead Child-Therapy Clinic. They considered this to be a basic affective state which can be "of long or short duration, of low or high intensity, and can occur in a wide variety of personality types and clinical conditions." They distinguished it from adult depressive illnesses, pointing out that it was an affect which can occur in a variety of clinical contexts. As they first used the term "depressive reaction," it consisted of some combination of behavioral, interpersonal, physiognomic, regressive, sleep and mood components, as well as defenses against the emergence of this affective state. They referred to it as "a basic psycho-biological affective reaction." Later (Joffe and Sandler, 1965) they stripped away the defensive elements from this definition of the "depressive reaction" or "depressive response" and used these terms to apply only to the primary psychobiological affective response which formed its core, a response which they regarded as basic as anxiety. They viewed this state as "an ultimate reaction to the experiencing of helplessness in the face of physical or psychological pain in one form or another." They felt that it should not be confused with clinical states of depression, which include further defensive and restitutive processes.

The common factor in the cases that showed this "basic psycho-biological affective reaction" was that it occurred when the child was confronted with a particular kind of threat to his well-being. "An essential aspect of this is the feeling of having lost, or of being unable to attain, something which was essential to his narcissistic integrity. Coupled with this was the feeling of being helpless and unable to undo the loss."

Many writers regard this loss as primarily an object loss. Central to Sandler and Joffe's concept is that what is really lost, even when object loss does occur, "is the state of well-being implicit, both psychologically and biologically, in the relationship with the object." The deprived infant sustains a "loss of psychophysical well-being." Older children who experience a depressive reaction after the birth of a sibling experience not an object loss but "a feeling of having been deprived of an ideal state, the vehicle of which was the sole possession of the mother." They may react to this loss in different ways, but if they experience helplessness and resignation they are regarded as depressed. These writers do not wish to minimize the importance of object loss but they do emphasize that what is lost is the state of well-being embodied in the relationship to the object. They thus stress the link between the loss of a sense of well-being, however precipitated, and depressive affect.

In a formulation reminiscent of other writers' definition of self-esteem as involving the discrepancy between the actual self-representation and the wished-for state of the self, Sandler and Joffe postulate that "mental pain reflects a discrepancy between the actual state of the self and the ideal state of psychological well-being." They go on to state that "if the presence of a love-object is an essential condition for approximating the actual self to the ideal, the loss of the object (or of any other essential precondition of this sort) must inevitably result in mental pain." And if the person feels helpless and resigned in the face of this pain, he then experiences the affective response which we call depression.

Thus they do not feel that depression is identical with this pain. "There are other reactions to mental pain which are varieties of unhappiness, but which are not, strictly speaking, depressive reactions proper." They see mourning, for example, as a complex process designed to reduce the pain of a loss, "to work through the situations which give rise to pain and the later depression." In this formulation Sandler and Joffe obviously see the depressive response as a clinical constellation or a complex psychobiological affective reaction, which might ensue *if the mourning process is not worked through successfully.*

The depressive reaction is often associated with behavior that can be understood as defensive measures to prevent or to deal with the development of the pain with which it is associated. Excitement and clowning, for example, may represent attempts to deal with the painful affect, or this affect may find expression in psychosomatic states.

They consider aggression that is directed against the source of distress to be a normal response to the kind of mental pain which can trigger a depressive reaction. This aggression may alter the situation so that the pain is diminished. "If the child feels impotent in the face of pain and cannot discharge his aggression, the accumulation of undischarged aggression may reinforce the painful state so that he is forced into a state of helpless resignation."

It is here assumed, contrary to their revised formulations of several years later (Joffe and Sandler, 1967a; Sandler and Joffe, 1969), that aggression represents a quantity of psychic energy which can accumulate and be stored up, as in a reservoir, and which must be discharged, lie quiescent or be reflected back on the self. That a person may be unaware of aggressive feelings or that aggressive feelings may be inhibited are certainly possibilities; that aggressive energy must always be present and ready to be discharged, however, seems to be an a priori assumption rather than an empirically observed clinical phenomenon.

In fact, in a paper published the same year, Joffe and Sandler (1965) explicitly noted that conflict over aggression and ambivalence, though an important source of pain and therefore also of the depressive response, is "only one of a number of possible sources of pain, and the depressive response is by no means specifically and uniquely related to it."

In this same paper, they express the idea that much of psychodynamics can be understood in terms of the effort to maintain or to acquire what they refer to as "the ideal state of well-being," a state to which they attach the significance of a biological goal. This goal is not to be equated with successful drive discharge which can sometimes or even often lead to psychic conflict rather than well-being.

In the attainment of this ideal state of well-being, they see the role of the love-object as being that of a "vehicle." This is as true of altruistic object constancy as it is of an anaclitic need-fulfilling type of relationship. Since the object's presence, physical or otherwise, is a condition for feelings of well-being, then it follows that the loss of the object represents the loss of the feeling of well-being. They make the point that "even if the highest level of object love has been reached, the object is ultimately the means whereby a desired state of the self may be attained in fact or in fantasy." The object becomes uniquely important for the maintenance of a sense of well-being. When the object is lost, what occurs is not only the realistic loss of the object but the loss of that affective state of well-being for which the object was so instrumental, or, in the writers' term, "the vehicle." Thus Joffe and Sandler establish a connection between object loss and mental pain that leads to grief and so often to depression. To paraphrase: What the person feels he has lost is the love-object. What he has actually lost is not only the love-object but also the well-being for which the relationship was responsible.

Gaylin (1968) makes a similar point when he writes about the loss of self-esteem or self-confidence: "What is important to realize is that depression can be precipitated by the loss or removal of *anything* that the individual overvalues in terms of his security. To the extent that one's sense of well-being, safety or security is dependent on love, money, social position, power, drugs or obsessional defenses—to that extent one will be threatened by its loss. When the reliance is preponderant, the individual despairs of survival and gives up. It is that despair which has been called depression" (p. 390).

Sandler and his colleagues have thus modified the stress on self-esteem in depression and have broadened the concept to refer to a psychobiological affective state which they refer to as a basic feeling state of well-being. This affective state of well-being seems to be a much more fundamental psychological state than self-esteem. The concept of self-esteem appears to have a somewhat too cognitive and even too intellectual flavor to fulfill the role which has been assigned to it in theories of depression. Sandler and Joffe (1965) suggest this when they refer to the concept of self-esteem as a "psychologically more elaborate concept" than their own fundamental, simple, almost physiological concept of a basic sense of well-being. In fact, as I will later suggest, one finds many instances of depressive illness where feelings or thoughts about self-esteem play no role whatsoever but where the psychic pain that represents the lack of a sense of well-being is only too evident.

In two later papers (Joffe and Sandler, 1968; Sandler and Joffe, 1969), they elevate the individual's attempt to attain or maintain an ideal state of well-being into a basic regulatory principle. They discuss this under the heading of psychic adaptation. This principle is considered to be superordinate to both the pleasure principle and the reality principle. It takes precedence over the pleasure principle in that instinctual drives pressing for unconflictual discharge result in "post-discharge satisfaction [which] can be conceptualized as well-being" (1969). However, when there is a conflict between the wish for pleasure and the need to maintain a feeling of safety, there may be an inhibition of the pleasure-seeking activity—an inhibition which in some cases may even lead to neurotic conflict. Activities which lead to pleasure may be inhibited if they lower the level of safety feeling. Similarly, to ignore the reality principle produces anxiety or some other unpleasurable feeling, whereas to take it into account leads to anticipated pleasure or to feelings of safety and well-being. As the authors (1969) put it, "The view of adaptation taken here implies that . . . experiences are constantly being aroused which disrupt the person's basic feeling state, and that the aim, function or purpose of adaptation is to maintain a basic stability of the central feeling-state."

It would be out of place here to explicate their position on these points. Their view of adaptation has been introduced into this discussion in order to indicate how important the concept of the ideal state of well-being is in their theoretical structure. I have tried to demonstrate how much better the concept of a basic state of well-being fits the role which previous writers attempted to assign to the concept of self-esteem.

It might be worth mentioning that some exceptions that have been taken to the emphasis on psychic adaptation seem to have been off the mark. Rubinfine (in Zetzel, 1970a), for example, belittled this concept as a mere superficial response to external reality and without the intrapsychic dimensions of a true psychoanalytic concept. Joffe and Sandler (1968), however, had made it very clear that the concept of adaptation encompasses "more than that of adaptation to the external world but includes adaptation to inner forces and inner states, as well as to the demands or promptings of external reality." They recognize the danger of being misunderstood, for they continue: "It is perhaps unfortunate that the way in which the term 'adaptation' is generally employed is to denote reality relationship. . . ." They state quite explicitly that the inner forces include the instinctual drives and the superego.

One point that Sandler and Joffe clarified in a number of papers was that the mental pain which led to a depressive response was not identical with that depressive reaction. They conceptualize it as a signal (analogous to the signal function of anxiety) which can lead on the one hand to depression but on the other to a number of defenses or countermeasures including acting out or the taking of drugs or alcohol, as well as to a number of healthier alternatives. It is only when these are not resorted to or when they fail and lead to helplessness that the depressive reaction ensues.

Alternative reactions to mental pain other than depression include an increase in discontent, with regression to unhappy, complaining behavior; anger or ambivalence toward the self, which must be differentiated from the hostility directed to the self via a process of identification with the ambivalently loved object; and displacement of anger or ambivalence from the self toward others.

Various authors, in the writer's opinion, have failed to differentiate mental pain from depression. The lowering of self-esteem or the mental pain deriving from a discrepancy between the ideal self and the actual self need not necessarily result in depression. It has often been noted that people with low self-esteem are not actually depressed, despite the literature that tends to equate these two states. I have often seen patients who were no longer clinically depressed but who retained their predepressive low estimation of themselves. An individual may defend against his mental pain by angry resentment or by overcompensation in fantasy or by exhibitionistic behavior. Joffe and Sandler (1965) emphasize that if an individual defends against pain in this way, "this does not imply that he is either experiencing a depressive response or defending against one." If, however, for whatever reason, he reacts with hopelessness and helplessness, he would then become depressed.

CONCLUSION

Freud referred to "the lowering of the self-regarding feelings" in melancholia. This chapter has in a sense been devoted to the evolution of this observation in the psychoanalytic literature on depression.

The writers reviewed in this chapter have addressed themselves to the role in depressive illness of a psychological state variously referred to as low self-esteem, negative self-concepts and the lack of a sense of well-being. Other aspects of depression, such as depression as an ego phenomenon, the centrality of aggression in depression and the etiological primacy of cognitive distortions in depression, have also been touched upon in this chapter. Some of these I have already discussed; others of these topics will receive a more extended discussion in a later chapter.

Rado and Fenichel had already stressed the importance of low self-esteem in depression when Bibring and Jacobson formulated their conceptions of lowered self-esteem as representing not just an important feature of depression but its most essential element. Since Bibring and Jacobson agreed that loss of self-esteem was basic to all types of depression and that a lowered self-esteem may have many different causes, they necessarily felt that depressed states can arise from a multitude of sources. Bibring felt that the loss of self-esteem in depression results from the tensions between highly important aspirations and an awareness of real or imaginary helplessness in fulfilling these aspirations. He identified these aspirations as involving more than the acquisition of the external narcissistic supplies that Rado had written about. He decisively broadened the concept of self-esteem by identifying others of its determinants using fixation points at the various psychosexual developmental levels as the background of his theory. In addition to establishing a broader context in which to view self-esteem, he asserted that depression should be conceptualized not in intersystemic terms but rather as an ego phenomenon.

Jacobson too defined the core of depression as involving a fall in self-esteem. She too saw more than oral elements entering into self-esteem, but, looking at depression from a fresh perspective, defined the determinants of self-esteem in structural terms rather than in terms of fixations at the oral, anal and phallic levels. Moreover, she deviated quite explicitly and extensively from Freud's formulation of melancholia, for which, as I have noted, Freud himself did not claim the universal validity that others later forced on it. Jacobson did not discard Freud's insights but rather included them within her own broader perspective on depressive illness. As she understood depressive disorders, they included more than just intersystemic tensions between ego and superego, a view to which others, e.g., Rochlin (1953), continued to cling. She brought into clearer perspective the importance of the ego ideal, appropriate or pathological, the actual ego functions and the developmental stage of the superego. She furthermore, as had Fenichel, distinguished clearly between instinctual and ego regressions and thus clarified Freud's view of narcissistic identifications in depression. In addition, she emphasized the contribution of constitutional factors to the vulnerability to low self-esteem in some kinds of depression, especially of the cyclothymic variety. Her concept of low self-esteem as the aggressive cathexis of the self-representation will be taken up in a later chapter.

Beck, on the basis of extensive empirical studies, developed a cognitive model of depressive illness. Avoiding the term "self-esteem" because of its complex mixture of affective and cognitive components, he singled out the latter for closer study. His work on the cognitive elements in self-esteem led him to take the theoretical step of postulating an etiological primacy for cognitive distortions and other cognitions. Thus, for him, negative self-concepts and other cognitions lead to low self-esteem which constitutes the core of depressive illness, although he, too, viewed depression as a complex syndrome involving biological and motivational as well as cognitive elements.

From another perspective, Sandler and his colleagues also dissected out the concept of self-esteem which they reduced to more basic elements but in a way different from Beck's. They postulated a more basic biological affective state than self-esteem. Sandler at one time called this state "a feeling of safety." It was later renamed "an ideal state of well-being." They visualized the loss of this state of well-being as resulting in psychic pain, thus reviewing a familiar concept of Freud's (1926, Addendum C). They conceived of this psychic pain as occurring when there was a discrepancy between the actual state of an individual and his ideal state of well-being. They thus defined it in a way that did not necessarily involve cognitive elements, as will be further discussed in a later context. They considered that psychic pain could exist even prior to the time when cognitions or self-representations developed. As was indicated earlier, they equated depression not with this psychic pain but rather with a state of helpless resignation when confronted by this pain.

It is interesting that neither Bibring, who focused on the depressive's failure to attain highly valued aspirations, nor Sandler and his colleagues, who interested themselves in the discrepancies between the actual and ideal states of individuals, regarded these failures or discrepancies as constituting the essence of depression. In both cases it is the helplessness that is felt in the face of these circumstances that defines for them the depressive reaction.

Thus Freud's "loss of self-regarding feelings," renamed "loss of self-esteem," moved gradually on to center stage in the gradually evolving intrapsychic drama which was progressively elaborated to understand depression. This loss of self-esteem was then broken down into its constituent elements, cognitive and affective, each of which, to change the metaphor, acquired an advocate to defend the central importance in depression of his respective client. This adversary situation was implicit rather than explicit, neither side taking direct issue with the other. In fact, there have been attempts at reconciliation. But the points of difference nevertheless remain.

Chapter IV

INTRODUCTION

CHILDHOOD MOURNING AND MELANCHOLIA—do they exist? This question represents the subject matter of this chapter. On the face of it, it would appear to be an easy question to answer, certainly easier than formulating the psychodynamics of depression. Again, on the face of it, it would appear to be basically an empirical matter, to be resolved by examing the data.

Alas, the psychoanalytic answers to this question turn out to be not quite so simple.

Bowlby, in an impressive series of papers and books, has attempted to view the question of mourning in children both empirically and theoretically. His work, however, has been challenged from both a theoretical and a clinical perspective. The very possibility of mourning in children has been questioned. In an attempt to resolve this issue, I have reviewed some of the literature on adult mourning and have surveyed the psychoanalytic literature on mourning in children.

This subject led naturally to the problem of depression in childhood. I have therefore examined the psychoanalytic literature on depression in children and have compared it with data derived from other sources.

All in all, the question of the existence of mourning or depression in childhood turns out to be a surprisingly controversial issue.

BOWLBY
[1]

Bowlby, in a series of papers (1958, 1960a, 1960b, 1961a, 1961b, 1963) and in two books (1969, 1973) of a series of three, the last of which has not yet been published, attempts to demonstrate:

1. that the child's tie to his mother is best understood as the result of a number of instinctual response systems, mostly nonoral in character, which represent part of man's inherited behavioral repertoire;

2. that when the mother figure is available, attachment behavior will ensue;

3. that when the mother figure is temporarily unavailable, separation anxiety and protest behavior will ensue;

4. that when the mother figure continues to be unavailable, a series of events both behavioral and emotional will ensue;

5. that this process, despite the general belief that mourning does not occur in infancy and early childhood, in fact constitutes grief and mourning;

6. that the loss of the mother in the early years of childhood is a pathogenic circumstance of relevance in the development of personality configurations prone to psychiatric illness, among which depressive illness is prominent;

7. that these illnesses are best understood as sequelae of pathological mourning.

He advances the thesis that separation anxiety, grief and mourning, and defense are phases of a process, each of which illuminates the other two. I will outline his view of attachment behavior and touch upon separation anxiety and defense, but will focus most centrally on his observations and concepts concerning grief and mourning.

Bowlby's work is only peripherally related to depressive illness, although he does make a contribution to the understanding of depressive affect and indirectly to the understanding of Bibring's hypothesis. His work is an amalgam of (1) clinical observations on the behavior of children separated from their mothers, (2) inferences about this behavior and (3) theoretical hypotheses about these observations and inferences. These inferences and hypotheses are at varying distances from the primary data. While mention will be made of these hypotheses, my primary interest will be on his observations and his inferences.

In an early paper, Bowlby (1958) brings to our rather surprised attention the lateness of Freud's full recognition of the importance of the child's tie to his mother (Freud, 1926, 1931, 1940). Before that, of course, he referred to the "oral component instinct" (e.g., Freud, 1922) which achieved gratification of its need for nourishment through the mother's breast. In addition there are a number of references to "anaclitic" object-choice, implying that an infant's earliest love-objects are those persons who have fed, cared for and protected him. Freud (1926) postulated that an infant experiences anxiety on being alone, because of the danger that his bodily needs will remain ungratified. This must be recognized as an inference about the infant's separation anxiety, just as Bowlby's own interpretation will be and, as we shall see later, just as Sandler's explanation of such anxiety will be. The clinical phenomenon is there to be observed by all. The explanations differ according to the observer's theoretical bias.

Freud's anaclitic and economic* understanding of separation anxiety had, by 1940, a very late date, evolved to an awareness of the child's tie to his mother depicted in language referred to by Bowlby as so "colorful and dramatic" that "the relationship to the mother is described [in] terms which, so far as I know, are not found elsewhere in his writings on the subject." Freud (1940, p. 56) described it as "unique, without parallel, laid down unalterably for a whole lifetime, as the first and strongest love-object and as the prototype of all later love relations—for both sexes."

Bowlby points out that Freud begins to explain this in terms of the familiar anaclitic formula of the child's need for food; he tells us that the relationship is originally with the mother's breast (which is initially not differentiated from the infant's own body) but that subsequently the relationship is carried over to the whole person of his mother. Then, "almost"—as it seems to Bowlby—"as an afterthought," Freud writes that "the phylogenic foundation has so much the upper hand in all this over personal accidental experience that it makes no difference whether a child has really sucked at the breast or has been brought up on the bottle and never enjoyed the tenderness of a mother's care. His development takes the same path in both cases." This last quotation from Freud is of such importance to Bowlby because it is in tune with his own phylogenetic formulations about instinctual release mechanisms and attachment behavior.

*"an accumulation of instinctual needs which cannot obtain satisfaction" (Freud, 1926, p. 168).

Bowlby notes that this isolated comment of Freud's is not representative of the thinking of the Viennese school, of which he cites Anna Freud as a representative example. She quite explicitly indicates (1954) that the love-object merely serves the child's need for satisfaction of his bodily needs and of wish fulfillment, "its status being no more than that of a means to an end, a 'convenience.'" Bowlby reminds us that this theory has been called the cupboard-love theory of object relations.

As an example of how she is "trapped" in her hypothesis, he draws attention to observations she and Dorothy Burlingham (1944) made of children in the Hampstead Nurseries. They noted that children will cling to mothers independent of their personal qualities, even to mothers who are harsh and cruel to them. They spoke of the emotions of the children in the nursery being latent and ready to leap into action the moment any opportunity for attachment is offered. Bowlby notes the "extent to which the attachment seems to be independent of what is received" by citing another observation of Anna Freud's. She and Sophie Dann (1951) described six children from a concentration camp clinging to one another to the exclusion of everyone else. "The children's positive feelings were centered exclusively in their own group . . . they cared greatly for each other and not at all for anybody or anything else," even though these children could not meet one another's physiological needs. Confronted by observations such as these, which Bowlby finds hardly compatible with the cupboard-love theory of object relations, Dorothy Burlingham and Anna Freud (1944) spoke of the child's need "for early attachment to the mother" as an important instinctual need" (p. 22).

Bowlby cites examples in which Anna Freud and Dorothy Burlingham (1942) use terms such as "grief" and "mourning" interchangeably, but because of what he regards as certain beliefs that they have about what a child can tolerate, they make fine discriminations between the two. Speaking of the "depth and seriousness of . . . grief in a small child," they comment that "mourning of equal intensity in an adult person would have to run its course through a year." But "childish grief is short-lived," they declare (pp. 51–52), no longer than forty-eight hours at most—at variance, according to Bowlby, with their own reports. This is also in direct contrast with Bowlby's findings in his study. He comments thus on such discrepancies: "Incompatibility between a theoretical expectation and observed data inevitably calls the theory in question."

Bowlby finds this same discrepancy between formulations

derived from clinical observations and those presented in the course of theoretical discussions to be the rule in the writing of analysts with firsthand experience of infants, analysts such as Melanie Klein, Ribble, Therese Benedek and René Spitz. "In each case they have observed non-oral social interaction between mother and infant and, in describing it, have used terms suggesting a primary social bond. When they come to theorizing about it, however, each seems to feel a compulsion to give primacy to needs for food and warmth and to suppose that social interaction develops only secondarily and as a result of instrumental learning."

He cites observation after observation from Klein, Winnicott, Benedek, Erikson, Sullivan and Spitz indicating that infants have attachments to mother figures that cannot be explained by pressing physiologic needs such as hunger or pain. But, "trapped" as they are by their own theories, writer after writer seems to overlook what is to Bowlby the most obvious explanation of such behavior, namely, an instinctual need for "attachment behavior" which manifests itself not only as sucking but also as clinging, following, crying and smiling. He finds Melanie Klein (1948), for example, preoccupied with food, orality and the breast; Benedek (1956), "a prisoner of orality theory" reporting behavior which she terms "emotional symbiosis" and which she acknowledges finding hard to understand but resorting in the end to the infant's need to be fed as an explanatory device; Fairbairn (1952, p. 47), despite evidence to the contrary, stressing orality: "infantile dependence is equivalent to oral dependence"; and so on.

An exception to this general trend is what Bowlby refers to as "the Hungarian school," the outstanding representatives of which are Michael and Alice Balint. Inspired by Ferenczi's interest in the mother-child relationship, the Balints eventually took the position that there is, in infancy, a primary, primitive object relationship which is wholly independent of the erotogenic zones. M. Balint (1949) stated that "this form of object relation . . . is not oral, oral-sucking, anal, genital, etc., love but is something on its own. . . ."

Bowlby's interest in attachment behavior stems from an adherence to a biological instinctual theory of such behavior. This biological theory in turn originated in the work on imprinting in birds by Lorenz. The latter's work was followed up by investigations of attachment behavior in guinea pigs, dogs, sheep and rhesus monkeys, culminating in the work of Harlow and collaborators (for references, see Bowlby, 1969, Chapter 12 and elsewhere). This theory of attachment behavior, insofar as it applies to man, is outside the scope of this book. To repeat, what is of relevance for the understanding of depression is his views on separation anxiety, grief and mourning.

In his paper on separation anxiety, Bowlby (1960a) outlines the sequence of events that follow upon the temporary separation from mother figures of children in institutional settings between the ages of one and four. He was greatly impressed and influenced in his understanding of separation by an ongoing study of James Robertson (1952, 1953, 1958a, 1958b, 1962) and later by the collaborative work of James and Joyce Robertson (1967–73, 1971). The sequence of events that follow separation were labeled "protest," "despair" and "denial" by Robertson (1953). The name of the last phase was later changed to "detachment."

The phase of protest, which lasts in children from a few hours to a week or more, is one in which the child experiences acute distress and appears to be making an effort to regain his mother's presence by crying loudly, angrily throwing himself about, shaking the cot, engaging in reproachful language and looking eagerly toward any sight or sound which might suggest the return of the missing mother.

This is followed by a phase of despair, which, while his preoccupation with his missing mother is still present, is characterized more by increasing hopelessness. The physical activity diminishes and the loud crying becomes more monotonous or intermittent. The child becomes withdrawn and inert. He becomes quieter and makes no or fewer demands. He looks depressed and appears to be in deep mourning.

In the succeeding phase of detachment, the child accepts the care of his nurses and the food and toys they may bring. He may smile and appear sociable. But when his mother visits there is a striking absence of attachment behavior. He may not greet her. He may hardly seem to know her. He may seem remote and apathetic. He turns away listlessly, seeming to have lost interest in her.

If he has lost a series of mother figures in the persons of a series of nurses who move from one shift or from one service to another, he may gradually commit himself less and less to succeeding mother figures. He may act as if mothering or human contact has little interest for him. He will cease to show feelings when nurses come and go or when his parents come and go on visiting days.

In a review of the literature on separation anxiety, Bowlby (1961a) indicates that it was not until 1942 and 1944 that Burlingham and Anna Freud first directed attention to the violent reactions and despair felt by children who are separated from their mothers. But in contrast to Bowlby, Anna Freud (e.g., 1953, 1960) continues to attribute this anxiety to worry about the fulfillment of needs. Bowlby notes that Benedek (1946) also became fully aware of the anxiety that is inherent in separation and of the yearning and the longing that accompanies this separation. But as he points out, "the increase in longing evident in adults at separation, which can hardly be considered other than a natural and normal response, is explained as due to a regression to oral dependency. Indeed, as in the theorizing of other analysts, Therese Benedek tends at times to theorize as though all attachments to loved persons were undesirable regressions to an infantile state."

Bowlby notes also that Freud, after many years of wondering about the consequences of object loss, brought himself to contemplate the subject once again (Freud, 1926, pp. 164–72) and formulated a hypothesis which, Bowlby acknowledged, permits him "to entertain the agreeable idea that towards the end of his life Freud was searching after a formulation not very different from that advanced [by Bowlby]." Bowlby summarized this formulation as follows: "Anxiety is the reaction to the danger of loss of object, the pain of mourning a reaction to the actual loss of object, defenses protect the ego against instinctual demands which threaten to overwhelm it and which can occur all too readily in the absence of the object."

[2]

In his paper on grief and mourning in infancy and childhood, Bowlby (1960b) notes that writers such as Abraham, Jacobson and Spitz, who were concerned with the child's object-relations in the early years of life, have tended to use words like "disappointment" and "disillusionment" rather than "mourning" to identify the sequence of events initiated by separation or loss of love, while those who conceive of the infant as being object-seeking from the start, such as Melanie Klein and her associates (1952), Balint (1953), Fairbairn (1952) and Winnicott (1958), who have recognized the reality of grief and mourning in early childhood, have tended to focus on the loss of the breast or other part-objects.

Unlike the classical psychoanalytic writers, Melanie Klein and her associates, as well as other British analysts, explicitly described mourning in childhood, but, owing to the tendency to link object-seeking with orality, "most of these analysts," according to Bowlby, saw the "loss of breast at weaning as not only the first but by far the most pathologically significant loss suffered by the child." And since this usually occurs within the first year, Melanie Klein saw the first few months of life as being the critical time during which a child either acquires or fails to acquire the capacity for tolerating loss. Bowlby, not subscribing to Melanie Klein's theory of the active adultomorphic fantasy life alleged to go on in the first few months of life, feels that there is simply insufficient evidence to enable him to theorize with confidence about a child's development before the second half of the first year.

He expresses his regret that Abraham (1924), who described "primal parathymia" in childhood, did not recognize it as mourning, and that those who have been influenced by him, such as Melanie Klein, who did recognize mourning as central, focused so much attention on the loss of the breast and on weaning that they tended to neglect the relationship to the whole object. An examination of Melanie Klein's data, as well as a review of the data on weaning in other cultures, leaves Bowlby unconvinced of the extraordinary importance of this "deprivation." Not that he regards it as of no importance; he insists, however, on seeing it in the context of the relationship of the child with his mother whenever it occurs, within the first few months or, as in other cultures, in the second or third year of life. As he views it: "The truth is that we are still singularly ignorant of the effects on young children of weaning per se. Its dispassionate evaluation has not been made easier by overconfident claims based on reconstructive theorizing."

He blames Rado's (1928) conception of the infant's relations to his mother as setting a poor example for future theorists. As will be remembered, Rado equated being loved with oral gratification, and the fear of the loss of love with the dread of starvation. His theory about the guilt, atonement and plea for forgiveness that he saw in melancholia was based on a model having to do with rage, hunger and drinking at the mother's breast. Bowlby indicates that some analysts do not go all the way with Rado in this paradigm, while others, chiefly Jacobson (1946), frankly dissent.

Bowlby believes that the significance of the loss of the breast and hence of orality has been exaggerated, partly because it occurs simultaneously with partial separation from the mother. In his view, the chief trauma is precisely this separation or loss of close contact with the mother. His view of the depressive position, which British writers so emphasize, is that it extends well beyond the weaning period into and beyond the fourth year. It is during this whole period, according to Bowlby, that observations indicate that the child is in danger of experiences which can result in separation anxiety, grief and mourning of sufficient intensity to dislocate the development of his personality.

He uses the word "mourning" to refer to the comprehensive series of behavioral and psychological consequences that are initiated by the loss of a loved object. These processes may take healthy or pathological courses; some, like mania, are so uncharacteristic that an all-inclusive term such as "response to loss" may be indicated instead. He uses "grief" to denote the sequence of subjective experiences that occur in mourning. And the term "depression" is used by Bowlby to denote the affect which constitutes one of the aspects of grief and which may be experienced by the individual as inertia, purposelessness and helplessness and may be seen by the observer as sad, curtailed and disorganized behavior.

This affect, though very much a part of the mourning process, is conceived by Bowlby to be not at all confined to the bereaved. Following Bibring (1953), he sees this as a basic affective state that occurs not only in situations of loss but in many other circumstances. Depression occurs in both healthy and sick personalities. It is to be distinguished from "the clinical syndrome of which a pathological degree of depression is the main presenting symptom" which he, like Zetzel (1960), refers to as "depressive illness" or "melancholia."

Although Bibring, Zetzel and others have made this distinction, perhaps no one has made it so unambiguously and so clearly as Bowlby. This may be on account of the clinical material which illustrates his use of the term. In fact, it illuminates Bibring's formulation with retrospective clarity, as we shall have occasion to point out again later.

Bowlby (1960b) reviews the literature on mourning in adult life by writers such as Lindemann (1944), Marris (1958) and others to demonstrate that the same sequence of psychic and behavioral events takes place in adult mourning as he has described in mourning in infancy and childhood. He has done this to refute the theories of those who do not accept the view that mourning can occur in early childhood. He has grouped the psychological responses described in the literature on adult mourning into five categories to demonstrate their similarity to the process of mourning in the first few years of life:

(a) Thought and behavior still directed toward the lost object;
(b) Hostility, to whomsoever directed;
(c) Appeals for help;
(d) Despair, withdrawal, regression, and disorganization;
(e) Reorganization of behavior directed toward a new object.

He believes that Anna Freud's disagreement with him about what she regards as the very limited duration of childhood mourning can be explained by her definition of "mourning." He states that this refers to the period before which "the child is ready to accept food and comfort from a new person"—a misleading view, according to Bowlby, since young children will accept food and a measure of comfort long before the mourning period is over.

[3]

In the next papers of his series, Bowlby (1961b, 1963) describes some pathological outcomes of the processes of mourning. In my review of these pathological sequelae, I will pay particular attention to those that have relevance to depressive illness or to certain theoretical issues related to depression, namely, intense and persistent anger and reproach against various objects, including the self, and persistent unconscious yearnings for the recovery of the lost object.

Bowlby emphasizes that the material he is presenting is empirical in nature, derived from the separation of young children from their mothers. He acknowledges that other variables enter into the picture, such as that the children are removed to a nursing home or to a hospital instead of remaining in their own homes, but notes that he has to make do with what clinical material is available. Furthermore, he feels that the observations made on these children are but exaggerations of what would occur at home and thus lend themselves more readily to examination.

Bowlby again divides the processes of mourning into three

phases: protest, despair and detachment. He feels that the phase of protest has an underlying function in separation anxiety and in mourning, that it represents a mechanism for recalling the lost object—an effort to effect reunion when separation threatens or has already occurred. Moreover, except in the situation of irretrievable loss, he regards it as a behavior that tends to be successful, in that it may cause the mother to put off temporary separation or to offer reunion. It may so impress her with the pain of the separation and may inspire so much regret or guilt by the intensity of the reproaches that she may hesitate to separate from her child again for long periods of time. As will be recalled, this phase of protest is made up of loud crying, shaking of the crib and vociferous expressions of anger and reproach, sometimes repeated, as in an example cited by Bowlby, as long as six months after the separation. He feels that this function of trying to prevent a separation or of effecting a reunion has been given too little attention in the literature devoted to the subject; yet he believes that it can be linked with Rado's (1928) picture of melancholia as "a great despairing cry for love."

Freud (1917), in *Mourning and Melancholia*, maintained that ambivalence and anger were absent in normal mourning. Bowlby feels that the data do not support his position, at least in childhood mourning but also, as Lindemann's (1944) and Marris' (1958) findings would suggest, in adult mourning. Bowlby sees anger in mourning to have two main objectives: to express strong resentment against those believed to be responsible for the loss and against those who seem to stand in the way of reunion. He (1961b) feels that "the lost object is almost always sensed as being in some degree responsible also. This means that anger directed against the lost loved object is practically inevitable and universal." The cardinal feature of this hypothesis is that the loss of an object almost always spurs an effort to regain it and that this effort is often more successful when spiced with a "dash of aggression."

Certainly there is no doubt that loss in childhood produces anger and reproaches in the bereaved child, or that in the adult anger may be directed at the doctors and at others held responsible for the loss. Self-reproaches may be experienced or expressed for real or imaginary measures that might have been but were not taken to avert the loss or for real or exaggerated mistreatment of the lost love-object while he was alive. Occasionally, especially in other more expressive cultures, reproaches may be hurled at the dead in the protest phase of mourning, for abandoning the mourner.

Sometimes this anger and these reproaches may be realistic. Other people, by their acts of omission or commission, may have contributed to the loss. The mourner himself may have actual feelings or acts to blame himself for. Even the lost object may, by acts of commission or omission, have made his own death inevitable.

But the more inappropriate such reproaches are, the more pathologic they are. If they are unrealistically displaced onto third parties, they may assume a paranoid flavor. As Bowlby (1963) states: "It was their inapplicability to the self in cases of melancholia that struck Freud so forcibly and led him to his famous hypothesis regarding the origin of pathological self-reproaches." Properly understood, these self-reproaches were not complaints but accusations—and accusations not against the self but against the lost object.

Thus melancholia is one possible pathological outcome of prolonged or displaced anger after the loss of a love-object. According to Bowlby, the pathology lies not in the evidence of anger in mourning, but in its displacement toward an inappropriate object. Experience suggests to Bowlby that if this anger, toward whomsoever, were openly expressed from the beginning, it would tend to fade away. It is only when it is not appropriately expressed toward its appropriate object that it tends to persist.

Guilt, too, may be appropriate or inappropriate. It may be appropriate when it refers to some part the bereaved may have played in his own loss. It is less appropriate when it is based on ambivalent thoughts and feelings experienced in the past toward the love-object. It is wholly inappropriate and psychotic when it arises from a haziness of ego boundaries and represents anger meant for the lost object and reflected back on the self with whose image the object-representation has merged.

As many analysts have recognized, in the mourning of healthy adults good reality testing and loving memories are sufficiently strong to hold angry reproaches in check, to allow them limited or even no expression and to permit the bereaved to recover from his loss.

The phase of protest includes crying, which serves at the most obvious level as a mechanism to recover the object. But the yearning that it reflects may persist long after the first phase is over, giving rise to feelings of sadness, depression and longing for the lost object. It is especially evident in the phase of despair, a less stormy phase but more marked by quiet depression, longing and disorganization. In due course, in the healthy resolution of mourning, the yearning may be expected to diminish and disappear. When repressed, however, it may linger, with the patient being unaware of it and perhaps resorting to one or another defensive maneuver to keep his longing for the lost object out of his awareness. The more open the yearning, the healthier it is; the more repressed or otherwise disguised, the more pathological. (See Fleming and Altschul, 1963, for clinical examples of such repressed longing and delayed mourning.)

When a child has been subjected to repeated losses or rejections and has experienced repeated anger and yearning, this may generate intense ambivalence toward current or later love-objects. Bowlby (1963) emphasizes: "This is a main plank in my explanation of why it is that some individuals become prone to respond to loss in a pathological way."

To summarize, then, Bowlby has directed attention to the importance of the child's tie to his mother. He has described from empirical data the separation anxiety and the sequence of behavioral and emotional events that occur when children are removed from their mother figures and placed temporarily in nursing homes or hospitals. He has called this sequence of events "mourning," contrary to the belief of most analysts that mourning cannot occur in childhood, and has attributed this mourning, contrary to Melanie Klein and others, to the breaking-off of attachment behavior rather than to the loss of the breast and to oral or sadistic pathology.

His explanations should be differentiated from his data. They are hypotheses as much as are Melanie Klein's or Anna Freud's or Rado's or Spitz's. Regardless of the hypotheses invoked to explain the data, the data are nevertheless there, even though they may be interpreted (as distinguished from hypothesized about) in different ways; that is, some might regard the data as evidence not of mourning, but of anxiety or depression or bereavement.

Despite Lindemann and Marris' observations, however, it is not as clear as Bowlby would have us believe that all adults, at least in most of Western Europe and North America, experience all the phases of mourning that Bowlby describes. Weeping and yearning —yes. Anger, displaced or not—that is not nearly so universal. I have seen many instances of mourning where neither the patient nor I have identified or recognized it. We have all seen despair in adults. But as to anger and the kind of indifferent detachment Bowlby describes, there is some question as to how general they are in adult mourning. I believe that more comprehensive empirical studies are required to confirm what Bowlby takes for granted.

Bowlby considers depression only in the context of object loss. But as Bibring (1953) has shown and as Bowlby would agree, depression can also occur in other circumstances. Jacobson (1971) has dealt with this extensively, and Sandler and his colleagues have offered their own relative formulations.

Some of the critiques of Bowlby's work (especially Schur, 1960) are mostly concerned with his biological conceptual model and with his rejection of so many psychoanalytic concepts. It is hardly surprising that someone who is so critical of basic psychoanalytic concepts—most of which criticism I have omitted in this review —should be attacked so vigorously on these very issues. Despite this, Bowlby has received at least one enthusiastic endorsement (Blanco, 1971) precisely on these controversial issues. It turns out, as will be seen in Chapter VII, that many of Bowlby's criticisms of psychoanalytic concepts, which I have not reviewed in this chapter, are increasingly shared by psychoanalytic writers. Nevertheless, it does appear that in the interest of his biological theory of attachment behavior, Bowlby seems guilty of oversimplifying very complex matters.

Anna Freud (1960), Spitz (1960) and Engel (1971) treat his contributions quite respectfully, though the former two writers, in addition to criticizing both his underlying hypotheses and his stand on psychoanalytic issues, also criticize his data.

I am especially interested in several important criticisms of Anna Freud's since they have since been subjected to an empirical test. She contends that for the work of mourning to occur, the child must have reached the stage of reality testing, and on the libidinal side, the stage of object constancy. Prior to this, she regards it as unlikely that a child can hold on to the image of his mother sufficiently to warrant calling his experience mourning rather than just bereavement. Furthermore, she regards it as unlikely that under these circumstances grief reactions could last for periods approximately corresponding to the adult internal processes of mourning. Jacobson (in Levin, 1966), too, asserts that, since children are unable to tolerate the persisting aspects of grief, they cannot undergo a satisfactory mourning process. Wolfenstein (in Levin, 1966) goes even further, hypothesizing that one must pass through adolescence in order for successful mourning to occur, since not until then can a child tolerate decathecting his parents.

Anna Freud notes that both her work and the data described by Bowlby have to do with infants and children transferred away from their own homes to places where they have to share many mother figures. She comments: "If we wish to determine how long an infant needs to transfer cathexis from one mother figure to a substitute mother in the full sense of the word, we need to supplement our observations, excluding group or ward conditions. For all we know, duration of grief might then be found to be either shorter or longer."

Robertson and Robertson (1971) performed just such a study. They observed thirteen children, aged seventeen months to two years, five months, who were separated from their mothers and cared for under circumstances in which the adverse effects of institutional conditions were absent. Four of these children were looked after in foster care by the Robertsons and nine were looked after in their own homes in a familiar setting. They report that none of the thirteen children responded with protest and despair. They feel that "the difference between their responses and those of children observed in institutional settings was qualitative and not merely of degree."

The four children fostered by the Robertsons and observed with special care showed variations in response which corresponded to differences in age, levels of ego maturity and object constancy and a number of other variables. "Their behavior conformed to the psychoanalytic view that the capacity to mourn is a function of ego maturity and object constancy." They found this to be consistent with Anna Freud's view that this capacity is dependent on the level of object constancy and ego maturity.

Bowlby (1973) has examined the Robertsons' data but has come to somewhat different conclusions. He acknowledges that although the sequence of protest, despair and detachment was greatly reduced in these favorable circumstances, it could not be regarded as absent. He feels that the two older children fostered by the Robertsons (the foster children were reported on in the greatest detail) showed "yearning and searching for the missing mother, sadness, increased protest at her absence and growing anger with her for staying away, increased ambivalence on return home, and evident fear of being separated again"—and it must be acknowledged that a reading of the data does confirm his impression.

Joffe and Sandler (1965) in their consideration of Bowlby's protest phase view it as a frequent kind of reaction not only to object loss but to all states of psychic pain, however produced.

They view the despair phase as corresponding to what they refer to as the "depressive reaction" that can occur as a response to psychic pain, yet they feel that the generalized inhibition which they postulate in this reaction is incompatible with the presence of yearning that Bowlby describes. I regard this, however, as reasoning deductively from a definition, rather than inductively from observed phenomena. Yearning either does occur in the despair phase or it does not. This can only be determined by observation. It will not do to argue that since the despair phase equals a depressive response, and since the depressive response does not include yearning, therefore yearning for the missing love-object cannot exist in the despair phase.

Again, incompatibility between a theoretical expectation and observed data inevitably calls the theory in question. If Joffe and Sandler equate the despair phase with the depressive response and if yearning is observed to occur in this phase (about which there seems to be general agreement), then the depressive reaction must sometimes include feelings of yearning. Why theoretically must a depressive response always consist of precisely the same psychic configuration? A full-blown depressive illness does not.

In contrast to Joffe and Sandler, Mahler (1961) expresses her belief that grief can occur in children once enough psychic structure has developed for the child "to mobilize sufficient vestiges of confident expectation" for him to tolerate some delay of discharge. For this to be possible, the child must be able to experience mental images of the temporarily absent mother. Mahler considers that this mental representation of temporarily absent love-objects is "the spark that ignites the ego's capacity for human affect." When this stage has been reached, *during the second half of the first year*, according to Mahler, it is possible for the child "to experience the subjective affect of longing, which to my mind, is a precursor to the ego-filtered affects of sadness and grief." Expressing this in another way, she writes that "grief is dependent upon that measure of human object cathexis which prevails from the second half of the first year on. . . ." In another part of this same paper she refers to "the period of grief and mourning." Thus, though she does not mention Bowlby, she appears to agree with him that grief and mourning, brief though these periods tend to be in children, according to her, nevertheless can occur in infants and young children. In a later paper (1966) she more explicitly states that a child's " 'depressed mood' may be represented predominantly by separation and grief reactions" described in much the same way that Bowlby describes what he refers to as the mourning process in children and which, she believes, very much as Bowlby does, creates the basis for later depressive states. And actually Joffe and Sandler, too, believe that the depressive responses of childhood are the precursors of later depressive illnesses.

Bowlby (1960b) makes it clear that when he is referring to the despair phase he is referring to depressive affect, an affect "integral to psychic life" in Zetzel's (1960) words, an affect which is experienced subjectively with many different subtle nuances and not in an arbitrarily defined way. What seems valid about Joffe and Sandler's definition is that it is "a reaction to the experiencing of helplessness in the face of psychic pain," but no one can delimit for another the nuances of this pain or of this reaction.

Actually some aspects of the phase of detachment, which Joffe and Sandler see as "an attempt to restore a minimum level of well-being and feelings of safety," are, as Bowlby (1960b) defines this phase, closer in certain respects than the despair phase to Joffe and Sandler's characterization of the depressive reaction: e.g., the child "communicated a sense of feeling rejected or unloved, and showed a readiness to turn away from disappointing objects."

We see once again the deadening effect of trying to squeeze human reactions too narrowly into arbitrarily delimited definitions.

All of this surely illustrates the need for more empirical data to confirm or disprove various hypotheses, psychoanalytic and otherwise, about children. It also illustrates how varying are the inferences that can be derived from data.

MOURNING IN ADULTS

Freud (1917), who first undertook to compare mourning with melancholia, defined mourning as "the reaction to the loss of a loved person, or to the loss of some abstraction which has taken the place of one, such as one's country, liberty, an ideal, and so on. In some people the same influences produce melancholia instead of mourning and we consequently suspect them of a pathological disposition. It is also well worth notice that, although mourning involves grave departures from the normal attitude to life, it never occurs to us to regard it as a pathological condition and to refer it to medical treatment. Profound mourning, the reaction to the loss of someone who is loved, contains the same painful frame of mind" as does melancholia, "the same loss of interest in the outside world —insofar as it does not recall him—the same loss of capacity to adopt any new object of love . . . and the same turning away from any activity that is not connected with thoughts of him."

In considering "the work which mourning performs," he postulated that reality testing forces the mourner to see that the loved object is no longer alive and compels him to withdraw all libido from its attachments to the deceased love-object. There will be opposition to the withdrawal of this libido, sometimes so strong as to produce "a hallucinatory wishful psychosis," but normally the reality principle prevails and this withdrawal of libido painfully proceeds, preceded or accompanied by a process of idealization (hypercathexis).

In his famous words, "each single one of the memories and expectations in which the libido is bound to the object is brought up and hypercathected, and detachment of libido is accomplished in respect of it," or, as he stated elsewhere in the same paper, "each single one of the memories and situations of expectancy which demonstrate the libido's attachment to the lost object is met by the verdict of reality that the object of reality no longer exists."

He explained the mourner's inhibition of activity and loss of interest in the outside world by the painful work of mourning in which the ego is engaged. He noted that in melancholia there was "a lowering of the self-regarding feelings to a degree that finds utterances in self-reproaches and self-revilings" but that this disturbance of self-regard was absent in mourning. In obsessionally predisposed individuals, however, the "conflict of ambivalence" did, he felt, give rise to self-reproaches and self-blame for the death of the love-object. Yet he considered the mechanism in the "obsessional states of depression following upon the death of a loved person" to be different from the one in melancholia since in the former the self-reproaches are due to the obsessional's magical thinking or omnipotence of thought—that is, the obsessionally depressed person believes that the death occurred because he himself willed it—whereas in melancholia the process of "narcissistic identification" already referred to explains the self-reproaches which are to be understood as aimed at the introjected object. To repeat, Freud conceptualized ambivalence and self-reproaches as occurring not in normal mourning, but only in obsessional mourners and in melancholia.

Bowlby (1963), who regards mourning as the sequence of events following upon separation or loss, indicates that anger and ambivalence are almost universally present in the mourning processes of young children. Anger is described as occurring in the protest phase of mourning and ambivalence in the detachment phase. In contrast to Freud's picture of mourning as devoid of anger and ambivalence, Bowlby provides clear evidence that rage, protest and ambivalence occur in what he labels the mourning process in small children. Robertson and Robertson (1971), despite their disagreement with some of Bowlby's generalizations, also provide evidence of anger and ambivalence in young children temporarily separated from their parents in noninstitutional settings.

As to the mourning process in adults, Lindemann (1944) published a short, empirical study of grief in 101 subjects which is remarkable in that so many of his findings have been confirmed by so many subsequent investigators. He demonstrated that acute grief is a definite syndrome* with both psychological and somatic signs and symptoms which can appear immediately, be delayed, exaggerated or absent, and can occur in typical or atypical ("distorted") forms.

The syndrome is described as follows: "Sensations of somatic distress occurring in waves lasting from twenty minutes to an hour at a time, a feeling of tightness in the throat, choking with shortness of breath, need for sighing, and an empty feeling in the abdomen, lack of muscular power, and an intense subjective distress described as tension or mental pain."

He found the lack of muscular power to be universal and he gave examples of this strength and exhaustion (e.g., " 'The slightest effort makes me feel exhausted' "; " 'I can't walk to the corner without feeling exhausted' ").

He also noted some feelings of unreality, a sense of emotional

*See Engel, 1961: "Is Grief a Disease?"

detachment from others, a lessening of feelings of warmth and closeness to other people, a tendency to irritability and anger. The subjects' hostility was frequently surprising to the bereaved persons themselves, who often made a great effort to control it and who sometimes wondered whether they were going insane.

He described a push of speech and marked aimless restlessness in acute grief rather than retardation. At the same time he noted a painful inability to initiate and maintain organized patterns of behavior. There was a lack of zest. Routine activities were carried on with effort. The bereaved were surprised to discover how many of their activities had been done in some meaningful relationship to the deceased and how pointless these activities now seemed in their absence. Lindemann also noted a process of identification with some behavioral or physical characteristic of the deceased or with some particular interest of his. And also quite prominent were feelings of guilt. The bereaved accused themselves of acts of omission and commission.

Lindemann summarized his findings as including: "(1) somatic distress, (2) preoccupation with the image of the deceased, (3) guilt, (4) hostile reactions, and (5) loss of patterns of conduct. . . ."

The reader will be reminded of the high similarity between these features and the protest phase of the mourning process that Bowlby observed in young children, except, of course, that guilt and the peculiar identifications with the deceased were not present in Bowlby's young subjects.

Lindemann listed certain morbid and distorted grief reactions, such as a delay or postponement of the grief reaction; overactivity without a sense of loss, his description of which conveys the flavor of denial carried to the point of hypomania; the acquisition of symptoms resembling those of the deceased, which seem to be hypochondriacal or hysteric in nature and which seem to involve identification with the deceased; psychosomatic symptoms in four patients; a conspicuous change in relation to friends and relatives characterized by irritability, avoidance of and a lack of interest in them; furious anger against particular individuals, especially doctors; an arduous struggle on the part of some subjects to control their hostility; and finally, a few instances in which the grief reaction took the form of a typical agitated depression.

Prognostically, he noted that individuals with an obsessive personality and a history of previous depressions were likely to develop an agitated depression, and that mothers who had lost young children seemed to develop particularly severe grief reactions. He observed that strong ambivalent trends toward someone with whom the person was in close contact might be followed by a severe grief reaction with marked hostility, but he did not indicate that this ended up in an agitated depression.

Thus Freud's comments about the resemblances between mourning and melancholia were largely confirmed by Lindemann, although the latter found much more hostility and guilt in mourning than Freud had described. Lindemann, furthermore, confirmed the pathogenicity of marked ambivalence and of an obsessive personality structure. Unlike Freud, he stressed the prognostic importance of previous episodes of depressive illness, and those instances of obvious identifications with the deceased that he observed were characterized more by hypochondriasis and conversion reactions than by melancholia.

Marris (1956), in a study of seventy-two working-class English widows, also described physical symptoms, difficulty in accepting the loss, a preoccupation with the deceased, a tendency to withdraw from people and a prominent element of hostility.

Krupp (1962), in an empirical study of what he refers to as "the bereavement reaction," confirms most of Lindemann's findings. He describes very similar physical signs and symptoms (weakness, restlessness, anorexia, etc.), along with an altered sensorium and occasional feelings of unreality. He notes great emotional pain, self-reproaches, hostility, guilt and a general loss of interest in the world. All thoughts and feelings are directed toward the deceased. The world seems poor and empty. He refers to the deep sense of loss and feelings of purposelessness and emptiness as among the most poignant characteristics. Unlike Freud, he noted a "considerable" loss of self-esteem, especially in the early phase of bereavement.

An interesting feature of his paper has to do with the dreams of the bereaved. He observed that those who previously had good and loving relationships with the deceased tended to have happy dreams involving union with the beloved followed by disappointment upon awakening. The bereaved who had had hostile or ambivalent relationships with the deceased tended to have dreams filled with hostility, fear and terror. The dead person might appear angry or persecutory. The bereaved or the deceased might be attacking.

Krupp reports the same general types of pathological grief reactions: namely, (1) prolonged or intense reactions sometimes blending into melancholia with suicidal behavior, (2) psychosis of a paranoid or persecutory type, and (3) pathological identifications. He sees pathological grief reactions as ones in which there are excessive amounts of hostility, guilt, anxiety and depression (depressive affect), all of which he found to be normally present in bereavement. He views the pathological reactions as being arrested in Bowlby's Phase 1 (protest) or Phase 2 (despair).

Gorer (1965), in his interviews of a large number of British people who had been bereaved within the previous five years, found neither guilt nor anger to be prominent in his subjects, although he acknowledged that they simply may not have verbalized such feelings. It is interesting that he, too, noted particularly severe grief reactions for children: "the most distressing and long-lasting of all griefs, it would seem, is that for the loss of a grown child" (p. 121).

The most extensive series of empirical studies on bereavement was made by an English psychiatrist, Parkes. His studies included:

1. the records of ninety-four patients who had been admitted to the Bethlem Royal and Maudsley hospitals during 1949 to 1951 with a psychiatric illness that had come on within six months of the death of a parent, spouse, sibling or child (Parkes, 1964a),

2. the effects of bereavement on the physical and mental health of forty-four English widows (Parkes, 1964b),

3. twenty-two London widows (Parkes, 1971), and

4. sixty-eight people in Boston fourteen months after their bereavement (Parkes and Brown, 1972).

In his book on bereavement, Parkes (1972) describes the physical characteristics of acute grief: anorexia, loss of weight, sleep disturbances, sighing, respiration, aimless restlessness, gastrointestinal disturbances, heart palpitations, muscular aches and pains, anger and irritability. He found the most characteristic feature of grief to be an episode of severe anxiety and mental pain during which the bereaved sobs or cries aloud for the deceased whom he misses intensely. Parkes refers to such an episode as a "pang" of grief. Such pangs usually begin with the first hours or days of bereavement and reach a peak of intensity within five days to two weeks.

He sees the aimless restlessness as involving a restless searching for the lost object. This is often done unconsciously, but many bereaved openly acknowledge this while being fully aware of the pointlessness of their behavior: "I can't help looking for him everywhere," "I'm just searching for nothing," "Everywhere I go I am searching for him" (pp. 44–46) are characteristic comments.

He found that there was a tendency to return time after time to thoughts of the deceased, thoughts which were remarkable for their clarity. This tendency was still present a year after bereavement in most of the London widows he interviewed. The widows would often misperceive people to be the husbands they were pining and searching for. These illusions and misperceptions would be promptly corrected. They were not more frequent among psychiatric patients than among the non-patient widows. Parkes regards them as characteristic of normal bereavement reactions.

Fifteen of the twenty-two widows reported feeling a sense of their husband's presence, would associate certain clothing or furniture with the bereaved and would act toward these objects in ways that would continue to evoke his presence or sometimes to banish it if it was too disturbing. Some would be drawn to the cemetery and feel concern for him in the discomfort of the grave, especially in inclement weather. Reunion would sometimes be sought through spiritualism and sometimes through thoughts of suicide, e.g., "If it weren't for the children I might consider it" (p. 53). Parkes notes that Rees (1970) found that 39 percent of 293 Welsh widows and widowers sensed the presence of their dead spouse and that 14 percent of them experienced intermittent illusions or actual hallucinations of their presence. These illusions were more common in those who were over forty, who had been happily married, were of a higher social class and had been widowed for less than ten years.

Parkes also reports dreams of the husband in 50 percent of the London widows, both wish-fulfilling, happy dreams and dreams connected with death.

Most of the London widows expressed the feeling that "I can't believe it's true" (p. 62), and even a year after the death of their husbands most of them could not, at times, believe that their spouses were indeed dead. Denial in one form or another existed prior to the death in twelve of the nineteen widows who had been warned of the impending death. One woman refused to recognize her husband's death for four days after it occurred.

Parkes describes various other defensive mechanisms ("mitigation" utilized to lessen the pain): feelings of derealization lasting most of one year, keeping busy, deliberately shunning thoughts of the husband, avoiding his possessions and the idealization of the husband.

He, like Lindemann, Krupp and Marris, noted anger, especially in the first month, but often extending intermittently throughout the first year. This anger was directed either at themselves in the form of self-reproaches for some fancied or real omissions or was directed at others, often the doctors, for some alleged failure on their part. Frequently there was a generalized irritability and bitterness which, if too sustained, drove people away and led to a greater degree of loneliness.

Comparing the unselected London sample of widows with the psychiatric patients, Parkes observed that the grief reactions of these two groups were quite similar except in one respect. More (two-thirds) of the psychiatric patients experienced guilt during their mourning than did the London widows, of whom one-half reported guilt feelings. There was also a tendency for the grief reactions to be prolonged in the psychiatric patients.

Summarizing his data, Parkes finds some evidence, unfortunately not too decisive, that ambivalence plays a role in pathological grief reactions. In a general way, he sketches a portrait of a high-risk case, that is, of a widow prone to a pathological grief reaction. She would be a young woman with children living at home without close relatives nearby. She would be a dependent, ambivalent young widow. She would have had previous excessive grief reactions or previous depressive illnesses. Her background would be such as to prevent her from openly expressing her feelings. She might have additional stress involving loss of income and status, change of homes and difficulties with children. Her grief reaction would tend to be delayed, but intense pining would soon emerge together with self-reproaches and guilt feelings.

This is a general picture and a complex one. It will be noted that situational circumstances are as prominent as intrapsychic factors. Some of these features, prognostic of a depressive illness, namely, guilt and previous depressive illness, were also found by Lindemann and Gorer.

Levin (in Levin, 1966) proposes an alternative explanation to the traditional view that intense hostility or ambivalence has a causal relationship to excessive grief or depression, an explanation that would appear to be compatible with Parkes' empirical observations. Levin suggests that people who develop excessive grief reactions may have been extremely attached to and dependent on their love-object: "[They] have concentrated excessive quantities of libido in one object." They may have made excessive demands on him which in turn would have led inevitably to excessive frustrations with accompanying inevitable hostility toward the object. When he dies, the excessively attached, dependent and ambivalent widow, having little ability to transfer her needs and affections elsewhere, feels proportionately deprived, leading to intense prolonged grief. The emphasis here is on excessive dependency rather than on the ambivalence that may be an inevitable consequence of this.

In this section, I have reviewed some empirical studies on bereaved adults. Freud's view that mourning, except for the circumstances under which it occurs, has all the earmarks of an illness, has been confirmed over and over again.

The mental pain inherent in mourning, the difficulty in accepting the reality and finality of death, the general inhibition of functioning and the loss of interest in the world, the preoccupation with the memories of the deceased, the eventual triumph of the reality principle (a victory that is won not all at once, but in conflict after conflict with the wishful fantasies), the defense mechanisms and outright denial—all these have been noted in study after study.

Freud's generalization that low self-esteem and ambivalence do not occur in normal mourning has not been entirely confirmed by these studies, nor has his tidy formulation that the work of mourning detaches all libido from the lost object so that it can be transferred elsewhere. Although I did not cite the explicit evidence very often in this brief review, these studies showed longing persisting year after year in nonpsychiatric patients. But I will have more to say on this subject at a later point indicating that Freud was less dogmatic on this theoretical issue than were some who followed after him.

Furthermore, these reports suggest that identifications with the lost but introjected objects are not nearly as pathognomonic of melancholia as Freud believed, at least in Freud's initial version of this formulation, although not incompatible, of course, with Jacobson's revision of this concept.

These studies throw clinical light on the predisposition to the melancholic consequences of grief but provide no more than a flicker of insight into ambivalence or guilt or other psychological predispositions to depressive illness.

MOURNING IN CHILDREN AND ADOLESCENTS

Mourning in children is a very controversial topic. Some writers deny its possibility. The reasons advanced for this stand vary considerably from author to author. On the other hand, there have been clinical reports on mourning occurring in childhood. These, in turn, have been challenged by critics who dispute whether the feelings that the bereaved children in these reports were experiencing could properly be called mourning.

Let us go back to the beginning of psychoanalytic concepts of mourning. As we have seen, Freud (1917) regarded it as the reaction to a loss. He conceptualized the work of mourning as the gradual painful removal of libidinal cathexes from the memories of the lost object. He regarded this process as a very painful one, absorbing the energies of the individual and resulting in a generalized inhibition of behavior and a loss of interest in the external world. During this process he visualized the claims of reality conflicting with the wishful denial of the loss and the reluctance to accept its finality.

Bowlby (1961b) defines mourning as the process that ensues after separation and loss, a process that consists of three phases: protest, despair and detachment. He defines grief as the subjective experience of this process.

Krupp (1962), like Freud, views mourning as a painful withdrawal of interest containing feelings of both anxiety and depression.

Sandler and Joffe (1965) emphasize "the ego's attempts to reduce the painful experience of loss of the love-object, to work through the situations which give rise to pain and threaten depression." They see an element of resignation and acceptance in sadness, and they visualize grief as similar in content except that the loss cannot be accepted.

Long before the studies of Lindemann, Gorer and Parkes, Helene Deutsch (1937) had observed, in a series of adult patients, that an absence of grief at the time of a loss was followed by pathological consequences. As to the motive for postponement or absence of grief, she speculated that among other possibilities the affect may have been unendurable "because of the ego's weakness, as in children." She emphasized that for a healthy outcome "the process of mourning as a reaction to the real loss of a beloved person *must be carried to completion* [my italics]."

Fenichel (1945), too, states that when a child loses a love-object, its libidinal ties, no longer attached to the object, may overwhelm the child and create panic. "Grief" is a mechanism or device which the adult uses to slow down or modulate this flood of yearning and pining by spreading out in time and diluting the process of loosening the libidinal ties to the object. Most ties are represented by hundreds of separate memories, and the detachment of libido from these memories takes time and modulates the full impact of mourning. He thus sees grief as a gradual "taming" of the violent affects that might otherwise overcome the mourner after a loss. "Our 'mourning' extended over a period of time, is a defense against being overwhelmed by this premature affect" (pp. 393–95).

Rochlin (1959), in a paper devoted to the argument that clinical depression and mourning do not occur in childhood, nevertheless does indicate "that children may become sad or grieve or appear briefly depressed over their object losses and revile themselves." He adds that lowered self-esteem and self-reproaches follow the loss of affection or of a loved person in childhood. However, he stresses the point that in childhood the ego is insufficiently differentiated for the more complex mechanisms of depression to be present. Instead, he points to the regressive processes, the pathological identifications, the hyperactivity and the arrest of certain ego functions that do take place in children as pathological responses to loss.

Two reports from Rochlin's Children's Unit at the Massachusetts Mental Health Center describe in some detail the various defensive mechanisms (identification, denial, rage, displacement, acting out, etc.) in two young sisters aged five and eight after their witnessing the death by decapitation of their father in a car accident (Scharl, 1961) and in a seven-year-old boy after the loss of his mother (Shambaugh, 1961). The latter author notes that the work of mourning requires a relatively strong ego not too burdened by other tasks. The boy in his report did not have the strength to retain consciously the image of his mother and to gradually decathect her memories. Instead, regression and anxiety interrupted his development for a considerable period of time.

While these writers speak generally of a child's insufficiently strong and inadequately differentiated ego to sustain the work of mourning, Anna Freud (1960) more specifically points to the necessary presence of certain capacities as prerequisites to the process of mourning. Among these prerequisites she lists reality testing, the acceptance of the reality principle, the partial control of id tendencies by the ego and the achievement of the stage of object constancy. She believes that the length of time it takes for a child to transfer his affections to a substitute love-object depends less on his chronological age than on his attained level of object-relationships and on the degree of ego maturity that he has developed prior to his object loss. She feels that the period of grief will last longer and more closely approximate the internal processes of adult mourning, the nearer the child's level of object-relations has approached the stage of object constancy. She mentions one year as the traditionally assumed period of mourning in the adult. She and Bowlby are in agreement that the mourning period of a child does not ordinarily approximate this one-year period. It will be noted that she does not deny the possibility of grief and mourning in a child. She merely indicates the developmental prerequisites for mourning in children and the briefer duration of the mourning process that one observes in them.

Wolfenstein (1966), like Freud, sees mourning as a gradual process of decathexis. Like Fenichel (1945), she views it as serving an important defensive function in "protecting the mourner from the too sudden influx of traumatic quantities of freed libido." She addresses herself to the question of whether mourning takes place in children and adolescents. In a general theoretical and clinical discussion, rather than a detailed empirical report, on forty-two children in the age range between six and nineteen (forty-one children being above six years of age and thirty children above twelve), she reports the curtailment of sad feelings, little weeping and the absorption of these bereaved patients into everyday activities. "Gradually the fact emerged" that denial was occurring and that the children were postponing the painful process of decathexis; that, instead, the lost object was invested with an intensified cathexis. She reports the strong impression of a developmental unreadiness for the work of mourning in these children and adolescents.

She then summarizes the case history of a fifteen-year-old girl in which just these features were manifested. She indicates that the device exhibited by this girl was seen in many others of her subjects. They could not tolerate the idea that their mothers or fathers were dead. "They reported seeing someone on the street whom they fleetingly mistook for the lost parent." Children would change the subject when the topic of the lost parent was introduced. She refers to a number of reports on the pathological aftereffects in adults who had experienced denial or postponement of grief in childhood (e.g., Freud, 1927; Helene Deutsch, 1937; Fleming and Altschul, 1963). She emphasizes the idealization of the lost parent that occurs in childhood which involves the splitting off of the negative components of the ambivalence previously felt for the deceased parent which now become displaced onto others, especially the surviving parent.

She considers some of the factors that predispose to the denial that she and others have reported. Parents are the source of external narcissistic supplies and also, in setting limits, play the role of external superego. Without these ego and superego supports, Wolfenstein believes that the child fears the disintegration of his psychic structure. Furthermore, adults have the capacity to gradually decathect the lost object, a capacity that Wolfenstein feels young children and adolescents do not have. She suggests that they "lack the capacity for this kind of dosage in letting go" and are therefore in danger of being overwhelmed by "massive amounts of objectless libido." Speaking about this in a rather all-or-none manner, Wolfenstein states that "children operate on an all-or-none basis."

She also draws attention to an observation that is undoubtedly valid in some cases, but which I have not seen noted by anyone else: namely, that children are deeply ashamed of having lost a parent. How often this is the case would seem to be a matter for empirical investigation.

She discerningly notes another factor predisposing to denial: the fear of regression. She observes that young children cry readily at any frustration, disappointment or hurt; that in latency there is a tendency to repudiate crying as babyish, an inhibition that extends into adolescence and is strengthened by the feeling that it is more shameful for boys to cry than for girls.

After postulating this developmental unreadiness to mourn in childhood, she hypothesizes that adolescence is a necessary precursor to the capacity to mourn. Root (1957), Anna Freud (1958) and Lampl-DeGroot (1960) had earlier pointed out, as the latter expresses it, that the adolescent's "loosening of the ties with the parents is a difficult and protracted process, *often* [italics mine] accompanied by genuine mourning." As Wolfenstein phrases it, "It is not until adolescence that the individual is forced to give up a major love-object." She believes that this giving up represents a necessary precondition for the ability to mourn. The adolescent has, in this process, learned how to give up a major love-object. It thus initiates him into how to mourn. She refers to the often observed sadness or depression of adolescents and suggests that although he does not know it, the adolescent is mourning for "the loss of his capacity to feel for his parents." She believes that an individual is unable to mourn until he has experienced "the trial mourning of adolescence."

In a subsequent paper, Wolfenstein (1969) reports on several interesting and different adaptations to loss. In one instance, Mary, who was fourteen when her father died, determinedly set out to prove that no one could help her or take care of her, a venture that was facilitated by her vindictive rage. After discussing a few other maladaptive responses to bereavement, the author then considers some instances in which children and adolescents reacted to the loss of a parent in more constructive ways. In one instance, a ten-year-old boy was able to accept his beloved grandmother as an acceptable surrogate. The boy had already shown a capacity to reach out to new people and had advanced beyond the need-satisfying type of object-relations. Even before his mother's death, he had shown evidence of wishing to provide for her and to be independent.

A girl whose physician father had died when she was ten identified in a constructive way with her lost father and became a doctor herself. He had become incorporated into her ego ideal and, as Wolfenstein notes, "she herself became the only substitute for a father." For her, her father remained a model for effort and achievement. In contrast, for Mary, her father remained a need-satisfying object. Wolfenstein also describes a boy who lost his mother when he was eleven and who incorporated her ambitions for him and aspired to scientific excellence.

In considering why such identifications with the lost parent is not more frequently a resource for further adaptive development, Wolfenstein, like Anna Freud (1960), believes that the point of development of object-relations at the time of the parent's death is a crucial factor. A relatively low level of ambivalence toward the lost parent is also a factor that is relevant.

Nagera's (1970) thinking on the subject of children's reactions to death is close to Wolfenstein's in many respects. He believes that there are important differences between the bereavement reactions of children and the mourning of adults. He finds that the process of decathexis which takes place in normal adult mourning is frequently interfered with by internal forces which recreate the relationship to the lost object, sometimes by idealization, at times of disappointment with the substitute object. He points out that opportunities for frustration with substitute objects come up regularly since children have to be educated and limits have to be set on their behavior and on their desires. Thus he, too, emphasizes the splitting of ambivalence into an idealization of the lost parent and negative feelings toward the substitute or surviving parent.

Finally, among the differences between children and adults in their reactions to loss, he notes the great frequency in children of such manifestations as anxiety, regressive processes and the development of abnormal forms of behavior. Instead of the sustained mourning process, bereavement in childhood frequently produces diverse pathological symptoms.

Examining the different phases of object-relations in children, he sees a loss occurring in the first few months as causing nothing more than the "loss of something pleasurable," since in the view of many workers in the field no differentiation as yet exists between the self and objects.

After the third month of life, when the infant is presumed to have acquired a mental representation of the mother as a need-satisfying object, it is the need-satisfying characteristics of the lost object that will be missed by the child.

Since object constancy is believed to develop toward the end of the first or the beginning of the second year (Anna Freud, 1952), the child experiences more distress if loss occurs then when it no longer attaches itself so automatically to substitute objects. Evidence is cited that indicates that the child misses its parent. In Nagera's as well as in Anna Freud's view, it is only when this stage of object constancy is reached that it becomes possible "to observe *some aspects* of mourning in children as the psychological response to the psychologically meaningful loss of an object." It is only at this point, he believes, that the child exhibits Bowlby's three phases of protest, despair and denial in a way that bears some resemblance to the mourning responses of adults. He cautions, however, against the belief that similar behavior in younger infants is based on the same reasons or mechanisms and against the idea that bereavement reactions from this point on are identical with those of adults.

Among the features that contribute to the differences between mourning in children and in adults, he lists (1) children's reduced tolerance of acute distress, and (2) the incomplete development in children of reality testing, reality awareness and reality adaptation of which he presents several examples, especially the children's belief in the omnipotence of their parents, which conflicts with the idea that Daddy can't come even though he is dead. Especially confusing to the child is the adults' tendency to refer to a parent as being in heaven or as having gone away, which may imply to the child that he can therefore return from wherever he is. Some children are unable to conceptualize the idea of death in its full significance.

Nagera postulates that in the latency period the child's need for a parental figure interferes with the decathexis that one can observe in adults. His emotional development requires a parent and Nagera believes that physical death does not alter this need. The latency child will therefore, in his opinion, entertain a fantasy life in which the lost object is experienced as alive and at times as ideal. This may go on despite the superficial behavior of such children which may seem to minimize the importance of the loss that has been suffered. Sadness or grief may be absent or short-lived.

In adolescence, the various preconditions for mourning seem to be well-established. The adolescent understands "the full implications and finality of death. His reality testing is firmly established. His awareness of reality and capacity to adapt to it are sufficiently developed." He feels nevertheless that adolescent mourning is still significantly different from adult mourning. He quotes Wolfenstein (1966) to the effect that adolescents hypercathect rather than decathect their lost love-objects. As she puts it, "fantasies of the parent's return are either more clearly conscious or more readily admitted in adolescence than at earlier ages." Furthermore, Nagera refers to case material of his own and of others (Wolfenstein, 1966; Laufer, 1966) to support his ideas on adolescents' reactions to loss.

In summary, those who take the stand that children and adolescents are unable to experience what Freud defined as mourning

express one or another of the following points about the insufficient development of children or adolescents:

1. Insufficient differentiation of the ego.
2. Lack of object constancy.
3. Lack of full development of reality testing and reality awareness.
4. Short sadness span with an incapacity to sustain mourning.
5. Extensive use of denial or reversal of affect (e.g., from sadness
to gaiety).
6. The search for substitute love-objects.
7. Extensive use of regressive defenses with development of
symptom formation or behavioral pathology.

Preeminent among those who affirm that mourning *can* occur
in young children is Furman (1964a, 1964b). Tackling the question
of whether children can comprehend the fact of death, he quotes
from Anna Freud and Burlingham's (1943) study of children during wartime: e.g., a five-year-old whose mother wanted to deny
the fact of his father's death insisted, " 'I know all about my father.
He has been killed and will never come back.' " Furman outlines
the preconditions for reality testing sufficient to master the concept of death. He points to the quantitative element that enters
into these preconditions which, he acknowledges, is hard to delineate in print. "For example, a two-year-old may understand
that the dead bird will never fly or sing again while at the same
time he may not always be certain after awakening from his nap
whether the happenings of the morning occurred that day or the
day before."

He refers to Anna Freud and Burlingham's observations of children after two years of age during the blitz in London to support
his position that children between two and three can understand
the meaning of death. It is on this ability to have a concept of death
that the work of mourning is initially dependent. In addition, he
believes that a child should have mastered the high degree of
ambivalence that is so characteristic of children. If the aggressive
component of this ambivalence is too strong, he feels that the
internal representation of the lost object will be obliterated, and
decathexis of an object representation can, of course, not occur in
the absence of that representation. In other words, he too stresses
the importance of the child's having attained the level of object
constancy before mourning can occur.

He feels that in order to master the pain associated with object loss, the child must have reached the point where he can identify and verbalize affects. He illustrates this together with the help that an analyst can give a child in the identification and verbalization of affects in a fascinating paper on the death of a six-year-old's mother during his analysis (1964b).

He further postulates that the child must have the confidence that his reality needs will be met; otherwise, his anxiety might force a denial of his loss. He particularly emphasizes the importance of the person or persons who fulfill his needs after the death of a parent being consistent and unchanging so that the replacement can be invested with affect; otherwise, there will be the danger of pathological identifications with the lost object or a heightened degree of narcissism or self-involvement.

After considering the variables that contribute to the capacity to mourn and the quantitative aspects of these variables and the importance of a reliable substitute love-object, he comments on the great discrepancy among children. "Some two-year-olds will have a concept of death, while some five-year-olds will not. There is no reason to question the apparently conflicting observations of different authors. *It is fundamental, however, to make a sharp distinction between a child's not mourning and his incapability of mourning.*"

In a recent paper, Miller (1971) notes a nearly unanimous consensus that directly contradicts Furman's position. This consensus holds that children do not pass through mourning as Freud defined it. More specifically, Wolfenstein (1966) has argued that although a child may intellectually accept the fact of death, there may be a split between his intellectual and his emotional acceptance of this reality. She strongly emphasizes this emotional (as well as intellectual) denial of death in children and the difficulty children have in gradually decathecting rather than hypercathecting the love-object. Referring to Furman's (1964b) description of a six-year-old patient mourning for his mother, she expresses skepticism about whether the boy was truly mourning or merely missing his mother. As she phrased it, "We can miss and long for someone we still hope to see again," to which the only appropriate rejoinder is that we can also miss and long for someone we have no hope of ever seeing again.

In reading Furman's paper on this six-year-old, however, one is struck by his comment about the relative absence of denial in this boy. And with respect to gradual decathexis, one is particularly impressed by the boy's question of his father five months after his mother's death. " 'Is it all right that I don't think about mother all the time? Sometimes now when I play, I just play and don't think about her. I used to [think about her] all the time.' "

An observer would presumably not have noticed mourning behavior while the boy was playing nor would he have been aware of the gradual process of decathexis that was going on. Perhaps Spiegel's (1966) distinction between "the state of mourning"—referring to what Freud described—and "the work of mourning" is relevant here. Spiegel makes the point that "in childhood and adolescence the grieving state of mourning is usually not observed. However, this does not permit us to infer the absence of the *work of mourning.*"

The occasional observation of the kind that Furman quoted is, of course, not conclusive. But, on the other hand, one is impressed by the peculiar nature of the literature on mourning in children and adolescents. Some of it is based on retrospective observations on adults in analysis for conflicts deriving precisely from the postponement or absence of grief in childhood or adolescence (e.g., H. Deutsch, 1937; Jacobson, 1957; Fleming and Altschul, 1963). Other papers have to do with the pathological effects on development of object losses in specific children or adolescents (e.g., Rochlin, 1959; Scharl, 1961; Shambaugh, 1961; Laufer, 1966; Nagera, 1970). Still others set forth doctrinaire standards by which to define mourning, such as complete decathexis (e.g., Deutsch, 1937; Wolfenstein, 1966).

Freud himself was not as dogmatic as his successors. As Siggins (1966) points out, when Freud in *Mourning and Melancholia* set forth the relinquishment of the lost object as a goal of the work of mourning, this formulation was intended as a theoretical model rather than as a realistic account of what goes on in actual mourning. Among the affirmations by Freud that a loved object is never really given up, Siggins quotes from a letter of Freud's to Binswanger (Freud, 1929, Letter 239) in which he says that although the acute state of mourning will subside after the death of a loved one, "we also know we shall remain inconsolable and will never find a substitute. No matter what may fill the gap, even if it be filled completely, it nevertheless remains something else."

In contrast, Wetmore (1960), in pursuit of the ideal unique essence of mourning, goes far beyond adolescence and even the normal adult life. He goes so far as to postulate that "effective mourning" can occur only in the context of a successful analysis, a context which obviously excludes most of the world's population.*

To go on with the psychoanalytic literature on mourning from which such far-reaching conclusions are drawn, case studies consist of one or several or even forty-two patients, but how they are selected—whether at random, or whether they experience their loss during the analysis of a neurotic problem or whether they are in analysis because of pathological mourning itself—is not always made clear. Of Wolfenstein's series of forty-two patients, twenty-six were seen from two to fourteen years after the parent's death. Of these twenty-six, eighteen were seen from four to fourteen years later. Of the forty-two, sixteen came under observation within a year after the parent's death. It is not clear how many of these sixteen were observed during the actual period when one might expect bereavement behavior to be manifest. Nor is it clear how many of these children came into treatment directly because of abnormal bereavement reactions. At least some of them were in treatment prior to the parent's death because of neurotic conflicts. One would hardly think that this would be an ideal sample from which to draw generalized conclusions about mourning in children.

Another study of bereavement in children (Arthur and Kemme, 1964) is a report on eighty-three children from four and a half to seventeen years of age. Again, it is a study of bereavement in emotionally disturbed children. "The problems for which the children were referred often ante-dated the death of their parent, although in thirteen instances the death itself was acknowledged as the precipitating incident." This is a most unsatisfying study in that it often leaves the reader uncertain as to when data are being reported and when inferences are being drawn.

Among some interesting observations in this paper is the confirmation of other writers' findings that young children tend to be confused by explanations having to do with heaven (visualized as a place), angels and sleep (" 'Daddy has gone to sleep' " or " 'Daddy has died in his sleep' "), explanations which may give rise to misconceptions, confusions or phobias.

As far as I know, no studies of bereavement in "normal" samples

*". . . I am talking not only of sadness, mourning, or the reaction to present loss which reawakens reaction to past loss, but of a unique emotional response experienced, perhaps, only in the psychoanalytic process. . . ."

of children, children not being treated for neurotic difficulties nor being treated for difficulties arising from their bereavement, have been reported. When one thinks about it, the literature on mourning in children and adolescents constitutes an imposing edifice of generalizations supported on the most sketchy of observations, hardly any of which have to do with random or normal samples.

One further criticism of this literature comes to mind. The criteria for mourning are related to Freud's theoretical model of mourning. Denial, absence of complete decathexis, idealization of the lost parent are all presented as examples of inadequate mourning. Yet, when one glances back at the previous section devoted to the study of mourning in random samples of adults, one sees numerous, indeed almost universal examples of precisely these defenses. The adult subjects attempt to deny the reality of the death. They "search" for their lost objects everywhere. They seem to recognize them in the street. They "feel" them around about them in the house. They idealize them. They keep them in mind for years. They experience anxiety and panic in the acute phase of mourning and mobilize available defenses. But if one reads the literature on children and adolescents after having read through the observations on normal adult mourning, one is aware that, besides the biased samples, the authors impose criteria for normal mourning on these children that most of the adults in the studies would not pass. Psychoanalytic writers on adult mourning seem to see the situation more flexibly. Lipson (1963), for example, notes that "the failure to complete mourning, accompanied by the feeling that the departed still lives, is actually quite common." Furthermore, he refers to a number of psychoanalysts who have pointed out that "denial of the reality of death is a general attitude in our culture." He adds: "It is easily enough observed in mourners." In contrast, the psychoanalytic child literature appears biased, doctrinaire, theoretical and, at bottom, unconvincing. Not that I am arguing that there are no differences between mourning in children, adolescents and adults. Adults experience different losses when they lose a spouse. They may, in addition to losing a love-object on whom they have become dependent, have lost a sexual partner or an economic support. They may have experienced a change in social status or in standard of living. Their burdens may be immeasurably increased and their aspirations may be realistically diminished. A child may have lost a need-satisfying object, a beloved mother or father or oedipal rival. There may or there may not be adequate substitutes. The children may be at different points of development and may have different ego strengths or weaknesses. All these factors make for varying responses to bereavement and perhaps for different types of mourning. But to generalize glibly about whether children or adolescents *can* mourn from the evidence contained in the literature seems peculiarly dogmatic and unempirical. Anna Freud (1960) long ago commented on how little we know about grief from direct observation in children who remain at home after permanent separation from a parent.

DEPRESSION IN CHILDREN
[1]

There seems to be a general but not absolutely unanimous agreement in the psychoanalytic literature that depressive illness does not occur in children. It is true that Abraham (1924) referred to "primal parathymia" in children, but he was referring to a set of depressive feelings and not to a clinical depression. And here, in anticipation of a fuller discussion later, it might be noted that a distinction has come to be noted between depressed feelings, symptoms, moods and depressive illness. As Jacobson (1971, Chapter 6) and others have insisted, confusion is generated when the word "depression" is used without clarification of the semantic ambiguities inherent in this term. Melanie Klein (1948) has referred to the "depressive position" in infants, but this again denotes not a depressive illness but rather a normal phase of development during which the child becomes aware that the bad object is identical with the good object; when he becomes aware, in other words, of the complexity of his hitherto purely good and bad objects.

Rie (1966) has written a useful survey of the topic of depression in childhood, and I intend to make use of his thoughtful paper as a point of departure for the consideration of this topic. He begins his discussion of depression in childhood by adding his caveat, "if indeed such a disorder exists." In the course of his review he goes on to consider the criteria for depressive illness which would determine whether indeed such a disorder exists in childhood.

First, however, he notes that in a representative number of general publications and texts on child psychiatry or depression, no mention is made of such a disorder in childhood. He refers to the "remarkable consensus" that "the *familiar manifestations* of adult, non-psychiatric depression are virtually non-existant in childhood."

With respect to the clinical manifestations of adult depression, he accepts Lehmann's (1959) characterization of depressive illness. Lehmann considers that the primary symptoms of this illness consist of "a sad, despairing mood; decrease of motor productivity and reduction of drive; retardation or agitation in the field of expressive motor responses." Of these primary symptoms he considers that "the sad despairing motor state and depressive mood seem to constitute the real core of all depressions." Finally, noting that although the diagnosis of a depressive syndrome is based on the behavior and the verbal reports of the patient, he acknowledges that the patient's appearance may be deceptive, in which case the diagnosis "depends entirely on the evaluation of a single symptom, which is possibly the most essential of all, namely the patient's verbal description of his mood and his feelings." Throughout his survey, Rie uses this "most essential of all" symptoms, "the patient's verbal description of his mood and his feelings" as the major criterion, the touchstone of what constitues a depressive illness.

He reviews the various psychodynamic items that are discussed in the literature on adult depressive disorders. He concludes that there is no consensus with respect to the significance of aggression in depression. He notes the absence of unanimity regarding the importance of orality in depression. He goes on to touch upon the significance attributed to the loss of self-esteem in depression by Freud, Rado and others, and he particularly refers to the emphasis placed by Bibring and Jacobson on the loss of self-esteem in depression. He finds "general agreement at least with respect to the following: The precipitating role of loss of a love-object, whether real or fantasied; the low self-esteem of the depressive; and the dependence of the depressive upon external sources for maintenance and reinforcement of his self-esteem."

Considering the implications of these dynamics for depression in childhood, Rie reviews Rochlin's (1959) extreme position with respect to depression, namely, that only those conditions which involve intersystemic conflicts between the superego and the ego can be properly considered to be depressions. This review, that all depressions are characterized by guilt, a view that is also expressed by Beres (1966), is in direct disagreement with the more authoritative views of Bibring and Jacobson and is in fact in conflict with empirical observations.

Beres (1952) makes a useful distinction between aggression in children directed toward the body (as in head-banging, hair-pulling, etc.) and aggression directed toward the ego (or what we would now term the self-representations). He does not consider that the former, aggression directed toward the body, represents an intrapsychic struggle, a point discussed even more comprehensively by Cain (1961). Beres does not believe that self-directed aggression of this kind serves as an index to depression in the way he believes self-directed aggression does in adult life. It might be added, however, that empirical observations suggest that punishing or injuring one's own body (other than in suicide attempts) even in adults is usually not a symptom of depression, nor, when it occurs, does it tend to occur in depressive disorders.

Furthermore, some British workers (Kiloh and Garside, 1963; Carney et al., 1965) have determined that guilt could be observed in only 31 and 59 percent, respectively, of their mixed series of depressives. And in cross-cultural studies, Venkoba Rao (1966) and Teja et al. (1971) found guilt to be present in only 27 and 48 percent, respectively, of their Indian subjects. Similarly Lambo (1956) found guilt to be almost entirely absent in his Nigerian depressed patients.

Noting the general consensus about the importance of self-esteem in depression and that self-esteem in Jacobson's definition represents the discrepancy or harmony between one's self-image and the wished-for concept of the self, Rie proposes the logical corollary that we cannot speak of loss of self-esteem until the child can form adequate self-representations. He finds, as Erikson (1950) believes, that the acquisition of a "sense of ego identity," the "ability to maintain inner sameness and continuity," comes about only when "childhood proper comes to an end." Furthermore, Rie quotes Loevinger's (1959) observations that the "ability to conceptualize one's self" does not fully occur before early adolescence, although she traces the beginnings of this capacity back to the age of eight in some children.

Since Rie finds considerable agreement that stable self-representations are found during adolescence at the earliest, he considers that a loss of self-esteem, dependent as this is on the discrepancy between these self-representations and the ideal self, cannot occur until early adolescence, and that, further, since "chronically low self-esteem . . . is regarded as a necessary condition for depression by *all* theorists," it follows that clinical depressions cannot occur until adolescence.

Similarly, since the wished-for concept of the self is so elastic and fluid in children—at one point the child aspires to be a policeman, at another an astronaut—Rie is skeptical about the "potential for relatively intensely and pervasively experienced discrepancies . . . which are relatively stable" between the child's self-representations and his wished-for concept of the self.

He dismisses orality as a criterion of depression in children since orality in its broadest sense—the need for comfort, assurance and external narcissistic supplies—is so much a part of childhood that an increase in its intensity does not stand out as obviously as does intensification of orality in adult life.

He also dismisses Spitz's (1946) observations on anaclitic depression in children because of the same objections that we will touch on later, namely, that these children's "untreated condition evolves in early childhood into a disorder which is *not* highly reminiscent of depression."

The plausibility of Rie's logic falters somewhat when he discusses a case study of a six-year-old boy with poliomyelitis (Bierman et al., 1958). The boy's condition is described in a way that, as Rie acknowledges, "seems to coincide in all major respects with the primary symptoms of depression summarized above" by Lehmann. He notes that Bierman et al. were least convincing in the evidence for loss of self-esteem, and reminds us that Freud (1917) felt that melancholia did but that grief and mourning did not involve loss of self-esteem. Rie then suggests that the boy's condition, since he lost not only the function of his legs but also the comfort of his mother from whom he was separated during his hospitalization, resembled grief or mourning more than depression.

His suggestion that the boy's depression is more probably grief or mourning stands in ironic contrast to the arguments that we have just reviewed by psychoanalytic workers to the effect that mourning does not occur in childhood. The boy's comments about himself (" 'I don't play any games, I just play with toys—I don't know how to play games' ") and his general clinical picture certainly, as Rie says, seems to coincide with the primary symptoms of depression. It would appear that no one, unless he were inspired to argue from first principles that depressive illness can not occur in childhood, would dispute the presence of a clinical depression in this child.

Rie is more appropriately skeptical about whether Harrington and Hassan (1958) have established their case for depressive illness in six girls aged eight to eleven, and about whether Toolan (1962) has presented a plausible case for depressive illness in the children in his report. He also appropriately raises the question of adequate criteria for depressive illness when he discusses a paper by Keeler (1954) in which a variety of reactions to the loss of a parent are described, and a paper by Sperling (1959) on depressive equivalents in children. He very cogently remarks, in reference to these papers, that "the simple fact that *a* reaction, whatever it might be, follows loss should obviously not serve as sufficient basis for calling it depression."

He discusses a review of suicide in children by Despert (1952) in which she examines four hundred records of children brought for treatment. She found only twenty-six children who " 'had manifested depressive moods and/or evidenced preoccupation with suicide, or else expressed realistic suicide threats.' " Of the five cases drawn from these twenty-six, who were presented in some detail in her article, Rie felt that only two children, one sixteen and one ten, both of superior intelligence, "satisfied the typical criteria of clinical depression or gave evidence of intrapsychic processes usually associated with depression."

In summary, he suggests that "there may be reason to believe that the fully differentiated and generalized primary affect characterizing depression, namely despair or hopelessness, is one of which children—perhaps prior to the end of the latency years—are incapable."

Addressing himself as he did to the concept of low self-esteem in children, Rie made the point that children do not develop stable self-representations on which self-esteem is allegedly dependent until early adolescence.

However, at the same time that his paper appeared, Sandler and Joffe (1965) offered a modified perspective on the question of self-esteem and loss, that on the face of it would seem to undercut Rie's position. In a consideration of the topic of childhood depression, they examined 100 cases of children treated psychoanalytically at the Hampstead Child Therapy Clinic. They discovered a number of children who, though not exhibiting the signs and symptoms of adult depressive disorders, did show what they termed a "depressive reaction" to various internal or external stressful circumstances.

This reaction was described as follows: The child appeared sad, unhappy, bored or discontented. He showed a degree of with-drawal and communicated a sense of feeling rejected and unloved and was inclined to turn away from disappointing objects and not to accept help or comfort. Also noted were a tendency to regress to oral passivity, sleep disturbances, and autoerotic or other repetitive activities. In addition, the child's therapist usually had difficulty establishing sustained contact with the child.

They considered the depressive reaction to be a basic or central affective state, "a basic psychobiological affective reaction," comparable to anxiety, rather than a symptom of an illness. In looking for a common factor in those children who displayed this depressive reaction, it appeared to them that the child was confronted with a particular kind of threat to his well-being. An essential element of this threat was the feeling of having lost or of being unable to acquire something that was essential to his well-being. Along with this, they observed a feeling of helplessness, a feeling of being unable to correct the situation.

They noted that what was lost was not always a love-object. Even when it *was* an object, they believed that what was *really* lost was the state of well-being inherent both psychologically and biologically in the child's relationship with that object.

What they are describing seems to be something more basic than self-esteem, which, as we have seen is, in Rie's estimation, dependent on the development of coherent self-representations and ideal images of the self. Sandler and Joffe speak of a young infant experiencing physical or emotional deprivation and showing a depressive reaction to the loss of psychological well-being even before mental representations have been adequately structured.

Using Freud's term (1926, Addendum C), they speak of a child or an adult experiencing "mental pain" when a discrepancy exists between an existing state of the self and a wished-for ideal state. Coming even closer to Jacobson's formulation of low self-esteem, they (Joffe and Sandler, 1965) define this psychic pain as "a discrepancy between the actual state of the self on the one hand and an ideal state of well-being on the other."

As we have noted, it is important to understand that they do not regard this mental pain as identical with depression. Depression, as they view it, is one possible reaction to this pain. It occurs when the individual responds to it with helplessness, hopelessness or passive resignation. They feel that many children who are described as unhappy or as displaying varying amounts of discontent or resentment have not "capitulated" and are therefore not actually experiencing or displaying a depressive reaction.

This brings us to the question of depressive equivalents. Rie, in his survey, reviewed the question of depressive equivalents with some care. His position was that since these equivalents were not characterized by the essential symptoms of depression, they could not therefore be defined as depression. Furthermore, in his view, the demonstration of so-called depressive equivalents in children did not prove that depressive illness occurred in children. Sandler and Joffe's views lend support to this position. Their conceptualization of depressive equivalents as defenses against psychic pain illuminates the difference between depressive equivalents and depression. No more than addiction or denial can be equated with depression can depressive equivalents be considered to be depression.

It is important, however, to differentiate between depressive equivalents and depressive symptoms. Depressive illness is a complex syndrome which involves affective, cognitive, autonomic and sleep components, among others. If a patient demonstrates middle-of-the-night or terminal insomnia, for example, this, in proper context, must be considered a depressive symptom and not a depressive equivalent.

Furthermore, it is important to remind ourselves that Sandler and Joffe, when they describe a depressive reaction or response in children, are not arguing for the existence of depressive illness in children. They regard a depressive reaction as a basic psychobiological response to mental pain. They go on to emphasize that "what does not appear to occur in young children are those forms of depression which are the consequence of further defensive and restitutive processes, and, in particular, of pathological identifications and introjections which characterize neurotic and psychotic melancholic depression."

It is this basic depressive response rather than depressive illness which they believe can occur in infants who suffer nutritional disease or who are deprived of adequate psychological stimuli. In fact, they believe it can occur at any point in an individual's life during the process of individuation, during the process of giving up previous desirable states of psychological well-being. But they distinguish this reaction from the more complexly visualized depressive illness which they also believe can occur at any time in the individual's life—except before adolescence.

Thus, in review, Rie notes the general consensus about the central importance of low self-esteem in depressive illness. He further points to the discrepancy between representations of the actual self and the ideal self that constitutes low self-esteem. Then, arguing that such self-representations are not adequately developed before adolescence, he concludes that clinical depressive illness can not occur before adolescence. The issue of whether children can or cannot attain stable self-representations is, in itself, not an established matter. Rie concludes this not from any definitive empirical studies but from the theoretical considerations of Erikson and Loevinger.

Disregarding this issue, however, Sandler and Joffe argue that what is central to depressive affects and depressive illness is not a loss of self-esteem but a loss of a sense of well-being defined as an affective state of harmonious and integrated biological and mental functioning, an affective state that is more basic than the complex combination of cognitive and affective elements that go into self-esteem. In addition, they indicate that this state of well-being or its opposite, the psychic pain that reflects the absence of this ideal state, can be found even in infants before an inner representational world is established. Thus far, their position would seem to rebut Rie's view of the matter. But they actually arrive at a position which is in full accord with Rie's, albeit by a different route, when they argue that, although a depressive reaction or response can occur in children, this is a basic affective psychobiological state and not a clinical illness. Clinical depressive illness, while it does contain this basic core of depressive affect, is, in their view, made up of much more complex components and does not occur before adolescence.

Sandler and Joffe's formulation, appealing as it does to common sense and to clinical observations, brings with it a satisfying sense of understanding and of closure. It clarifies so many issues. Compared to the concept of self-esteem, the concept of psychological well-being seems so much more basic and down to earth. And the idea of a depressive reaction representing the affective core of a depressive illness and yet different from it appears to be so clear and illuminating.

And yet a nagging doubt persists. The distinction between a depressive reaction and a depressive illness seems so clear-cut and decisive. But does psychopathology have quite such well-demarcated boundaries? As Sandler and Joffe say: "The depressive reaction, considered as a basic affective state, can, like anxiety, be of long or short duration, of low or high intensity. . . ." If anxiety is experienced as more than signal anxiety, it may be regarded as a symptom. If it persists, if it is of long duration and high intensity, we refer to the experience as an anxiety neurosis. The anxiety may be displaced to an object or to a place and we call it a phobia. It may, on the other hand, persist in a way that we refer to as free-floating anxiety. It may be experienced as disabling chronic anxiety.

What of the depressive reaction? True, as Sandler and Joffe also state, psychotic melancholia is made up of "further defensive and restitutive processes and, in particular, of pathological identifications and introjections"; thus a depressive reaction is not equivalent to melancholia. But what if the depressive reaction persists? What if its intensity is high and its duration long? Doesn't it at some point cease to be a depressive reaction and become at least a depressive neurosis? And if not, why not? Cytryn and McKnew (1972), in a discussion of childhood depression, "think in terms of depressive illness rather than of depressive affect when the depression is of long duration (of at least several months) and is associated with severe impairment of the child's scholastic and social adjustment and with disturbances of the vegetative functions, especially those of food intake and sleep."

Since this is their opinion, what are we to think of Sandler and Joffe's position that these prolonged and intense states of depressive neurosis do not occur in children? One response might be that depressive illness has not been observed to occur in children. But this is an empirical response, not a theoretical one. And to such a response there can only be an empirical reply. I intend, therefore, to examine this issue in the next section of this chapter in the hope of providing some clarification of this perplexing topic.

[2]

The psychoanalytic literature on the question of depressive illness in children carries the impressive impact of almost complete unanimity. The literature clearly indicates that depressive illness cannot occur in children. However, the matter must not be dismissed quite so easily. In a recent stimulating paper, Arlow (1970) argues for "the need to bring psychoanalytic hypotheses in line with established findings in other, that is, related fields," among which he mentions ethology, experimental animal psychology, developmental psychology and communications theory. He very appropriately notes that "a proper wedding" of psychoanalysis with other disciplines "would require respect from the party of the first part as well as from the party of the second part."

In this matter of depressive illness in children, it would have been helpful if the writers had looked beyond their own borders and disciplines, not necessarily as far away as experimental animal psychology or communications theory but to disciplines no further away than adult and child psychiatry.

Rie, in a way, did this but regrettably with results that turn out to be misleading. He adopted Lehmann's ultimate criterion for depression, "the patient's verbal description of his mood and his feelings." Although this criterion has general validity for most of the clinical depressions we see in our daily practice, it is unfortunately not universally valid. I have seen patients suffering from depressive illness who had such inadequate access to their own moods or feelings as to be unable to describe themselves as depressed. It will be remembered that depressive illness is made up of a constellation of symptoms of which the experienced affect is only one component. I have seen a patient who knew only that he was suffering from an illness that interfered with his sleep, concentration, energy and functioning but who never over a period of almost ten years of intermittent visits could say that he felt depressed. As Jacobson (1971) notes, such patients, "unaware of their depressive affective state, complain only about their mental and physical fatigue and exhaustion" (p. 174).

I have seen one patient who after five years of psychoanalysis for "chronic anxiety" had no awareness of depressed spirits despite the fact that he was suffering from a depressive illness with all the usual signs and symptoms, including early-morning awakening, diurnal variation of his symptoms (anxiety but not depression), impaired concentration, etc. This patient's pervasive anxiety as well as his biological signs and symptoms responded promptly to antidepressant medication.

If this patient, only one of a number of such, who was an assistant professor at a large university, had so much trouble identifying or experiencing his illness as depressive, then how do less sophisticated and presumably less educated individuals experience their depressions? The answer to this question might throw some light on the adequacy of Lehmann's criterion and Rie's adaptation of it for children who are hardly as articulate or as sophisticated as this scientist after five years of psychoanalysis.

One place to look for an answer to this problem is the literature on cross-cultural psychiatry. Most cross-cultural studies of depression focus on aspects other than presenting symptoms. They frequently concern themselves with epidemiological factors and with the kinds of affective diagnoses found in a given population. They devote a considerable amount of attention to the presence or absence of guilt in non-Western or non-Westernized populations.

Yap (1965), however, does comment on the different ways in which depressed people of different cultures conceptualize their sick-role. He notes that "illiterate groups, such as the lower classes in advanced countries, tend to define the sick-role in somatic terms, so that they will present themselves to the doctor as physical cases." He remarks that Lambo (1956) and Field (1958), among others, have "pointed out that depression might be missed because of a veneer of psychosomatic symptoms."

Bazzoui (1970), in his study of affective disorders in Iraq, addresses himself more directly to the point under discussion. In his study of fifty-eight cases of hospitalized and privately treated patients with depressive illness, he makes the observation that "the average Iraqian patient describes his depression as a sense of oppression in the chest, a feeling of being hemmed in, or in other cases, a hunger for air. On being asked if he feels sad, downcast or depressed, one is struck in many cases by the unawareness of the patient of his mood. . . . The chest, head and abdomen are frequently considered to be the core of the troubles."

Lewis (1974) cites the instance of "an obviously depressed Tahitian [who] told his doctor he could not state what was wrong with him—he just felt 'sick' (the Tahitian language has no words for depression, grief, nostalgia and the like, though it has more than 40 words for various shades of anger)."

One need not go so far afield, however, to discover that depressed patients may describe their symptoms in physical rather than in psychological terms. Foster Kennedy (1944) drew attention to the fact that manic-depressive patients may present with physical symptoms with or without complaints about their mood. Watts (1947) has indicated that British patients with endogenous depression will often present themselves for treatment with physical rather than emotional complaints. And Campbell (1953) devotes a chapter of his book on manic-depressive disease to the many ways in which "patients have attempted, through their own descriptive language, to interest physicians in the many intriguing manifestations of a disturbed autonomic nervous system" (p. 52).

Thus, patients with affective disorders may not complain of what Lehmann considers their primary symptoms and may not bring to their psychiatrist's attention the "most essential" symptom of all, namely, a verbal report of mood and feelings.

Nevertheless, it does not, of course, follow that the reverse is true, that because children also may not complain of depression that they are therefore necessarily depressed. To substantiate a claim for depressive illness in children without their complaining of conscious depressed affect, requires, as it does in adult patients, the presence of some combination of the other primary symptoms of an endogenous depression, namely, retardation of thought or behavior, sleep disturbance (especially middle-of-the-night or terminal insomnia), loss of interest in activities or hobbies, self-critical feelings, etc. To consider this issue properly, one must examine the psychiatric literature on depression in childhood. Since the most conclusively recognizable of depressions are manic-depressive depressions, I will now review the literature on this subject though I will stray away from exclusive attention to this type of depression.

It should be pointed out that there are several issues involved here: the theoretical issue of whether depressive illness *can* occur in children; the empirical issue of whether in fact it does; and, if it does, whether it occurs in late or early childhood or both, how frequently it occurs and, finally, whether it appears to be similar to or different from adult depressive disorders.

I have reviewed some of the psychoanalytic arguments against the possibility of depression occurring in childhood. These arguments include the lack of adequate psychic development, especially the development of stable self-representations and ideal-representations of the self. Jacobson (1971), in addition, notes that young children exhibit somewhat more intense affective manifestations than adults do, but because of the relative instability of their object-relationship, their intolerance for pain and tension and the readiness to accept substitute love-objects, they are unable to sustain painful moods (p. 76).

There are a number of psychiatric studies which support the

view that manic-depressive illness does not occur in children. Lurie et al. (1936) found no such patients in a series of twenty cases of functional psychoses in children. Bender and Schilder (1937) found no manic-depressives in sixty-five children with suicidal preoccupations. Hall (1952) diagnosed "affective" illness in only six of one thousand patients between five and sixteen years of age.

Bellak (1952, Chapter 7) mentions, amidst some doubtful case reports, a small series of bipolar manic-depressive illnesses in children ranging in age from eight to fourteen. One such example was that of a fourteen-year-old patient of Rice's (1944) at the Phipps Clinic who had cycles of psychotic behavior swinging from severe depression to great excitement and back within forty-eight-hour periods, each cycle lasting forty to fifty days. Another convincing case (Cronick, 1941) was that of a manic-depressed, depressed child with "extremely rapid, explosive mood shifts" with suicidal threats.

Harms (1952a) published a very polemical paper on the subject of manic-depressive illness in children. He (1952b) issued a challenge to "the present autocratic opinion of academic psychiatry that there does not exist manic-depressive disease pattern(s) among children." He (1952b) presented brief sketches of ten children who indeed exhibited periods of depression and restlessness or excitement. However, the clinical descriptions of these patients failed to carry conviction with respect to their manic-depressive diagnoses.

Anthony and Scott (1960) suggest that "childhood proper" be limited to the period prior to the appearance of secondary sex characteristics. Unfortunately, the data respecting this do not always appear in the literature. I intend to limit the term "children" to those under twelve years of age as Bradley (1937) suggested, although a less controversial upper limit might be ten years of age.

Unfortunately, as Anthony and Scott concluded, the criteria for manic-depressive illness in childhood are poorly delineated in much of the literature. To correct this situation, these writers go to the opposite extreme and propose very strict criteria for this condition. To qualify for this diagnosis, one must have a positive family history, a premorbid, extraverted personality, a clinical picture that conforms to Kraepelin, Bleuler and Meyer's descriptions of a bipolar, recurrent, endogenous (defined as "with minimal reference to environmental events") illness of sufficient severity as to warrant "in-patient treatment, heavy sedation and ECT," with an absence of features that might suggest conditions such as schizophrenia. Furthermore, they included among their criteria "evidence of an early tendency to a manic-depressive type of reaction" such as oscillating, cyclothymic moods and "delirious manic or depressive outbursts occurring during pyrexial illness."

These are strict criteria, so strict that few *adult* manic-depressives would be admitted to this select group. For one thing, it disqualifies the unipolar manic-depressives. Also, clinical observations clearly establish that not all manic-depressives have premorbid extraverted personalities, (e.g., Winokur et al., 1969, pp. 101, 107). I have seen a goodly number of shy, even "schizoid" introverted patients who had undoubted bipolar swings that responded satisfactorily to lithium carbonate, and even more of such personality types who had unipolar manic-depressive depressions. Third, as has become increasingly clear since the introduction of lithium carbonate, manic-depressive illness may present in many atypical forms, some very much resembling schizophrenia (e.g., Lipkin et al., 1970; Taylor and Abrams, 1973). Fourth, despite the fact that manic-depressive illness is an "endogenous" disorder in the sense that its symptomatology conforms to that described by Kraepelin and other authorities, depressive episodes may occur in reaction to life circumstances (e.g., Winokur et al., 1969, p. 84). Fifth, although one welcomes a positive family history of manic-depressive illness as a help in confirming the diagnosis, it simply does not always happen that such a family history is forthcoming in patients who are undoubtedly manic-depressive. Sixth, since the introduction of lithium carbonate, the phenothiazines and the antidepressants, many undoubted manic-depressives are treated successfully outside a hospital and without ECT, although if the above-mentioned medications can be accepted as the equivalent of what Anthony and Scott refer to as "heavy sedation" then this criterion is, of course, valid.

Thus these criteria for the diagnosis of manic-depressive psychoses are rigid indeed. I cannot recall many, or perhaps any adult manic-depressives of whom I happen to see many in my clinical practice, who referred to delirious manic or depressive episodes occurring during a high fever, although it is true that I do not routinely inquire about this.

Anthony and Scott were able to find only three cases in the literature who qualified by more than five of these criteria. These cases were all eleven years of age. Thus these were below twelve but could not be considered as belonging to *early* childhood. They nevertheless presented a twelve-year-old boy who, as might be guessed, qualified for the diagnosis of manic-depressive psychosis by virtue of fulfilling all of these criteria, even including feverish delirious episodes.

As they put it, then, they allied themselves with the supporters of the clinical existence of manic-depressive illness in childhood, albeit late childhood. They state their opinion that this case, followed through its various cycles up to the age of twenty-two, "offers ample proof that an affective psychosis may begin *before puberty.*" It is important to notice that during and shortly after his first admission to the hospital at age twelve, he exhibited both manic and *depressed* episodes. Thus the theoretical issue of whether a depressive illness of an endogenous type *can* occur before puberty seems conclusively settled by this psychoanalytic case report. Anthony and Scott believe it has as yet to be demonstrated that manic-depressive illness can occur in early childhood.

If one chooses to adopt criteria no more stringent than one does in ordinary adult clinical practice, one has only to turn to Campbell's (1952) cases for additional examples of childhood depression. Of these, twelve patients varying in age between thirteen and eighteen had what appeared to be, from the clinical descriptions, undoubted prolonged depressive illnesses. At least four of these twelve were bipolar in type, while some of the others had cyclothymic but not pathological mood swings. ECT was of decisive help in at least five of these twelve patients. One was retrospectively diagnosed as having had brief but definite depressive states as early as ten.

Campbell also reported one "daughter of manic-depressive" parents who was seen with a definite depressive illness at ten years of age. "She became very depressed, bowed down with feelings of guilt, and declared that 'fears have almost made me crazy.' " She had sleep disturbances, obsessional worries and some ideas of reference. There were some atypical features to this picture, though the follow-up indicated that there were two subsequent recurrences during the next few years. But whether or not this patient was properly diagnosed as manic-depressive, depressed, of which actually there seems little doubt, there is no doubt that she experienced a sustained period of depression.

A seven-year-old "friendly but timid" girl with no previous psychiatric history became ill with "loss of appetite, crying spells, a tendency to worry about death." During the Christmas period, the patient " 'had not been at all like herself' . . . took no interest in her Christmas presents and would stand quietly moaning with her hands folded in a position of prayer. She worried over having committed a sin. . . ." She would cry for several hours before going to bed and would have insomnia. She would switch off the radio when it played Christmas music since it made her sad, as did blessings at the table. No explanations or reassurances had any effect on her "morbid moods." She felt that the world looked hopeless to her.

A previously vivacious six-year-old girl "became depressed and despondent, talking about death and people who were deceased." She became mentally and physically sluggish. She became more depressed in church and in Sunday School and also during prayers and when hearing sad music.

All of these young children became frightened of the dark and complained that they saw various distortions in the dark.

The information supplied about these last three children did not conclusively confirm that they were suffering from manic-depressive illness. However, there is no doubt that they were suffering from sustained depressive illnesses, however diagnosed. Moreover, two of these children were suffering from guilt of almost or actual psychotic intensity. In each instance, these three patients had not been previously psychiatrically ill in any obvious way and in each instance the patient gradually recovered from her depression. The ten-year-old girl had two recurrences of her depression by the time of the report.

McHarg (1954) reports the case of a prepubertal girl of eleven who was admitted to the hospital with a typical case of mania which lasted for approximately eight weeks. It was followed shortly by a depressive episode in which she clung to her mother, wept loudly and declared "that she was 'the cause of the world going to be destroyed.' " She worried about what was going to happen to the world, said that God was punishing her, and wanted to die. She became very depressed and lost interest in her usual activities. This depressed phase also lasted for approximately eight weeks. There was a family history of manic-depressive psychosis. The illness was followed by complete remission up to the time of the report two years later.

Winokur et al. (1969) cite a paper by Barrett (1931) in which he reported five cases of manic-depressive illness in children aged ten (three children), eleven and twelve years of age. In three of the patients there was a history of three generations of manic-depressive psychosis. One of the ten-year-old patients whom Winokur et al. discussed in more detail had her first attack of depression at age ten at least one and a half to two years before her first menstrual period. This severe depression lasted for seven months. She then became excited and flighty. A period of four months followed during which periods of depression and excitement alternated every two weeks. A three-month-long depression then followed. After a normal period of one month her illness recurred with alternating periods of excitement and depression. She was well for two years and then again for four years. After an excited period lasting a few weeks, eight years passed before she again had to be admitted to a hospital (pp. 23–24).

It will be remembered that Anthony and Scott (1960) indicated that manic-depressive illness in early childhood had not yet been demonstrated, though they did not specify what exact ages they were referring to. Poznanski and Zrull (1970) list children aged three, five (three children), six, seven, eight, nine (two boys), along with older children in their paper on depression. Unfortunately, the information about these children is very skimpy, e.g., " 'unhappy, withdrawn and depressed' described by school and parents. Sat isolated during interview, avoids face-to-face contact. . . ." together with some behavioral notes and a paragraph on the family background. The information supplied is distressingly insufficient but again there seems no doubt that many of these children were capable of sustained depressed symptoms or moods.

A more interesting but again insufficiently documented study is that of Frommer (1968). She reports on three groups of depressed children, one group of fifty-four so-called enuretic depressives, a second group of seventy-four children with "uncomplicated depression" and a third group of sixty-two phobic-depressives. I will omit any further comment on the enuretic and phobic depressives because of their more complex symptomatology.

The group of seventy-four children with uncomplicated depression included two four- to six-year-olds, six six- to eight-year-olds, eleven eight- to ten-year-olds, fifteen ten- to twelve-year-olds and forty children from twelve to sixteen. Frommer's comments on this group are of interest: ". . . nearly half of this group have difficulty in getting off to sleep, or a poor night because of restlessness, nightmares, sleepwalking, talking or screaming. No less than a quarter wake in the middle of the night, or unusually early, in just the same way as do adult patients who are suffering from an endogenous depressive illness. This is also the only group of children in which a sizeable number complained quite spontaneously of feeling depressed, and the majority of suicidal ideas, feelings and attempts occurred in children of this group."

The treatment provided for these children is of considerable relevance. The uncomplicated depressed children were treated by antidepressive medications usually of the monoamine oxidase inhibitor group. The details of the treatment and responses are strikingly similar to the successful use of these drugs in adults with the exception that the children responded earlier and were not maintained on the medication for nearly as long as are adult patients. Just as with adults, if the medication was phased out too soon, "deterioration usually sets in rapidly . . . and full dosage must be maintained for considerably longer" in such cases. Frommer also notes that "children of this group who show a marked pattern of early morning waking may respond well to a tricyclic antidepressant."

It is of interest, again, as in the treatment of adult patients with antidepressants, that "the duration of illness up to the time of referral did not seem to influence the results of treatment to any great extent in these depressives." This is of special interest in that some of these children had been depressed for as long as ten to eleven years. If this applied to the oldest of them (there were eight children aged fourteen to sixteen), this meant that they were depressed since they were five or six. If some, younger than sixteen, had been depressed for ten or eleven years, their depressions would have, of course, begun when they were even younger than five.

With respect to Anthony and Scott's (1960) skepticism (written prior to the time when lithium carbonate was available in England) relative to the documentation of manic-depressive children, it is of interest that a number of Frommer's depressed patients with "hypomania," sometimes of a disruptive nature, were treated successfully with lithium carbonate. Some of these children, when they were no longer hypomanic, became again depressed within days or weeks on lithium carbonate, just as happens sometimes with adult manic-depressives. Such patients did better with a combination of lithium carbonate and an antidepressant, just as some adult manic-depressives do. Frommer reports that "several children have found this drug combination so helpful in controlling themselves that they have insisted on continuing with it until they felt really well again."

The question of the specificity of lithium carbonate for manic-depressive illness is relevant here. Although no one can as yet assert that this has been conclusively demonstrated, the fact is that nearly all clinicians experienced in the use of lithium carbonate have no doubt that this medication is indeed specific for manic-depressive disorders. Frommer almost too conservatively notes that "although the response to treatment does not prove the diagnosis . . . it may help to further identify the children who need study." Incidentally, in the total group of "uncomplicated depressions" she reports a "success (i.e., apparent full recovery)" rate of 74 percent.

What does all of the above prove? I think that it proves that those authors who argue from first principles that depressive illnesses cannot occur in children take up their positions by deductive reasoning from theoretical propositions. In other words, they are doctrinaire rather than empirical. They have not followed Arlow's (1970) advice. They have not even looked next-door to the child psychiatric clinic and the child psychiatric literature. Reading their arguments, one has the same kind of bemused feeling that one might have reading a well-reasoned text arguing against the possibility of heavier-than-air machines while flying across the Atlantic.

It might be well to remind ourselves of the confident assertions that one finds in the literature. Rochlin (1959) flatly asserts that "clinical depression, a superego phenomenon as we psychoanalytically understand the disorder, does not occur in childhood." Remembering Sandler and Joffe's (1965) observation that object loss is not a necessary precursor to depressive reactions, an observation incidentally confirmed over and over again in the psychiatric literature, we can compare this with Rochlin's statement that "clinical experience shows us that we are compelled to look for 'loss' when we find depression." This statement is followed by an argument that for children to experience loss with pathological depression "presupposes that certain phases of psychic development have occurred," a presupposition that he, of course, dismisses.

Some comments by Sir Denis Hill are applicable here. In his Adolf Meyer Lecture of 1968 he refers to Freud's paradigm in

Mourning and Melancholia "in which loss or the sense of loss of loved objects was a primary constituent. This places the emphasis upon events external to the patient and has led to the present day-to-day search in the patient's life situation for such events. As we know, very often such stressful events cannot be found. . . ."

Cytryn and McKnew (1972) published a classification of childhood depression which permits the reader to form some grasp of the clinical pictures involved. Although they cite Sandler and Joffe (1965) on the "syndrome of childhood depression," they unfortunately seem not to have grasped that these authors regard their "depressive reactions" not as depressive illnesses but as "responses" to psychic pain; nor that Sandler and Joffe would have regarded one of their classifications, "masked depressive reaction of childhood," not as a depressive reaction (let alone a depressive illness) but as a defense mechanism against psychic pain.

Be that as it may, Cytryn and McKnew do describe "a more clearly identifiable depressive syndrome," the symptoms of which "include a persistent sad affect, social withdrawal, hopelessness, helplessness, psychomotor retardation, anxiety, school and social failure, sleep and feeding disturbances, and suicidal ideas and threats but only rarely suicidal attempts. The clinical picture . . . usually lasts at least two to three months before medical help is sought. The children with this clinical picture can be further subdivided into those with *acute* and *chronic depressive reactions.*"

The acute depressive reactions of childhood seem to occur in children who had been functioning relatively well until they were exposed to a severe trauma. Some maladjustment such as signs of a passive-aggressive personality structure were noted in their premorbid history.

The chronic depressive reactions of childhood, on the other hand, occurred in children with marginal emotional development. "They were helpless, passive, clinging, dependent, and lonely and often had had depressive episodes in the past that lasted from several days to several months." All of these chronically depressed patients had at least one parent with a history of recurrent depressive illness. Immediate precipitating factors were not found in most of the chronic depressive reactions.

Cytryn and McKnew stress that their patients were neurotic and not psychotic. This is an example of the semantic ambiguity that obscures diagnostic discussions. Their comment that these children were not delusional or hallucinated and had no bizarre thoughts, speech or behavior is beside the point, in the sense that primary depressions may or may not be psychotic according to these authors' use of the word. The fact that they are not psychotic does not automatically mean that they are neurotic.

And, in fact, the description of the chronically depressed children with their positive family histories and absence of clear precipitants in addition to the psychomotor retardation, sleep disturbances, suicidal ideas, etc., that they share with the acutely depressive children certainly carries the flavor of primary, endogenous depressions. But the authors' conceptual scheme unfortunately permits them to obscure this important issue, one which is in the center of current clinical discussion.

It would seem that even though Anthony and Scott's multiple criteria for the diagnosis of manic-depressive psychosis in childhood have not been met by Campbell, Frommer and others, nevertheless these and other writers including Anthony and Scott have demonstrated that a sustained depressive illness, often in a bipolar manic-depressive context, sometimes in a recurrent unipolar pattern, often in diagnostic categories not made more explicit than by the adjectives "endogenous" or "neurotic," *can* exist.

The question of its frequency is another matter. The statistics are very confusing. Frommer easily accumulates a large series. Hall finds only six cases in one thousand outpatients. Kraepelin (1921) reported only 0.4 percent of manic-depressive psychoses as beginning before the age of ten. Cytryn and McKnew assert that children with clear-cut depressions are rare. The semantic irony is that by "rare" they mean that they see only ten to twenty such depressions each year.

Is depressive illness, whether endogenous or neurotic, a rare illness in children? I think that it is fair to say, in view of the conflicting data provided by different observers, that we don't know. As long as a depressive illness is called a "loss complex" by one writer (Rochlin) and a "depressive response" by others (Sandler and Joffe), and as long as it can be argued that a depressed child is not depressed but is "mourning" for his lost physical integrity and his absent mother, we can't know.

There are still other unresolved issues. Although most of the cases that I have described in this section seem to be examples of early onset of depressive illness, it is not yet clear whether endogenous depressions manifest themselves in other and more atypical ways in childhood, in ways that some writers call "depressive equivalents," a term that loses some of its plausibility when examined by means of Sandler and Joffe's concepts. Nevertheless, are there "childhood depressives" just as there are "childhood schizophrenics" with symptomatology different from the adult depressives? As I have demonstrated earlier, not every depressed patient declares that he is depressed. How many childhood depressions present with symptoms other than depressed affect? We don't know. This is one reservation that I have concerning Sandler and Joffe's (1965) insightful concept about the difference between defensive operations against psychic pain and a "depressive response." Will it conceal from us atypical childhood versions of depressive illness? This would seem to be a fruitful area for empirical and follow-up studies. There is very little about this in the literature, unless Bowlby's "detached" pathological mourners are examples of atypical childhood depressives.

Although my practice does not include children or adolescents, I have at the request of patients and colleagues occasionally seen high school students who were clearly endogenously depressed, sometimes in the context of a bipolar manic-depressive psychosis. What is more, I have seen such psychotically depressed patients with several generations of manic-depressive forebears behind them, diagnosed as schizophrenic. Many more depressed patients, some no further away from their childhoods than college, have told me that they have "always" been depressed, dating their depression back to early childhood. One such college-age patient insisted that she could remember depressed feelings comparable to her current profound depression as far back as age three. She may have had inexact recall. But it is obvious that despite a priori arguments against the *possibility* of an endogenous depressive illness existing in childhood, sustained, long-lasting states of depressive illness *do* occur in childhood and are overlooked or are diagnosed as something else.

I have seen a middle-aged business executive with an absolutely typical endogenous depression being treated elsewhere for a "passive-aggressive personality disorder." If this happens, it is not difficult to believe that depressed children are not being recognized for what they are. But how many? That is a matter for sophisticated research by workers fully aware of the theoretical and clinical issues involved and without any ideological axes to grind or theses to prove.

CONCLUSION

The topics reviewed in this chapter are not among the most intellectually satisfying in this book. Bowlby has described what he has variously referred to as mourning and pathological mourning in children following separation. He has explained his observations with a theory derived from ethology. Not only his observations but the inferences from his observations as well as his theoretical stand concerning his observations and inferences have met with sharp criticism. His theoretical position seems to have aroused more ire than his clinical reports. The latter and the inferences drawn from them have been subjected to moderate and thoughtful criticisms (e.g., Anna Freud, 1960; Joffe and Sandler, 1965). His designation of what he observed as "mourning" has not yet met with general acceptance.

A review of observations on mourning in adults was followed by a survey of the psychoanalytic literature on mourning in children. The observation was made that certain writers (e.g., Wolfenstein) set up criteria for mourning in children that were so arbitrarily rigid and doctrinaire that the actual adult mourners discussed in the prior section would not have qualified as mourning acceptably. These theoretical positions all derived from a formula of Freud's which he was too realistic to take literally, but which eventually took precedence over actual observations. Moreover, these generalizations were seemingly derived from patient samples so scanty as to be hardly credible.

One can argue for the existence of a certain phenomenon if one finds it in only one case. One cannot argue that a phenomenon *cannot* exist even if one fails to find it in one hundred or, for that matter, one thousand successive cases. If one could argue in this way, then a study of one thousand successive medical inpatients in Philadelphia might prove that leprosy was as imaginary as a unicorn. And a sample of one hundred cases might fail to substantiate the existence of disseminated lupus erythematosus, or for that matter, childhood schizophrenia.

The samples of children reported on in the papers on mourning consisted of one or two or forty-two psychiatrically ill patients, some of them seen years after the actual loss of their parents.

And so it is with depression in children. The arguments against the existence of depressive illness in childhood were scholarly and persuasive—except that they ignored the reports on depressive illness and manic-depressive illness in children.

It would seem that in no other area of the psychoanalytic litera-ture on depressives are the theoretical papers so far removed from the observations that any clinician can make in the course of his daily practice. There is the occasional writer in the literature on adults who will insist, despite all evidence and opinion to the contrary, that guilt must exist in any respectable depression worth its salt. But generally this literature has been characterized by an increasing awareness of the broad range of depressive illness. The theoretical formulations have gradually but inexorably encom-passed more and more of the clinical phenomena. Bibring, Jacob-son, Beck, Sandler and Joffe have progressively increased our un-derstanding of depression. And Jacobson especially has continued to insist on the validity of nosological differences, an insistence that is in keeping with the growing awareness in clinical psy-chiatry (e.g., Winokur et al., 1969) of the necessity of making these distinctions if successful research is to be carried on.

This literature on childhood, at its worst, demonstrates the prob-lems that can develop when dogmatic and arbitrary positions, derived from first principles, intrude between the observer and his observations; when one's clinical spectacles are clouded with theoretical preconceptions; and when little attention is paid to the reports emanating from child psychiatric clinics. Not that these psychiatric reports are adequate. One hopes that really sophis-ticated studies with adequate reporting would begin to be pub-lished in the psychoanalytic literature. Anthony and Scott's (1960) report could serve as a model, although the strict criteria em-ployed by these writers, undoubtedly useful in view of the slipshod diagnostic criteria in so many papers, are so narrow that they would inevitably lead to single case histories rather than to the well-documented reports of scores of cases that might otherwise appear. These reports need not be about fully analyzed cases, but hopefully they would contain adequate and knowledgeably de-scribed and discussed case histories of manic-depressive or en-dogenously or neurotically depressed children.

Chapter V

INTRODUCTION

W̲E̲ ̲H̲A̲V̲E̲ ̲T̲R̲A̲C̲E̲D̲ the psychoanalytic concept of depression, noting its theoretical vicissitudes from the earliest reflections on oral traits in depressed patients through to the extensive ramifications of the later, more complex theoretical constructs. The aim has consistently been to delineate the major contributions to this theory, to set them in their proper perspective and to indicate their genetic relationship to previous observations and conceptualizations. There have been many aspects of the theory of depression which have been referred to rather fragmentarily. In studying the details of any one writer's contribution, there is some danger of losing perspective with regard to the more general direction and shape of the body of theory. It is difficult to examine a subject both longitudinally and in cross-section at the same time. In this chapter, therefore, in order to think about depression from another vantage point, we will consider separately the various strands that have gone into the weaving of this theoretical structure. Dissecting out its various components and examining each one of them separately in the light of the subject matter already reviewed should aid in allowing one to understand more clearly this sometimes confusing body of theory. We will briefly recapitulate and reexamine such elements of the theory of depression as the concepts of predisposition, prepsychotic character structure, unconscious fantasies, aggression, orality, etc., with the aim of throwing more light upon them than was possible in the chronological account of the development of this theory.

HEREDITY

With regard to predisposition, although writer after writer has attempted to explain the etiology and mechanisms of depression in psychological terms, there has been evident a lingering feeling of discomfort and an underlying but varying degree of awareness that there was more to the depressive reaction than could be explained by environmental and experiential factors. Kraepelin regarded depression in its various manifestations as essentially a constitutional disease process. Meyer pointed out the therapeutic uselessness of such a focus and determinedly turned toward an examination of the potentially treatable factors in the reaction. Freud did not exclude the possibility that some types of melancholia were constitutional but of course proclaimed his field of interest to be the psychologically understandable features of the condition. Yet even in types of melancholia which he considered essentially psychogenic, he felt that some symptoms like diurnal variation were basically somatic in nature. Abraham, in his effort to understand the choice of neurosis, postulated that there was in depressives an inherited constitutional increased oral eroticism, a heightened capacity of the mucosa of the mouth to experience pleasure with an accompanying increased need and a consequent greater possibility of frustration of this need. Gero broadened the meaning of the term "orality" to include all manifestations of the need for dependency, love and warmth, with the implication that in depressives a heightened constitutional need of this kind stood in greater danger of frustration. Melanie Klein, with her particular interest in early aggressive phenomena, postulated a "constitutionally strengthened oral sadism" as a possible factor in "the most serious deficiencies of development and psychic illnesses." Thus these writers assumed that there exists in some people a constitutionally determined greater-than-average need for what is varyingly expressed as gratification of the oral erogenous zone or oral supplies in the wider sense. These increased needs, it was postulated, may lead to greater frustrations with a consequent greater tendency for fixation at the oral phase.

Jacobson (1953), with her interest in the ego psychological aspects of depression, considers the question of predisposition in a somewhat different light. She first of all clearly distinguishes neurotic from psychotic depression and feels that the latter "represents not only a mental but an unknown psychosomatic process";

she expresses the belief that this hypothesis will serve as an incentive to collaborative research on the biological, physiological and psychological aspects of psychosis. She believes that psychotic patients are predisposed to total regressive processes by an arrested, defective ego and superego development, the result of their inherited constitution and their infantile history.

Zetzel (1960), too, commented on this topic. She felt that depressive illness, "because of its frequent occurrence in patients with a positive family history and its common association with specific periods of biological significance poses crucial problems as to the relation between psychogenic, environmental, and constitutional factors in the development and structure of mental illness."

Those geneticists who are interested in psychiatric problems do not attempt to isolate the individual factors that are inherited and constitutional in manic-depressive psychosis. They have been more concerned with determining if it is true at all that hereditary factors play a part in the etiology of this psychiatric disorder. Kallman (1948), until the 1960's perhaps the foremost American psychiatric geneticist, stated his views as follows: "The implication is that some persons have the genetic capacity for reacting to precipitating stimuli with either a schizophrenic or a manic-depressive type of psychosis, while others have not. Whether or not a real psychosis will be developed by such a 'predisposed' person usually depends on an intricate interplay of constitutional and environmental factors. . . . The specific nature of the respective genes is indicated by the observation that no twin partner has as yet been found with a schizophrenic psychosis in one member and with a manic-depressive psychosis in the other, if a consistent system of classification is used."

There were other writers, however (e.g., Penrose, 1945), who, while agreeing that this psychosis is hereditary, questioned the genetic specificity of the manic-depressive heredity.

Kallman (1953) defended his position by maintaining that the presence of "small contingents of schizophrenics found among the relatives of manic-depressive patients" in some of the European studies merely reflected the looseness of the criteria for the diagnosis of manic-depressive psychosis in these studies. In his work, he carefully restricted the diagnosis to those "cyclic cases which showed periodicity of acute, self-limited mood swings before the fifth decade of life and no progressive or residual personality disintegration before or after such episodes."

The 1960's introduced a wealth of new genetic studies on the affective disorders, especially manic-depressive illness. They are too numerous and specialized to be reviewed in this book, which considers depressive illnesses from a different perspective. The reader, however, can be referred to the reviews of Beck (1967), Winokur et al. (1969), Rosenthal (1970) and Mendels (1974).

Beck concludes that "the available research data does not establish conclusively whether affective disorders are genetic, environmental, both or neither" (p. 132). Winokur et al. both review the literature and report on extensive work of their own to support the hypothesis that heredity plays a very important role in manic-depressive illness. Their proposed major mode of transmission ("from an X-linked dominant kind of gene," p. 121) has, however, not met with general acceptance.

Rosenthal, after a thorough review, concludes that there is "strong evidence in favor of considering manic-depressive psychosis to be genetically influenced in good part" but is "unable to come to any conclusion regarding its mode of inheritance" (p. 221).

Whether or not one is convinced by the work of the geneticists, one point that Kallman (1953) made is worth noting. He argued against the tendency to identify human genetics with a fatalistic outlook which would discourage therapeutic activity. He maintained that inheritability is not at all inconsistent with symptomatic treatment. He suggested that a polydactylous hand or a cleft palate may be rendered normal by operation, whereas a gangrenous foot may not respond to surgery. He pointed out that "the effect of anticonvulsant drugs is virtually independent of the etiological type of epilepsy treated. Similarly, the knowledge that diabetes mellitus is usually inherited has not interfered with the discovery of insulin or its clinical usefulness." He argued further that a rational therapy for many hereditary conditions—including presumably psychiatric ones—may not be discovered until it is clearly determined how the genetically controlled factors are transmitted, reproduced and brought into play.

PSYCHOLOGICAL PREDISPOSING FACTORS

Turning from hereditary and constitutional to psychological predisposing factors, we find that the literature provides an abundance of speculations and observations, most of them in considerable agreement with one another. There have, however, been a few points of controversy. Ever since Abraham (1924) first described a "primal depression" occurring in childhood as the result of early disappointments in the child's relationship with his parents, "before the Oedipus wishes have been overcome," writers have consistently subscribed to the idea that the predisposition to depression is formed very early in childhood.

Jacobson, among the more orthodox contributors to the theory of depression, has given perhaps the most detailed exposition of the conditions allegedly necessary for the development of depressive feelings. She has described how an optimal level of self-esteem develops "only in an atmosphere of parental love and care with sufficient libidinous gratification." In such an atmosphere manageable quantities of frustration and disappointment tend to promote the process of self-discovery and reality testing, to throw the child back on his own resources and to facilitate the establishment of solid endopsychic boundaries between self- and object-images. Such an atmosphere gradually allows the child to learn to tolerate his own ambivalence and is conducive to the establishment of a realistic ego ideal and a maturely self-critical superego.

She moreover has focused attention on the importance of severe early disappointments in the development of depressed patients. She defines disappointment as the experience that results from nonfulfillment of expectations of gratification from an object. In other words, she labels as disappointment the feeling that a child has when he fails to get the affection and love and other gratifications that he is expecting. Now, in some measure this is the fate of every human child. And small quantities of disappointment, coming at a time when the child has developed sufficiently to tolerate these deprivations, are indispensable in helping the child learn about the limitations of his own and his parents' omnipotence. Disappointments and frustrations in manageable doses help him to evaluate the world more realistically. It is as if small doses of disappointment in an optimal setting are useful in immunizing the child against the much larger doses of disappointment, anxiety and frustration that he is bound to be exposed to later in life.

But Jacobson emphasizes that the child who has been disappointed too massively and too early in life cannot profit from his experience. Instead, he sustains a deep narcissistic injury. This narcissistic injury corresponds to the feeling of being unvalued, unwanted and unloved. The child thus sets up inside himself the judgment of his parents concerning him. In other words, he develops a harsh and critical superego. Furthermore, this narcissistic injury occurring before the child has learned how to tolerate his ambivalence interferes with the optimal cathexis of self- and object-representations, i.e., with the development of normal self-esteem and satisfactory interpersonal relationships.

Immoderate frustrations experienced too early may also interfere with the establishment of adequate boundaries between the self- and object-images and between these and the ego ideal. The magical idealized omnipotent components of the pre-oedipal ego ideal remain prominent and in later life the patient has to live up to this exaggerated ego ideal before he can experience satisfactory self-esteem. Whitehorn (1952) drew particular attention to the depressed patient's excessive demands upon himself. He pointed out that these patients "have characteristically been demanding of themselves and of others a very extreme degree of self-control, amounting, in effect, to omnipotence. Failing in the omnipotent control of themselves or of events, they feel guilty and insecure."

Thus, in summary, Jacobson attributes the predisposition to depression to the occurrence of excessive disappointments at a time before the child has learned how to handle his ambivalent feelings toward himself and his love-objects and at a time when the endopsychic representations of his self and his objects have not yet been firmly established or distinguished.

Melanie Klein (1934, 1940) also offered a sweeping and general hypothesis to explain the predisposition to depressed states. She too emphasized the importance of the infant's coming to terms with his own feelings of ambivalence in the process of his personality development. Her theory centered around the child's attempt to achieve satisfactory object-relationships in the presence of conflicting feelings of love and hate. The infant was believed by Klein to enter a phase which is characterized by a complex mixture of feelings consisting chiefly of grief and sorrow over the feared loss of his love-object, a state of affairs which he attributes to his own greedy hostility and because of which he feels guilty and self-reproachful. The period when the child experiences this combination of guilt and fear and sorrow and self-reproach is called by her "the depressive position." She believed that those infants who fail to pass successfully through this so-called depressive position remain liable to succumb to this same set of depressive feelings again and again throughout their lives.

It is in this period, Klein believed, that the infant must come to terms with the realization that the object that he hates, the "bad object," and the object that he loves, the "good object," are in reality one person, a "whole object." This depressive position was believed by her to be characterized by fears on the part of the child that his hatred and aggression will prove stronger than his love and will result in the lasting loss of his object. Klein believed that in a favorable outcome the child becomes confident of his mother's love for him and of his own capacity to love; in other words, he succeeds in establishing his "good objects" securely within his ego. She postulated that a predisposition to depression arises only if the infant fails to establish his loved object within his ego, i.e., only if he fails to develop feelings of trust and belief in his objects and in his own capacity to love.

There has been considerable opposition in the psychoanalytic literature (e.g., Glover, 1945) to the concept of a "normal" infantile depressive position. Melanie Klein's contention has often been misunderstood to mean that every infant goes through a psychotic depressive episode in the course of his development. Zetzel (1953) helped to clarify Klein's hypothesis. She understood it to refer simply to "the growth of object relationships in an ambivalent setting." More specifically she suggested that Klein was referring to a phase through which every infant must pass, the weaning process. She felt that Klein was "offering the hypothesis that the attainment of a predominantly positive object relationship prior to this first object loss is crucial for future development. The infant, that is to say, during the weaning process must come to terms with a real object loss—i.e., the breast or its substitute. This is the basis for the concept of a 'depressive position.' "

Therese Benedek (1956) described "a significant variation in the primary psychic organization" which sounds very analogous to Klein's "depressive position" and which she termed the "depressive constellation." She, too, considered this to be of "a universal nature" and to represent the "intensification of the hostile-aggressive component of the ambivalent core in the child." She felt that in later life specific stresses may reactivate this "universal core organization" and produce a depression. Benedek believed that an infant can best be protected against a psychological accentuation of the depressive constellation by "confidence" developing through multiple repetitions of gratifying nursing experiences. "Confidence," as she used the term, is analogous with Klein's conception of the introjection of good objects.

Klein's picture of the infant's eventual achievement of self-esteem and satisfactory object-relationships in the midst of conflicting feelings of hate and love bears an obvious resemblance to Jacobson's theory of how these same goals are achieved. And despite the marked difference in terminology there are perhaps more basic conceptual similarities than differences in their theoretical outlines of this process, even though Jacobson goes far beyond Klein in her discussion of the intermediate steps of this development. Nevertheless, they differ to some extent in their conceptions of how the infant may fail to achieve a state of good object-relationships and adequate self-esteem. Jacobson speaks of excessive disappointments experienced too early, thus bringing into consideration the effect of the quality of the parent-child relationship on the development of the child. She, as Zetzel (1953) pointed out, "postulates an identification with these devalued useless parents, leading to diminution of the ego and the sense of worthlessness so characteristic of the depressive. She would . . . regard the precipitating event in this pathogenic chain of events as emanating from some real failure on the part of the parents." On the other hand, Klein, while not disregarding the actual behavior of the parents, tended to attribute the child's depressive reaction to his feeling that all goodness and love and security are lost, "and lost as a result of his own uncontrollable greedy and destructive phantasies and impulses against his mother's breasts" (Klein, 1934). In other words, according to Klein, the child attributes the disappointing parental behavior mainly to his own excessive greed and sadism.

Most writers have been content to refer vaguely to the preoedipal period as the one in which predisposition to depression is formed, and by this period they mean the first few years of life. Klein (1948) differed with this view on two counts. She considered the critical period to be as early as the first few months of life, and she referred to this period not as pre-oedipal but as indeed already oedipal. She postulated that the infant is at this time already experiencing oedipal fantasies. Moreover, she considered that these fantasies, or these early introjects, as she would refer to them, are derived from the mother's breast and the father's penis, about which the infant is already presumed to have some conceptualizations.

Zetzel (1953) suggested that Klein arrived at this controversial conclusion because in her clinical work with children she found superego-like introjections preceding the classical oedipal period and, instead of considering that precursors of the superego antedate the oedipal period, chose to conclude that the oedipus complex antedates the genital level. However, outside the so-called English school of psychoanalysis, there is almost complete disagreement with Klein on the theoretical implications of these clinical observations. Be that as it may, she believed that it is these early months of life culminating around the period of weaning that are decisive in determining whether or not a predominantly good object has been successfully introjected, i.e., whether or not a depressive predisposition has been averted.

In summary, then, a number of writers other than Melanie Klein have visualized childhood experiences as predisposing to adult depression—each, however, from his particular theoretical perspective. Abraham (1924) believed that since all the melancholic's "subsequent disappointments derive their importance from being representations of his original one, the whole sum of his anger is ultimately directed against one single person—against the person, that is, whom he had been mostfondofasachildandwhohadthen ceased to occupy this position in his life." He went on to postulate that the melancholic's self-reproaches and self-criticisms were not only aimed at his abandoned love-object but were also directed "against that former object." He viewed adult depressions as repetitions of the primal disappointment, the "primal parathymia."

Rado (1928) saw the intrapsychic situation in adult depressions as repetitions of the infant's nursing experiences. Following in Abraham's footsteps, Jacobson (1946) hypothesized that oedipal disappointments revived earlier unresolved pregenital conflicts and predisposed the individual to repetitions of these disappointments in later life.

It should be stressed that these authors do not only argue that childhood experiences predispose to depression. They also view the adult depressions as repetitions, more or less, of the original infantile disappointments. Zetzel (1960) referred to this general "psycho-analytical developmental hypothesis" that "adult symptomatology directly repeats infantile experience." More explicitly, she stated: "The common premise in short, underlying these theories is that adult depressive illness closely resembles an infantile prototype," a premise which she was not inclined to accept unquestioningly.

Still other writers, while not suggesting that adult depressions are repetitions of their infantile precursors, nevertheless feel that early experiences predispose to later adult depressions. Rochlin (1959), Mahler (1961) and Nagera (1970) all stress the importance of early childhood losses and disturbances in predisposing to developmental failures with effects on subsequent object-relationships and the capacity for deeply felt affects.

Bowlby (1963) has suggested that children who have been separated from their mothers in childhood may eventually experience a degree of detachment that will affect their subsequent lives in an undesirable way. Although he refers to evidence that the loss of the mother in childhood "is an antecedent of relevance in the development of personalities prone to depressive and other psychiatric illnesses," his own comments suggest that a child who has no one person to whom he can relate, rather than becoming depressed, "as a rule . . . becomes increasingly self-centered and prone to make transient and shallow relationships with all and sundry."

Sandler and Joffe (1965), in their discussion of childhood depression, note that many depressed adults may have experienced losses or separations in their childhoods. However, they believe that it has been by no means demonstrated that the predisposition to depression is "universally or frequently" correlated with early losses or depressive *illnesses* in childhood.

As we have seen, they do describe a basic psychophysiological affective state in childhood which they refer to as a "depressive reaction" or "depressive response" which they regard as constituting one of the possible reactions to psychic pain. Psychic pain is defined by them as the discrepancy between the actual state of the self and the ideal psychological state of well-being. When this discrepancy is met with helplessness and resignation rather than with a variety of other possible reactions, they refer to the ensuing affective state as a "depressive reaction."

The loss of the ideal state of well-being can, of course, occur with the loss of a love-object, though Sandler and Joffe argue that it is more the loss of the previous state of well-being of which the lost object was the "vehicle" than the loss of the object itself which produces the psychic pain. As we have seen, they point out that similar losses of a previous state of well-being can occur with the birth of a sibling who may bring an end to the previous exclusive possession of the mother which was responsible for the prior state of well-being.

Sandler and Joffe (1965) also dwell on the process of individuation in development during which previous ideal states are given up for the sake of forward moves into fresh developmental phases with their phase-specific states of well-being. This process of individuation involves an increasing independence from parental figures and an increasing autonomy of ego functions. It involves the giving up of infantile goals and the acquiring of more reality-oriented goals and satisfactions. But it can involve some loss of previously experienced well-being and, in some instances, can produce depressive reactions.

"The child who fails to individuate" by acquiring more reality-oriented ideals and gratifications "is prone to react to later disappointments with depression, which cannot readily be worked through but which can only be experienced as clinical depression or alternatively warded off in a pathological way." Sandler and Joffe believe that the prognosis becomes progressively more dismal for the children and adults who regularly respond to disappointment with a depressive response, "who fail to individuate and who cannot withdraw their attachment from infantile ideals."

Furthermore, they see this process of individuation as occurring not only in childhood but continuously throughout life, in school, adolescence, college, in making vocational choices, in love relationships, marriage, parenthood, in moving to a new house, in retirement and old age. All of these occasions and many more involve the giving up of earlier states of psychological well-being and are potential triggering points for depressive illness in individuals predisposed to react to the loss of earlier states of well-being with helplessness, resignation and a depressive response.

In considering his own conceptualization of this depressive response, namely, the depression-withdrawal reaction, Engel (1962) makes the same observation that Sandler and Joffe do, that this is only one of the ways in which infants and children respond to pain or frustration. He refers to Fries and Woolf's (1953) discussion of different congenital activity types in newborns, and notes that those infants, described by her as inactive, respond to withdrawal of the nipple during nursing with inactivity and sleep rather than with crying and struggling. He cites similar observations having to do with sleep withdrawal by Ribble (1943) and by Burton and Derbyshire (1958).

He views this withdrawal pattern as "essentially a conservative one in which the infant reduces activity, heightens the barriers against stimulation and conserves energy, as, for example does a hibernating animal." And, as I have indicated, he views the depression-withdrawal reaction as one of the two primary affects of unpleasure. He cites evidence (Frank, 1954) to indicate that these two affective patterns depend on different neurological substructures and that "constitutional factors may determine an excessive development of one system over the other, an imbalance."

Engel believes that the role of aggression in depression has been exaggerated. He sees the depression-withdrawal reaction of infants and children as the biological anlage, the prototype of adult depressive illness. He refers to those depressive feelings described by adults as "sad, empty, bereft, heavy, tired, weak, fatigued, no energy, no interest, no feeling, lost, and so on" to support his belief that the depression-withdrawal reaction of the child was prototypical of adult depressive illnesses even though "the adult's feelings are also mixed with other affects. . . ." He feels that most depressive reactions encountered in clinical practice are characterized by "giving up" rather than by the morbid guilt and self-directed aggression described by Freud and Abraham.

Most (but not all) of these speculations about predisposition to depression are retrospectively derived from the study of adult patients. However, there is in addition an abundance of clinical evidence in the literature to document in a general way the pathological effects on personality development of severe deprivations in early childhood.

Brown (1961), for example, reported a significantly higher incidence of loss of parents in childhood among depressed patients not differentiated into neurotic and endogenous groupings. Beck et al. (1963) found that patients not diagnostically differentiated but rated as more severely depressed had a higher incidence of bereavements in childhood than was found in nondepressed patients, a finding that was also reported by Munro (1966) and Wilson et al. (1967). In connection with this, one must remember that other studies had indicated that severity of depression did not correlate with diagnostic groupings; i.e., a neurotically depressed patient could have a more severe depression than a patient with an endogenous depression. Dennehy (1966) also confirmed the increased incidence in depressed patients of bereavement during childhood. This was especially true with respect to the loss of the father between the ages of ten and fourteen, a finding also reported by Brown (1961), Munro (1966) and Hill and Price (1967).

Oltman et al. (1951), however, found no significant difference in the incidence of parental deprivation between manic-depressive patients and normal subjects. Hopkinson and Reed (1966) also failed to find correlations between childhood bereavement and manic-depressive illness. They found that the "loss of one or both parents before the patient reached the age of 15 is no commoner in manic-depressive patients than it is for the general population. Their findings supported a previous study by Stenstedt (1952). It was their opinion that what Brown had actually demonstrated was an association between bereavement in childhood and a subsequent general depressed mood later in adult life.

Furthermore, Pitts et al. (1965) found the frequency of childhood bereavement was not significantly different in medical patients as compared with depressives or members of any other diagnostic category. Gregory (1966b), using generation life tables which provide information about the expected frequency of orphanhood in the general population, was unable to find any significant differences between the observed and expected frequency of childhood bereavement in 321 adult psychiatric patients. More specifically, his study did not suggest that bereavement during childhood was associated with depression or with any specific pattern of neurosis or psychosis in adult life. Similarly, Brill and Liston (1966) failed to demonstrate a linkage between childhood parental losses and depressive illness.

On the other hand, the investigations of Glueck and Glueck (1950), Gregory (1965a, 1966b) and Munro and Griffiths (1969) indicate that delinquency was most likely to be the consequence of childhood loss of the parent of the same sex as the child, whether this loss is due to death or divorce. Gregory suggests that the control functions and identification models provided by the parent of the same sex were among the significant elements missing after the loss of such a parent.

Gay and Tonge (1967) tested a hypothesis that bereavement in childhood predisposes to psychogenic rather than to endogenous depressions in later life and did find such an association between parental deaths and reactive depressions. As they put it, "it is possible that the experience of childhood bereavement affects the quality of the mourning reaction and predisposes to depression in the adult," but they reported an unexpected finding, namely, an association between neuroses without depression and the loss of the parent of the same sex while parents with neurotic depressions tended to lose parents of the opposite sex.

Thus there is virtual unanimity that early parental loss is not associated with endogenous depression, although Beck et al., Munro and Wilson et al. do report such an association with the severity of depressions. Also, there is some evidence that early parental loss may have an influence on subsequent depressed moods and outlooks and on neurotic depressions.

These studies would seem to stand in direct contradiction to the plausible assumption that early losses and deprivations would predispose to depressive illness in later life, although they may influence subsequent development in other ways such as predisposing to depressed or pessimistic moods or to neurotic types of depression. A much clearer link has been established between childhood losses and what has variously been referred to as delinquency, sociopathy and psychopathy.

An interesting alternative possibility has been suggested by Gregory (1966a), namely, "that hardship and deprivation, including orphanhood, may lead to increased adaptability and creativity, with diminished vulnerability to adult psychopathology." He refers to work by Goertzel and Goertzel (1962) and a prior report of his own (1965b) to provide some support for this possibility. Actually, as Dennehy (1966), Hill and Price (1967) and Munro and Griffiths (1969) suggest, just to speak of bereavement as a determining factor in development is to greatly oversimplify the issue. Of enormous relevance is how the child is helped to endure his bereavement, the stability of the family after the death, the economic situation of the family and the availability and supportiveness of the remaining or substitute parents.

Most (but not all) of these speculations about predisposition to depression are retrospectively derived from the study of adult patients. However, there is in addition an abundance of clinical evidence in the literature to document in a general way the pathological effects on personality development of severe deprivations in early childhood.

Valuable and pertinent as these observations are, they are not to be viewed as evidence in support of any one particular psychogenic theory as opposed to another.

In the first place, although retrospective (e.g., Bowlby, 1944; Bender, 1952) and follow-up studies of very severely deprived children (Lowrey, 1940; Goldfarb, 1945; Beres and Obers, 1950) have clearly demonstrated the pathological effects of such early experiences on these children, these effects have mainly turned out to be of the schizophrenic or psychopathic variety rather than manic-depressive in type.

Second, although some workers (e.g., Spitz, 1946) have shown that early deprivations produce depressive conditions in childhood, it must be borne in mind that the word "depressed" in these cases was used in a behavioristic sense since the children under observation were still preverbal. Whether these reactions actually correspond to adult depressive states is still, at best, questionable. Certainly Rochlin (1959) argues that they do not.

Third, as Rochlin (1953b) points out, the psychotic or atypical children that have been recently described in the literature by Rank (1949), Geleerd (1949), Mahler (1952) and others cannot be said to have regressed to this psychotic phase as adult psychotics are presumed to do. They have actually never developed beyond it and therefore cannot strictly be compared to adult manic-depressives and schizophrenics. Although they dramatically demonstrate, in a general way, the effects of very severe early deprivation, they can hardly be used as evidence to support any one particular current theory as opposed to another, about predisposition to manic-depressive psychosis or to any other depressive reaction.

THE CENTRAL ANXIETY SITUATION IN HUMAN DEVELOPMENT

It was mentioned previously that Melanie Klein (1940) referred to the depressive position with its mixture of guilt and fear and sorrow and longing as the central anxiety situation in human development, "the deepest source of the painful conflicts . . . in the child's relation to people in general." The conception of this complex of feelings as the central anxiety situation in human development warrants examination in considerably more detail.

Fairbairn (1952), another British writer whose views were in large measure related to Melanie Klein's, agreed basically with her conception of the depressive position as a composite of feelings which the infant experiences as the result of inevitable frustrations sustained at the hands of his love-objects. Like Klein, he saw this position as made up of feelings of lovelessness and unhappiness infused with anger toward the love-object and guilt and fear over this anger. He saw the great problem of the depressive individual, the individual who has never resolved the difficulties of the depressive position, as how to love without destroying by hate. In every love relationship into which such an individual enters, there is always the danger that the inevitable frustrations will arouse such feelings of rage and destruction that the relationship will be threatened. Fairbairn differed somewhat, as will be seen below, from Klein in his conception of the schizoid position, the developmental phase which, he believed, precedes the depressive position. But, like Klein, he attributed to these infantile "positions," or states of feeling, a very central importance in all neurosis. He felt that these states are not defenses "but have all the characteristics of conditions against which the ego utilizes paranoid, obsessive, hysterical and phobic techniques." In other words, he felt that the depressive and the schizoid positions are the two fundamental dangers against which all neurotic phenomena and character traits are defenses.

Michael Balint (1952) in an interesting paper examined the depressive position with its mixture of paranoid and depressive anxieties and dissected it even further into purer elements. He regularly observed that many of his patients in analysis pass through a phase of suspicion and mistrust of what they see as a careless, loveless, indifferent environment. If they can be helped out of this paranoid position, he noted that another state develops during which "there is the feeling of a deep, painful, narcissistic wound which, as a rule, can be made conscious without serious difficulty, somehow in this way: It is terrifying and dreadfully painful that *I am not loved for what I am,* time and time again I cannot avoid seeing that people are critical of me; it is an irrefutable fact that no one loves me as I want to be loved." Balint identified this set of feelings with Klein's depressive position, although he differed from her in not considering (at least not explicitly and, as far as the writer could determine, not implicitly) the depressive position as, in part, reactive to previous sadistic fantasies. He did not give these depressive anxieties quite the central position in all psychic phenomena that Klein did but nevertheless agreed with her that they give rise to a variety of defenses and reactions.

It is interesting to note that other writers with superficially quite different theoretical approaches also spoke of affective states which, although described differently, bear certain obvious resemblances to the depressive position in that they are described as being in one sense or another "basic" or "central." Karen Horney

(1936), for example, had the concept of a "basic anxiety" which, she believed, plays a fundamental role in neurosis and which "underlies all relationships to people." This basic anxiety consists of an all-pervasive feeling of being lonely, helpless and unlovable in a hostile world. This fundamental anxiety was seen by Horney as being "inseparably interwoven" with a basic hostility.

Sullivan (1947), too, speculated with regard to a central core of anxieties around which the personality structure is built and which neurotic techniques help to keep from awareness. "The self," he believed, "comes into being as a dynamism to preserve the feeling of security." He went on to say that "from the disappointments in the very early stages of life outside the womb—in which all things were given—comes the beginning of the vast development of actions, thoughts, foresights, and so on, which are calculated to protect one from a feeling of insecurity and helplessness in the situation which confronts one." This precariously acquired self-esteem which Sullivan considered so important, and which corresponds largely to the introjected good objects of Melanie Klein, is referred to by Silverberg (1952) in his attempted synthesis of Sullivanian and Freudian thought as "the psychic equivalent of somatic survival." This bears a striking resemblance to Klein's statement (1934) that "the preservation of the good object is regarded as synonymous with the survival of the ego."

We find, therefore, a common area of agreement among writers of many different persuasions that there is a "central anxiety position," a "basic anxiety" or whatever it is called, "against which the ego requires to be defended" and which consists of the "feeling of sorrow for the loved objects, the fears of losing them and the longing to regain them," "the irrefutable fact that no one loves me as I want to be loved," the feeling that comes from being unloved, and of being alone and helpless in a hostile world. This is, in other words, the lack of self-esteem which is the result of the reflected appraisal of the early love-objects.

These concepts are by no means identical, but underlying all of them is the overwhelmingly acknowledged importance of the quality of early object-relationships in the type of character structure that evolves.

Glover (1945), in his comprehensive critique of the Kleinian body of theory, disputes the central importance in neurosogenesis of this depressive position and feels that it is contrary to Freud's view. It will be helpful to look at Freud's own words on the subject of what neurosis defends against.

In *Inhibitions, Symptoms and Anxiety* (1936), a comparatively late formulation of his theory, he described anxiety as a danger signal, i.e., a signal that a situation of danger was impending. This danger situation, as he conceived it, was the danger of losing the object. He amplified this concept when he remarked that "grief is therefore the reaction specific to object loss, anxiety to the danger which this object loss entails, or, by a further displacement, to the danger of the object loss itself." In this view, "all symptom formation would be brought about solely in order to avoid anxiety; the symptoms bind the psychic energy which otherwise would be discharged as anxiety, so that anxiety would be the fundamental phenomenon and the central problem of neurosis."

However, Freud went on to say that object loss took different forms at different stages of development. In early childhood he conceived of the danger as simply object loss itself, i.e., loss of the mother. But in the phallic phase, as is well known, he thought of this danger as a castration danger. At first glance it might be difficult to reconcile this with the danger of object loss, but as he looked at it, "the high narcissistic value attaching to the penis may be referable to the fact that the possession of this organ contains a guaranty of reunion with the mother (or mother substitute) in the act of coitus. Deprivation of this mother . . . has again the significance . . . of being delivered over helpless to the unpleasurable tension arising from non-gratification of a need." The danger of object loss in the latency period was formulated by Freud as "the anger, the punishment, of the superego, the loss of its love, which the ego apprehends as a danger and to which it responds with the signal of anxiety," a view with which we are very familiar.

Thus Freud conceived of anxiety, "the central problem of neurosis," as but a signal of the real danger, the danger of loss of the object as it is experienced in its various forms in the different phases of development. Obviously this Freudian view of anxiety and the danger of object loss should not be twisted into too close a correspondence with the views outlined above, but the writer suggests that there are more than superficial resemblances to these theories in Freud's progressively increasing conceptualization of the central problem in neurosis as the danger of the loss of the actual and introjected love-objects.

To summarize this section briefly, we have seen that many writers, primarily British, have observed clinically a set of intensely painful feelings of sorrow and loss and unlovableness fused with hate and guilt that they have variously termed "depressive anxieties" or "position" or "state" and which they have felt to be not a defense, but a fundamental danger situation against which defenses and restitutive measures must be mobilized. These writers further maintained: (1) that every infant went through such a state of depressive anxieties (if he successfully passed through the variously described preceding persecutory or schizoid state); (2) that the infant's further development and proneness to depression depended on how successfully he "worked through" this position, this working-through process being characterized by firmly establishing the good objects within himself, i.e., in becoming confident of love and security.

Furthermore, there was surprisingly widespread agreement that the central danger position, with regard to which anxiety was a signal and neurosis a defense, was this set of depressive anxieties which were variously termed but which all had to do with the loss of the object, external or internalized, and with the associated feelings of helplessness, unlovableness, desolation and lack of self-esteem.

What can be said of these attempts to attribute central importance in normal and neurotic development to one or another of these developmental problems, whether it be the depressive position of Klein or the Oedipus complex of Freud? Is one more important than the other or is the whole controversy a pseudo-problem, a perfectionistic and unrealistic attempt to assign critical priority to one of several crucial life phases, each of which is of overwhelming importance at some particular period in life? To the reviewer, it would appear that the developing infant and child has many developmental crises to weather. He has to come to terms with his own ambivalence. He has to face the problem of acquiring a rewarding and satisfying relationship with his first love-object with its implications for self-esteem and confidence. He has to attain an effective mastery over his physiological processes and his developing ego functions. He has to arrive at a solution of the "three-body relationship," as Rickman (1951) refers to it, the fateful oedipal situation which is so important in determining his subsequent ability to lead a gratifying emotional and sexual life. The growing child is confronted with the task of solving the problems of jealousy and envy that are also connected with sibling rivalry. Nor is that all. As we all know and as Sullivan (1953) and Erikson (1950) have shown, the problems of adolescence are by no means negligible in their relevance to the development of the individual.

Are any of these stages or problems or periods the most important? Or would it not be more reasonable to think of these as nodal points in human development, the successful mastery of each being largely dependent upon the degree of success in coping with previous phases? After all, one who has not successfully mastered the tensions of unrestrained ambivalence can hardly integrate the most satisfying kind of object-relationship. And one who has never successfully solved the problems of the "two-body relationship" will be at a disadvantage in engaging in the conflicts of the oedipal situation. It is clear that each phase in life is colored and influenced by the previous life experiences of the individual.

This is not to suggest that there are not critical phases and important nodal points in human development. One need not subscribe to a strictly monistic theory of neurotic causation to appreciate the key importance of several of the phases and several of the problems of psychological development. The achievement of a good relationship with the mother is one of these phases, and the struggle to attain a measure of self-esteem is one of these problems. And needless to say, the satisfactory working through of the oedipal situation is one of the critical tasks of the developing child.

It is interesting to note in this connection that Gitelson (1952), in his comments on opening the symposium on the reevaluation of the Oedipus complex at the Seventeenth International Psychoanalytic Congress, stressed the importance of pregenital conflicts. He felt that it was only on the basis of a satisfactory mother-child relationship that an individual could enter into and solve the problems of the oedipal period. He drew attention to the presence of so many borderline patients in current analytic practice who far from being able to deal with oedipal problems have never even successfully solved the problems of the primary mother-child constellation. Implying then that one who has begun to cope with the oedipal situation has already traveled a very considerable distance along the pathway of development, he significantly concluded that "the Oedipus complex thus has apical importance not so much as the nucleus of the neuroses but as the nucleus of normal character structure and as the basis of mature life."

OBSESSIONAL CHARACTER STRUCTURE

We will now consider the obsessional character structure that has been attributed to the depressive person in his "free intervals" by various writers. It was Abraham who first made this correlation. After having made previous observations to the effect that the obsessional neurotic and the manic-depressive had in common a marked ambivalence toward their love-objects, Abraham (1924) stated that the manic-depressive patient "is found to have an abnormal character-formation during his 'free interval' and that this character-formation coincides in a quite unmistakable way with that of the obsessional neurotic." He found in his manic-depressive patients during their nonpsychotic periods the same attitudes about cleanliness, order, money and possessions and the same defiance and obstinacy alternating with docility and submissiveness that he observed in obsessional neurotics.

Rado (1928) confirmed the presence of obsessional traits in the character of melancholics between attacks. He thought of them as reaction formations serving the purpose of psychic bulwarks for the restraint of ambivalence and as devices to "minister to narcissistic gratification" by draining off aggressive energy into socially acceptable channels.

Gero (1936) objected to the conceptualization of the obsessional character as the sum of isolated qualities such as order, cleanliness, etc. He felt that to understand this character structure properly it was necessary to see these different traits in a more comprehensive and unified way. Unlike Rado, who tended to think of obsessional traits as devices to drain off aggressive energy into useful channels and, in this sense, a healing mechanism, Gero thought of them collectively as simply a defense, in itself part of the neurosis. He regarded the obsessional character structure as a defense designed to guard against the coming into awareness of hostile impulses and thoughts, and a defense, moreover, which must be analyzed immediately so that the patient's warded-off impulses could become conscious and be experienced and so that changes could then occur.

He regarded this type of defense as "a continuous state of being on one's guard against oneself, a complete inability to break loose. Such people's typical reactions are mistrust of themselves and an incapacity to let themselves go. Their impulses are always reined in. They feel in themselves something excessive and passionate which they fear without knowing what it is. They are afraid to lose control lest these dark passions should carry them away. We know that above all it is the abnormal sadistic impulses that render these defensive measures necessary. These patients suffer from a chronic damming up of the feeling of aggression. On the one hand their repressed feelings of aggression are tremendously strong, on the other hand their excessively strict superego does not permit them even innocent acts of aggression. Always held back, continually hurt, they long for revenge, but they can never satisfy these feelings." However it must be noted that his case material led Gero to question the universality of this type of character structure in depressed patients.

Stengel, who reported extensively on the association of obsessional neurosis with psychotic reaction types (1945, 1948), stated quite categorically (1948): "I do not agree with those writers who maintain that the typical features of the obsessional character can be found in every case of manic-depressive illness."

Edith Jacobson's (1953) case material also leads her to question the thesis that the manic-depressive shows obsessive or compulsive traits during his free intervals. She finds that even during these intervals there are vacillations in mood and efficiency that are not at all characteristic of compulsives. Nor is there in the cyclothymic patient the independence which exists in the compulsive and which is the result of the latter's dependence on his own superego for self-esteem. She finds that the manic-depressive does, at times, lean on his superego. This, it is true, gives him the appearance of independence. However, this is illusory since he also simultaneously or alternately depends upon some idealized love-object which, she feels, does not happen in the true compulsive.

Mabel Blake Cohen and her co-workers (1954), in their study of manic-depressive psychosis, also felt that there are important differences between the manic-depressive character and the obsessional character, although they focused attention on rather different aspects of the obsessional character than does Jacobson. The main difference they saw was that the manic-depressive has a marked lack of interpersonal awareness which makes him overlook the particular characteristics and qualities of the other person, whereas the obsessional, although hostile, controlling and envious, does nevertheless have an awareness of the other person as a person.

Attention must be drawn to the observation that all of these judgments refer specifically to manic-depressive patients and not to other kinds of depressives. There seem to be scarcely any comparable psychoanalytic references to other groups of depressed patients with data relevant to this aspect of their character structure. However, as was indicated in an earlier chapter, several clinical psychiatric studies (Titley, 1936; Palmer and Sherman, 1938; Malamud and Sands, 1941) seem to show that the obsessional character structure is much more typical of the prepsychotic involutional melancholic than of the prepsychotic manic-depressive.

AGGRESSION IN DEPRESSION

Concern with the obsessional character is in large part concern with the defenses of the depressed or depression-prone person. But psychoanalytic writers have been even more concerned with the impulses against which these defenses operate. The most important of these impulses is aggression.

Abraham (1911) first noted the presence of hostility and ambivalence in the psychopathology of the depressive. Freud (1917) gave classical expression to this theme in his interpretation of the meaning of the melancholic's self-reproaches. He saw these self-reproaches as hostile feelings which the patients unconsciously felt toward their love-objects and which, with the abandonment of these objects, they redirected toward their own persons with which the objects had now become identified. Abraham (1924) later provided clinical documentation of these observations.

Rado (1928) later also supported Freud's conception of the depressive's hostility and reported an irritability and embittered rebelliousness in depressives even before the so-called melancholic introjection. By now the theme of aggression played a central role in psychoanalytic writing on depression. It was a theme that was particularly emphasized by Melanie Klein (1948). Her view of a "death instinct" as innate in every person from birth onwards influenced her to assign even greater emphasis to the alleged association of hostility and aggression with every depressive reaction. She conceived of the infant as turning the self-directed aggressive energy of the death instinct outwards and reacting to frustration with hostile, sadistic feelings. Indeed, she labeled as the "depressive position" that phase in human development when the infant can allegedly feel guilt and sorrow over the feared loss of the love-object which it attributes to its own sadistic impulses. She believed that this depressive position is the prototype for all clinical depressions, and the concept of hostility and aggression was thus for her intimately bound up with the concept of depression.

The association of aggression and depression has become so common in psychoanalytic and general psychiatric thinking that it is of interest to find four writers who challenged the universality of this association. Balint (1952), for example, utilized the concept of a depressive position and yet, unlike Klein, saw it as free of aggressive coloring. He conceived of a pre-ambivalent infantile state which he called the period of archaic object love. The depressive position follows the loss of this state and he spoke of it in terms of "a deep painful narcissistic wound." Despite Balint's thesis that such an infantile state exists, he referred to bitterness and resentment about an undeserved injury as occurring "in every form of depression" but spoke of these feelings as secondary narcissistic features. He considered them reactions to, rather than essential elements of, depression.

Bibring (1953) also regarded aggression as a secondary phenomenon and as not necessarily a component part of every depression. He stated that "it seems justified to generalize that the turning of aggressive impulses against the self is secondary to a breakdown of the self-esteem. . . . However there are depressions which are not accompanied by any self-aggression and there are cases of angry self-hatred which do not show any manifest signs of depression."

He was echoed in these remarks by Cohen and her colleagues (1953), who said about their patients' hostility: "We feel that it has been considerably overstressed as a dynamic factor in the illness." They relegated the hostility that does appear to a secondary position. "We see hostile feelings arising in the patient as the result of frustration of his manipulative and exploitative needs. . . . But we feel that much of the hostility that has been imputed to the patient has been the result of his annoying impact upon others, rather than of a primary motivation to do injury to them."

Gero (1953) challenges the view that all self-devaluation can be considered self-directed aggression. In a patient whom he was treating, one kind of self-devaluation and self-dissatisfaction was not, according to him, a superego reaction (i.e., a manifestation of aggression) but "the expression of a perception based on the withdrawal of libidinal cathexis from the genital region and secondarily from the whole body." In other words, this particular patient's complaints about the ugliness of her body were characterized as "a generalized feeling of being castrated," a statement of grief.

Thus, as we can see, there appear to be radical differences of opinion about the role of aggression in the depressive reactions. However, a review of the pertinent literature reveals the presence of two semantic and conceptual difficulties which contribute a very considerable share to the theoretical difficulties we have been discussing.

The first of these difficulties has to do with the definition of depression, the second with the definition of aggression. The first difficulty is the easier to resolve for it is largely a question of definition. Some authors require the presence of aggression for the diagnosis of depression. It is therefore hardly surprising that they find it. Indeed, were they not to find aggression they would be forced, as Beres (1958) has acknowledged, to deny that the illness was depression. Two leading exponents of this viewpoint are Jacobson and Fairbairn. For Jacobson, depression and the vicissitudes of aggression are inseparable. In the more psychotic depressions she sees a massive redirection of hostile feelings from the object to the self-image. In other depressions there may be a less explicit deployment of aggressive energy between the ego and the ego ideal with accompanying feelings of unworthiness, inadequacy or inferiority. In still other depressions which are characterized by feelings of guilt and moral unworthiness, the aggressive tension is between the superego and the ego.

Those states which other writers refer to as depressions and which consist primarily of feelings of loneliness and longing are not considered by Jacobson to be depressions at all. She acknowledges (1957) that these states are mostly free of aggressive elements and that they are often characterized primarily by the lack of gratification of libidinal impulses.

For Fairbairn (1952), too, depression was intimately associated with aggression. However, he believed that there is an earlier and more basic reaction than anger to the loss of the object. This he called not "depression" but the "schizoid" way of reacting. Patients who react in this way to object loss will frequently describe themselves as being depressed. Yet when they describe what they mean by depression, they will use such words as "lonely," "empty," "a feeling of futility," "feeling out of touch," "hungry," etc. There is frequently no communication or indication of guilt or anger—just a sad, empty loneliness that appears quite different in quality from the retarded depression of the cyclothymic person. Since Fairbairn believed that there is no element of anger in this reaction, he excluded it from the category of depression.

Nacht and Racamier (1960) are also very explicit on this point. For them, "the depressed person—except no doubt the stuporous melancholic—is always *truly aggressive* towards others through the very medium of the manifestations of his depression."

The second semantic difficulty to which we have referred has to do with the various meanings assigned to the concept of "aggression." In the first place, "aggression" may be used either as a description of behavior or as an explanation of behavior with no clear distinction between these two uses. In the second place, "aggression" may be used either for impulses or feelings or for a highly abstract concept of psychic energy, again with little distinction between these uses.

René Spitz provides an example of these difficulties. In his paper *Anaclitic Depression* (1946), he attempts to make this type of depression conform to the mechanism which Freud (1917) postulated in *Mourning and Melancholia.* He declares that "in the infant the superego is absent, so that it is impossible to assume destructive hostility of the superego. However, the loss of the love-object in itself is equivalent to a hostile deprivation for the infant." The infants that he studied were restricted in their locomotion and thus blocked from making contact with other children or adults. "Inhibited in its motor release, the pent-up aggressive drive is turned against the ego." The manifestation of this self-directed aggression is assumed, in conformity with Freud's theory about melancholics, to be the anaclitic depression itself. Here Spitz resorts to the concept of a retroflexed aggressive drive to provide an explanation for the anaclitic depression primarily on the basis of accepted theory, rather than on the basis of observable behavior.

In his later paper (1953), Spitz uses the term in an additional way. He postulates that in the infant in the second half of the first year, the libidinal and the aggressive drives are both directed toward the same object. He believes that if this object is removed from the infant, the aggressive drive, for a time, finds no target. "It is the relationship with the love-object which gives the infant the opportunity to release its aggressive drives. . . . If the infant is deprived of the libidinal object, both drives are deprived of their target. This is what happened to the infants affected with anaclitic depression. . . . If we follow the fate of the aggressive drive, we find these infants slowly becoming self-destructive. It is in such cases that we have found the frequent manifestations of headbanging."

Spitz goes on to remark that infants, after regaining their libidinal object and after recovering from their depression, become even more aggressive against others than normal children of their age. It is inferred from this externally directed aggression which occurs in the period of recovery from depression that previously, during the depressed state, this aggression must have been directed inwards. Spitz suggests this when he remarks that "after coming out of the anaclitic depression the restored infant no longer hits or scratches itself. It now begins to bite, to scratch, to kick others."

In both of these latter two examples, Spitz seems to be speaking in a far more behavioristic sense when referring to aggression. He no longer theorizes that the depression itself is simply the manifestation of self-directed aggression. When he speaks of the aggression turned against the self, or against others, he refers to observable self-destruction, or aggression toward others, rather than to a hypothetical drive.

In this same paper, Spitz uses the concept of aggression in still another way. He describes how continued institutionalization can lead to physical deterioration and death. In explanation for this, he states that "theoretically we may posit that in these children the aggression has been turned against the self, resulting in the shockingly high percentage of deaths."

Thus Spitz speaks of aggression as leading to clinical depression in infants when the "pent-up aggressive drive is turned on the ego." First, aggression is conceptualized as *psychic energy*. In the second example, "aggression" refers to such self-destructive *behavior* as head-banging. And in the third example he postulates that aggression, now a veritable *death instinct*, becomes turned against the self to cause physical deterioration and death.

Solnit (1970), too, uses the concept of aggression in this last way. In his paper, the aggressive drive becomes an instinctual biological drive so tangible that it can be turned against the "self" and bring about marasmus and death in such infants.

We have noted that a second confusion in the use of the term "aggression" is occasioned by the failure to distinguish between aggression as an impulse or feeling and aggression as a highly abstract concept of psychic energy. This confusion is well illustrated in the use of the term by Jacobson. When a manic-depressive abandons his love-object and withdraws into a psychotic depression, for example, she postulates that all of the hostility that he has felt toward the object becomes experienced as directed against the self, since, by a regressive dissolution of identifications, the object- and self-images have merged.

This manner of deploying aggressive energy is quite different from what she presumes to happen to an individual who fails in some way to live up to his ego ideal. Here she considers that the superego cathects the self-image with aggressive energy and that self-esteem drops. But the objects are still retained and there is no massive withdrawal of libidinal cathexis from them. In such a case, it would not seem correct to say that the aggression meant for an object has now been redirected or retroflexed. The aggressive energy with which the self-representation is cathected to bring about the drop in self-esteem is certainly related to the original disapproval experienced by the individual from his parents. According to the theory, his superego has taken over their role. But this aggressive energy with which his self-image is now presumed to be cathected is a much less positively identifiable affective entity than the hostility which the manic-depressive feels for his disappointing object and which he reflexes on himself. To speak of both of these situations simply as manifestations of aggression would seem only to confuse the issue.

Nacht and Racamier (1960) provide a good example of clinicians reading aggression into the very symptomatology of the depressed patient. For them, "depression [is actually] one of the clinical manifestations of aggression." As they interpret it, the depressed person's "suffering is an accusation. His sense of incurableness is a reproach. His demands are perhaps humble, but devastating. His dependency is tyrannical. . . ." For these authors, the patient cannot be sick without being aggressive—and at others, not at himself.

What they are here expressing is obviously not a description of aggressive behavior but an explanation of behavior which may or may not, depending on the individual case, be aggressive in intent. For them depression is always aggressively motivated. They know before they have examined the patient, and therefore aggression is always present in the patient's behavior. But then, by the same reasoning, every illness, and especially every chronic illness, can be thought of "as one of the manifestations of aggression."

Hartmann (1955) made an attempt to conceptualize the manner

in which various manifestations of aggression are related to one another. It had long been considered that libidinal energy is transformed into nonsexual energy and made available to the ego for nonsexual purposes. This transformation is referred to as "sublimation." Hartmann suggested that a similar transformation occurs with aggressive energy, a transformation that he terms "neutralization." He further proposed that the word "neutralization" be used in a general sense to refer not only to the deaggressivization of aggressive energy but also to the desexualization or sublimation of libidinal energy. Moreover, he thought that "it comes closer to observable facts to speak . . . not just of two modes of energy of each drive: instinctual or neutralized. Both clinical experience and theory point to the probability that there exists a continuum of gradations of energy, from the fully instinctual to the fully neutralized mode." In this connection he speaks of the aggression that the superego uses in its relations to the ego as being already partly modified from its purely hostile, destructive "instinctual mode."

The dangers inherent in this reification of energy have been critically considered by Kubie (1947), and in a conference on psychiatric education Whitehorn (1953) warned against taking seriously "any applied identity or too close analogy with the concepts of energy, tension or pressure in the sense that the physicist uses these terms."

As the reader can see, the study of the theoretical models constructed to help understand the depressive reactions sometimes carries one into regions that can most charitably be described as metapsychological. It is in this particular aspect of the depressive problem that one most frequently encounters a level of discourse far removed from clinical reality. Freud's explanation of the melancholic's self-reproaches and Abraham's description of the manic-depressive's ambivalence became universally and, it is feared, uncritically and uniformly applied to all depressive phenomena. And later authors frequently sought to justify these constructions rather than to investigate their applicability. This subject will be discussed much more extensively in a later chapter.

In summary, there is very little consensus in the literature on the relation of aggression to depression. There is no agreement as to whether aggression is an innate primary human drive or whether it appears only secondarily in reaction to frustration—or indeed as to whether this antithesis has any real meaning. There is no agreement as to whether or not aggression is related to a hypothetical death instinct. There is no agreement as to whether aggression is central to the problem of depression or secondary. And there has been very little notice paid to the various ways in which the word "aggression" is used. In short, speculation is rife, consensus minimal and confusion distressingly common.

ORALITY IN DEPRESSION

Let us now turn to an examination of the theories about the presence of "orality" in depression. Abraham (1916), in corroboration of Freud's (1905) original formulation about the role of the erogenous zones in psychosexual development, provided numerous clinical examples of patients whose mode of achieving libidinal gratification was by stimulation of their oral zone. He theorized that oral eroticism in neurotic depressives has two functions: to prevent an episode of depression and to remove one once it has occurred. He reported one depressed patient who was inexplicably soothed by drinking a cup of milk that his mother brought him. Abraham further postulated that the melancholically depressed patient regresses in his unconscious to the oral phase of psychosexual development and that he directs upon his love-object the wish to incorporate it, a wish that is colored by hostility so that it is simultaneously a desire to devour and to demolish the object. Abraham felt that it was the guilt associated with this hostile cannibalistic wish that accounted for the melancholic's refusal to take food and for his fear of starvation.

Freud (1917), as we know, interpreted the melancholic's self-reproaches as being in reality directed against the abandoned love-object which had been introjected into the ego. For Freud this introjection represented a regression of libido from object-choice to the earliest and original form of object-relationship.

He felt that this earliest type of relationship was essentially an oral phenomenon since one of the infant's most primitive reactions to objects was to put them into his mouth. This was considered by Freud to be the earliest method of relating to an object and one which he referred to as "identification" since it represented for Freud an attempt to be magically at one with the loved object. And in what way could the infant be more at one with the loved object than by actually putting it into his mouth and incorporating it into himself?

After the abandonment of the object by the melancholic, Freud believed that it was this process that took place, namely, a regression to an identification with the object by means of its introjection into the ego, the introjection being conceptualized as an oral act. And he understood the self-reproaches to be reproaches against this introjected object. He furthermore agreed with Abraham's explanation of the melancholic's refusal to eat, since he too considered this introjection of the object to be essentially an unconsciously hostile cannibalistic act. In turn Abraham (1924) attempted to corroborate Freud's hypothesis that introjection takes place by an oral mechanism with numerous clinical examples drawn from his patients' fantasies and dreams. He furthermore postulated a constitutional and inherited overaccentuation of oral eroticism in potential melancholics, i.e., an increased capacity to experience pleasures in the oral zone. He thought that as a result of this alleged constitutional intensification of oral needs and consequent oral frustrations, such patients suffered a special fixation of psychosexual development at the oral level.

Rado (1928), as was mentioned earlier, performed two services to the understanding of orality. He was one of the first workers to broaden the concept of orality by trying to show that "pleasurable stimulation of the mouth-zone does not constitute the whole of the oral-libidinal gratification but should rather be regarded as its more conspicuous antecedent." He referred to the climax of the process of which the mouth pleasure was the precursor by the suggestively descriptive term "alimentary orgasm," a term which has, by and large, failed to enter into the everyday currency of psychoanalytic language. He suggested that the pleasure which the infant experiences at his mother's breasts and which includes components of security, warmth and nourishment, is the prototype of the narcissistic gratification that is later experienced as self-satisfaction and self-esteem.

Rado argued that "the deepest fixation point in the [melancholic] depressive disposition is to be found in the . . . hunger-situation of the infant," by which he meant that the "intensely strong craving for narcissistic gratification" which he found so characteristic of depressives had its roots in the hungry feelings of the ungratified infant. And just as the "oral-narcissistic bliss" of the infant is dependent upon supplies of nourishment from the outside, so does the narcissistic gratification of the depressive, he felt, depend upon love, appreciation and recognition by others—what Fenichel (1945) was to refer to as "external narcissistic supplies."

Rado considered that the narcissistic people who are so predisposed to depression "have a sense of security and comfort only when they feel themselves loved, esteemed, supported and encouraged."

Gero (1936) made this broader interpretation of orality more explicit by dissociating it even further from its purely buccal and alimentary connotations and by extending its meaning to cover all aspects of the early mother-child relationship. "Inseparable from it is the pleasurable contact with the skin, the comfortable feeling of warmth emanating from the mother's body. . . . The specifically oral pleasure is only one factor in the experience satisfying the infant's need for warmth, touch, love and care." It is in this wider sense that he believed that the depressive type is oral: he "longs for shelter and love, and for the warmth of the mother's protecting body."

It was Fenichel (1945) who more fully described the narcissistic oral character of the depressive, the "person who is fixated on the state where his self-esteem is regulated by external supplies." He sketched a vivid picture of the depressive's perpetual greediness, his extremely dependent need to be loved and his inordinate demands upon his love-objects. He considered that "a severe depression represents the state into which the orally dependent individual gets when the vital supplies are lacking."

In opposition to this general theoretical trend, Bibring (1953) first openly questioned the universality of oral fixation and oral orientation in depression. Since his demurral reopened an issue that seemed for a long time to be a closed one, let us glance more carefully at the issue of oral fixation in depression.

The alleged orality of depressives seems to have three theoretical and historical sources. In the first place, it has long been pointed out that depressives have oral fantasies and are inclined to oral gratifications. About this, Jacobson (1953) says, "It has seemed to me to be of lesser importance [than other factors that she emphasizes] that the melancholic divulges cannibalistic incorporation and anal-sadistic ejection fantasies. All psychotics, schizophrenic or manic-depressives manifest such deeply regressive id material." Thus she indicates that such fantasies are by no means characteristic of depression.

Glover (1955), moreover, points out that one should guard against being misled by the mere presence of oral manifestations. He feels that they may actually represent a defensive regression

to cope with the "anxieties connected with a later fixation point."
He reports two cases, examples of "lesser depressive states," in
which "the oral constructions represented only a defensive regression from an Oedipus conflict, which by an unusual coincidence
was associated in both cases with a circumcision trauma following
the birth of a rival brother at an early stage of his Oedipus phase,
namely almost three years of age. . . . We should always bear in
mind the possibility that a seemingly deep regression may be a
cover for a later fixation."

Secondly, ever since Rado (1928), writers have repeatedly described the depressive person in terms of his excessive dependence for self-esteem on external narcissistic supplies of love, affection and attention—supplies which, by virtue of Rado's
elaboration of the term, are considered to be essentially oral in
character. Chodoff (1972) has recently concluded from a review of
the literature that orality appears to be the most agreed-upon
predisposing factor to depression. Bibring (1953) acknowledged
that the " 'orally dependent type' which constantly needs 'narcissistic supplies' from the outside represents perhaps the most frequent type of predisposition to depression" but denied that all
persons who develop depression have this type of predisposition.
As was outlined previously, Bibring's view was that "depression
can be defined as the emotional correlate of a partial or complete
collapse of the self-esteem of the ego, since it feels unable to live
up to its aspirations." He acknowledged that some of these narcissistic aspirations ("the need to get affection, to be loved, to be
taken care of," etc.) are developed or built on the oral level,
though even here he stressed the point that "the emphasis is not
on the oral frustration and subsequent oral fixation, but on the
infant's or little child's shocklike experience of and fixation to the
feeling of helplessness." However, his clinical material forced him
to conclude that depressions can also occur due to the inability to
live up to aspirations linked with other phases of psychosexual
development, e.g., the anal ("the wish to be good, not to be resentful, defiant, but to be loving, not to be dirty," etc.) and the phallic
("the wish to be admired, to be the center of attention, to be strong
or victorious," etc.).

Doubtless, an argument could be made that at bottom these
latter types of aspirations are actually derived from oral needs, i.e.,
that one might wish to be good, clean, loving, strong, admired, etc.
because one wished to be loved and taken care of or because one

had to defend oneself against these needs. Actually, it seems very unlikely that any depressive in treatment will not eventually produce "oral material" despite the nature of the presenting grievance. But, as was indicated above, the mere presence of oral material does not necessarily imply an oral fixation.

Be that as it may, it would seem that the value of Bibring's observation lies in his calling attention to the difference in maturity and development implied by the clinical fact that one person's equilibrium seems to be based exclusively on the attainment of narcissistic supplies from an outside love-object and another's on the attainment of narcissistic supplies from an internalized source by the fulfillment of certain aspirations and ideals.

A third basis for the theory of oral fixation in depression was Freud's (1917) original designation of the process that occurs in melancholia as an identification of the ego with the abandoned love-object, a process that was believed to represent a regression to "the way in which the ego first adopts an object," namely, incorporation. Since this kind of emotional tie was considered to represent the type of object-relationship characteristic of the earliest phase of life, and since incorporation was considered to be an oral phenomenon, Freud concluded that "among the special characteristics of melancholia [was] a regression from object-cathexis to the still narcissistic oral phase of the libido." Subsequently, all depressions in which introjection or identification were believed to take place, and this particularly included psychotic depressions, were considered to be based on oral mechanisms.

However, as was seen earlier, there is considerable evidence (e.g., Fenichel, 1931, 1937) that incorporation fantasies need by no means be only oral in nature, since respiratory, anal, ocular and many other types have been described.

As to the designation of the typical melancholic restitutive mechanism as an oral phenomenon because introjection is involved, perhaps it would be more profitable to by-pass the whole thorny question of whether this phenomenon takes place by instinctual processes and to think about it as Jacobson (1953) does. She has adopted the point of view of modern ego psychology and thinks about the "pathognomonic introjection" not so much in psychosexual terms as in terms of ego mechanisms. As has been discussed, she conceptualizes the mechanism in melancholia not so much as an identification achieved through oral means but rather as a regressive dissolution of ego identifications, a "break-

down of realistic object- and self-representations, of object relations and of ego functions" in which reality testing is lost and the
self-images confused with object-representations, and in which
the latter no longer adequately reflect the actual objects.

INTROJECTIVE MECHANISMS
IN DEPRESSION

To treat this subject exhaustively, the reviewer should discuss in
much more detail the various controversies centering around the
relationship between introjection and orality and between introjection and identification. These matters have occupied the attention of numerous authors (e.g., Fuchs, 1937; Knight, 1940; Sandler
and Rosenblatt, 1962; Schafer, 1972) and have given rise to many
sophisticated attempts at definition and differentiation. The present writer will refrain, however, from attempting to review fully
this confusing theoretical issue except to indicate that Jacobson
(1954b, 1964) uses the term "introjection" in a manner that is quite
different from that of other writers.

In her quest for terminological precision, she takes issue with
the previous usage of the terms "introjection" and "projection."
Melanie Klein (1948), for example, makes frequent references to
the introjection of good and bad objects by which she means the
internalization of good and bad aspects of the love-object.

Jacobson objects to giving "introjection" this vague connotation
of internalization, although it must be said that this has been the
meaning assigned to it in the psychoanalytic literature of even the
most classic variety. Knight (1940), for example, defined introjection as "an unconscious inclusion of an object or part of an object
into the ego of the subject." And Fenichel (1945) stated that "introduction is an attempt to make parts of the external world flow into
the ego."

Jacobson takes issue with what she regards as the terminological
and conceptual imprecision of speaking of objects, rather than
object-images, being included in the ego. Furthermore, she
(1954b) prefers to speak not of object-images being formed by a
process of introjection, but less magically of object-images emerging "from the ever-increasing memory traces of pleasurable and
unpleasurable experiences and of perceptions with which they
become associated." By the term "introjection" she refers strictly

to the endopsychic process in which the self-image assumes characteristics of the object-representations. If, according to her, object-images accurately reflect external objects, then their introjection will endow the self-representations—and the self—with attributes of real persons. She considers that in the introjective process in psychotic states the self-images assume characteristics of very archaic object-images which reflect current external reality very poorly. It is in this sense that she speaks of the mechanism in melancholia as consisting of a dissolution of ego identifications in which the object-images no longer accurately reflect actual objects and in which the self-representation, by a process of introjection, takes on the characteristics of these unrealistic object-images. In other words, the self- and object-representations, which are never at any time adequately delineated from one another in the prepsychotic personality, according to Jacobson, now with the onset of the psychotic state, fuse and merge with one another.

Chapter VI

INTRODUCTION

Now THAT WE HAVE examined these various aspects of the mul-subject of the depressed states, it might be well to step back a pace and to consider these conditions not in the microscopic manner of the preceding pages but, instead, macroscopically, from the point of view of diagnostic entities. There has been a remarkable advance in psychiatric sophistication since the days when it was thought that there were a host of clinical entities waiting to be recognized and isolated from one another, each with its different toxic or histopathological etiology. Diagnostic entities are not always accorded quite the same respectful attention in psychiatry as they are in other medical specialties. Nor is this surprising in view of the fact that there is actually no uniform system of diagnostic classification. Some conditions are characterized on the basis of behavior in the narrower sense of the word, others on the basis of thoughts and sense perceptions, while others still are classified according to the dominant mood. One speaks, for example, not of a disease called "obsessionalism" but rather of obsessional traits in so-called normal character structure, of obsessional neuroses and of obsessional defenses against a schizophrenic or manic-depressive breakdown. One no longer faithfully subscribes to the old clean-cut divisions between diagnostic categories. The human being and his life experiences cannot always be neatly compressed into a diagnostic compartment.

For a few decades after the Second World War, the emphasis in psychiatry was more on the psychodynamics of the individual patient than on diagnostic distinctions which often appeared irrelevant to the treatment of a particular patient. In the last ten or fifteen years, interest in diagnosis has revived. Diagnoses are again becoming the daily currency with which psychiatrists, in common with their medical colleagues, conduct their affairs. And even if this currency does not represent the pure gold of another era, neither can it be said to be entirely debased. The diagnostic categories must represent some approximation to clinical reality or else they would have gone the way of devils and humors in psychiatric thinking. Even those clinicians who focus on the motivational and experiential, in contrast with the formal and diagnostic aspects of psychiatric illness, implicitly and explicitly acknowledge the usefulness of the clinical categories.

DIAGNOSTIC ASPECTS OF DEPRESSION

We have previously given some consideration to the diagnostic aspects of the depressive reactions. We have noted the controversy over whether it is possible to differentiate neurotic from psychotic depression and have indicated that psychoanalytic writers have tended to concur in this differentiation. Yet there has been no absolute unanimity among psychoanalysts about whether manic-depressive psychosis does or does not represent a distinct diagnostic category. Zilboorg (1933), for instance, declared that "on the basis of my clinical experience I am under the definite impression that manic-depressive psychoses despite their age-long existence do not actually represent a separate clinical entity."

Most current psychoanalytic writers on the subject, however, acknowledge with relatively little hesitation the usefulness of this Kraepelinian category. Cohen and her colleagues (1954), for example, considered that "the manic-depressive syndrome does represent a fairly clear-cut system of defenses which are sufficiently unique and of sufficient theoretical interest to deserve separate study." And Jacobson (1953; 1971, Chapter 6) indicates quite explicitly that she regards manic-depressive psychosis as a distinct clinical entity.

The question of whether involutional melancholia is an entity that is different from manic-depressive psychosis has been previously reviewed in these pages. It will be recalled that there tended to be a consensus that there was indeed a difference between these conditions, a difference both in the prepsychotic personality structure and in the symptomatology of these two depressive psychoses, a consensus that no longer exists.

Recent psychoanalytic descriptions of the prepsychotic manic-depressive personality correspond rather closely to the older clinical psychiatric pictures. Jacobson (1953; 1971, p. 231), for example, mentions that before their psychoses, these patients "may be delightful companions or marital partners, a feature that Bleuler mentioned especially. In their sexual life they may show a full genital response, and emotionally . . . a touching warmth or . . . an unusual, affectionate clinging to people they like."

This description, as we have seen, is markedly different from that of the prepsychotic personality of the involutional melancholic as reported by such writers as Titley (1936), Palmer and Sherman (1938), etc. However, no comparable psychoanalytic studies or descriptions exist. As for the actual psychoses, Glover (1955) remarks that "involutional states represent a mixture of reactions chiefly characteristic of depression but frequently having some resemblance to maniacal and schizophrenic discharge. No *specific* conflict factors have been determined."

In view of this observation it is interesting to note that Kallman (1953), on the basis of his research in heredity, stated that "the principal genetic relationship of that type of emotional instability which may lead to an involutional psychosis is [not to manic-depressive psychosis but] to the group of schizoid personality traits."

Fenichel (1945) admitted that "psychoanalytically not much is known about the structure and mechanisms of involutional melancholias. They seem to occur in personalities with an outspoken character of an especially rigid nature."

This relative ignorance of involutional melancholia from the psychoanalytic point of view is only too frequently overlooked. Facile interpretations are frequently based on studies which were actually conducted on manic-depressive patients. In view of the depressive mood and the self-accusations common to both of these reactions it is not improbable that similar psychological events occur in them, but the fact remains that the literature is practically —but not entirely (see Kaufman, 1937)—devoid of psychoanalytic studies of involutional melancholia.

Nor, surprisingly enough, can there be said to exist an impressive volume of contributions on the subject of neurotic depressive reactions. Freud (1917) explicitly recognized the difference between neurotic and psychotic depression but preferred to concern himself chiefly with the latter. Abraham (1916) threw some incidental light on neurotic depression but also mainly addressed himself to the problem of manic-depressive psychosis. Rado (1928) indicated that the former type of depressive reaction differed from the latter chiefly in the extent of the narcissistic regression but abstained from considering in any detail what further differences, if any, existed. Bibring (1953) made some general remarks about all types of depression but provided no clinical documentation of his very plausible thesis. And Jacobson (1953, 1971), though making some very pertinent and clarifying generalizations about depression, nevertheless makes it clear at several points that she is chiefly concerned with psychotic depression. It therefore happens that although it is by no means true to say that the neurotic depressive reaction has been overlooked in the literature (see especially Fenichel, 1945; Lorand, 1946; Glover, 1955), the tendency has nevertheless been to generalize about it from the theories derived from the investigation and treatment of psychotic patients. There are very few clinical studies (as distinguished from theoretical essays) designed to confirm or refute these generalizations or to indicate what, if any, deviations from standard treatment are necessary.

Among psychoanalytic writers on depression, Jacobson (1971) stands out for her insistence on the importance of differential diagnosis in the group of depressive illnesses. As we have seen, she has been critical of Bibring (1953) and Rubinfine (1968), who failed to make such distinctions, and even of Zetzel (1960), who also stressed the importance of being more precise when speaking of "depression" because the latter used the term "depressive illness" in an insufficiently precise way.

She describes what she regards as quite distinct differences between neurotic and psychotic depressions. She views this distinction as based on "constitutional neuro-physiological processes" (pp. 183–84). She (Chapter 6) describes how differently the psychotic depressive experiences his depression compared with a neurotic depressive. She notes "an impoverishment of the ego" characterized by feelings of blankness and detachment, inner weariness and apathy, a mental and physical inability to enjoy life and love, sexual impotence (or frigidity) and feelings of deep inferiority, inadequacy and general withdrawnness" (p. 172). She refers not only to symptoms such as insomnia, anorexia, amenorrhea, weight loss and other "vegetative" symptoms but also to the psychosomatic features in the retardation which affect the way that cyclothymics, for instance, experience their inhibitions, a subjective experience quite different from that of neurotic depressives. "They commonly feel that the retardation, as well as the keyed up state, befalls them like a physical illness. They experience it as strange to their nature. . . . One such patient . . . said: 'You know, this is a real "illness." One morning I wake up and have no appetite. I cannot think, I cannot move. . . . And then one day I wake up and I know it is over.' " Such patients may be unaware of depressed spirits or a depressed mood and may complain primarily about their fatigue and exhaustion. "They may compare the slowing up to a fog settling down in their brain; to a veil drawn over their thinking; to insurmountable walls blocking their feelings, their thinking, and their actions" (pp. 173–74).

I have quoted so extensively from her description of the typical subjective experiences in a cyclothymic depression because I believe this is the best such description in the psychoanalytic literature on depression. It is a testimonial to her clinical as well as conceptual perspicacity. It corresponds in every detail to what I have observed myself in such patients. And I agree that these experiences are very different from those of the neurotic depressive. I find myself standing firmly beside Jacobson on the issue of differential diagnosis. And although these diagnoses may turn out to represent merely different points on a depressive continuum, as Kendell (1968) believes he has demonstrated, there is no doubt that patients at different points on this continuum seem and feel different.

However, I would disagree with the labeling or perhaps the understanding of the differences between neurotic and psychotic depressions. Jacobson refers to the depressive experiences described above as "psychotic." "Psychotic" has two levels of meaning in every day psychoanalytic speech. At the more obvious level, it refers to gross distortions of reality such as delusions and hallucinations. There is no disagreement about delusional depressive illnesses being psychotic. However, at a subtler level, "psychotic" refers to a fixation at or a regression or decompensation to levels of ego functioning which are considered more pathological than uncertainly defined other levels of ego functioning.

A depressed person whose ego boundaries (or more strictly, whose self-representations) are so fuzzy that he confuses his self-image with that of the disappointing object-image can be thought of as psychotic. But what of the patient who is so retarded that he finds it hard to concentrate? And what of the patient who feels too fatigued to cope with his work? Are these cognitive and executive ego functions impaired in a psychotic way? What if he couldn't concentrate or function due to a fever? Or to hypothyroidism? Or what of a previously healthy person who becomes undelusionally depressed but can't concentrate due to having taken reserpine? Is he psychotic? What of the patient of mine with what Jacobson refers to as a "simple" (nondelusional) endogenous depression who experienced his retardation as a physical illness, who couldn't concentrate or function at his work but who did not experience low self-esteem or self-critical feelings, because like Jacobson's patient, he considered that he had an illness, and his self-esteem was not ordinarily affected by being sick. Having an illness for him was an accident of fate, not a moral weakness. Or what of the much more sophisticated physician who regarded his depression as a psychophysiological illness, who acknowledged that he was depressed and couldn't function, but who did not experience self-critical feelings (again, because his disability was experienced by him, and acceptable to him, as an illness)? In a more complicated example, what of the physicist who couldn't function due to his impairment of concentration and his finding work to be an intolerable burden when he was depressed, who did acknowledge guilt because he was "letting the side down." His collaborators had to take up the slack produced by his absence. He knew that he had what he regarded as a neurophysiological illness and knew that logically he was not responsible for not being able to work. But emotionally and, as he said, "illogically," he could not help reproaching himself and feeling guilty about not going to work. In other words, his guilt was secondary to his illness, which involved adding to the workload of his colleagues. There was no other guilt about the past or the present. Was he psychotic?

I prefer in these instances to avoid the adjective "psychotic" with its descriptive but also pejorative connotations and to think of such a patient, in line with Jacobson's own thinking, as having a psychobiological depression with the descriptive and etiological implications of a term that has no pejorative overtones. Of more importance is the fact that I believe it is more accurate, in the instances of which I speak, than the term "psychotic." Not that I am entirely satisfied with the word "psychobiological." It has Meyerian overtones that do not fit the use that I am making of it. In Adolf Meyer's sense of the word, it would apply just as appropriately to neurotic depressions as to cyclothymic ones. Sometimes, in recognition of the absence of obvious psychotic manifestations, this kind of depression is referred to, in the European literature, as an atypical or nonpsychotic or mild endogenous or manic-depressive disorder. And, of course, Winokur (1973) carefully avoids this terminological problem by speaking of primary affective disorders which he expressly differentiates from reactive or neurotic depressions. I agree with Jacobson that some distinction should be made between neurotic depressions and what she refers to as the "simple," nondelusional endogenous depressions that she describes as "psychotic." I grant that there may be a gray area in which the depressed patients are not delusional but whose image of themselves or of the future is distorted, yet whether the extent of these distortions is psychotic in degree seems to me a matter of clinical judgment and not an a priori decision.

Attention should again be drawn to the ways in which the adjectives "reactive," "neurotic" and "endogenous" are misused in the literature on depression. "Reactive" is too often used as if it were synonymous with "neurotic." Jacobson (1971) calls attention to this error. "Reactive" merely implies that the disorder that the word modifies has occurred in reaction to clearly identifiable circumstances. If a depression occurs in reaction to the death of a spouse, this depressive illness may be either neurotic or psychotic, or, for that matter, psychobiological, depending on its characteristics. As we all know, a post-partum psychotic depression may develop in reaction to the birth of a child. It is a fallacy, then, that all reactive depressions are neurotic, a fallacy that may lead to errors in the mode of treatment adopted for the illness. I should point out that in the new classification proposed by the St. Louis group (Winokur, 1973) the word "reactive" is used differently, i.e., only in the special sense of a short-lived secondary depressive disorder occurring in reaction to an obvious psychological cause such as bereavement.

Similarly, "endogenous," whatever it may have once meant, does not mean "nonreactive." An endogenous depression is simply a depression with the characteristics of what Jacobson calls a psychotic depression, or what I refer to as a psychobiological depression with or without psychosis. The death of a spouse or parent may, for example, trigger off a cyclothymic, psychotic "endogenous" depression which is "reactive" to the loss. Among the clinical signs and symptoms are middle-of-the-night or terminal insomnia, diurnal variation of mood, impaired concentration, reduced or absence of interest or pleasure in one's ordinary pursuits, difficulty in making decisions, slowed or racing thoughts, suicidal ideation, self-critical feelings, low self-esteem, hypochondriacal complaints, psychic and motor retardation or agitation, and in extreme instances delusional ideas of sin, guilt or poverty. Not all of these need be present. Very few of them may be present. The depression may be so mild that as Jacobson points out (1971) it may be mistaken for a neurotic depression, especially if it occurred in reaction to some event.

To repeat, "reactive" and "endogenous" are terms that are not mutually exclusive. A "reactive" depression can be psychotic, and an "endogenous" depression may occur in reaction to external circumstances. As we are all aware, retirement may be followed by that "endogenous" depression which we call involutional melancholia.

RELATIONSHIP OF DEPRESSION TO SCHIZOID AND SCHIZOPHRENIC STATES

One speculative, fascinating but as yet imperfectly understood problem is the relationship between the depressive and the schizoid and schizophrenic states. Kretschmer (1931) attempted to distinguish schizoid and cyclothymic personalities as two fundamental types of contrasting kinds of body structure and temperament.

Fenichel (1945) did not find Kretschmer's attempt at differentiation very helpful, feeling that more important than the differences between these two types was what they had in common, namely, a tendency toward narcissistic regression and loss of objects and of reality testing. However, he believed that "the pathogenic fixations of schizophrenia may tentatively be considered as related to a still earlier stage than those found in depressions."

Melanie Klein (1948) and Fairbairn (1952) subscribed to the same thesis which they amplify in considerable detail. Klein theorized that it was only when the mother could be identified as a whole, real and loved person that the infant could be said to be in the depressive position. It is then that he perceives that the loved object is at the same time the hated object. It is at this time that the infant finds himself confronted with the psychic reality that his hate is directed toward his loved object. The despair and the guilt and the anxiety that this recognition produces go to make up the depressive position.

However, before he experiences the feeling of being loved, i.e., before he can identify the mother as a whole object who loves him, Klein believed that he is in a phase which is characterized by anxieties about his extreme rage and sadistic fantasies. She postulated that this anxiety is experienced by the infant as a feeling of helplessness and fear in the face of the immense tensions inside himself and of the external persecutors who are the projections of his hate and anger. She believed that a person who has never worked his way through this persecutory-schizoid position and who has never experienced a love relationship in his infancy may all his life have a markedly distorted sense of reality since his persecution-anxiety causes him to see people mainly from the aspect of whether or not they are persecutors. She believed that for such an individual a satisfactory relationship with another object, in the sense of seeing it and understanding it as it really is and loving it, is not possible. And it is this position, she held, that underlies paranoid and schizophrenic disorders.

Fairbairn differed from Klein in several important theoretical points. He, too, considered the depressive position as underlying manic-depressive psychosis but his view of this and of the preceding position was considerably different from Klein's. He felt that the child's oral relationship with his mother is his first experience of a social relationship and the foundation upon which he builds all future relationships. According to Fairbairn, a person who is fixated at the late oral phase, after the acquisition of teeth, remains in the depressive position in which his great problem is how to love without destroying by hate. But Fairbairn postulated that in the pre-ambivalent early oral phase, when the child relates to his mother only by sucking, it might appear to the infant who feels that he is not loved that the reason for this is that he has destroyed his mother's affection and made it disappear by the very act of his sucking, i.e., by his first way of expressing love. The intolerable situation in which he then finds himself is that he perceives his own love as destructive and bad. The result is that he comes to regard expression of his love as bad, and comes to feel that love relationships in general are at the very best precarious. Such a person tends to keep his relationships with his objects in the world of internal reality with a resulting general overevaluation of the inner at the expense of the external world. This is the schizoid position which Fairbairn believes to underlie not only schizophrenia but the very comprehensive schizoid group.

Jacobson (1954c; 1971, Chapter 10), in her metapsychological examination of psychotic identifications, studies the problem from quite a different point of view and, in the opinion of the writer, from a much more stimulating one. Her ideas about schizophrenia are, like Klein and Fairbairn's, closely related to those about manic-depressive psychosis. About the latter she says that in order to maintain their self-esteem, manic-depressive patients must at all costs maintain "a continuous libidinous hypercathexis of the love-object, designed to prevent its aggressive devaluation in which their self is bound to participate." Even in psychosis the manic-depressive aims at and succeeds in remaining dependent on a strong powerful object-image, the superego. This is presumed to take place, as we have seen, by means of a regressive transformation of identifications.

Jacobson postulates that in the schizophrenic this regressive process, by virtue of an even more defective ego development, goes much further. Self- and object-images fuse, not partially as in manic-depressive psychosis, but much more completely and in a much more disintegrated manner. In Jacobson's words, "if the melancholic *treats* himself as if he were the love-object, the schizoid or pre-schizophrenic type imitates, he *behaves* as if he were the object, whereas in a delusional schizophrenic state the patient may eventually consciously *believe* himself to be another object." Not only are self and objects confused but the object-representations may break down into more primitive, infantile, archaic object-images. "Thus omnipotent, male-female, breast-phallus figures and castrated, breastless, injured, dead figures" may be created, combining features and traits of various male and female individuals and of the patient himself.

Jacobson refers to the defective ego ideal and superego development in the schizophrenic. His ego ideal is often only an ambitious fantasy of participation in the longed-for omnipotence of the love-objects. In states of psychosis his superego, unlike that of the manic-depressive which gains control of the self, undergoes a regressive transformation back into threatening, murderously primitive parental images. Instead of guilt the patient may experience fears of being persecuted and destroyed or of dying or being dead.

To sum up, Jacobson also agrees that schizophrenia represents a fixation to an earlier stage of development than manic-depressive psychosis. However, she implicitly concurs with Knight (1953) in his suggestion that "a one-sided, libidinal theory of human functioning . . . needs to be supplemented extensively with the findings of ego psychology." She has therefore offered a theory of psychosis in terms of ego psychology. It is in this ego-psychological sense and with reference to the development of ego and superego identifications that she considers schizophrenia to represent a fixation at and a regression to an earlier developmental phase than manic-depressive psychosis.

Some workers, Cohen and her group, for example, felt that manic-depressive psychosis is not only a regressive decompensation to an early stage of personality development, but "can be thought of as serving a defensive function against the still greater personality disintegration which is represented by the schizophrenic state. Thus, in persons whose conflicts and anxiety are too severe to be handled by depressive or manic defenses, a schizophrenic breakdown may be the end result." The implication is that the manic-depressive patient can decompensate even further into a schizophrenic reaction, although the authors cite no instances of this in their series.

Jacobson (1954a) fails to provide support for this thesis. She refers to her depressed patients sometimes becoming very confused and sustaining violent psychosomatic reactions while working through deep pre-oedipal material. However, she explicitly states that she has "never had the experience of a patient going into a psychotic state provoked by the breaking through of deep id material" except for the recurrence of psychotic depressive episodes.

This same issue has occupied the attention of clinical psychiatrists. Lewis and Hubbard (1931), for example, reported on seventy-seven schizophrenic patients at St. Elizabeth's all of whom had originally been diagnosed as manic-depressive. They presumed that they had been erroneously diagnosed on their first admission but the paper did not really conclusively prove that they had not simply become schizophrenic despite correct diagnosis when they were first seen. Similarly, Hoch and Rachlin (1941) examined the records of 5,799 cases of schizophrenia at the Manhattan State Hospital and found that, of this number, 415 cases had been "originally and often repeatedly diagnosed as manic-depressive psychosis." In other words, "every 13th case of schizophrenia was originally diagnosed as manic-depressive psychosis." They felt that most of these cases had had malignant features from the very beginning which had somehow been overlooked. "The description of many cases was often that of schizophrenia, but the diagno-

sis was manic-depressive, disregarding the basic clinical symptomatology. The diagnosis was probably made because of the
quick recovery and periodicity of the attacks, or the presence of
so-called psychogenic factors which impressed the examiner so
much that he overlooked the fundamental symptoms."

Shortly afterwards, Rennie (1942) reported a study of 208 cases
of manic-depressive psychosis admitted to the Henry Phipps Psychiatric Clinic and in his review posed the following question:
"Does the typical manic-depressive reaction ever change its character sufficiently that one has a right to speak of ultimate schizophrenic development?" He replied that four cases in his series
pointed definitely in that direction. There is no implication in his
paper that these cases were originally misdiagnosed.

Lewis and Piotrowski (1954) went back to this old problem in an
effort to determine whether it was just wisdom after the event that
led some psychiatrists to imply that a schizophrenic who had been
previously diagnosed manic-depressive had really been schizophrenic all the time or whether there actually were some pathognomonic schizophrenic signs which could guide an experienced
observer to the correct diagnosis even in the early deceptive
phase of some schizophrenic illnesses. They studied a group of
seventy patients originally diagnosed as manic-depressive of
whom 54 percent had later developed a clear-cut schizophrenia.
They contended that these schizophrenic patients had all had
clinical signs—which they classified—at the time of their original
diagnosis which should have identified them as schizophrenic
even then. They noted that "nearly all errors of diagnosis were
made not because of insufficient observation of symptoms but
because of failure to interpret the diagnostic significance of the
symptoms." They emphasized that "even a trace of schizophrenia
is schizophrenia and has a very important prognostic as well as
diagnostic significance."

This view is in agreement with that of Bleuler (1911) expressed
many years before: "The symptomatological differentiation of
schizophrenia from manic-depressive psychosis can only be based
on the presence of the specific schizophrenic symptoms. All the
phenomena of manic-depressive psychosis may also appear in our
disease; the only decisive factor is the presence or absence of
schizophrenic symptoms. Therefore, neither a state of manic exaltation nor a melancholic depression, nor the alteration of both
states has any significance for the diagnosis. Only after careful

observation has revealed no schizophrenic features, may we conclude that we are dealing with a manic-depressive psychosis."

In conflict with this view is the accumulating evidence (Lipkin et al., 1970; Taylor and Abraham, 1973) that many manic-depressive patients have paranoid, catatonic and even hebephrenic symptoms in their acute psychotic phases, and that the only reliable diagnostic criteria are the patient's history of mood fluctuations, his personality configuration during his well periods, his family history and, in the opinion of many clinicians, his response to lithium carbonate.

Jacobson (1971, footnote, p. 171) asserts: "I do not believe in the continuity between manic-depressive and schizophrenic conditions. I have kept track of a series of cases that always remained affective disorders."

In support of the above observations, one might also cite the observations of Kallman (1953) and Winokur et al. (1969) that schizophrenia and manic-depressive psychoses do not occur in the same family unit if the diagnostic criteria for these conditions are properly restricted.

SEMANTICS OF "DEPRESSION"

Attention should here be drawn to a paradoxical situation, namely, that although the numerous writers discussed in this review have all written copiously about depression there is nevertheless no widespread agreement in the literature as to what the phenomenon of depression actually comprises.

Whitehorn (1939) commented on the naïveté of uncritically believing that one can easily label a patient's "emotions" by listening to the conventional terms which he uses to describe them. It would seem that nowhere is this danger more threatening than when the patient states that he is depressed.

The difference between two depressive syndromes impressed one observer so markedly that he argued that although these disparate clinical pictures are both designated "depression" one of them is in reality something quite different. Fairbairn, according to Guntrip (1952), felt that "complaints of feeling cut off, shut off, out of touch, feeling apart or strange, of things being out of focus or unreal, of not feeling well with people, interest flagging, things seeming futile and meaningless" all describe a state of mind which patients often call "depression" but which "lacks the heavy, black, inner sense of brooding, of anger and of guilt, which are not diffi-cult to discover in depression." Fairbairn referred to the states of mind described above as "schizoid states." Hammerman (1963) describes a type of depression obviously related to Fairbairn's "schizoid" state of depression in words that are often very similar to Guntrip's. In these patients with what Hammerman refers to as an ego-defect, "there is a lifelong pattern of apathy and chronic lack of any real enjoyment in living. . . . Life tends to be seen in dull gray tones accompanied by feelings of emptiness and weight-lessness. Such people give to others an impression of leaking and being full of holes." They "go through life feeling cheated from lack of gratification. Every disappointment is experienced as the repetitive loss of the need-fulfilling object."

Similarly, Good (1946) divided depressions into two groups. The first group consists of those conditions ordinarily classified as the depressed phase of manic-depressive psychosis. The patient be-longing to this group has lost touch with reality, is retarded, com-plains in a low monotonous voice of having committed grave and unforgivable sins, of being eternally damned and destined to en-dure the tortures of hell. He reproaches and vilifies himself and may refuse food or may demand that he be done away with.

A typical patient in the second group retains the ability to smile and to communicate and may appear deceptively normal. He may describe his complaints in various ways: " 'I don't get the same kick out of things as I used to,' 'I feel as if I had a big disappoint-ment only it lasts,' 'things don't seem worthwhile,' 'fed up,' 'browned off,' 'as if the joy had gone out of life,' of the color having faded from life, from the things which constitute life, of life being insipid, tasteless, full, and monotonous; 'things don't matter' or 'I don't give a damn—nothing left to bother about—not worth carry-ing on for,' etc. Seldom do self-reproaches accompany the verbal expression of these feelings." Good referred to this second type of depression as "schizophrenic depression" in contrast to the first type, which he designates as "melancholic."

By 1951 we find that Rado had lost his earlier (1928) more simple view of depression sufficiently to remark: "We encounter depres-sions in drug-dependent patients, neurotics, schizophrenics, gen-eral paretics, patients afflicted with severe physical illness, etc. The question arises whether or not significant psychodynamic dif-ferences exist between depressive spells that occur in different pathogenic contexts. Further psychoanalytic investigation may provide an answer to this question."

Indeed, it was a very pertinent question. Whether the formulations chiefly derived from the study of a small group of manic-depressive patients are as applicable to the restlessly agitated depressive psychoses of the involutional period, the empty, lonely depressed conditions found in young schizophrenics and the listless apathetic post-viral depressions as they are to the deeply retarded periodic melancholias of the manic-depressive type is a very pertinent inquiry. It is one which workers had tended to ignore or to answer with misplaced and unwarranted confidence.

Gero (1953) addressed himself to this same question. He uttered a warning about the dangers inherent in not clearly recognizing the nature of the clinical material forming the basis of any particular theory. He pointed out that "we do not always realize that we are talking about different phenomena and arrive at theories which contradict each other." He not only believed that all depressed patients do not necessarily belong to the same clinical groups which Freud and Abraham studied, but he also felt that even "in the same type of depression different aspects of the symptomatology necessitate different explanations." This view was explicitly contested, erroneously in my opinion, by Nacht and Racamier (1960), who state that "allowing for variations of intensity and degree . . . *all* truly depressive subjects display that special organization of the personality that many authors have described as 'manic-depressive' . . ."

It is noteworthy that Engel and Reichsman (1956), in their extraordinarily interesting study of the infant Monica, conclude that their observations led them "to the position that there is not only the active, oral, introjective anlage emphasized in classic theory" (characterized by "the varieties of internalization of aggression") but "also an active, pre-oral, pre-object anlage which is psychologically . . . well expressed by Bibring's (1953) phrase, 'the ego's shocking awareness of its helplessness in regard to its aspirations.' " These conclusions appear to bear striking kinship to those of Fairbairn and Good, though expressed in different terms and derived from different patient material.

Stunkard (1957), too, is impressed with how little the classical psychodynamic formulations of depression are applicable to the depressed obese patients whom he has been studying. He describes these patients as follows: "The predominant symptomatology was depressive, but they were not typical depressions. The closest parallel is perhaps those curious periods of apathy and sadness which occur during the adolescence of schizoid people." He particularly notes the absence of expressions of self-condemnation.

It has become increasingly clear that the term "depression" has been used to refer to a transient mood, to a symptom found in a variety of clinical states and to any one of a variety of affective illnesses. Writers on depression often confusingly fail to distinguish between these various uses of the word. Consequently, it is often difficult to know which usage of the term "depression" their writing has reference to. Zetzel (1960) referred to the failure in so many psychoanalytic discussions of depression "to distinguish clearly between depression as a symptom which may arise in the widest variety of clinical conditions ranging from normal grief to overt schizophrenic disorder and depressive illness as a specific psychiatric syndrome."

Jacobson (1971), too, expresses herself solidly in favor of distinguishing between depressive moods and depressive illness. She is very critical of any tendency to neglect differential diagnostic criteria. She impatiently points out the futility, for example, of doing research on " 'endogenous' types of depression with a group of patients consisting of neurotic, manic-depressive and schizophrenic patients. This kind of research," she emphasizes, "cannot yield scientifically correct, acceptable results" (p. 170). She criticizes Bibring (1953) and Rubinfine (1968) for failing to make this distinction. And she finds even Zetzel's (1960) term "depressive illness" insufficiently specific. She disagrees with Beres (1965) about restricting the diagnosis of depression to those conditions which are characterized by guilt, a disagreement which would obviously also apply to Rochlin's (1959) view of depression.

Turning to another area of disagreement, we see that while psychoanalytic workers have held that clinical depressive illness does not occur before adolescence, Spitz (1946) described a condition in hospitalized infants which he designated as "anaclitic depression." A disagreement has arisen as to whether the depression observed in children should be designated as a clinical illness or as a variously defined "depressive response or reaction." Similarly, what Bierman et al. (1961) described as a depression in a six-year-old boy with poliomyelitis was said by Rie (1966), who was upholding the view that depressive illness did not occur in children, to resemble grief or mourning rather than depression, though ironically psychoanalytic writers have tended to deny the possibility that children can mourn.

Engel and Reichsman (1956), reporting on their famous infant patient, Monica, described a condition which in this paper they termed "depression" but which was also referred to as a "depression-withdrawal reaction" and which Engel (1962) later came to regard as one of the two primary affects of unpleasure. The other such affect was, of course, anxiety. It would be presumptuous for the writer who, of course, did not see Monica, to take a stand on whether her condition represented an illness or a "reaction." However, on admission to the hospital at the age of fifteen months the infant was called cachectic "and was described by the pediatric house officer as 'very depressed'" (Engel and Reichsman, 1956). Her improvement from this marasmic and depressed condition proceeded over a period of five and a half months, though the authors do not indicate at just what point Monica was considered no longer depressed. Photographs which were included in the paper, taken three months after admission, demonstrated "contentment and joy." Elsewhere in the paper, the authors refer to the child's capacity for forming relationships "which probably contributed to her recovery from the depression." All this suggests —yet, of course, does not prove—that Engel and Reichsman were observing something more in the nature of an illness than of a depressed mood or a transient affect.

However, what was more obviously a transient affective reaction was what occurred when Monica during her hospitalization was confronted by a stranger. When this happened, Monica would demonstrate "prompt loss of muscle tone, the limbs literally falling where they were," profound immobility, initial glances at the stranger, followed by closing of the eyes, at first intermittently but then up to periods of ten to thirty minutes. Oral activity was mostly restricted to swallowing movements. Her facial expression produced empathetic feelings in observers of "sadness, depression, hopelessness."

If the stranger remained more than twenty to thirty minutes, this stage would be followed by sleep in which the facial expression and posture assumed the normal response to sleep. If the stranger was still present on awakening, Monica promptly responded with a resumption of the depression-withdrawal pattern.

As I have indicated, Engel (1962) later conceptualized depression-withdrawal as one of two primary affects. He thought that "the attitude and expression most indicative of depression-withdrawal" was "to give up." He pointed to Bibring (1953) as evidence that Freud and Abraham's classic formulations for melancholia were no longer universally applicable. "Indeed," he added, "the bulk of depressive reactions encountered in clinical practice are more indicative of 'giving up' and do not include as a major component morbid guilt and aggression turned on the self."

Sandler and Joffe (1965), as we have seen, also describe a "depressive reaction" which they distinguish from depressive illness, and which they feel is more characteristic of depressive-like conditions in children than is what they regard as the more complex condition of depressive illness. As will be remembered, they define psychic pain as the experience which reflects the discrepancy between the actual state of the self and an ideal state of psychological well-being. They observed varying responses to this psychic pain, "from angry protesting unacceptance of this painful state to states of passive helpless resignation" which they term a "depressive reaction." In their later discussion of this depressive reaction or depressive response they, too, consider it a basic affective response, like anxiety, "a basic psycho-biological affective reaction." In considering the depression-withdrawal reaction, Engel (1962) makes the same observation that Sandler and Joffe (1965) do, namely, that this is only one of the ways in which infants and children can respond to pain or frustration. He refers to Fries' discussion of different congenital activity types in newborns and notes that those infants described by her as inactive respond to withdrawal of the nipple during nursing with inactivity and sleep rather than crying and struggling. He cites similar observations having to do with sleep withdrawal by Ribble (1943) and by Burton and Derbyshire (1958).

He views this withdrawal pattern as "essentially a conservative one in which the infant reduces activity, heightens the barriers against stimulation and conserves energy, as, for example, does a hibernating animal." And as I have indicated, he visualizes it as one of the two primary affects of unpleasure. He cites evidence to indicate that these two primary affects are mediated by different neural organizations and are hence determined by inborn constitutional factors.

"DEPRESSIVE EQUIVALENTS"

In a series of papers, Kaufman (1955; 1956 with Elizabeth Makkay; 1958; 1958 with Lora Heims) elaborates his concept that delinquency is frequently the juvenile delinquent's method of coping with his underlying depression or his "depressive nucleus," as Kaufman refers to it. He sees the child's delinquency as partly an attempt to avoid confronting and experiencing his overwhelming depression, in other words, as a sort of equivalent of depression or, more precisely, as a defense against depression. "Masked depression" is another term used to imply that a variety of symptoms or behavior patterns may actually be "masks" for an underlying depression (e.g., Fox, 1967; Goldfarb, 1967; Lesse, 1967).

Sandler and Joffe, in a number of publications (Sandler and Joffe, 1965; Joffe and Sandler, 1965, 1967a, b), have postulated a conceptual scheme which seems to offer a way of clarifying the theoretical and semantic ambiguities inherent in terms such as "depressive equivalents" and "masked depressions." As I have indicated, they refer to the discrepancy that is experienced between one's actual affective state and one's ideal psychological state of well-being as "psychic pain." They conceptualize the depressive reaction as just one possible reaction or response to such pain. The depressive reaction occurs when the psychic pain is experienced with a feeling of helplessness, hopelessness or resignation. But these authors point out that there are a number of defensive and adaptive measures, other than the depressive response, to which an individual can resort. He may seek to increase his state of well-being by means of external narcissistic supplies; he may overcompensate in fantasy; he may resort to promiscuity, nymphomania, or to a variety of perversions; he may become delinquent, alcoholic or addicted. All these are defensive measures to reduce the psychic pain. An individual may on the other hand turn to more realistic ideal states of well-being or he may use his developing or already acquired abilities or talents to strive for a new state of well-being. Joffe and Sandler (1967a) note that "if the individual's adaptive and defensive manoeuvres fail, and if he is left helpless and hopeless in the face of the (conscious or unconscious) state of pain, he may then develop a depressive reaction. . . ."

In this theoretical model, the depressive equivalents and the masks of depression that many authors have written about are actually defenses against a state of psychic pain and should therefore not be labeled "depressive equivalents." The latter term implies that the defense is the "equivalent" of the failure of the defense. It suggests, for example, that a defensive operation such as delinquency is the equivalent of the affective response which may ensue if this defense fails. If it fails and *if* the individual responds to his pain with helplessness and resignation, he will experience a depressive response. But the defense, according to Sandler and Joffe, is not against the depression but against the pain. The depressive reaction develops only if the defense against the pain fails and *if* the individual feels helpless and resigned. This conceptualization of defenses against psychic pain does help to resolve the incongruity of referring to an undepressed nymphomaniac as exhibiting a depressive equivalent. To repeat, a defense cannot be equated with the failure of that defense or with the affective response to that failure.

However, not all the symptoms that are referred to as depressive equivalents are defenses against psychic pain. It has been repeatedly pointed out that a depressive illness represents a multifaceted syndrome which includes affective, cognitive, sleep, behavioral and physiological components. If a patient presents with constipation as part of the symptomatology of a psychotic depression, *with or without the affective component of this illness,* the constipation is a *symptom* and not an equivalent of this depressive illness. It should not be confused with a symptom that is a defense against psychic pain but should be identified as part of the illness which can result when defensive operations fail.

Physical complaints may be difficult to classify. They may serve as defenses against psychic pain or may actually be symptoms of a depressive illness. Hypochondriasis may present as a defense against psychic pain. As Joffe and Sandler (1967b) express it, in the face of psychic pain an "individual's self-esteem may be completely restored by the belief that he would be capable of functioning well in all areas, were it not for the fact that he is physically afflicted. Similarly such feelings as guilt and responsibility for failure may be considerably lessened. . . ." Asch (1966) mistakenly refers to such instances of hypochondriasis without depressed affect as representing a clinical variation of depression. On the other hand, hypochondriasis may be one of the symptoms of a depressive illness rather than a defense mechanism. But even while experiencing a depressive illness, for reasons just described by Joffe and Sandler, an individual may prefer to complain about his physical health rather than his depressed mood. As we have seen, in other cultures—Iraq, for example (Bazzoui, 1970)—a depressed patient may present with hypochondriacal or somatic complaints because of cultural conditioning or because he has no conscious access to the affective component of his depressive illness.

The term "manic-depressive equivalent" was actually coined in 1944 by Foster Kennedy to designate somatic complaints following a periodic course in the absence of or with mood changes. Long before this, it was clearly understood that depressed patients, manic-depressive or otherwise, often complained of somatic sensations in addition to or as a substitute for their depressed mood. Every psychiatrist has seen such patients admitted to one medical ward after another for the fruitless investigation of constipation or gastric distress. And countless patients have been subjected to surgery because of the failure to recognize the depressive nature of the somatic complaint. Many psychiatrists (e.g., Jones, 1949) writing in the general medical literature have warned of the dangers of overlooking such "depressive equivalents."

Lorand (1946) and Gero (1953) have contributed to the elucidation of one particular equivalent of depression, anorexia. It is unnecessary to dwell upon the details of this except to note with Gero the difficulty in explaining any particular choice of symptom. He points out that "the nature of the oral drive pattern does not determine the symptom. Not all depressive patients with the same cannibalistic or oral-sadistic drives, with the same incorporative needs, develop eating disturbances. A complicated set of factors, not all of them necessarily recognizable, will decide whether or not an eating disturbance results."

The term "depressive equivalent" carries the connotation that the particular symptom complained of exists without the corresponding mood accompaniment. A patient may complain of constipation without being aware of its affective significance, without clearly knowing that he is depressed. But whether the patient is or is not conscious of his depression, this type of somatic complaint represents in general a change in function or body sensation rather than a detectable tissue alteration. When a depressed and constipated patient, for example, is investigated by x-ray or sigmoidoscope, no tissue pathology is visible.

There are cases, nevertheless, where the physical symptom or state does seem to exist in some significant relationship to a pathological process in the body tissues. Sandler and Joffe speak of psychosomatic illness as one of the defensive mechanisms against the underlying psychic pain. Alexander (1950) cited many instances of psychosomatic disorders occurring after object loss when one might ordinarily have expected depressed feelings to manifest themselves. However, there seem to be instances when psychosomatic illness and depression are both reactions to the failure of defensive measures against psychic pain. For example, McClary, Meyer and Weitzman (1955) observed a very significant relationship between loss and disseminated lupus erythematosus in a series of fourteen patients. These patients appeared to have a characteristic series of reactions to the loss or the threat of loss of a significant person. These situations were at first reacted to with denial, especially denial of the intensity of the emotional experience. This denial was followed by a tense need for increased activity, and when this did not suffice or could not be maintained, depression and pain and joint disability appeared. In this series of cases, defensive measures were utilized one after another to ward off the psychic pain. Only when these defenses failed did *both* depression and the symptoms of the lupus appear together.

And Engel (1955a), in his study of ulcerative colitis, considers it "an arresting observation" that the feeling tone at the time of onset or relapse of symptoms in every instance in which he could obtain the appropriate data in his series of thirty-nine patients (there were forty-five such instances) "was designated by such expressions as 'helpless,' 'despair,' 'hopeless,' 'overwhelmed,' 'too much to cope with,' 'too much to expect of me.' " "In general," he goes on to say, "there was a fairly good correlation between the severity of the symptoms and the degree of helplessness or hopelessness felt by the patient."

Incidentally, his case material as well as that of several other writers quoted by him contain instances of colitis coexisting with psychotic depression. These observations do not provide support, as Engel points out, for an impression frequently encountered in the literature that psychoses and psychosomatic disorders have a reciprocal relationship.

In a study of forty-two semiprivate hospitalized medical patients, Schmale (1958) reports on the relationship that he has observed between separation and depression on the one hand and disease on the other. He refers to "separation and depression" as "the psychic pattern of unsuccessful resolution of object loss." In forty-one of the forty-two patients in his series, the author felt that "there was verbal and/or nonverbal evidence for feelings of helplessness or hopelessness prior to the onset of the disease." This investigator sees disease as "one possible manifestation of depression" but acknowledges that it is by no means understood why these patients responded to separation with medical illness rather than just with depression.

Engel (1954), too, calls attention to the importance of determining how the psychological processes in ulcerative colitis are related to the somatic (and, of course, the same holds true for every similar disorder): "The jump from the psychic phenomena to the physical phenomena at the end organ is conceptually the most difficult. . . ." Engel has heeded his own summons to study the physiology of hope and despair and has recently (1955a) reported an extensive and rigorous investigation of the effect of mood on gastric physiology.

However, an understanding of the biochemical changes that take place even in depressions not complicated by overt psychosomatic disturbances is still incomplete, although the literature is now filled with studies and surveys of this aspect of depression. It should be noted that the illnesses that McClary et al., Engel and Schmale describe are accompanied by the feeling of helplessness that Sandler and Joffe postulate is characteristic of depressive illness. In other words, to the extent that these illnesses are accompanied by feelings of helplessness and depression, they should not be regarded as "depressive equivalents," no matter how the latter term is understood.

Chapter VII

INTRODUCTION

SINCE THE PUBLICATION of the first edition of this book, an important group of psychoanalytic writers have concerned themselves with a sustained critical reevaluation of certain psychoanalytic concepts. These concepts constitute integral elements in the formulations of depression that we have been examining. I intend to review these theories of depression, taking advantage of the insights afforded us by this critique of analytic constructs. Up to the time of writing, psychoanalytic concepts of depression have not been reevaluated from this perspective.

I intend to examine some aspects of Bibring and Jacobson's theories of depression that these writers considered of central importance in their formulations. I believe, and hope to demonstrate, that these aspects of their theories are conceptually unsatisfactory. I will start off by examining Bibring's concept of depression as an ego phenomenon and will then move on to analyze Jacobson's conception of aggression as central to depression. Both of these views will be considered from the perspective of the critique to which I have just referred.

There will be a necessary element of repetitiveness encountered here as I examine these formulations first from one aspect and then from another. In a flight of fancy, my procedure might be compared with the study of a many-sided and multicolored crystal. I will be peering first at one of its facets and then, slowly turning it over, will be examining one after another of its apparently translucent surfaces. I will turn it over and over, gazing and peering, chipping away and analyzing, and in the course of this painstaking endeavor I will unfortunately not fail to repeat myself as I examine it first from one side and then from another, then from one angle and still again from another.

Not that Bibring and Jacobson's formulations throw the only significant light on depression. I will be focusing down on their views of depression not so much for their own sakes but because the careful examination of the various components and facets of their paradigms will permit me to consider in depth some very provocative aspects of recent analytic thinking and to apply these insights to the study of depression. This was not possible in the chronological account of the development of these theories.

I suspect that this chapter will appeal most to those with a taste for metapsychology—a rather specialized taste, to be sure. It may be more accurate to say that it will appeal most to those who enjoy critical, conceptual or linguistic analysis. By the same token, this chapter may appear arid to those whose taste is for different delights. But then this book is not meant for them. I suspect that they will not have read this far.

THE EGO IN DEPRESSION
[1]

Bibring refers to depression as an "ego-phenomenon," an "ego-state." What does he mean by this? To gain more perspective on this question let us take a backward glance at Freud's use of this term.

Freud published *The Ego and the Id* in 1923. This work contains what has come to be called his structural theory, which conceptualizes the mental apparatus as being made up of the ego, the superego and the id. It contains his well-known formulation that "in every individual there is a coherent organization of mental processes which we call his ego." In earlier papers, Freud had used the term "ego" in a variety of ways (see Hartmann, 1956). At times he used "ego" interchangeably with "one's own person" and "the self." In *Mourning and Melancholia*, for example, he noted that "in the clinical picture of melancholia, dissatisfaction with the ego on moral grounds is the most outstanding feature. The patient's self-evaluation concerns itself much less frequently with bodily infirmities. . . ." His major clinical observation about melancholia, "the key to the clinical picture," is described in these words: "We perceive that the self-reproaches are reproaches against a loved object which have been shifted away from it onto the patient's own ego." The interchangeability of "ego" and "self" in these quotations is obvious.

Freud's new definition of the ego as an organization of mental processes unfortunately did not put an end to the use of this term in less precise ways. The literature is full of protests against the use of this construct to mean a person, the self or an anatomical location in the central nervous system.

Hartmann, Kris and Loewenstein (1946), referring to the structural concepts of psychoanalysis, acknowledged that a danger existed in the use of metaphors in science. They felt that "the danger obviously begins if and when metaphor infringes upon meaning; in the case in point, when the structural concepts are anthropomorphized." It was Hartmann (1950) who made a distinction between the analytic term "ego" and constructs like "personality," "the individual" and the "the self." The ego is, he emphasized, "a substructure of personality and is defined by its functions." He made it clear that the "ego" was a theoretical abstraction and not an existing entity. And Jacobson, as we have seen, also maintained this distinction. In a terminological examination of the Freudian sentence "The Ego presents itself to the Superego as a love object," Hartmann et al. (1946) first replaced the word "ego" by "the self" and then, more rigorously, found it preferable to avoid terms like "love," "approval" or "disapproval" when speaking of the superego. Instead, they spoke of "different kinds and degrees of tension between the two psychic organizations, according to the presence or absence of conflict between their functions." They acknowledged that restricting the use of metaphors in this way "considerably impoverishes the plasticity of language as compared to Freud's mode of expression." They suggested that the metaphor evokes a more immediate response since "the anthropomorphism it introduces corresponds to human experience."

Nash (1963), too, defends the role of metaphor in psychological theory, arguing that "tangled thinking occurs in the absence of metaphor, as in its presence." He wonders also, in relation to structural theory, "about the advisability of supplanting a vivid and fertile figure—once relations between ego and self have been clarified—by a technical formulation distinguished neither for stimulating imagery nor for well-defined observations anchored firmly in the world of observation."

But to illustrate the slipperiness of metaphoric imagery, Grossman and Simon (1969), in the course of a very thoughtful paper, examine the reformulation that was just noted above. In their opinion, "the substitution of tension for the clearly anthropomorphic terms of self-love, self-approval and of the ego being the love object of the superego does not seem to be entirely successful. 'Tension' in this setting appears to be evocative and not strictly denotative. It is a subtle form of evocation, however, since its use depends on the fact that it refers both to the experience of psychological tension and to tension as a physical concept. Note that tension as a physical concept is defined mathematically and that its use otherwise is to a great extent anthropomorphic. Hence 'tension' serves merely as a statement of the proposition that there is a conflict between two psychic agencies. As such, it is no more or no less metaphorical than the term "conflict." The criteria for 'tension' are, as far as can be seen, the same as the criteria for conflict."

Grossman and Simon are but among the most recent exponents of the dangers of anthropomorphism and reification. Freud himself (1933), despite his actual practice, warned of this danger. Brierley (1951) noted that "the temptation to personify is insidious" (p. 33). Beres (1956) warned that the concept of the ego is a working concept and that risk of personifying it must be avoided. Several years later he (1962) was even more explicit about the danger of referring to the psychic structures as if they have spatial location. He disapproved of locutions or verbal usages implying the presence of fantasies or other contents "in" the ego or id, which, he insists, are theoretical abstractions. "They do not have existence in space" and to speak of ego, id or superego contents, he argues, "is an act of reification and a contradiction of the original definition." And again in 1965 he continues to warn against the "danger of reification of the components of the 'structural theory,' the id, ego and superego, the danger of 'misplaced concreteness'. . . ."

Holt (1967a) also notes that writers often do not avoid the methodological fallacies of personification and reification. They too easily fall into the trap of attributing actions and psychic operations to the three structural systems. Schafer (1970), too, in a discussion of Hartmann's claim that "the language of functions helps to avoid the anthropomorphism that tends to creep into references to the psychic structures," asks: "Is it, however, any the less anthropomorphic to speak of functions . . . that can collaborate with or oppose or suspend other functions? What is the difference between saying that the ego revolts against the tyrannical superego and saying that the defensive functions of the ego direct counter-cathexis against superego influence? I maintain that the anthropomorphism has merely been concealed behind aseptic language."

In his ambitious attempt to recast psychoanalytic theory on an information-systems model, Peterfreund (1971), too, complains that psychoanalytic theory is contaminated with anthropomorphism. He elaborates this criticism at considerable length in his book and even examines the term "tension" in much the same way as did Grossman and Simon and from a perspective that is in agreement with Schafer's comments in the previous paragraph. "Hartmann, Kris and Loewenstein apparently do not recognize that they are still using anthropomorphizations in speaking of 'tension' between psychic organizations. 'Tension' is no less an anthropomorphization than 'approval' or 'disapproval.' These words are the language of people; it is clinical language" (p. 73).

Since we find this same kind of caution and criticism being sounded by Schafer once more in 1972 and again in 1973, we have to recognize that this continued tolling of the bell warning us against the dangers of personification, reification and anthropomorphism should not be taken lightly—else why would not the first alarm have sufficed?

In the light of these warnings and admonitions, it will be instructive to take a backward glance to observe how the theorists we have reviewed, have used the term "ego." It is only fair to point out that these authors wrote their papers too early to be affected by these later strictures. But it might introduce some conceptual clarity if we take note of their ways of using this term.

The first important paper on depression after Freud's structural theory was introduced in 1923 was Rado's (1928). Some examples of his personification of the term "ego" are vivid and even poetic but they do demonstrate the dangers that Beres, Schafer, Holt and others warn against: "The ego does penance [and] begs for forgiveness"; "In its remorse the ego turned, full of confidence, to a benevolent being"; "The repentant ego desires to win the forgiveness of the offended object"; "The ego . . . heaves a sigh of relief and with every sign of blissful transport unites itself with the 'good object' which has been raised to the position of the super-ego"; "The ego, its wits sharpened by its painful experience. . . ." These examples sound picturesque and delightful and bring back the flavor of a past era of psychoanalytic writing.

Melanie Klein's imaginative but terminologically imprecise conceptual style has been so often commented on, criticized and defended that it is hardly worthwhile examining it again in this connection.

Twenty-five years after Rado's paper, Bibring (1953) showed evidence of deftly interchanging, for metaphoric purposes, a systemic and personified use of the term "ego," though the result does seem to warrant the kind of criticism cited above. He referred, for example, to "the ego's acute awareness of . . . helplessness" closely followed by a sentence including the words "whenever . . . the person comes to feel that all effort was in vain." In referring to the type of depression associated with the wish to be strong he wrote about "the ego's weakness," whereas when writing about the type of depression associated with the wish to be good and loving he spoke about "aggressive tendencies within the self."

Jacobson has made it her deliberate goal to contribute to the clarification of psychoanalytic concepts. In her volume *The Self and the Object World* (1964) she explicitly makes "special efforts to avoid confusing terminological inaccuracies" (footnote, p. 6). She discriminates carefully with respect to "the meaning of the concepts of the self and self-representations as distinct from that of the ego" (p. 19). Nevertheless, one can, without too much trouble, find sentences like the following: "In fact, the ego cannot acquire a realistic likeness to the loved object unless admired traits of this object become enduringly introjected into the child's wishful self images"; "In so far as the realistic self-representations become a mirror of the ego. . . ." (p. 51).

But Jacobson disarms criticism on this point. In the above-mentioned footnote where she declares her intention to make "special efforts" to avoid such imprecisions, she adds, "However, this is not always possible" and points out that Freud too was guilty of just such confusions as have been quoted from her book.

Yet one begins to see why Holt (1967b) argues so strongly that "further progress [in psychoanalytic theoretical development] will be exceedingly difficult unless a concentrated effort is made to avoid the methodologically indefensible and all-too-common practice of personifying [terms like the ego] and treating them as concrete entities that are capable of initiating action or more generally of acting as efficient causes" (p. 5). In his reforming zeal, he adds that much of current usage is actually redundant and easily avoided: " 'The ego's defenses' conveys no meaning not contained in simply 'defenses'. . . ." In his capacity as editor of a book of essays in honor of David Rapaport, that "leader in a continuing effort to advance toward theoretical precision" (p. 4), he (1967b) took "a sharp second look at any passage in which ego, superego, or id was used as a noun, instead of adjectively, and to see that activity was referred to the behaving organism or person" (p. 5).

There are hints in Jacobson's writings of locutions about the ego as if it were a concrete entity or perhaps a pseudoanatomic location. She refers to the "partial or total fusions of self- and object-representations in the system ego" (1953, p. 55) and in a revised version of the same paper, but in a different context, she mentions "the object- and self-representations in the system ego" (1971, p. 231). She speaks of the "endopsychic representations of the bodily and mental self in the system ego" (1964, p. 19).

This danger of concretization might be lessened if Sandler and Rosenblatt's (1962) concept of a representational world were to be more generally adopted. In their handling of this theme, they consider the construction of a representational world to be one of the functions of the ego. As they view it, "The child creates, within its perceptual or representational world, images and organizations of his internal as well as external environment. . . . In the course of development, the child creates stable images of objects existing in the external world. These images are located within the representational world of the child, but refer to what the child learns to experience as the 'external' world." As well as object-representations, this representational world includes the self-representations, by which the authors mean "that organization which represents the person as he has consciously and unconsciously perceived himself and which forms an integral part of the representational world. . . . The construction of the representational world is a product of ego functions, and the self- and object-representations are part of the representational world." I believe that this conceptualization adheres very closely to Jacobson's except that its terminology skirts somewhat more widely those dangers of reification that seem to lie in wait when the term "ego" is used too loosely or casually. It would, however, not satisfy Schafer, who in a recent paper (1972) argues strongly against any concession to pseudospatial metaphors.

Going back to Bibring (1953), let us look more carefully at his view of the role of the ego in depression. As we have seen, he thought of depression as "an ego-psychological phenomenon, a 'state of the ego,' an affective state."

Rapaport (1959), no mean theoretician, is on record as emphasizing the importance and decisiveness of this conception of depression. In an effort to find a precedent for Bibring's theory in Freud, he noted that "according to Bibring, to be loved and to be loving are among the narcissistic aspirations whose role in depression is crucial" and that Freud (1915) had written ". . . the attitude of love and hate cannot be said to characterize the relations of instincts to their objects, but are reserved for the relations of the ego as a whole to objects." He acknowledged that "the relationships implied in Freud's formulation have not been explored" but added that one of the merits of Bibring's theory is that it makes such exploration "a patent and urgent necessity." Rapaport spoke of Bibring opening up new vistas and new theoretical possibilities.

Granted that these comments of Rapaport's were made in the course of a Bibring Memorial Meeting of the Boston Psychoanalytic Association, these comments are not to be taken lightly. Rapaport treated psychoanalytic theory with great seriousness and made impressive contributions to this body of theory.

But what does it all mean? What does it mean to say that depression is an ego-psychological phenomenon and that it is an ego state? Bibring himself explains it in part as follows: "Depression is primarily not determined by a conflict between the ego on the one hand and the id, or the superego, or the environment on the other hand, but stems primarily from a tension within the ego itself, from an inner-systemic 'conflict.' Thus depression can be defined as the emotional correlate of a partial or complete collapse of the self-esteem of the ego, since it feels unable to live up to its aspirations (ego ideal, superego) while they are strongly maintained."

I intend to subject this picture of depression as representing an intrasystemic rather than an intersystemic conflict to a critical analysis. I hope to demonstrate that this issue, which has won such unhesitating approval from writers such as Rapaport (1959), Rubinfine (1968) and Mahler (1966) and that has been criticized as only partially valid by Jacobson (1971), is in reality neither valid nor invalid, but rather a pseudo-issue that represents a red herring in the theorizing about depression. More generally, I hope to demonstrate that Bibring's attempt to conceptualize depression as an ego phenomenon serves merely to conceal the true value of Bibring's contribution to the evolution of psychoanalytic concepts of depression.

The problem of examining and clarifying Bibring's explanation is made a little complicated by his tendency to personify the term "ego" as when he refers to the "collapse of the self-esteem of the ego, since it feels unable to live up to its aspirations" or, elsewhere in his paper, to "the ego's awareness of its helplessness." Nevertheless, what is clearest about Bibring's formulation is that he did not consider depression to consist of *inter*systemic conflicts or tensions, i.e., conflicts between the system ego, superego or id. He viewed depression as an *intra*systemic conflict, a conflict within the system ego itself. To elaborate on this, Bibring disagreed with the concept that aggression directed by the superego against the ego in any form—guilt, self-castigation, self-criticism or self-loathing—represented the essence of depression. He saw aggression as a "complicating" factor, secondary to the depression and to the collapse of self-esteem, "the narcissistic core of the ego."

The ego is considered to be a psychic system that is defined by its functions. One of its functions, as we have seen, is the organization of self-representations, and, more generally, of the inner representational world. Rapaport, in his Bibring paper delivered in 1959 but only published posthumously (1967b), stated that "the term self-esteem was not defined explicitly by Freud, nor by anyone else, including Bibring." Jacobson (1954 and 1964), however, did describe self-esteem as "the ideational, especially the emotional expression of self-evaluation and of the corresponding more or less neutralized libidinal and aggressive cathexis of the self-representations." Stated more simply, self-esteem implies self-representations that are positively experienced. And it is the failure of the self-representations to maintain their positive affective coloring or quality that characterizes the "collapse of the self-esteem of the ego" that Bibring refers to. In other words, it is the loss of self-esteem with the accompanying feeling of helplessness that represents the "state of the ego" or the "ego-psychological phenomenon" that Bibring believed depression to be. Comparing depression to anxiety, which Freud considered to be an ego reaction, Bibring held that "since they cannot be reduced any further it may be justified to call them ego reactions."

As we have seen, Bibring defined the basic mechanism of depression as the "ego's shocking awareness of its helplessness in regard to its aspirations" or as "the emotional correlate of a partial or complete collapse of the self-esteem of the ego, since it feels unable to live up to its aspirations (ego ideal, superego). . . ."

As will be remembered, Bibring classified these so-called narcissistic aspirations into three groups: "(1) the wish to be worthy, to be loved, to be appreciated, not to be inferior or unworthy; (2) the wish to be strong, superior, great, secure, not to be weak and insecure; and (3) the wish to be good, to be loving, not to be aggressive, hateful and destructive." Brushing aside for the moment Bibring's outdated personification of the ego ("the ego's shocking awareness," "the self-esteem of the ego"), let us focus on his definition of depression as the ego's inability "to live up to its aspirations (ego ideal, superego). . . ." It will be seen that despite Bibring's focus on depression as an ego phenomenon, he does have occasion to refer to the ego ideal or superego when he touches upon the "ego's . . . aspirations."

A narcissistic conflict having to do with an individual's failure to attain his aspirations would seem to mean, in classical psychoanalytic terminology, a conflict between his ego and his ego ideal. Stated more precisely, this would involve a discrepancy between his self-representations and his ego ideal. But since the ego ideal is traditionally associated with the superego, would this not make of this discrepancy an intersystemic conflict? In considering this matter of narcissistic aspirations and their relationship to the ego ideal or superego, it will be necessary for me to turn aside to examine with some care the role of the ego ideal or superego in such aspirations and in the frustration of these aspirations. The necessity for this digression has, of course, to do with Bibring's insistence that depression is an intrasystemic rather than an intersystemic condition.

Before moving on to this matter, however, I would like to consider Jacobson's view on this issue. In her recent book (1971, p. 176) she agrees with Bibring that in "simple," i.e., undelusional but psychotic depressions, "the narcissistic conflict is a conflict within the ego." She believes that this is the case also in many schizophrenic depressions "as well as those neurotic or even normal kinds of depression in which feelings of inadequacy and inferiority play the main role. In such cases the conflict is between the wishful self-image and the image of the failing self." She excludes from narcissistic conflicts "within the ego" those conflicts which include feelings of guilt and which, by the usual definition, are intersystemic conflicts involving the superego as well as the ego. She points out that "obsessional-compulsive depressives usually complain about their guilt feelings." As we know, guilt feelings are also quite common in involutional melancholia as well as in many other depressions, both delusional and nondelusional. She also correctly observes that many patients who appear to have conflicts about inadequacy "within the ego" may also have underlying guilt feelings.

Thus Jacobson agrees with Bibring that in some depressions the narcissistic conflict resides "within the ego." But since these conflicts would seem to consist of discrepancies between the self-representations and the ego ideal, on what grounds does she agree with Bibring even to the limited extent to which she does? The metapsychological assumptions underlying this agreement have not been made clear in Chapter 6 of her book, where she deals with this problem, though there are some considerations elsewhere that do bear on this matter and which will be reviewed presently.

To explore this issue with some grasp of the metapsychologic problems involved, it will be necessary, as I have said, to turn aside for the moment and to note how the terms "ego," ego ideal" and "superego" have evolved in the writings of psychoanalytic theorists. I have found it helpful to follow Sandler, Holder and Meers' (1963) outline of this development but have not restricted myself to their very useful paper.

[2]

As will be remembered, Freud (1917) in *Mourning and Melancholia* referred to "the conflict between one part of the ego and its self-criticizing faculty," the "faculty" that was to evolve into the concept of the superego. Before this, in *On Narcissism* (1914) and in *Introductory Lectures* (1915–17), he had written about the ideal which an individual sets up in himself as a standard by which to measure himself and had distinguished this ego ideal from the conscience. In *Group Psychology and the Analysis of the Ego*, he (1921) used the term "ego ideal" in a different sense, including in it not only what he had previously referred to as the "ego ideal" but also the "critical agency within the ego," "the moral conscience."

When he (1923) formulated his structural theory in *The Ego and the Id*, this broadly defined ego ideal was now used synonymously with "the superego," with more emphasis than hithertofore being placed on the critical and punitive aspects of this "agency" or structure. As Sandler et al. (1963) indicate, Freud "used the two terms synonymously and when he spoke of the ego ideal in relation to the superego it was in the sense of the superego's function of maintaining and enforcing standards on the ego."

In recent years, a number of proposals (e.g., Annie Reich, 1954, 1960; Novey, 1955; Lampl-deGroot, 1962) have been made to separate out the ego ideal as a psychic structure distinct from the superego, or as a term encompassing only some of the functions of the superego. But with reference to Bibring's views, this picture of the ego ideal as a system distinct from the superego would still seem to involve intersystemic conflicts when "the ego feels unable to live up to its aspirations."

Bing, McLaughlin and Marburg (1959) view the matter a little differently. They propose that the two structures, ego ideal and superego, be conceptually separated, but they contend that "the ego ideal is 'anatomically' a part of the ego, conscious or unconscious, whereas the superego has become a structure apart from the ego with functions of its own." If this view, that the ego ideal should be considered "anatomically" a part of the ego, prevailed, it would indeed be compatible with Bibring's idea that the narcissistic conflicts he referred to—or most of them—were intrasystemic.

However, authorities as eminent as Hartmann and Loewenstein (1962) decisively maintained that they "consider the superego, as Freud did, as *one* system of personality, despite its various aspects. We would not, as has occasionally been suggested, consider the ego ideal as a separate system. . . . The connections between the ego ideal and the prohibitive aspects of the superego are so close that both should be considered as aspects of one and the same system."

Jacobson's (1954, 1964) position on this subject is paradoxically both straightforward and ambiguous. She, too, maintains strongly that the ego ideal and the superego cannot be conceptually separated. Yet she repeatedly refers (e.g., 1964, Chapter 6) to the child's "wishful self-images" (with respect to which he strives to model his realistic self-images) as related to the ego. She sees these wishful self-images as forerunners of the ego ideal. In commenting on the forestages of superego development, she refers not too explicitly to "processes . . . which transform the primitive, wishful images of the self- and the love-objects into a unified ego ideal" (1964, p. 93).

She conceives of these ego-related wishful self-images as childhood precursors of the adult ego ideal. Nevertheless, when she has occasion to speak of *adult* failures to attain narcissistic aspirations in simple and in neurotic depressions, she persists in declaring, in agreement with Bibring, that "the narcissistic conflict is a conflict within the ego." This yielding to Bibring's formulation would seem to be in direct contradiction to her own views about the superego and its development.

Rapaport (1957), with characteristic awareness of theoretical fuzziness, drew attention to "the perplexities which attend this [superego] concept." To speak of one's inability to live up to his aspirations seems to imply the failure of the individual's realistic self-representations to live up to his ego ideal. This would mean that the ego ideal "contains" ideal self-representations against which the person's own self-representations do not measure up. However, Rapaport pointed out in a manner similar to Hartmann (1939) and Sandler and Rosenblatt (1962) that it is the "inner world [that] contains the representations" and furthermore that "the inner world is a substructure of the ego" and that "in regard to the superego . . . we would not attribute to it any of the functions of the inner world."

This view is, of course, compatible with Rapaport's commendation of Bibring's theory of depression quoted above. The implication is that the self-representations—both realistic and ideal—are "contained" in the "inner world," a view which supports Bibring's intrasystemic conception of depression. But for Rapaport the matter was not so simple. For him, the whole concept of the superego was a "Gordian knot" which only in the future would "yield to theoretical discernment."

Sandler (1960) and his colleagues (1963) have attempted to make some inroads into the intricate and painstaking untangling of this Gordian knot. Sandler (1960) refers to the tendency on the part of the theorists to by-pass "the difficulty which exists in integrating the superego concept into the psychoanalytic model." Part of this difficulty, as we have seen, has to do with ideal-images to which the individual aspires and which are assigned by some writers to the ego and by others to the ego ideal. Another part of this difficulty consists in conceptualizing and differentiating between classes of object-representations that are classified as ego-related and classes of object-representations of parental and authority figures which are assigned to the superego.

Sandler, for example, at one point (1960) sees the superego as developing separately from object-representations which make up part of the representational world. In this paper, in a traditional analytic formulation, he links the formation of the superego "with a partial and relative reduction of interest in and dependence on the real parents. The major source of self-esteem is no longer the real parents, but the superego. *Introjection* of the parents has taken place. . . . What distinguishes the introject [from previous object-representations of the parents] is precisely the capacity of the introject to substitute, in whole or in part, for the real object as a source of narcissistic gratification. . . . Through introjection, the *relationship* to the object is maintained and perpetuated, but the real object is no longer so vital to the relationship. It follows that what is introjected is neither the personality nor the behavior of the parents, but their *authority.* . . . What was previously experienced as the threat of parental disapproval becomes guilt . . . [with a] drop in self-esteem." Sandler also draws attention to the affective state which exists "when the ego and superego are functioning together in a smooth and harmonious fashion . . . best described as a state of mental comfort and well-being, of *eupathy.*"

There is nothing new in this formulation. It is a nice summary of accepted psychoanalytic thinking on the subject. In this view of the situation, the superego is linked not only to guilt and low self-esteem but also to the feeling of being loved—all states, by the way, which Bibring explicitly thought of as intrasystemic.

However, faced with the problem of classifying and indexing case material in the Hampstead Index, Sandler, Holder and Meers (1963) had to expand this neat and tidy model of the superego. Faced with the complexity of labeling their clinical observations, they now referred to the "ego–ego ideal–superego system." They found the process of actually indexing stubborn and complex case material very different from aseptically theorizing about psychic structures. They found that they "could not differentiate an ego-ideal system or structure as functionally distinct from the ego and superego."

At this point, after hastily skimming over the concept of the superego, it might be useful to remind ourselves once again of the purpose of this examination. Our point of departure was Bibring's theoretically radical assertion that depression represented an intrasystemic conflict; that it was an "ego phenomenon," representing "the ego's shocking awareness of its helplessness in regard to its aspirations." This was in sharp contrast to the views of other theorists who had seen the superego as central to the psychodynamics of depression. We are therefore dissecting out the systemic or structural implications of one's failure to attain one's aspirations.

In all of this it is important to be reminded that what we are discussing here are not observable facts or clinical data. What we have been considering are concepts, abstractions and theoretical constructs. They are definitions, first proposed and then revised and then sometimes revised once again. At best, they derive, as in the work of Sandler and his collaborators, from an attempt to order and classify clinical data. They are what Schafer (1967) has referred to as "ordering abstractions," and it is Schafer (1967) who, up to this point, has presented the most persuasive, enlightening and sophisticated discussion of ideals, the ego ideal and the ideal self.

Schafer distinguishes between superego standards and ideals and ego standards and ideals. By superego standards he means the classic standards of moral perfection which Freud (1933) conceptualized as the "ego ideal," one of the aspects of the superego namely, its ideals. Schafer applies the term "ego standards" to all those standards of performance, beauty, health, effectiveness, excellence or skill that are by definition not related to the kind of moral standards that characterize superego ideals. These ego standards derive initially from parental example but later develop also in relation to peers, teachers and others. When superego standards are not met, we observe feelings of guilt and unworthiness. When ego standards are not met, we observe feelings of dissatisfaction, uselessness, purposelessness and uncertainty.

Acknowledging that "in metapsychology the self is still minimally defined," Schafer suggests that it might be useful to think of the self as the organization or integration, to whatever extent it exists, of all the self-representations. The degree of synthesis or integration would then represent one measure of ego strength or weakness, and one could then refer to the integration of partial ideal self-representations as the ideal self. This term, Schafer emphasizes, refers to mental contents. It is a phenomenological term, not a system term like ego, id or superego. He points out that ideal self-representations can be inconsistent, e.g., "determined self-assertion and saintly forbearance," or an ideal of scholarliness co-existing and conflicting with an ideal of masculinity represented by hard manual labor. The ideal of sharp intelligence may be in conflict with that of appealing naïveté. The ideal of self-contain-ment may clash with that of demonstrativeness.

The laying down of self-representations has been regarded as an ego function. Therefore, to return to Bibring's concept of depres-sion, the discrepancy in ego standards between what Schafer re-fers to as one's experienced self and one's ideal self would, of course, be regarded as an intrasystemic conflict; whereas a dis-crepancy in the realm of moral or superego standards would, by definition, be intersystemic.

Thus we are back to the same recurring disagreement about whether aspirations and ideals should be assigned to the ego alone or also to the ego ideal or superego. This is a disagreement—usually implicit, sometimes explicit—that we have repeatedly en-countered between Bibring and other writers. But Schafer, even more decisively than Sandler et al. (1963), breaks out of the recur-ring circle of theoretical controversy. He strongly argues that to conceptualize the matter in this way is to be guilty of oversimplify-ing a complexly ramified set of data. He reminds us that although we may, for didactic purposes, speak of ego or superego ideals, this distinction is essentially artificial. "In practice we find that ideals frequently—and possibly always—simultaneously express factors we refer to the id, ego, and superego."

Gill (1963, Chapter 8), from another perspective, also argues against a too arbitrary separation between the three major sys-tems. Although he focuses mainly on the ego and the id, his com-ments have more general application. He visualizes the ego and the id as a continuum rather than two separate and hostile states or provinces. He, too, contends that any given behavior can be classified under the system id, ego or superego depending on its relationships, characteristics and functions at any given point, rather than by the inherent nature of the behavioral unit.

Apfelbaum (1966), too, in a thoughtful paper argues that the work of Gill (1963) and of Arlow and Brenner (1964) seems to show that "structural distinctions are difficult to maintain." As Harrison (1970) puts it, "The structural hypothesis is nothing more than a means of ordering data in what is really a semiarbitrary though extremely useful fashion."

As an example of the clinical realities as distinguished from the didactic practice, Schafer observes that in the ideal of being the "toughest guy on the block," not only may "id aggressivity" be present, but also ego defenses against castration anxiety as well as superego strictures against homosexual or passive dependent tendencies.

It might be argued that what Bibring referred to as the mechanism of depression was not the loss of self-esteem per se following upon the patient's failure to achieve his narcissistic aspirations, but rather the helplessness, the narcissistic shock following upon the loss of self-esteem. And it might be pointed out that Schafer's statement that "feelings of helplessness . . . uselessness, purposelessness, and if we agree with Bibring, even depression all may indicate a failure to meet ego standards" seemingly supports Bibring's view of depression as an ego phenomenon. But later on in the same paragraph (1967, p. 139), Schafer adds: "Usually we do not find clear-cut instances of these intersystemic and intrasystemic affects; typically affects are complex, fluid and multiply determined."

Schafer reminds us that our clinical raw data are "ideas, fantasies, feelings and strivings and that only by a process of abstraction are these phenomena classified along systemic (id, ego or superego) lines. He argues that Waelder's (1936) principle of multiple function makes it necessary to view "each psychic phenomenon as a simultaneous expression of tendencies of the system's id, ego and superego." In the light of Schafer's sophisticated discussion of this topic and the evolution of more fluid conceptions of the structural model, a debate about whether a patient's narcissistic conflict lies "within" the ego or whether it also involves the superego appears simplistic and arbitrary.

Apfelbaum (1966), in a thoughtful paper, argues that the work of Gill (1963) and of Arlow and Brenner (1964) seems to show that "structural distinctions are difficult to maintain." It seems clear that the term "ego" like the terms "superego" and "id," properly understood, are ordering abstractions, theoretical devices to classify data according to semi-arbitrary but clinically useful categories. They are not mutually exclusive structures which do or do not "contain" affects, defenses or self-representations.

And if all this is so, and it appears self-evident that it is, does it not appear that Bibring was guilty of overly simplifying the problem of depression by assigning it exclusively to the ego, and that

Jacobson has—almost in passing, it is true—allowed herself to be drawn into a debate about what is in reality a pseudo-issue?

After this long digression, let us turn to another aspect of Bibring's formulation of depression. It is of some importance that Bibring refers to depression as an affective state. We are so accustomed to think of depression as an affective illness that the implications of Bibring's seemingly obvious statement may escape us. Therefore, it is important to note that not one of the major theorists on depression had, prior to 1953, as far as I have been able to discover, tended to refer to depression as an affective state.

Freud (1917) used the term "melancholia" almost exclusively, referring neither to "depression" nor to affective states when speaking about this condition, which he viewed as a clinical entity with complex ramifications. Abraham did in the course of one paper (1911) refer to "affects" of anxiety, depression and anger. The word was used as if it were synonymous with "feelings." Rado (1928) did not refer to affective states nor did Gero (1936) in the course of a quite lengthy paper.

Rapaport (1959) drew particular attention to Bibring's view: "What is bold and new in Bibring's [theory] is the assertion that *all* depressions are affective states. . . ." The importance of all of this has to do with Freud's use of the term. In *Inhibitions, Symptoms and Anxiety* (1926), for example, he stated: "Anxiety is an affective state and as such can, of course, only be felt by the ego" (p. 113). Freud in 1926 had clearly established the ego as "the seat of anxiety." In a very late reference (1933) he again stated very explicitly that "the ego is the sole seat of anxiety—that the ego alone can produce and feel anxiety . . . and indeed it is difficult to see what sense there would be in speaking of an 'anxiety of the id' or in attributing a capacity for apprehensiveness to the superego" (p. 85). Once he labeled depression as an affective state, Bibring, of course, had an important precedent in referring it to the ego.

However, in this connection Zetzel (1960) and Jacobson (1971) were later to comment on the confusion that results when writers blur the distinctions between depression as an affect, a mood, a symptom and an illness.

With respect to Freud's declaration that the ego is the seat of anxiety, he was, of course, slipping into the tendency to reify this psychic system. Despite the fact that in a personal discussion (Herold, 1941) Freud "expressed his astonishment that so many analysts used terms like id, ego, superego as if they were real entities," he was as prone as anyone else to personify and reify these terms. Examples of this from the same book (1926) in which he wrote that an affect can only be felt by the ego are: "the ego scores its first success in its defensive struggles against the demands of the libido" (p. 114); "the ego will recoil with astonishment" (p. 116); "the ego knows that is innocent" (p. 117). On the subject of the ego as the seat of anxiety, Freud wrote interchangeably about "the subject's estimation of his . . . physical . . . and psychical helplessness" (p. 166) and "the motor helplessness of the ego" (p. 168).

As we have seen, Bibring was similarly prone to personify the ego, e.g., "when the ego was made to feel helpless"; "the ego is paralyzed because it finds itself incapable to meet the danger"; "everything that lowers or paralyzes the ego's self-esteem." Bibring also wrote interchangeably of "the ego's acute awareness of its . . . helplessness" and of "the infant's or little child's shocklike experience of and fixation to the feeling of helplessness."

Speaking about this tendency to personify, Holt (1967b, footnote, p. 136) insists that "to say that either the ego or the superego perceives is an unfortunate misusage which is at best tolerable clinical sloppiness, at worst, a mischievous fallacy . . . only the person acts (or perceives, etc.) [my italics]."

And in a reexamination of the concept of signal anxiety, Schur (in Löfgren, 1968, p. 648), a very sophisticated metapsychologist, clarified the obvious point that "the ego cannot be said to produce an affect—such a statement is essentially finalistic and anthropomorphic—any more than it can produce a percept or a memory."

Thus, to say that because depression is an affective illness, that the ego is therefore the seat of depression on the model of Freud's reference to the ego as the seat of anxiety, is an obvious example of reification. In fact, to speak of the ego experiencing either anxiety or depression really belongs to a previous less semantically sophisticated era of psychoanalysis. If we are to speak logically and coherently, we have to say that it is *the person*, and not the ego, *that is depressed*.

My intention, as I indicated earlier, was to demonstrate that the whole issue of depression as an ego phenomenon, as reflecting an intrasystemic rather than an inter-systemic conflict, was a pseudo-issue. I believe that I have done this. Going even further, Sandler, in a paper which is still in press at the time of writing, argues with convincing illustrations that "the conceptualization of conflict in terms of the interaction of the various psychic 'agencies' of the structural model is insufficient for our clinical needs."

Bibring, as Jacobson (1971) has pointed out, failed to differentiate clearly between depression as an affect, a symptom and an illness. Moreover, he blurred the distinctions between the various types of depressive illness.

What Bibring did do, and what represents his major contribution to the evolution of psychoanalytic theory of depression, was to elaborate the important role that self-esteem plays in depression, glimpses of which had been seen previously by Rado and Fenichel. More importantly, he conceptualized self-esteem in broader terms than those that prevailed when he wrote his paper. He went beyond the stereotyped theoretical fixation on external narcissistic supplies on the one hand and hate and guilt on the other hand. He broadened the concept of self-esteem in a clinically useful way that was to be surpassed only by Jacobson. And it is as a clinical contribution rather than a theoretical one that Bibring's paper deserves to be remembered. His attempt to clothe his astute clinical observations in theoretical terms unfortunately contributed to two decades of conceptual confusion about depression as an ego phenomenon.

AGGRESSION IN DEPRESSION

In a footnote on Bibring's view of depression, Jacobson (1953, p. 60) states quite firmly that "whereas he refuses to ascribe the central part in the pathology of depression to aggression and its vicissitudes, I am convinced, on clinical and theoretical grounds, that this view is correct." She reiterates this position at somewhat greater length in her recent book (1971, pp. 178–81) and thus outlines the dimensions of this basic conceptual disagreement. Since so much in the psychoanalytic theory of depression hinges on the presence or absence of aggression in depression, let us then be as clear as we can be about what this term means and how it is understood.

Having reviewed in Chapter 5, in a rather summary fashion, the ambiguities and confusion inherent in the idea of aggression, I now intend to take a closer look at this concept. The purpose of this more careful examination is, of course, to attempt to gain as precise an understanding as possible of the meaning and implication of theories of aggression in depression.

Bibring (1941), Ostow (1942), Hartmann (1948) et al. (1949) and others have traced the evolution of Freud's theories of the instinctual drives. It will serve no purpose to review this again here. It is sufficient to say that in *Beyond the Pleasure Principle* Freud (1920), pursuing the implications of certain hints that can be found in his previous publications, clearly set forth his hypothesis of two distinct instinctual drives: the sexual, derived from Eros, the life force, and aggression, derived from the death instinct. Freud had previously (1905) identified the sexual instinct as the source of mental or psychic energy which he called "libido." When he postulated a second instinct he coined no analogous word for the energy of this other drive. We are left then with the term "aggression," with its confusing connotations of instinctual drive, the energy generated by that drive and the feelings and behavior derived therefrom. To confuse the picture still further, a sizable minority of writers (e.g., Gillespie, 1971) believe that aggression and aggressive feelings and behavior do not, in fact, derive from an instinctual drive at all but are merely reactions to frustrating circumstances and events.

From the very beginning, the concept of a death instinct met with considerable opposition, e.g., Fenichel (1935). Gillespie (1971) quotes Jones (1957, p. 287) to the effect that "of 50 or so papers devoted to the topic of the death instinct half of those published during the first decade after 1920 supported Freud's view, in the second decade only a third, and in the third decade none at all— thus implying that it is dying a natural death." But Gillespie points out that Jones neglected to mention that practically every paper by Melanie Klein or by members of her school has explicitly or implicitly endorsed the theory of the death instinct.

According to Heimann and Valenstein (1972), "The followers of Melanie Klein accept as literal Freud's most speculative venture into global theory. . . . They apply the concept of the death instinct directly to their clinical evaluations and technique as if it were clinical theory, immediately verifiable in the microscopic field of the psychoanalytic situation. . . ."

In fact, at the Twenty-seventh International Psychoanalytic Congress in Vienna, Garma and Rosenfeld were continuing to give clinical examples of the workings of the death instinct (see Lussier, 1972).

Even among non-Kleinians we find, as late as 1971, Eissler and

Stone respectively arguing the case for and against the death instinct.

Hartmann, Kris and Loewenstein (1949) represented a position that is now quite widely accepted among writers in the mainstream of American psychoanalysis. They readily accepted aggression as having the status of an instinctual drive but tactfully and antiseptically relegated the issue of the death instinct to the domain of "biology proper." They therefore refrained from entering into a discussion of "Freud's biological speculation," taking the position that their comments on the nature of aggressive drives were independent of the hypothesis that aggression is derived from the death instinct. They noted that some authors, such as Fenichel (1935), experienced "a kind of genuine discomfort" with respect to speculations about the death instinct, a discomfort which caused them to discard also the concept of a primary aggressive drive. Waelder (1956) and Brenner (1971) may also be cited as exponents of this attitude to the concept of the death instinct, a disposition of the problem that Stone (1971) equates with its being intellectually "kicked upstairs."

Those analysts who subscribe to the idea of a primary aggressive drive, whether or not related to a death instinct, have attempted to come to terms with its failure to resemble the sexual drive with respect to issues of source, aim and object, which formed part of Freud's (1905) definition of a drive. Hartmann et al. (1949), Brenner (1971) and Stone (1971), among others, have struggled with this problem. The source of the sexual drive is obviously much better understood than the source of a hypothetical aggressive drive. Brenner (1971) and Gillespie (1971), on opposite sides of the controversy over the existence of a primary aggressive drive, nevertheless agree on the absence of an obvious "source" of aggressive impulses. Stone (1971) regards the musculature as the source of aggressive behavior, a stand which is vigorously contested by Gillespie, who regards the musculature as the executive organ and not the source of aggression.

With respect to this much debated linkage between the drives and biology, Anna Freud (1972) attempts to establish a bridge between theorists of different persuasions. She makes the point that Freud never implied that the life drive was the actual source of sexual urges and feelings. These were always acknowledged to be either hormonal or anatomical. "Nor need the death drive be the actual source of aggression. Clinically speaking, both have

their own material sources, known or unknown, while simultaneously being what might be called the 'representatives on earth' of
the two supra-ordinated biological forces with contrary goals, the
presence of which they presuppose. We may say equally, with
regard to 'aim,' that clinically speaking, i.e., on earth, both libido
and aggression pursue their own limited and mundane aims while
serving at the same time the vaster biological purposes of life and
death." Here Anna Freud relegates the concepts of life and death
instincts to what might be called a supra-terrestrial status. Edward
Glover had earlier (1966) used the term "metaphysical" in the
same connection.

It might be worth noting that the alleged quasi-philosophical
aim of the aggressive drive, namely, the destruction of the object,
has troubled at least two writers. Hendrick (1943) long ago felt that
the urges and impulses of a constructive nature could not realistically be subsumed among the aims of a drive that was theoretically
destructive in nature. He therefore proposed the concept of an
instinct to master, "an inborn drive to do and to learn how to do."
This concept has failed to win a place in psychoanalytic theory.
Hartmann et al. (1949) dealt with this problem by hypothesizing
that just as libido can be sublimated, so can the aggressive drive
be subjected to various degrees of neutralization, some very far
away from the destructive implications of the term "aggression."

White (1963), in the course of a thoughtful and interesting monograph, also rejected the idea that goals of mastery, curiosity and
exploratory play could be considered manifestations of a destructive aggressive drive. His position "does not . . . require a transformation of energies originally instinctual, nor does it assure a new
instinct in any ordinary sense of the word. . . .[His proposal] corresponds roughly to the idea mentioned by Freud, but never more
than casually, that the ego apparatus might have intrinsic energies
of its own and that there might be a natural satisfaction in the
exercise of ego functions" (p. 184). He labeled the energy behind
the kind of behavior to which he was referring, "effectance." This
term too has hardly met with enthusiastic acceptance by analysts.

Brenner (1971) suggested that the destructive connotations of
aggression derived actually from its Freudian association with the
death instinct. Once that association was rejected and one depended on clinical observations for the definition of aggression,
the discrepancy between aggression and constructive activity dis-
appeared.

However, there are analysts who are opposed to, or at least ambivalent about, the very idea of a separate and primary aggressive instinctual drive. Fenichel (1945) was among this group. Gillespie (1971) and Stone (1971) have most recently rejected the necessity of postulating such a drive. Waelder (1960) argued the matter out in his book and eventually but without enthusiasm conceded that "to see in essential destructiveness the manifestation of an inborn instinctual drive is probably the simplest hypothesis. . . . But the theory of a destructive drive is not the only way in which essential destructiveness could be understood" (p. 149); "If there is an inborn destructive drive. . . ." (p. 150); "This hypothesis [neutralization] is, of course, contingent upon the assumption that destructiveness is the manifestation of an instinctual drive" (p. 153). He was obviously no ardent exponent of the concept of a primary aggressive drive.

Solnit (1972) argues that rather than looking for sufficient evidence for the existence of a primary aggressive drive, we should make a decision about this hypothesis on the basis of its technical usefulness. But by this criterion it could be argued that any concept, even the death instinct, should be retained. And, in fact, Hannal Segal (in Lussier, 1972) contends that "such a concept as 'death instinct' cannot be seen as true or false but only as useful or not useful in illuminating clinical phenomena." And, of course, being a Kleinian, she concludes that there is "a great clinical usefulness in the concept of a primary self-destructive drive [her locution for the death instinct] as well as of a primary destructive drive." This criterion of usefulness can be spread out to form a broad canopy indeed.

Thus, as Lussier (1972) and Heimann and Valenstein (1972) indicate in their reports and summaries of the panels and papers on the subject of aggression at the Twenty-seventh International Psychoanalytic Congress in 1971, great differences of opinion were expressed by various speakers on this topic. And this lack of agreement exists, it might be added, more than fifty years after Freud first introduced this hypothesis.

It will be remembered that this digression was made in order to clarify and to elucidate Jacobson's stand on the universality of aggression in depression. I have demonstrated some of the disagreements and conceptual uncertainties that still becloud this concept. But this theoretical ambiguity goes beyond the issues discussed in this section. As I have noted, Jacobson has not only used the term "aggression" to refer to an instinctual drive and to behavior and feelings but also and very centrally she conceptualizes aggression as a form of psychic energy. When she refers to an "aggressively cathected self-image" found so generally in depression, she means a self-image cathected with aggressive energy. It is necessary, therefore, in order to come to grips with this use of the term, to examine the concept of psychic energy as it has been used in psychoanalytic theory.

Yet it is very important to note that neither the existence nor the clinical or theoretical importance of aggressive drives depends on the validity of the concept of psychic energy. Stated differently, aggressive motivations are extremely important in human behavior whether or not we conceive of them as being propelled by psychic energy. The question of the presence or absence of aggression in depression is a matter to be determined on clinical rather than theoretical grounds. And insofar as aggression refers to motivations or feelings or behavior, the limited role that these play has already been determined, as I have indicated, by Jacobson and others.

In Jacobson's model of depression, however, aggression has been to a large extent conceptualized as psychic energy. When Jacobson states that aggression is central in depression, what she means is that low self-esteem is caused by the cathexis of the self-representation with aggressive psychic energy. So, by definition, aggression (i.e., aggressive psychic energy, not aggressive feelings or behavior) must always be present in depression.

But must it? To depict the self-image as cathected with aggression is not synonymous with postulating the presence of aggressive feelings or motivations in depression, nor is it equivalent to explaining the cause of low self-esteem.

PSYCHIC ENERGY
[1]

In a recent panel discussion on the economic viewpoint in psychoanalysis (Calder, 1970), speaker after speaker testified to the usefulness of the economic point of view. Schur, Greenson, Loewenstein, Rubinfine, Kohut and Wexler, among others, all emphasized the importance of the concept of psychic energy. Calder did comment that less opposition to energic concepts was expressed by the speakers on the panel than he believed to be current in the psychoanalytic world in general, and on this point he was certainly correct.

There has been an accelerating degree of dissatisfaction with the concept of psychic energy in the psychoanalytic literature, no matter how vigorously the concept has been defended by its supporters.

For a proper understanding of the issues involved in the controversy over psychic energy, it is necessary for me to sketch in some of the history of this concept. The reader can be referred to Bibring (1941), Hartmann (1948) and Schur (1966), as well as to Freud's own works (e.g., 1905, 1914, 1915, 1920, 1923, 1924), for a more comprehensive review of this subject. Freud's theory of instincts—or drives, as Hartmann (1948) but not Strachey, in the Standard Edition, prefers to translate *Triebe*—is essentially a theory of motivation.

Freud (1905) considered the subject of instincts from the points of view of source, aim and object. During the time that he was primarily interested in the sexual drive, he treated the source, the sexual chemical substances, as the most important of these aspects. However, when he included the aggressive drive with the two primary drives, his focus shifted to the aim of these drives. It was more difficult to conceptualize a somatic source of aggression, although for a while the muscular apparatus was so designated.

Freud was clearest in his views of psychic energy when he referred to libido, not that he displayed no ambiguities in his consideration of sexual psychic energy. He (Freud, 1910) indicated that the sexual drive generated a "quantitative variable force," an energy, libido, which because of its special chemical origin was qualitatively distinguished from other kinds of "psychical energy" that he then believed to be at the disposal of the mental apparatus.

Libido, by becoming attached to or cathecting spheres of activity other than the love-object, was said to undergo sublimation. Thus sublimation indicated a process in which the aim of the instinctual drive was displaced from the love-object to alternative interests. In the early analytic literature—and for that matter in a very recent paper (Gross and Rubin, 1972)—sublimation implied "higher" activities such as literature and art, a view which was considered by many writers to contaminate the process with value judgments. Glover (1931), in an examination of this topic, came to the conclusion that "some qualitative change in energy may prove to be the only metapsychologically valid criterion for sublimation." Hartmann (1955), following up on this concept, redefined sublimation to involve not so much a change of aim as "a change in the mode of energy away from an instinctual toward a noninstinctual goal." Furthermore, since aggression had been included among the instinctual drives (Freud, 1920), Hartmann, as we have seen in a previous chapter, coined the term "neutralization" to designate the change of aggressive as well as libidinal energy away from an instinctual to a noninstinctual mode. "Neutralization" was used as a general term to designate this change in both drives, while "sublimation" was retained as a specific term referring to the neutralization of libido.

Neutralization was conceptualized not as an all-or-none process but as occurring in varying degrees. Freud (1923) had suggested that sublimation is mediated by the ego. Hartmann (1950) and Hartmann et al. (1949), theorizing about the process of sublimation, echoed Freud's comment and generalized it to indicate that the neutralization of both drives occurs through the mediation of the ego. How instinctual energy is transformed into different grades of neutralized energy is nowhere satisfactorily explained (see Applegarth, 1971, on this point), though concepts of displacement, reaction formation and a shift of object libido to narcissistic libido have at times been invoked to afford such an explanation. Nelson (1967) caustically comments on this issue as follows: "The healthy ego functions as a sort of decontamination plant, which neutralizes instinctual energy and utilizes the purified end product to pursue object-related goals."

Although Freud (1910) originally described libido as an energy generated by the "special chemistry" of the sexual processes, he remained inconsistent about how somatic this energy was. At times he related it to biology. At other times he regarded psychic energy as purely a theoretical construct. Despite the fact that psychic energy is often referred to in terms that imply an existential entity, the most authoritative opinion today regards it as a theoretical concept. Loewenstein, for example, in a discussion of neutralization (Arlow, 1955), pointed out that the concept of psychic energy is only a theoretical construct based on analogies with the physical world. And Rapaport (1960) noted that psychic energy was "not equated with any known kind of biochemical energy." Another element of ambiguity has been noted by Loewald (1971). He points out that there has been some confusion with respect to how instincts are conceptualized. Freud (1915) in *Instincts and Their Vicissitudes* describes an instinct as "a stimulus applied to the mind." Instinct is here regarded as a physiological factor from within the organism which operates upon the mind, but from "outside" the mind. However, in the same paper Freud refers to an instinct as "the psychic representative of the stimuli originating from within the organism and reaching the mind." Here the instinct is not the stimulus itself but the "psychical representative" of the stimulus.

Freud's inconsistency with respect to these two interpretations of instinct is widespread throughout the literature. Schur (1966) was an important advocate of the second of these meanings of instinct or drive. He regarded the instinctual drives as "mental representations of forces originating within the soma" (p. 45). And Loewald, too, endorses the view that instincts are mental or psychic representations and not the organismic stimuli that generate these mental representations.

[2]

It is necessary to go back quite far to understand Freud's inconsistent references to psychic energy. Holt has devoted several papers (1965, 1967a) to the concept of psychic energy, "a concept [that] has steadily ramified into a conceptual thicket that baffles some, impresses many, and greatly complicates the task of anyone who tries to form a clear idea of what the basic theory of psychoanalysis is" (1967a). In this same paper, following upon Bernfeld's (1944, 1951) enlightening studies of Freud's scientific education, he described how Freud attempted to outline a psychology for neurologists.

Freud was a convinced disciple of his teachers Meynert and Brücke in their Helmholtzian mechanistic revolt against the vitalism of their predecessors. Vitalism involved the introduction of some nonmaterial supra-organic vital force, life substance, entelechy or élan vital which acts as a *deus ex machina* or "ghost in the machine" (Ryle, 1949) to breathe motivation and purpose into the behavior of the organism. It was Helmholtz who launched the attempt to understand physiology in "mechanical," material terms without resorting to vitalistic devices to explain data. As Holt (1965) pointed out, although Freud (1895) was decades ahead

of his time in introducing a cybernetic self-regulating servomech-
anism into his model with at least five feedback loops, he "was too
much [his era's] prisoner to see that the informational return provided by a feedback loop could obviate any hypothetical non-
conscious process of attention; ironically he concluded that he had
failed to provide" a mechanical explanation "and committed his
first great infidelity to the anti-vitalism of his teachers; he postulated an observing ego." True, Freud used this concept in its early
meaning of "the totality of cathected neurones" (1895). But finally,
as Holt (1965) points out, he was forced to revive a basically philo-
sophical concept of the kind that was so familiar to vitalists, "in
which the ego is a prime mover, the willer and ultimate knower,
and thus a vitalistic homunculus with some degree of autonomy."

Holt has demonstrated that when Freud gave up his attempt to
devise a neurological psychology, he had to come to terms with
the issue of motivation. Struggling to escape a vitalistic teleological
framework, Freud formulated a model of human functioning
which involved energies pressing for discharge. In part, as Apfelbaum (1965) has indicated, it was designed to resolve the thorny
problem of motivation with its teleological connotations by resorting to a model of psychic energy which "offered the possibility of
accounting for psychic activity without references to purposes.
. . . Psychic energy like its parent conception in physics could have
no inherent aim or purpose. . . . Psycho-analytic explanation could
be expressed in terms of the physics of forces, i.e. the 'economics'
of psychic energy. However pure motive force must be harnessed
by containing and transmitting structures."

As we know, Freud introduced the concept of an ego apparatus,
with the functions of defense and of delaying the peremptorily
pressing energies, in the interest of adaptation to the external
world. This model did not spring full-grown from his brow but was
gradually built up and molded over a period of decades by the
exercise of observation, by conceptual leaps and by periods of
careful revision until the so-called structural hypothesis was finally
evolved. This in turn was further refined by theorists such as
Hartmann and Rapaport.

But as Holt (1967a) has demonstrated, Freud retained a nineteenth-century conception of the nervous system derived from his
medical and neurological training that was to become outdated
even in his own lifetime. The assumption of his teachers was that
the nervous system, which was believed to have no energies of its

own, was merely a passive conductor of some unknown kind of physical energy which entered the system either from the outside or from within the body itself from sexual and other sources. Twentieth-century neurophysiology, however, informs us, according to Holt, that "the nerve impulse is generated anew everywhere along the fibre, which transmits [electrical impulses] only in the sense that a train of gunpowder transmits heat—by propagating a train of energy transformations." This energy is very different, as Holt and as Peterfreund (1971) have shown, from the psychic energy that Freud postulated.

The neurophysiology that Freud had learned became incorporated into his thinking and survived the change in his theorizing when he gave up his attempt to create a psychology for neurologists in favor of formulating a "pure" psychology. But "this change had the paradoxical effect of *preserving* these [metapsychological] assumptions by hiding their original nature, and by transferring the operations of the [psychic] apparatus into a conceptual realm where they were insulated from connection by progress in neurophysiology and brain anatomy."

To confuse the matter still further, the psychic energy that drives the mental apparatus is, depending on the context, referred to, as we have seen, sometimes as a physical quantity traveling along the fibers of a somatic nervous system and sometimes as a nonneurophysiological, purely psychological concept.

Holt (1967a) contends that "psychic energy is a vitalistic concept in the sense of being similar to and influenced by vital force, and being to a large extent functionally equivalent to it." Both he and Peterfreund (1971) emphasize the contrasts between psychic energy and the energy known to science. They and other critics point out that unlike the energy of science, and like vitalistic forces, psychic energy is directional, i.e., it is said to exist in both sexual and aggressive forms with, respectively, sexual and destructive aims, and that it is contained within a mechanistic structure called "the psychic apparatus" within which it operates.

These qualities of psychic energy are very different from the energy of science. Heat, light, sound and electricity are not qualitatively different forms of energy. Energy is transformed from heat to light or to chemical or electrical energy by various forms of mechanical or physical operations and in precisely quantifiable ways.

However, it can be—and has been—argued that everyone

knows this, that psychic energy is but a construct, a metaphor, and a useful one at that. As we have seen, the panelists (Calder, 1970) of several years ago argued for the usefulness of this concept. In a previous section we have noted that Hartmann et al. (1946), while acknowledging that some danger exists in the use of metaphor in science, argued that this danger only exists if and when "metaphor infringes upon meaning." They spoke up vigorously for the richness of metaphor, pointing to the impoverishment of language when metaphor is too vigorously avoided. They referred to Freud and to the French psychiatrists of the nineteenth century as masters of the vividness of metaphoric language, although they agreed that "metaphors should not obscure the nature of the concepts and their functions in psychoanalysis as a science." Their implication is that, as used by sophisticated theorists, this does not happen.

Nash (1963), too, as we saw, maintains that metaphor vivifies discussion and that it enables the theorist to arouse and maintain interest. He provides very interesting examples of the contributions that metaphors can make in the generation, elaboration and analysis of theory. As he persuasively puts it: "Metaphor clearly has its advantages and its hazards. Does one forego adventure for the risks?" But he concedes that one can compound error by proceeding from one inappropriate or obscure metaphor to another. Conclusions may be reached that are erroneous not only in degree but in kind.

Thus the stage is set for a review of the debate that has been in progress on the economic point of view and on the concept of psychic energy.

[3]

Let us first examine the issue of quantitative concepts in psychoanalysis. It seems quite obvious that psychic activity and behavior actually do have quantitative aspects. One person may try "harder," think "more deeply" or work "more vigorously" than another. Some people are "more passionate," "more virile" or "more sensuous" than others. Some patients are "more" phobic, compulsive, anxious or depressed than other patients. Others become "less" repressed or constricted than they used to be. One person's ego is spoken of as "stronger" or "weaker" than another's.

More consistent with current metapsychology, certain ego functions are said to be "more" or "less" strong, weak, impaired or
regressed than others.

However, as Kubie and Lewin (1936) pointed out, "when it is
observed that one patient has a greater 'drive' towards a certain
activity than another, it would be a most naïve explanation of this
fact to deduce that the difference in the 'drive' must depend solely
upon differences in the amounts of specific energy invested in this
direction. Such an explanation would be fallacious. . . ." Eleven
years later Kubie (1947) was arguing against the practice of explaining variations in behavior by invoking quantitative variables.
He saw this as a serious but seductive fallacy. He added: "When
in doubt one can always say that some component of human psychology is bigger or smaller, stronger or weaker, more intense or
less intense, more or less highly charged with 'energy' or with
degraded energy and by these words delude ourselves into believing that we have explained a phenomenon which we have merely
described in metaphors."

Kubie acknowledged that quantitative variables hold some special fascination for analysts, a fascination which he attributed to
the emotional conviction that a science has not reached maturity
"until it can count." He felt that the habitual use of quantitative
terms gave them an illusory reality. "Ideas and terminologies become a part of the very air we breathe, something whose truth and
presence we accept without question as we become used to them
through frequent repetition."

These initial attacks on the use of quantitative concepts in psychoanalysis were soon followed by an accelerating range of criticism against the economic point of view in analytic theory. Kardiner et al. (1954), outside the mainstream of orthodox analysis,
were quite categorical: "The energic hypothesis is tautological and
provides no new knowledge. . . . For example, suppose we observe
an infant's relation to its mother. We can say from this clinical
observation: The infant is intensely interested in the mother who
is the source of all his gratifications. . . . Suppose now we make use
of the energic hypothesis and say: The infant intensely cathects
the mother with libidinal energy. This statement does not add
anything to our knowledge about the relationship between the
mother and the child. We have merely restated the original observation in hypothetical energic terms. Hence the tautology. . . . If
the observer infers that the interest in the mother is 'intense' he

will say the cathexis is 'intense'; if he infers the interest is 'weak,' he will say the cathexis is 'weak.' Here, again, the notion of any quantity of energy is purely tautological."

In 1960, even Rapaport, reflecting on the survival value of economic concepts such as cathexis, binding and neutralization, felt that it was "uncertain whether they will survive in their present form" (p. 128).

In a report on a 1962 panel on psychic energy (Modell, 1963), Holt was quoted as asserting that "a basic objection to concepts such as psychic energy is that they are tautological and thus ultimately useless," although he conceded that "we obviously will do best to keep patching together the old theory and getting what mileage we can out of it until we can trade it in on a new model." Hardly an enthusiastic endorsement and hardly a banner under which to fight vigorously for the universality of aggressive energy in depression.

In this panel, Kubie, that old antagonist of quantitative explanations in psychoanalysis, protested that he did not reject the concept of psychic energy just because it could not be measured. "He objected to the use of a metaphor as though it were evidence or had explanatory significance."

On this occasion, Waelder expressed himself as "ambivalent about the concept of psychic energy." He objected to its vagueness. He also seriously objected to the concept of the transformation of energy from one form to another. That psychic energy could not be measured, he considered an even more fundamental objection. His ambivalence was further indicated by comments such as "he was not opposed to its use but he was not enthusiastic about it," and "he had planned to warn against the concept of psychic energy but found himself entering into its defense."

On the other side of this debate, Ostow, Schur, Beres and others defended the clinical usefulness of this concept. They deprecated the risk of confusing an analogy with an explanation and insisted that psychic activity did have quantitative aspects even if they could not be measured.

In rebuttal Apfelbaum (1965) published a paper, the title of which, *Ego Psychology, Psychic Energy and the Hazards of Quantitative Explanations in Psycho-Analytic Theory,* clearly conveys its tone. Referring to the calculated risk of conceptual error in the use of metaphors and models, he declared that "this risk becomes a danger because the quantitative model can subtly shed its hypothetical status" and begin to assume almost physiological implications.

Beres (1965) added his voice to the chorus of concern over the danger of metaphoric language being used uncritically as explanations: "We have become accustomed in psycho-analytic theorizing to use certain words and phrases which on closer examination prove to be tautological, analogical or pseudo-explanatory." He, too, warned against the false sense of understanding that was engendered when metaphor was used concretely as an explanatory device.

The attack on the dangers of metaphoric language in general and on the concept of psychic energy in particular continued to accelerate. In the panel referred to above (Modell, 1962), Holt had claimed some clinical usefulness for this concept. Several years later (1965) he felt that working with the concept of psychic energy was no longer completely defensible. By then he was questioning the use of economic concepts involving, as they did, "the successive postulation of a bewildering variety of types and modes of psychic energy (e.g., bound, fused, neutralized, aim-inhibited, etc.)." Other writers were to compare this "bewildering" piling-up of hypothesis upon hypothesis to the practice of the pre-Copernican astronomers who added epicycle to epicycle in a vain effort to make their data conform to their cherished Ptolemaic model.

Holt in his 1967 paper refers to his 1962 statement about the clinical usefulness of the concept of psychic energy and explicitly notes that he has "become more fully aware of the numerous ways in which emphasis on economic considerations may be clinically deleterious. . . . It would be difficult to strike a balance and to say whether the economic point of view has been more helpful clinically or more misleading." However, apart from whatever clinical usefulness it may have, Holt feels that scientifically it is an anachronism. "The burden of proof is on anyone who defends psychic energy to show that it can be measured in a useful way, so that it is estimated independently of the very phenomena it is to explain."

Waelder, too, who had been ambivalent about the concept of psychic energy in 1962, was expressing himself more decisively four years later (1966): "There must be many so-called 'orthodox' analysts in whose writings one will search for the term in vain. I am among them." He went on even more explicitly: "We cannot measure it, we have no reliable criteria to estimate it, and we do not know the factors that would determine its total amount. Above all, as there is no evidence for it beyond the very phenomena which necessitated its invention, its explanatory value is questionable. . . . It is . . . tautological." He referred to it as a concept "peripheral" to the body of psychoanalytic propositions, and, noting that Freud (1924)* had once even listed the division of the mind into the ego and the id as among psychoanalytic "nonessential propositions," exclaimed, "How much more this would apply to the concept of psychic energy."

The mounting criticism of psychic energy as a viable concept continued. Schafer (1968), in a closely reasoned volume on the metapsychology of internalization, scrutinizes the concept of psychic energy (Chapter 3). He disagrees with the view that psychic energy can be qualitative, i.e., libidinal, aggressive or neutralized. He consequently regards the concept of the libidinal or aggressive cathexis of representations as unnecessary and misleading. He retains the words "cathexis" and "cathected" but applies them to motives by which he means "cathected aims, which is to say, aims that are held more or less strongly by a person" (p. 44). In other words, the term "cathexis" retains for him a quantitative but not a qualitative connotation. Despite this seeming interest in the quantitative aspect of psychoanalysis, Schafer feels that the economic point of view can be dispensed with and adequately replaced by motivational, dynamic language.

Bowlby (1969, Chapter 1), too, believes that the psychic energy model can be discarded without affecting the concepts that are truly central to psychoanalysis. He emphasizes that this model originated outside psychoanalysis and that Freud introduced it in order to conform to what he considered to be the best scientific thinking of his time.

Grossman and Simon's (1969) paper on anthropomorphism, which is actually a sustained and thoughtful polemic on the dangers of metaphoric language in psychoanalysis, also contains many penetrating criticisms of the economic theory and of the language of psychic energy.

A year later, Schafer (1970) continues his attack against "this primary, mobile, inherently vectorial, peremptory, dischargeable, bindable, transformable and fusible energy." In this sustained appreciation of the strengths and weaknesses of Hartmann's enor-

*In a letter to Otto Rank. See Taft (1958).

mously influential contribution to psychoanalysis, Schafer argues that nowhere did Hartmann present and weigh the arguments pro and con the concept of psychic energy. "That is, he accepted Freud's basic assumption concerning instinctual drive energy uncritically and conservatively while so freely revising and reformulating other basic assumptions of Freud's." It is as if without psychic energy there can be no recognition of the central roles of sexuality and aggression in human life and thus no possibility of psychoanalytic explanation. He states again that "a psychic energy with qualitative aspects is not needed." He argues that energic statements are tautological. "Economic propositions about specific events invariably *follow* their clinical analysis, and so amount to no more than a restatement of the discovery."

Rosenblatt and Thickstun (1970), in a paper that has attracted an impressive amount of attention, subject the concept of psychic energy to a penetrating critique. They note that there has been increasing dissatisfaction with this concept in psychoanalytic circles and that the tempo of the debate over this issue has been increasing. They repeat the familiar criticisms. They point out that the metaphoric constructs have subtly become conceptualized as objective phenomena and are therefore "linguistic traps." They argue that psychic energy is used as an explanatory device in a tautological fashion offering actually only pseudo-explanations, and that this provides a false sense of closure blinding us to the need for more meaningful solutions. They, too, "see the concept of energy, a directionless quantity, being imbued with implicit aims and differing qualities, as in libidinal energy, aggressive energy, desexualized energy, etc. . . . quite different from the use in the physical sciences of the terms 'chemical energy,' 'thermal energy,' 'nuclear energy,' etc." which are not intended to imply different qualities of energy. They deny that, as has been sometimes maintained, an incomplete or defective theory is better than none. They quote Cassirer (1961) to buttress their case: "It is better to be without knowledge on some point than to be blind to a problem because we have contented ourselves with an apparent solution." They assert quite unequivocally that the theory of psychic energy should be abandoned.

Peterfreund (1971) broadens the semantic argument somewhat by discussing the different conceptual languages that are used by analysts. He analyzes one paragraph taken from Jacobson's book *The Self and the Object World* (1964, pp. 14–15) and demonstrates how she uses three languages interchangeably: "the language of persons (tension and self); the language of a hydrodynamic psychic apparatus (cathexis, the ego, psychic energy, fusion, and neutralization); and the language of biology and physiology (physiological energy, physiological channels and biological prepatterns). Indeed all these languages appear in the brief phrase, 'undifferentiated psychophysiological energy within the primal, structurally also undifferentiated self.'" He maintains that she uses three languages as if they were one (p. 62).

He suggests a striking and amusing analogy from the field of medicine. "Imagine a traumatic event with bleeding, and the patient experiencing a feeling of horror at the sight of the blood. Imagine if one were to explain these phenomena as follows: In this traumatic event the blood was pumped by beating PQRST waves, and electrical impulses in the nervous system transmitted the feeling of horror to the self" (p. 63). He regards the confusion of conceptual languages in this example as quite analogous to Jacobson's failure to separate out quite different conceptual frames of reference.

In another but somewhat more tolerant critique of the theory of psychic energy, Applegarth (1971) subjects this concept to most of the now familiar criticisms. In considering the subject of neutralization, she asks, "Is perhaps a descriptive word being used as an inquiry-stopping explanation, much as the élan vital used to be in biology? I think this is the case." She reverts to this "inquiry-stopping" theme again and again. For example, in referring to the language of psychic energy (fusion, binding, etc.), she comments in her rather understated fashion, "Their primary danger, besides the fact that they are probably incorrect, is that they appear to explain the phenomena and therefore stop inquiry." She, in agreement with Holt, Rosenblatt and Thickstun, Peterfreund and others, argues that the hypothesis of libidinal, aggressive, neutralized, fused and bound energies is just not compatible with present-day neurophysiological knowledge. She presents a very persuasive case "for not casting our theory in terms which are incompatible with neurophysiology, as we must eventually achieve some closure with it."

Schafer (1972) returns to the attack more succinctly but more assertively: "It might be assumed—correctly!—that I am dispensing with the hypothesis of an instinctual drive of aggression whose psychic energy (also called 'aggression') is accumulated and discharged in anger (among other responses). I, along with many others . . . have advanced at some length reasons for discarding 'psychic energy' as a fundamental hypothesis in psychoanalytic theory. . . ."

There is still another front along which the concept of psychic energy is subject to criticism. Although others have referred to this, Apfelbaum (1965) is perhaps the most explicit exponent of this line of attack. Like Holt, he understands the economic view in psychoanalysis to have developed as an attempt to eschew a purposive psychology which would have been experienced as too dangerously close to vitalistic thinking. On the clinical level psychoanalysis concerns itself with motives, wishes and conflicts. However, he views Freud as attempting to frame psychoanalytic theory in a purer, more aseptic physicalist language in which explanations are based on the effect of physical forces on material particles. This language was, of course, the language of the economic point of view. Explanations were based on the fate of energic forces pressing for discharge, thus partially avoiding the necessity of references to purposes. Psychic energy, like the energy of physics, could be thought of as having no inherent purposes. "Psychic conflict and repression are represented as the collision of 'blind' somatic impulses with quasi-organic thresholds, barriers and transmission structures." In the effort to exclude the concept of purpose, "the subjective world of intention and meaning was . . . shut out except where reduced to highly restricted formulations based on physical forces and material structures."

However, these forces had to be harnessed in containing and transmitting structures. Much of Hartmann's (1964) and Rapaport's (1967) work was devoted to a consideration of the system of confining, guiding and transmitting apparatuses, "systems of channels and valves with intrinsic stimulus and response thresholds," dams and dikes, hierarchic levels of control and discharge, which have the sound and the feel of engineering devices far removed from the clinical data with which psychoanalysis deals.

Loewald (1971) expresses similar complaints about the use of energic terminology in place of the language of purpose. Speaking about the evolution of the kinds of instinctual theory in which psychic life is explained in terms of confluent, fused or defused instinctual forces, he appears to cry out: "There seems to be no room for *personal* motivation. Yet I have claimed that personal motivation is the fundamental assumption of psychoanalysis. We now seem to see that, on the contrary, psychoanalytic psychology postulates instinctual, unconscious impersonal forces as the motives of our psychic life. Where is the person? Where is the ego or self that would be the source and the mainstay of personal motivation?" He does not believe that the problem of motivation is dealt with by hypotheses making use of so-called energy concepts which are, in his view, essentially nonpsychic, i.e., nonmotivational. His is a sustained appeal to return from the preoccupation with biological or pseudobiological issues back to the proper concern of psychoanalysis, personal motivation.

[4]

Jacobson (1953), as we have seen, considers that the loss of self-esteem represents "the central psychological problem in depression"; furthermore, she views lowered self-esteem as being due to the aggressive cathexis of the self-image, a view which then causes her to see aggression as of central importance in depression.

In this section I wish to move away from my general consideration of psychic energy in order to examine the clinical application of energic principles to problems of self-esteem. In their continuing effort to index their clinical material under a variety of psychoanalytic headings, Sandler and his colleagues at the Hampstead Clinic in London have become increasingly aware of the limitations of these headings and of the complexity of clinical phenomena. They consequently have been publishing a series of papers concerned with the progressive refinement of psychoanalytic concepts in their application to clinical material. In their consideration of the concept of psychic energy, they provide an outstanding example of an evolving attitude toward the adequacy of this concept and toward the phenomenon of self-esteem.

In an early paper (Sandler and Rosenblatt, 1962), they make use of these concepts in the traditional manner. They define primary narcissism as "the libidinal cathexis of the self-representation as it is formed from an initially undifferentiated sensory matrix." They go on, in the classic tradition, to explain that part of this libidinal cathexis of the self-representation becomes transferred to the object-representation, as libidinal object cathexis. This, of course, means that the original supply of libidinal cathexis, the primary narcissism, becomes differentiated or divided into two compartments. One division consists of the libidinal cathexis of the object-representation (object cathexis). The other portion consists of the remaining libidinal cathexis that still invests the self-representations. Subscribing as they did at this time to the traditional closed energic model, they go on to postulate that the libidinal cathexis that later becomes withdrawn from the object-representation and again cathects the self-representations corresponds to what is referred to as secondary narcissism. A similar process is understood to occur with aggressive energy. This conceptualization is sometimes concretely referred to as the pseudopod model in which part of the original pool or quantity of primary narcissistic libido becomes extruded to attach itself to an object-representation and then later is retracted back into the original reservoir.

Joffe and Sandler (1967), in their consideration of the disorders of narcissism, illustrate the difficulties that arise when they apply the concept of libido distribution to their clinical material. For example, insecure, dependent children might be expected to have low levels of narcissistic cathexis of their self-representation since they attach themselves so closely to their objects. Freud (1914), with his view of a fixed quantity of libido, had felt that there was an antithesis between libidinal cathexis of the self and object libido. "The more the one is employed, the more the other becomes depleted." In other words, loving another depletes one's self-esteem and being loved restores it. However, these needy children tend to demonstrate great self and bodily preoccupation and may indulge in compensatory heroic fantasies, all of which can be formally described as involving a high level of narcissistic cathexis. Indeed, these children may have the characteristics of so-called "narcissistic characters." Moreover, the high level of object cathexis that these children display may turn out to be a mere dependence on others for admiration, support and praise.

Conversely, as Joffe and Sandler point out, the self-confident, secure children who should, according to the theory, have little libido to spare for objects, are often the very children who are capable of stable, mature, caring, considerate relationships with their love-objects and who have to be assessed as having high levels of object cathexis.

Observations such as these made it obvious to them that the clinical material subsumed under the category of narcissistic disorders displayed qualities which would simply not be "adequately encompassed by drive-energic formulations." In testing the limits of such formulations in the study of narcissistic disorders, they try to determine whether a distinction between primary and secondary narcissistic cathexes of the self-representations may be of value, and whether one can usefully apply such formulations to account for different aspects of the self-representation, parceling out the quantities of libidinal and aggressive cathexis to various components of a person's actual and ideal self- and object-representations. They discover that they find themselves "in a position of such complexity in regard to clinical assessment that it would take a mathematician to disentangle us. And even with all this refinement, we cannot be at all certain that we have encompassed more than a small part of the relevant aspects of our clinical material in an adequate theoretical fashion."

They contend that it is quite obvious that concepts "auxiliary to those of energy distribution" must be called upon to account for the state of an individual's narcissism in a meaningful way. They find that when they speak of love or hate of the self or of an object in terms of psychic energy, they are "certainly in danger of obscuring and blunting both our clinical and theoretical formulations." They prefer the concept of an affective cathexis of a representation in which affective qualities become linked with aspects of both self- and object-representations. This is reminiscent of a formulation by Kaywin (1960), who advocated the use of concepts involving "positive and negative affect representations" to understand the clinical phenomena of narcissism and masochism rather than postulating differentiated libidinal and aggressive energy in the traditional way.

Sandler and Joffe (1969) expressed themselves even more strongly and explicitly in a footnote: ". . . the concept of narcissism as the 'libidinal cathexis of the ego' or even as the 'libidinal cathexis of the self- or the self-representation' was untenable from the point of view of a psychoanalytic psychology, as was the concept of a fixed quantity of libido distributed between self and object [or self- and object-representations]." Pulver (1970), too, in a thoughtful critique of narcissism, concluded that he "would resist the temptation to think of narcissism as simply the libidinal investment of the self." And, of course, what these authors say about libido also reflects their view of aggressive energy.

[5]

In summary, then, some writers have agreed that the concept of psychic energy is vulnerable to criticism because of its vitalistic character; some, because of the use that is made of it for tautological pseudo-explanations that tend to block off further inquiry by seeming to provide an explanation. There are others (Rubinstein, 1965, 1967, and Peterfreund, 1971) who reject the concept of psychic energy because it tends to set up a body-mind dichotomy by conceptually separating the mind from the body and because of its absolute incompatibility with present-day neurophysiology. And still others have criticized the concept because it lends itself to a kind of linguistic confusion to which even sophisticated theorists who prize conceptual clarity fall victim.

An interesting example of this last-mentioned semantic danger is provided by Engel (1971) in a review of Bowlby's views on psychic energy. Engel insists that "there can be no doubt that energy terms are indispensable to understand 'spontaneous' activity and the peremptoriness of behavior." Elsewhere in the same paper he notes that " 'psychic' merely identifies the form" which the energy assumes just as convention permits us to speak of energy as "electrical" or "mechanical." A rebuttal to this argument can be found in another discussion of psychic energy by Peterfreund (1971), who speculates on how behavior could be understood "if physiological and psychic energies were equatable, interchangeable or in any demonstrable way connected or related. . . ." He comments that "unfortunately, these concepts cannot be equated, and no connection or relationship between them has ever been found. The similarity of names does not justify an equation. Gravitational attraction and sexual attraction, for example, are in no way equitable. Nature does not play games with words" (pp. 67–68).

It is of interest that in an addendum to the same previously mentioned paper, Engel notes that he had, subsequent to submitting his review for publication, read Rosenblatt and Thickstun's (1970) criticism of psychic energy. He qualifies his own previous comments by stating: "I agree with Rosenblatt and Thickstun that attempts by psychoanalysts to apply energy concepts borrowed from outmoded models have failed, and indeed I make little use of them in my own thinking other than as convenient ways of classifying certain categories of psychic phenomena."

We see that there has developed an increasing drumbeat of criticism of the concept of psychic energy in recent years. And the critics are not foes of analysis. With hardly an exception the criticisms that have been reviewed in this chapter have been expressed by writers whose publications have found hospitality within the covers of the official journals of the American or the International Psychoanalytic Associations or in the volumes of the *Psychoanalytic Study of the Child,* which has practically the same status in psychoanalytic scholarship. Occasionally, criticisms have been quoted by authors (e.g., Rubinstein and Peterfreund) whose works have not appeared in these publications. But even their contributions have appeared in volumes or in series (such as *Psychological Issues*) entirely edited by distinguished analysts.

Obviously, there is no consensus among psychoanalysts about this rejection of psychic energy as a viable concept. But the literature is, at the time of writing, void of any comprehensive reasoned rebuttal of these criticisms. The defenders of the concept freely acknowledge that it is a theoretical construct, and that, as such, it bears no resemblance to biological or physical energy. They do, however, deny the vitalistic qualities of which it is accused and insist on its clinical usefulness.

It would seem that although this concept may indeed have some clinical usefulness, the drawbacks inherent in the concept far outweigh any usefulness it may have. The very name of this concept, "energy," invites endless comparisons and confusions with physical energy. As we have seen, some writers insist that it is entirely a psychological construct, whereas others (e.g., Hartmann, 1950; 1964, p. 130) speak of eventual compatibility with neurophysiology just as Freud in fact did so often in referring to his theoretical concepts (e.g., 1914, p. 78). The name and nature of this concept are thus misleading and breed scientific mischief and seemingly interminable debates about its value and significance.

In the light of the increasing suspicion or outright dismissal of the concept of psychic energy, what are we to think of Jacobson's (1953) comment about the central importance in depression of aggression and its vicissitudes? That Freud's insights into certain melancholics' self-directed hostile verbalizations were valid has long since been acknowledged. But, as he hastened to note, he claimed no universal validity for his observations. Jacobson (1957; 1971, p. 95) herself emphasized that "depressed states do not always develop from attempts to resolve ambivalence conflicts by a veering away of aggression from the love-object [the object world] to the self." Nor does she think of what might be referred to as aggressive tension between the superego and the self-image as the central factor in depression. She (1971, p. 171) states quite explicitly, "I realized as early as 1943 that the emphasis laid upon the guilt problem as the core of the conflict did not do justice to all the cases." As has been mentioned previously, what Jacobson seems to mean is that low self-esteem is central in depression, and since low self-esteem is caused by an aggressive cathexis of the self-representation, then, by definition, aggression must always be present in depression.

But must it? To depict the self-image as cathected with aggressive energy is not equivalent to explaining the cause of low self-esteem. It is just another way of saying that self-esteem is low. As so many critics of the concept of psychic energy have emphasized, it is tautological, not explanatory. It says the same thing in different language. And it exquisitely represents the chief danger that so many have spoken of in using energic terminology. Its metaphoric quality soon becomes forgotten and it assumes existential properties in the minds of its users. It misleads the writer into thinking he has understood the cause of a phenomenon and therefore produces premature closure.

The cause of low self-esteem has to do not with the vicissitudes of psychic energy, but, as Jacobson has so discerningly observed, with a number of important variables including early deprivation, deficiencies in the individual's actual talents or abilities and his expectation of himself, realistic or unrealistic, both in the moral sphere and in the sphere of his effectiveness. Later on, we will also consider some pharmacological and biochemical variables that appear to be correlated with low self-esteem and depressive illness. But among all these variables we should not include the vicissitudes of aggressive energy.

This long detour into the foggy swampland of ambiguities that envelop the concept of psychic energy, merely to take the measure of Jacobson's assertion of the centrality of aggression in depression, may appear to be disproportionate and excessive. But aggression in one form or another has had a long association with melancholia in psychoanalytic theory. For the most part this has been an uncritical association, although the theorists reviewed in this book have successively refined the theory. The one area which had not been clarified is the association between aggressive energy (as distinguished from aggressive behavior, feelings or statements) and depressive illness. Bibring, as we have seen, dismissed aggression as secondary to or as a "complication" of the helplessness and low self-esteem that he observed in depression. But Jacobson, who contributed so much to the theory of depression and whose conceptions so clarified the determinants of self-esteem, seems to have remained entangled in an increasingly anachronistic conceptual framework.

As has been noted several times, various authors have defended metaphoric language as a harmless way to enrich and vivify arid scientific discourse. But, as has been demonstrated over and over again in this chapter, the metaphors become slippery linguistic devices subtly and gradually assuming existential solidity in the minds of their users. They become phenomenological entities with real qualities. Functions are assigned to them and debates rage around them. Theoreticians and clinicians take up positions with respect to them. Clinical entities are defined and explained by these metaphors, and patients are treated with techniques derived from them. Because of all this, I have felt it to be imperative to conduct the reader on this long complex detour through the murky but passionately argued metapsychological debates on psychic energy with the ultimate aim of understanding its relevance in theories about depressive illness.

CONCLUSION

In this chapter I have subjected the concepts of the ego, the superego, the ego ideal, the instinctual drives, aggression and psychic energy to a searching examination. I have done so not merely for the sake of indulging in an analytic exercise. The subject of this book is the psychoanalytic understanding of depression. This understanding has broadened and deepened in step with the advances in the general body of analytic theory.

One of the central themes of psychoanalytic theoretical writing over the past fifteen years has been a critical evaluation of precisely the topics reviewed in this chapter. This ongoing critique has engaged the attention of some of the best and most creative minds in the psychoanalytic world. And this concern with conceptual clarity has been proceeding at an accelerating pace.

In the first edition of this volume I had occasion to comment on the nonpolemic nature of the psychoanalytic writing of that period. I was, of course, disregarding the controversy about Kleinian theories that had so preoccupied the English analysts as well as a few American ones (e.g., Bibring and Zetzel). Be that as it may, this comment certainly does not apply to the years between 1959 and 1974. The open debates and polemics that have filled the literature and that are in part reflected in this chapter have had the inevitable effect of enlivening psychoanalytic intellectual life. It is important that it has not led to a growth of new schools. There is no duplication of the years of Adler, Jung, Rank, Horney and Sullivan's dissents and heresies. This debate is taking place well within the mainstream of psychoanalytic thought. This continuing examination of analytic theories, in contradistinction to many earlier revisions, is taking place within the pages of official and representative psychoanalytic publications.

As others did with earlier psychoanalytic developments, such as the structural theory, I have attempted to apply the new insights of the last fifteen years to the analytic concepts of depression. Up to the time of writing, psychoanalytic concepts of depression have not been reevaluated from this perspective. As is inevitable in a period of criticism and review, this has involved subjecting psychoanalytic concepts of depression to a detailed examination under a conceptual microscope. In practice, this has meant a careful study of some of the most sophisticated and most quoted of the psychoanalytic theories about depression, those of Bibring and of Jacobson, in the light of the critical perspective of the last decade and a half. All this was done with the aim of searching beneath and beyond the verbal surface of Bibring and Jacobson's formulations in order to grasp their underlying meaning. As has been repeatedly argued by the many analytic critics cited in this chapter, many of the theoretical constructs underlying Bibring and Jacobson's formulations appear to be basically metaphoric and analogic in quality. As I have indicated, these constructs have tended imperceptibly to become reified.

However, it is a testimony to the remarkable perceptiveness of these authors that their clinical contributions, encrusted though they are with anachronistic and often anthropomorphic language, have remained as valuable as when they first wrote them. These writers have thrown open, by virtue of their clinical acumen, conceptual windows through which we can grasp a clearer and sharper vision of the dynamics of depression.

Chapter VIII

TREATMENT

DESPITE THE ORIGINAL psychoanalytic pessimism about the treatment of the so-called "narcissistic neuroses," one finds in the early literature a recurring cautious advocacy of analysis for patients with manic-depressive psychosis. Abraham (1911) perhaps set the tone with his rather determined optimism. He declared that psychoanalysis was "the only rational therapy to apply to the manic-depressive psychosis." Of the six patients in his series, two had already completed their analyses. One of these analyses had taken what seems now to have been the unusually short period of six months. Abraham acknowledged that "it is usually extraordinarily difficult to establish a transference in these patients who have turned away from all the world in their depression" and he advised that treatment should be begun during the free intervals between their attacks because he did not feel that analysis could be carried on with severely inhibited depressed patients.

Other papers on the analyses of manic-depressives began to appear as early as 1914. In that year Clark reported the successful treatment of two cases of "periodic mental depression." Contrary to the views generally held at that time on the treatment of such patients, Clark observed that "the transference occurs rapidly and is extraordinarily strong." In a later communication (1919) he considered, like Abraham, that severe depressives were not analyzable, but by 1923 he was able to add ten more successful cases to his series. All of these patients had had serious depressive illnesses and none of them had relapsed up to the time of his report. He felt that the periods when the patient was entering into or emerging from a depression were the most propitious times to start treatment.

Barkas (1925) also disagreed with current analytic opinion on the subject of the transference in the treatment of psychotic patients: "It has been said that the fundamental difficulty in the treatment of the psychoses lies in the difficulty of establishing a transference relationship; no one who has worked in a mental hospital can uphold this statement. Transference, both positive and negative, occurs violently towards the persons of the environment and is used intuitively by the staff of any asylum, and patients of all types respond to some extent."

By 1924, Abraham had come to feel that, in addition to relieving symptoms, the treatment of the manic-depressive should safeguard the patient from further attacks of illness. Ideally, the treatment should do away with his regressive libidinal impulses and should "effect a progression of his libido until he reaches the stage of genital organization and complete object-love." Abraham was able to report that one of his patients had become able to enter into normal object-relationships and had ceased to regard himself as a monstrosity, which he had previously done even in his free periods. Two of his patients, in situations where they would previously have withdrawn into melancholia, had developed instead transitory phobic, obsessional or hysteric symptoms. Abraham regarded it as highly noteworthy that these patients had ascended from a melancholic to a hysteric level.

There followed in the next decade or so a series of reports (e.g., Feigenbaum, 1926; Peck, 1939) which confirmed many of the observations of Abraham, Freud and Rado with regard to treatment. As was characteristic of that period in the history of psychoanalysis, the main focus of treatment was on the patient's id. Treatment consisted mainly of making the unconscious conscious, i.e., of making the patient aware of his repressed impulses.

However, in 1933, Reich called attention to one type of resistance to analytic treatment which he labeled "character resistance." By this term he meant a kind of resistance which was deeply embedded in the personality structure of the patient and which was indeed characteristic of that patient. There were presumed to be as many types of character resistance as there were types of character structure. This resistance could, for example, take the form of compliance or rigidity or aggressiveness. Reich felt that an analysis could not be carried on successfully until these resistances had been exposed and rendered inoperative. He described the analysis of character resistance as taking place systematically through the layers of its historical development, a process which he termed "character analysis."

Under the influence of Reich's work, Gero in 1936 made the next major contribution to the treatment of depression. He considered that the depressive's infantile demands for love remain unfulfilled because the normal adult method of gratifying these infantile wishes for warmth and tenderness, namely, the genital love-relationship, remains barred to these patients. He felt that this method of experiencing and acquiring love remains closed to them because of the anxieties and guilt associated with this libidinal phase. He believed that these patients, therefore, "long for something unattainable, being grown up, they want to be loved like children." Gero considered that the fundamental analytic task in their treatment was the mastery of the genital anxieties which "press the libido back into the pregenital positions" and which cause the patients to long for immoderate infantile satisfactions which they cannot obtain.

In the treatment of such patients, Gero stressed the importance of character analysis, i.e., the discovery and loosening of the specific characterological defenses that these patients employ. After these defenses against the underlying intense infantile cravings have weakened, the patient becomes aware of and experiences his deeply repressed oral wishes. Gero emphasized that it was not enough for the analyst to call attention to these unconscious wishes. He must bring it about that the patient actually experiences these cravings, an experience that is always, according to Gero, "accompanied by the appearance of bodily sensations, by violent affects and by great anxiety."

The solution of the oral fixation now becomes possible. Gero observed that "experiencing the oral wishes means at the same time becoming conscious of the object towards which these wishes are directed. . . . The solution of the oral fixation is attained less by the adult neurotic becoming conscious of his infantile wishes, and being thus able to resign these wishes which he now recognizes as infantile, than by his consciousness that he desires the breast—that is to say—the mother; and having become aware of this, the infantile wish to nestle close to the mother, the longing for the warm caressing body of the mother arouse also those dark and ardent wishes of a later time of childhood when he fell passionately in love with his mother. Consciousness of oral wishes turns into genital excitement. That is why the actual experiencing of oral wishes in analysis brings with it genital sensations. The solution of the oral fixations is therefore attained if one succeeds in making the patient experience the repressed oral impulses, for this experience does not stop at the oral aims, but activates the genital object-relation of the Oedipus-situation."

The next important technical problem in the analysis of depressives, according to Gero, is the bringing of the aggression into consciousness. It is again not sufficient simply to interpret the aggression. It is necessary to loosen the patient's defenses so that he can consciously experience his rage and hostility in the transference situation. It is finally necessary for this aggression to be worked out through its many layers and fixation points until the "aggressive impulses originating from the central conflict of the Oedipus situation" are made conscious and the genital anxieties and guilt mastered so that "the capacity of experiencing genital life and object-relations to the full, and without ambivalence, is re-established."

In 1945 Fenichel summarized the current views on the therapeutic analysis of manic-depressive conditions. He cited three special types of difficulties which must be overcome in the treatment of these patients. The first was the oral fixation, "the remoteness of crucial infantile experiences which the analysis must uncover." The second was the looseness and ambivalence of the transference. And the third was the inaccessibility of the severely depressed patient. He therefore, like Abraham (1924), recommended the free interval as the period of choice for treatment but drew attention to the observation which had also been made by Abraham and other workers that even inaccessible patients who do not appear to be in contact with the world are grateful and may sometimes derive benefit from a patient listener. Fenichel's tempered optimism about the treatment of manic-depressives is revealed in his remark that "even if the analysis fails, the patient is temporarily relieved through the opportunity of unburdening himself by talking." He was much more sanguine about the treatment of neurotic depressives. He felt that they needed no special techniques and presented no problems not found in other neurotic conditions.

Somewhat at variance with this view is Lorand's (1946) report of his experience with a case of neurotic depression in which he had found it necessary to deviate considerably from standard analytic technique, at least in the early states of treatment. For example, he had found it advisable to prescribe medications and to change appointments "according to [the patient's] inconsequential personal program." He had, moreover, at first made considerable use of encouragement and guidance.

To come back to the subject of psychotic depressions, Lampl-de Groot (1953) also feels that a deeply melancholic patient is not amenable to analytic therapy. In her paper she reviews the factors that she considers of importance in determining success or failure in the therapy of depression. In her opinion, the presence of sadomasochistic urges or fantasies militates against success. "An intimate fusion of [aggressive drives] with libido" worsens the prognosis, whereas aggressive urges which are not fused with the libidinal drive "can be liberated from repression and eventually integrated into the personality."

She considers the patient's capacity for sublimating his aggression to be a measure of his ability to improve. Taking a position similar to that of Hartmann, Kris and Loewenstein (1949), she feels that aggression, like the libidinal drive, can be sublimated in pursuits like exploration, the acquisition of knowledge, the control of nature, surgery, engineering, etc.

Finally, she believes that the form of discharge of aggression predominantly present in a patient is of importance in prognosis. According to her, aggression can be discharged directly as destructive or aggressive acts or outbursts of rage, or more indirectly by " 'gaining possession of,' conquering, mastering, getting hold of an object" in which the object is not destroyed but rather serves to increase the subject's power. She feels that when the patient's aggression is discharged in the latter way, by gaining possession of the object, his prognosis is better than when his aggression is discharged via "the mode of destruction," particularly when his sublimatory capacities are limited.

Mabel Blake Cohen and her colleagues (1954) and Edith Jacobson (1954; 1971, Ch. 12) have recently reported on their experience with the psychoanalytic treatment of manic-depressive patients. They consider this topic largely from the point of view of transference and countertransference phenomena. Cohen et al. felt that these patients have two outstanding transference patterns. The first of these patterns is their coercive manipulative dependency. Manic-depressive patients demand gratification by a verbalized and unverbalized exploitative demonstration of their own misery and need and of the other person's selfish indifference and culpability if he does not respond to this need.

The second of these patterns is their striking insensitivity to the individual characteristics of other people. They respond to others in a stereotyped way which clearly indicates that they simply do not see them as individuals in their own right. Like Melanie Klein (1948), Cohen and her colleagues believed that the manic-depressive is fixated at that depressive position where the mother has just begun to be recognized as a whole person, i.e., when it is discovered that the former "bad mother" and the former "good mother" are in reality the same individual. There are many anxieties associated with this position. The child experiences gratifying feelings of fulfillment and "goodness" when the mother is "good." But when she is rejecting or frustrating or, in other words, a "bad mother," this "makes the child hateful, enraged, bad, and fills him with bad emotional content that he tries to get rid of by elimination or denial." Melanie Klein believed that the manic-depressive has never successfully worked through this position, i.e., his early good experiences have not been sufficient to permit him to overcome his depressive anxiety when his mother is "bad." He has, in other words, not learned how to maintain his self-esteem through this period of maternal "badness." He is therefore continuously engaged in an operation of transforming the bad mother into a good one, and of denying her "badness." It is this that constitutes his interpersonal stereotypy.

The lack of interpersonal sensitivity which these patients display in their dealings with people is, of course, clearly observable in their relations with the therapist who is regarded "(a) as an object to be manipulated for purposes of getting sympathy and reassurance, (b) as a moral authority who can be manipulated into giving approval, and (c) as, in actuality, a critical and rejecting authority figure who will not give real approval but can be counted on only for token approval which can be achieved by proper behavior or manipulation."

The authors at first tended to regard this interpersonal obtuseness as a real learning defect in their patients but gradually came to understand it as actually a defense against the anxiety of having to recognize the simultaneous presence of good and bad traits in the same person. These patients have not yet come to terms with the anxiety of acknowledging the presence of "bad" traits in "good" objects. The recognition of unacceptable components in the other person would entail the abandonment of such an individual by the manic-depressive. In order to defend himself against this anxiety, the manic-depressive avoids the recognition of this complexity of personality structure, of the mixture of "good" and "bad" traits in every person and thus deprives himself of the possibility of entertaining a wide spectrum of complex feelings.

The writers gave serious consideration to the technical problems of dealing with these two transference patterns. They discussed the danger of the unmodified classical technique, with its relatively passive therapeutic role, which seems to mean to these patients a promise that their dependency needs will someday be met and that the therapist will eventually be manipulated into the parent role which they want him to play. Sooner or later the patient will interpret something in the therapist's behavior as a rejection, and, having to give up his gratification fantasies, he will become hopeless and suicidal. The same result may occur if the therapist is openly rejecting of the patient's demands. At first there will be a redoubling of efforts to please the harsh authority figure and to extort signs of approval, but, this failing too, hopelessness and perhaps a suicidal attempt will follow.

One of the countertransference difficulties reported by Cohen and her group is precisely in the area of the patient's demandingness. Some therapists, particularly those prone to playing benign roles with patients, may find that these patients are actually succeeding in manipulating them. The recognition of this fact may bring about a sudden resentment and perhaps rejection of the patient. It was discovered that even therapists who seemed to have no trouble dealing with the demandingness of these patients actually manifested a certain degree of apprehension of which they were unaware.

Another countertransference problem was that analysts who work with psychotics prefer to treat schizoid and schizophrenic patients. The extraverted, interpersonally stereotyped manic-depressive seems shallow, superficial, insensitive and unresponsive to such analysts, who, themselves, tend to be obsessional or schizoid people.* It was the impression of the group that cyclothymic therapists actually do better with such patients. However,

---

*For example, Clark in 1923 stated: "While it may sound unsympathetic, and also the facts may have been drawn from too few data, yet intense preoccupation with the manic-depressive group as a whole gives the impression that such individuals do not take a deep-rooted grasp upon the foundations of life, and though usually pleasing in personality have no great staying qualities. Just as the epileptic has many of these stabilizing qualities even to excess, the depressant is more superficial and possesses too little tough fiber for life's stress and storm."

it was noted that the interest of all of the workers in the project increased considerably when some conceptions of how to deal with these patients came into being. It was agreed by all the members of the group that the first step in therapy was to get beyond the interpersonal stereotypy and conventionalized barrier of these patients and into the area of meaningful emotional exchange. In other words, the first step was to come to grips with the characterological defenses of these patients. Various therapeutic maneuvers were proposed and utilized for this purpose: nonverbal techniques, a more patient, intense application of the usual techniques, pressing the patient for material that was presumed to be present and available, occasional outbursts by the therapist, etc.

The latter event occurred a few times, and with one patient the spontaneously expressed anger succeeded in putting a halt to the stereotyped complaining and allowed an exchange of feeling to occur. The fact that the therapist was human enough to get angry seemed to make the episode significant for the patient. However, the authors caution that "it is, of course, highly speculative whether such a sudden, spontaneous eruption of the therapist could be fashioned into a planned technical approach."

The research group found itself in agreement about the matter of handling the patient's demands. There was a consensus that this was a problem involving dangerous risks but that it was safest and most therapeutic for the irrational demands to be recognized, brought out into the open, labeled, discussed with the patient and refused. Furthermore, it was also agreed that the patient's manipulation of the therapist by acting out in the form of failure either at work or in the life situation or by threats of suicide should be handled by "a denial of responsibility for the continued existence of the patient," coupled with an implication or admission that the patient was important or meaningful to the therapist. The patient may feel that the therapist cannot be interested in him unless he needs him, e.g., unless he needs to succeed therapeutically with the patient for the sake of his own reputation. The writers suggest that the patient be made to understand that the therapist can be interested in the patient as a person without at the same time being dependent upon him for his reputation. They also recommend that the therapist should continuously attempt to convey his own feelings and attitudes to the patient so that the latter can gain some sense of his own meaningfulness to the therapist.

In short, these workers stressed the importance of the demand-ingness and the emotional stereotypy in the transference patterns of these patients. They also described their experiences with coun-tertransference problems and with techniques for establishing meaningful communication with these patients and for handling their dependency needs. They acknowledged the desirability of further study in these areas.

These writers worked largely in the conceptual framework of Sullivan's interpersonal theory, although they did not hesitate to take advantage of the contributions of the more orthodox analytic workers and, as a matter of fact, acknowledged a par-ticular debt to the theories of Melanie Klein. Their work, as re-ported, is notable for its exclusive concern with patterns of interpersonal relationships and for its neglect of the usual pregenital fantasy material that was reported so copiously by previous writers.

However, Jacobson (1954b), too, despite her different theoretical orientation, explicitly states that in some depressed patients it is simply not possible "to carry the analysis of such patients to the point where their pre-oedipal fantasies and impulses are produced and interpreted," although her experience suggests that "the more thorough and lasting therapeutic results could be achieved in cases where this deep fantasy material could be fully revived, understood and digested."

The central theme of her paper also concerns the problems arising from the demandingness of these patients. She discusses the technical difficulties associated with the fact that they inevita-bly make the analyst their central love-object and the focus of their pathological demands. It is interesting that Jacobson and Cohen and her colleagues have recognized similar problems and dangers and, in many cases, have advocated similar technical procedures in the treatment of these patients.

Jacobson, like Cohen and her co-authors, emphasizes the danger of seeming to offer these patients "seductive promises too great to be fulfilled." To avoid this, she advises that early in the analysis, in connection with interpretations regarding the illusory nature of the patients' expectations, one should utter warnings about the future. She, too, advocates deviations from the classical technique. For example, she advises only three or four sessions per week, because she believes that this tends to reduce rather than increase the ambivalence of these patients. She has noted that daily sessions are interpreted by them either as unspoken and really unfulfillable promises or as intolerable obligations which must be masochistically submitted to.

However, in accordance with her recommendation for a flexible application of analytic technique, she acknowledges that more frequent or longer sessions may sometimes be necessary with very deeply depressed patients. And she notes that during such periods the analyst may serve merely as a patient listener providing the patient "maybe for weeks or months not more than support from a durable transference, which may carry them through the depression."

One of the analyst's difficult tasks is to adjust his responses and remarks to the patient's psychological rhythm. This is essentially an exercise in subtle empathy. "There must be a continuous, subtle, empathatic tie between the analyst and his depressive patients; we must be very careful not to let empty silences grow or not to talk too long, too rapidly and too emphatically; that is, never to give too much or too little. . . . What those patients need is a . . . sufficient amount of spontaneity and flexible adjustment to their mood level, of warm understanding and especially of unwavering respect; attitudes which must not be confused with over-kindness, sympathy, reassurance, etc. In periods of threatening narcissistic withdrawal we may have to show a very active interest and participation in their daily activities and especially their sublimations." Like Cohen et al., Jacobson remarks that analysts who tend to be detached in temperament seem to have greater difficulty in treating these patients.

Interestingly enough, Jacobson also takes up the matter of the apparently almost inevitable occasional spontaneous flash of anger on the part of the therapist. She believes that this is a most precarious event since it, too, in a sense is a response to the patient's demandingness, for not only does he demand love and affection but at times he unconsciously demands a show of power from the analyst. As she observed in an earlier paper (1953), when the patient finds that the analyst is no longer able to live up to his expectations of love, he may, in his fear of a complete loss of his object, regress a step further. "The patient may now attempt to hold on at least to the reanimated image of an omnipotent, not loving, but primitive sadistic object." He may try to bring down upon himself a show of strictness, anger and punishment. Thus Jacobson adds an additional dimension to the explanation given by Cohen et al., for the occasionally therapeutic result of an outburst of anger by the therapist. They felt that it demonstrated to the patient that the analyst was human and that he cared. Jacobson adds, in effect, that the patient prefers an angry therapist to a nonparticipating one, a punitive object to no object. This explosion of anger sometimes serves to carry the patient over a dangerous depressive stage, but, in view of the provocativeness of these patients, she advocates "the most careful self-scrutiny and self-control in the analyst."

Jacobson places great emphasis on the vicissitudes of the transference in these patients. The problem is, as she sees it, to let the intensely ambivalent transference of these patients develop sufficiently for analysis to take place without the patient eventually discontinuing analysis in a phase of spurious transference success or, on the other hand, in a phase of severe depression. To emphasize these difficulties, to which she confesses she can offer no completely satisfactory solution, she outlines typical phases in the analysis of these patients.

The first phase may be marked by the establishment of prompt, intense rapport with the analyst, reflected in idealized fantasies about him and in marked enthusiasm for the treatment. Improvement may follow rapidly. But it is a deceptive improvement which depends on the unrealistic magical quality of the transference feelings and on the "exaggerated idealization and obstinate denial of possible or visible shortcomings of the analyst," distortions not dissimilar to those described by Cohen and her group. No real change occurs in the patient but his mood is one of hope and optimism. A successful analysis seems certain to him, though perhaps not until a time long in the future.

This phase may then be followed by a period of growing disappointment which is marked by sporadic doubts about the excellence, wisdom and kindness of the analyst followed by immediate efforts to transform him again into the loving, idealized image of his former fantasies. Feelings of hopelessness and self-doubt increase. Manifestations of ambivalence become more marked and may be displaced for a time to a third person, perhaps the spouse. A long typical period may follow in which the patient becomes more and more involved in the analysis and withdraws dangerously from other interpersonal relationships. Dependent, masochistic attitudes now characterize the transference, accompanied by demands for self-sacrificing devotion. The transference becomes more ambivalent and the patient, with his attempts to arouse guilt in the analyst for his alleged mistreatment of him, becomes more exhaustingly provocative.

Such a phase may be followed by a deepening of the depression in which the patient may totally abandon the "bad" object and enter a stage of pathological introjective defenses and narcissistic withdrawal, i.e., his restitutive maneuvers may now be enacted entirely in the psychic plane. The danger of discontinuation of therapy in this phase is great.

However, despite the unanswered questions that she freely raises, Jacobson is able to report some considerable success with these trying and difficult patients. She emphasizes the importance of a slow and careful analysis of their transference conflicts, their ego distortions and their superego defects, which would seem to be essentially equivalent to what Cohen and her group refer to as their demandingness, their provocativeness, their interpersonal insensitivity and their distortion of every person into approving or disapproving parental figures.

With reference to the demands that these patients make on others, Jacobson (1971) points out some interesting observations on the pathologic interplay that often exists between manic-depressives and their marital partners. She also outlines some of the favorable combinations that may be formed, for example, partners who share interests or hobbies or even professional work. But she notes that the mutual dependence that exists between patients and their spouses may instead combine mutual overdependence with a surprising lack of common interests. Despite their great need for one another, they may have little to say to one another, a situation that may be pathogenic to a manic-depressive patient. She observes that such patients may progressively build up mutual demands of a kind that lead to inevitable disappointment. She has noted that occasionally, when both partners are manic-depressive, they become sick alternately.

She illustrates with several examples that, when both partners can be studied, the patient's complaints about the spouse, which may be disguised as depressive self-accusations, precisely describe the marital problem. The healthy partner may represent the source of the love and praise for which the patient may play a seemingly self-sacrificing role. The partner may express feelings of gratitude for this, but when he is actually selfish and demanding his behavior may belie his words. All this leads her to suggest that no matter how exaggerated the complaints of the patients may be, how magnified their derogation of their partners, the complaints are often more justified than they appear at first glance.

She also points out that a depressed patient's prolonged period of complaints, self-reproaches and dependency may eventually wear even a healthy spouse down to the point where he defensively counterattacks with complaints of his own, which, in turn, intensify the patient's guilt and feelings of inadequacy, setting up a vicious cycle of aggression, complaints and depression. She vividly describes the guilt and depression into which a chronically complaining depressed patient can plunge his entire family. Attempts by the spouse to escape from the debilitating depression of the patient into work, social interests or extramarital sexual affairs may intensify the patient's feelings of unworthiness and unlovableness. A careful therapist will, of course, try to be aware of these possibilities.

Jacobson offers an insightful comment on marriages between manic-depressive and schizoid types. She declares that she has never seen such a marriage work out, since the manic-depressive's needs for warmth and affection are usually thwarted.

A number of other helpful papers on the treatment of depression have recently appeared (e.g., Gibson, 1963; Levin, 1965; Lorand, 1967). It is interesting that many topics which so exclusively preoccupied previous writers on depression—such as the depressive's self-reproaches, his hostile introjection of the abandoned object, the freeing of his hostility in treatment—now, in the broader perspective of the recent workers, find their place as mere phases in the interpersonal and transference conflicts of these very difficult patients.

Beck (1967, 1973), whose cognitive perspective on depression we considered earlier, has introduced one major new note in the treatment of depressive illness, a technique which he refers to as the cognitive therapy of depression. In brief, his view is that the patient's depression is activated either by the effect of specific stresses or by the overwhelming accumulation of nonspecific stresses on his idiosyncratic cognitive patterns. When activated, these tend to dominate the patient's thinking and produce depressive affective and motivational phenomena.

He believes that cognitive psychotherapy may help the patient symptomatically during the depression by helping him gain objectivity and some control over his automatic pattern. When the patient is not depressed, the treatment is directed toward modifying his idiosyncratic patterns in order to reduce his vulnerability to future depressions.

In this insight therapy, an important step is to identify the major maladaptive patterns through a study of the patient's life history. It is usually possible to demonstrate to him that he does not over-react indiscriminately to all situations but that he responds selec-tively to certain events and experiences. The therapist attempts to help the patient understand these overreactions as the conse-quences of early-life experiences which produced idiosyncratic sensitivities to certain kinds of stress. Thus the patient is enabled to understand his disturbances in terms of specific problems, rather than as an amorphous collection of symptoms. This in itself gives the patient a beginning sense of mastery over his problems. He may, for example, understand his reaction to an unusual slight by his spouse or by an employer as a stereotyped response dating back to an early feeling of being slighted or perhaps of not receiv-ing preferential treatment.

Beck outlines a number of common situations that trigger off disproportionate or inappropriate reactions in the vulnerable pa-tient: "failing to reach a particular goal, being excluded from a group, being rejected by another person, receiving criticism, and not receiving expected approval, encouragement, or guidance" (1967, p. 320; 1973, p. 132). If the patient can be helped to recognize his typical patterns of overreaction, he may be, to some extent, protected from the specific stress.

A more microscopic approach to this therapy consists of helping the patient identify his depression-generating cognitions. These cognitive distortions, according to Beck, cause the patient to expe-rience dysphoria. The identification of these distorted cognitions can produce some objectivity toward them with some possibility of neutralizing their pathogenic propensities. Part of the identifi-cation of distortions includes the identifications of the links be-tween the stimulus and the affect: stimulus $\longrightarrow$ cognition $\longrightarrow$ affect.

As the patient becomes more experienced at recognizing these links, Beck believes that he will be less influenced by them. Fur-thermore, he may become more able to identify those themes among his cognitions that lead to dysphoria. Beck usually helps the patient to categorize these themes by labeling the typical depress-ing themes such as deprivation, self-reproach or sense of inade-quacy. A patient's cognitive pattern is usually fairly stereotyped, making it easier to identify the repetitive themes. There is often a considerable gap, of course, between the identification of these themes and an awareness of their inaccuracy.

When it is helpful, Beck may draw a distinction for the patient between secondary-process cognitions, which he labels as a "higher-level" type of thinking for the patient, and primary-process cognitions, which are labeled "lower-level" forms of thinking and which are described as fairly automatic and involuntary and not the result of logical reasoning.

The less severely depressed patient comes to recognize that these latter cognitions are not the result of any logical reasoning or deliberating and is able to regard them as intrusive obsessions which are not valid despite their seeming plausibility.

Another device that Beck uses is helping the patient distinguish between his "ideas" and objective "facts." "By checking his observations, by taking into account all the data, and by considering other hypotheses to explain the events, he is less prone to equate his automatic thoughts with reality" (1967, p. 324; 1973, p. 135). As he recounts the details of a distortion, the patient is helped to look at the evidence and to examine alternative explanations for his distortions. Beck has found that once a patient has identified a particular cognition as invalid, it is important for him to neutralize the effect of his distortion by verbalizing exactly why it was erroneous and to counter the thought with an effective rebuttal. Beck illustrates these and other techniques by interesting anecdotal material.

At first glance, as one reads about this mode of therapy, one feels like the person who discovered that, unbeknownst to him, he had been talking prose all of his life. Many of the techniques that Beck identifies and labels are part of our daily therapeutic work which we do not ordinarily label or identify with technical terms. But technical language of this kind does have as one of its functions the bringing into clear awareness the nature of the therapeutic work that one does. To name, as even primitives know, is to acquire power over what is named.

But obviously Beck's therapy is more comprehensive than just attaching labels to familiar therapeutic techniques. One of the problems with it, however, as it is presented in his writings, is that it appears to be a first-order formulation. The therapist deals with more than just the manifest material but does not seem to analyze the cognitions much beyond their relations to patterns of assumptions or distortions. In cognitive therapy (which is probably more simplistically outlined in Beck's description than his actual clinical practice), the therapist does not seem to look beyond the distortions to quite different and latent meanings which may have only the most tenuous connection with the manifest cognitions.

Furthermore, as described, there seems to be a special emphasis on cognitions having to do with success, failure or guilt. Cognitions having to do with loneliness, emptiness and loss—not so much distortions as perceptions of painful states—would seem to lend themselves less well to cognitive techniques, except in those instances where negative self-concepts are largely responsible for the patient's inhibitions or lack of self-confidence in establishing satisfying relationships.

One other reservation presents itself. Despite Beck's reference to his theory applying to the whole spectrum of depressive disorders, he seems to be referring in his chapter on treatment (1967, Chapter 21) primarily to reactively depressed neurotic patients. Sometimes he seems to be referring to the lifting of a depressed mood rather than to the treatment of a depressive illness. In his comments on this subject, however, Beck (1967, p. 319; 1973, p. 130) acknowledges that the major usefulness of cognitive therapy *during* a depression is with those reactively depressed neurotic patients who are not severely ill, whose depressions are precipitated by identifiable events and who do not have the characteristics of endogenous depressions. "The depressed patient who is amenable to cognitive psychotherapy generally shows wide fluctuations during the course of a day and also from day to day. These fluctuations, moreover, are related to specific environmental events; positive experiences diminish and negative experiences increase the degree of depression" (1967, p. 379; 1973; p. 130). This is the description of a neurotic depression with the "reactivity" first described by Gillespie (1929). Despite these reservations, however, it would appear that Beck considers cognitive insight therapy in the *postdepressive period* to be not limited in its usefulness by these diagnostic and phenomenological characteristics.

Beck seems to visualize the difference between neurotic and psychotic depressions primarily in quantitative terms: "The more intense the affective state, the more credible the depressive cognitions are to the patient. When the intensity of the affect is reduced through anti-depressant drugs, there is a diminution in the compelling quality of these cognitions" (1967, p. 324; 1973, p. 135). This,

as Beck goes on to suggest, "seems to indicate an interaction between cognition and affect." Indeed it does. But the fact that
pharmacologic intervention in the absence of cognitive therapy
often (though not always) eradicates the negative self-concepts
hardly seems to provide support for the etiological primacy of
cognitions in endogenous depressions.

What psychoanalysts may find missing in Beck's outline of his
method of therapy is any consideration of the transference problems to which other writers have devoted such extensive attention. Although one can see how the patient's negative expectations or the projection of his negative self-concepts onto the
therapist may represent transference phenomena, and although
one can appreciate that problems related to an unrealistic ego
ideal or to superego aspirations may be encompassed within his
mode of therapy, there is little explicit reference in his writing to
this very important aspect of the treatment of depression. There
is no doubt that, from a psychoanalytic perspective, cognitive
therapy appears as a first-level approximation of an adequate
treatment approach. And from a general psychiatric perspective
there appears to be a blurring of diagnostic differences between
the neurotic and endogenous depressions.

However, I believe that Beck's approach can be defended as the
initial phase of an investigation devoted to the discovering of what
can be accomplished by focusing on the patient's self-concepts.

A general criticism that can be made of the literature on the
psychoanalytic treatment of depressive illness is that it virtually
ignores not only the astonishing effectiveness of the antidepressant medications and of lithium carbonate in the treatment of and
prophylaxis against depressive illness but also the theoretical implications of these psychopharmacological effects. Beck's work
stands out like a beacon as an exception to this oversight. Apart
from his work, it is almost as if the subject of treatment goes on
in a schizophrenic world. The psychoanalytic literature (by a process of denial?) seems barely to mention psychopharmacology,
whereas that portion of the general psychiatric literature on
depression that is not given over to diagnostic studies of depressive illness is almost entirely devoted to the exciting but confusing
neurobiochemical research on affective disorders and on the psy-
chopharmacotherapy of these conditions.

Chapter IX

CONCLUSION
[1]

THIS EXAMINATION OF psychoanalytic concepts of depression includes more psychiatric data than did the previous edition of this work. Such an expansion proved to be necessary in order to see some of these concepts in a broader perspective. This is compatible with the recommendations and the practice of very able psychoanalytic workers. Arlow (1970) has advocated the desirability of looking beyond the psychoanalytic conceptual world and Jacobson (1971, p. 170), too, refers approvingly to "a sound collaboration of psychological-psychoanalytic and somatic-neurophysiological research."

There have been an increasing number of occasions when the psychiatric and the psychoanalytic literature illuminated one another; other occasions when disconcerting unawareness or ignoring of psychiatric data has led to doctrinaire psychoanalytic pronouncements; and still other instances when the psychoanalytic approach exposed obvious defects in psychiatric data collecting, which in turn produced observational artifacts.

In a biting criticism, Home (1966) charged that "in the event of disagreement in [psychoanalytic] discussion, the appeal was almost invariably to 'the literature' and not to the fact. Indeed the place of 'the literature' in psycho-analysis has no parallel, as far as I know, in any other science. . . . Similar recourse to 'the literature' seems to occur only in religious writing and in our own day in Communist theory."

He is arguing, of course, that in the event of disagreement, appeals are made not to the relevant data but to the authority of the written word to confirm a hypothesis or to defend a position; in the same paper he comments also on the disparate psychoanalytic languages and the lack of conceptual clarity that this implies.

Part of the problem lies, of course, in the unusual circumstances of psychoanalytic clinical investigation. Patients and disorders are studied in great depth and over a period of years. This prevents the accumulation of sizable samples of homogeneous clinical entities from which one can derive the kind of replicable data that are the rule in other fields of study. The emphasis is instead on fully reported fragments of treatment complete with theoretical inferences, or on personal perspectives on a particular clinical state or spectrum of disorders onerously derived from a lifetime of interest and experience in these areas.

To one familiar with the open confessions of ignorance in other scientific disciplines it is a little disconcerting to read so many confidently offered global conclusions in the literature on depression. This tendency to make definitive pronouncements makes it appear as if legitimate uncertainty has acquired the bar sinister.

According to Whitehorn (1955): "It could be said with some justification that the scientist's first duty is to doubt." And perhaps high in priority among those things that a sophisticated worker should doubt is the absolute validity of his own conceptualizations. Konrad Lorenz (1955) has said that he takes pains to make himself as stupid as possible and to misunderstand everything that he could possibly misunderstand.

By contrast, the psychoanalytic literature on depression exhibits a tendency to produce confident and definitive formulations on every aspect of this complex illness.

One factor detracting from the scientific workmanship of the literature on depression is the frequently inadequate delineation of the case material. A *sine qua non* of scientific presentation is the description of the clinical group under discussion. Abraham and Freud were careful to identify diagnostically the depressed patients they were discussing. On one occasion, in order to corroborate the diagnosis of two of his patients, Abraham (1924) went so far as to report that they had "repeatedly been put in asylums or sanatoriums where they were under the observation of able psychiatrists and that they had been examined by eminent mental specialists. The clinical picture was absolutely typical of manic-depressive psychosis and the circular course of the illness quite characteristic in both cases."

In contrast with such careful reporting, many theories are based on case material that is described no more precisely than by the word "depressed." Emotional disorders are not clearly identified and the size of the sample is rarely mentioned. Instead, the theoretical conclusions are announced *ex cathedra*, as it were, based on the writer's presumably extensive experience.

One could be appreciative of any particular worker's range of experience and still wish more precise knowledge about his sample of patients. Kubie (1952), for example, noted that "even in the course of a lifetime of exclusive devotion to the psychoanalytic treatment of patients no analyst will have been able to analyze deeply more than a few representatives of any one psychopathological constellation." Mabel Blake Cohen and three colleagues studied a group of manic-depressive patients over a period of several years and were able to report on a series of no larger than twelve cases.

Another failing in the literature on depression is the assumption that features noted in one's own patients must necessarily be found in all similar patients. Gero (1936), for example, in his report on two patients, assumed that their failure to achieve genital relationships was characteristic of all depressed patients. Yet Jacobson (1953), in her description of manic-depressives, notes that "in their sexual life they may show a full genital response."

In contrast, as one glances back at the earliest papers on depression one becomes appreciative of the tentative nature of the formulations. I have already referred to Freud's (1917) disclaimer of universal validity for his observations on melancholia. Abraham (1924), too, was careful to avoid overgeneralizing. As he said: "It is no part of my intention in this essay, based as it is on a very limited number of psychoanalyses, to make a general and final pronouncement about the psychogenesis of the circular insanities. Nevertheless I believe that the material at our disposal does warrant us in making certain statements of whose provisional and incomplete character I am fully aware."

Thus these imaginative explorers pushing their way carefully into hitherto unexplored regions were quite aware of the preliminary nature of their sketch maps. Later travelers into these territories, such as Rado, Gero and Fenichel, mapped out more fully certain areas that had been only sketchily drawn by their predecessors. Already one begins to detect a prematurely confident note of certainty in their reports. Later surveyors more fully equipped

with sophisticated conceptual instruments were able to reach observational heights from which they could perceive and describe
how much broader and more complex the landscape of these
depressive disorders actually was. Bibring, Jacobson and Sandler
and Joffe fall into this category.

For many of the explorers of this clinical realm there has been
perhaps an understandable tendency to hold on to landmarks
staked out by earlier pioneers who had not fully comprehended
that they had often mistaken the West Indies for the Indian sub-
continent that they were seeking. The overgeneralizations, the
unawareness that the continents they were describing were only
islands or archipelagos, the anthropomorphic language and the
reifications were very understandable and acceptable in the tentative reports of the early discoverers. It is only when contemporary
writers in full possession of more modern conceptual and critical
apparatus still write their formulations as if they were medieval
scholastics, mistaking their partial insights for universal statements, that one becomes impressed with their scientific parochialism and their restricted vision. It is as if they were anthropologists
reporting ethnographic data about a Himalayan village unaware
that what they have described is not true even of other Indian
hamlets let alone European towns or American cities.

When one writer begs the question of the presence of aggression in depression by declaring that the very existence of depression proves the existence of such aggression; when another argues
that unless guilt is present, the so-called depressive states that one
observes are actually states of loss or apathy or anomie; when
others announce that depressions cannot occur in children because of what the literature has to say about depression and that
what looks like childhood depression is really mourning, which
still other writers declare cannot exist in children because of what
the literature has to say about mourning; when the authors don't
look up from their notebooks long enough to glance at the landscape and the data—then one begins to acknowledge some truth
in Home's harsh impatient reproaches.

[2]

There is now ample evidence that the term "depression" covers
a variety of affective states which differ not only overtly, but also

subjectively. Many of the previous formulations of depression and of the depressive character structure are simply not comprehensive enough to do justice to the variety of clinical types. Depressed patients are to be found not only among those who are excessively dependent for self-esteem on external narcissistic supplies, and on the other hand depressed patients are to be found not only among rigid over-conscientious perfectionists who expect the impossible of themselves. The spectrum is not nearly so narrow.

This relative multiplicity of depressed states—associated in some instances perhaps with private biases on the parts of the authors—has led to a variety of psychodynamic formulations and conceptualizations of the depressive reactions, each with partial validity but with only too many of them implicitly claiming general application. For different writers "depression" has not only different components but also different purposes. For one author it is, in essence, emptiness and loneliness; for another it is rage and guilt. For one observer it is a passive consequence of having sustained a loss in self-esteem; for another it is an active though distorted attempt to undo this loss.

A more widespread awareness of the complexity and variety of the depressive reactions will perhaps give rise to less dogmatic and more sophisticated theoretical models.

A striking feature of the impressionistic word-pictures of depression painted by many writers is that they have the flavor of art rather than of science and may well represent profound personal intuitions as much as they depict the raw clinical data.

Abraham, for example, saw the depressed state as a complicated process of psychic digestion shot through with primitive desires and impulses and fantasies. For Freud melancholia was a loud, lamenting, self-tormenting period of mourning in which each and every tie with the introjected love-object is painfully loosened and abandoned. Melanie Klein and Fairbairn viewed depression as a mixture of sorrow over the loss of the love-object and of guilt over the hostility and rage that brought about this loss. Balint, by way of contrast, thought of depression as essentially a state of starved unhappy lovelessness not necessarily reactive to previous sadistic fantasies. For Fairbairn such a condition in which hostility and guilt are absent was not depression at all but merited a special term the "schizoid state."

Rado pictured a depression as a great despairing cry for love and forgiveness, a drama of expiation acted out on the psychic plane following upon a fall in self-esteem. Fenichel, too, conceptualized depression as being simultaneously a fall in self-esteem and an attempt to coerce the love-object into delivering the narcissistic supplies necessary to restore the self-esteem. He and Rado both felt that this formulation was broad enough to apply to all cases of depression.

Both Bibring and Jacobson felt that there was a mechanism common to all cases of depression but differed from Rado and Fenichel in their conception of it. Bibring saw the fall in self-esteem as the essential element in depression with all else—including the restitutive attempts when they occur—as secondary phenomena. Jacobson, on the other hand, ascribed "the central part in the pathology of depression to aggression and its vicissitudes."

The tendency which we have noted in Engel and in Sandler and Joffe to conceptualize the "depressive reaction" as a state of helplessness and resignation derives, of course, from Bibring's view of depression as an affective state, defined as "the emotional expression . . . of a state of helplessness and powerlessness of the ego." Engel, Schmale, Bibring, Sandler and Joffe all regarded this affective state as the basic core of all depressive illnesses which Bibring saw as mere "complications" of this basic affective state.

Jacobson (1971, p. 176), however, observes helplessness existing without depression and, as we have seen, believes that aggression is central to depression. This conceptualization of aggression in depression is metaphychological in essence. Clinically, she subscribes to a much more broadly conceived formulation of depressive illness both from a psychological perspective and from a psychosomatic viewpoint.

Nacht and Racamier (1960), in contrast, believe that the loss of love is fundamental to depression. Beres (1966) denies that either loss of love or helplessness is the primary basis of depression. He postulates, along with Rochlin (1953), that guilt is a necessary condition for depression. Furthermore, in response to Bibring's belief that aggression is secondary to loss of self-esteem, he counters that it is just as likely that lowered self-esteem may be due to guilt brought on by aggression. To this, Jacobson (1971, p. 171) replies that she realized as long ago as 1943 that the emphasis on guilt did not do justice to all depressive cases.

Beck, as we have seen, sees negative cognitions as the common factor producing characteristic depressive affects. This etiological hypothesis, though plausible in many neurotic depressions of a reactive variety, has not gained general acceptance as a description of the situation in endogenous and especially manic-depressive depressions.

In other words, Nacht and Racamier emphasize loss of love. Beres challenges this. He and Rochlin argue for the centrality of guilt. Bibring and Jacobson encompass such partial conceptualizations in their much broader formulations. Bibring, however, along with Engel, Schmale, Sandler and Joffe, stress the central importance of helplessness in depressive affect. Beres and Jacobson join in disagreement. Jacobson, while metaphychologically standing for the centrality of aggression in depression, clinically believes the fall of self-esteem to be the central theme in depression, a theme which she formulates in a comprehensively thought-out fashion. This matter of self-esteem, however, has been broken down by Beck and by Sandler and Joffe into more elementary cognitive and affective components each of which is believed by its proponents to be the really basic element in depression.

From each personal vision of depression stem derivative explanations of one or another depressive symptom. The guilt of which the depressive complains, for example, was viewed by Abraham in conformity with his particular picture of this condition as related to the patient's cannibalistic impulses. Rado, with his conception of depression as a prolonged attempt to win back the love-object, understood the patient to be guilty because by his aggressive attitude he has himself to blame for the loss of the object. Mabel Blake Cohen and her group think of the patient's guilt as essentially a device to manipulate the object and to win approval. As they put it, "The patient merely resorts to the magic of uttering cries to placate authority." This particular view of depression as a manipulative device is shared by Smith (1960, 1971), who is also from the Washington area. He sees the depressive as one who has developed astonishing and intricate artistry in the use of "helplessness" as a defensive pattern.

In summary, it is clear that depressive illnesses such as manic-depressive illness and involutional melancholia involve much more than feelings of helplessness and resignation, or guilt, or loss of love or negative cognitions. They involve much more than depressive affects, however defined or understood. They represent, as Jacobson, Beck and Grinker et al. have indicated, multifaceted syndromes or disorders involving cognitive, behaviorial and physiological components as well as depressive affect.

[3]

The psychoanalytic understanding of depression is made up of certain recurring themes which weave in and out of the theoretical tapestry. These themes are the basic human themes of love and loss and hate and vulnerability and happiness. These themes are elemental aspects of human life. Expressed clinically they take on designations, simultaneously both aseptic and value-laden, such as dependency and aggression and narcissism. They lead to joy and despair, to elation and depression. In this work I have, of course, been primarily concerned with those enduring or long-lasting states of depression that we call depressive illnesses of one kind or another.

I would like to review the specific conceptual elements that, subtly linked together, constitute the psychoanalytic concepts of depression: Freud's recognition of the *identification* that occurs regressively in melancholia has long been seen as but a special case of a process that is part of normal development. The regressive identification of Freud's description has been reformulated by Fenichel, and more explicitly by Jacobson, as a lack of clear differentiation between the self- and object-images. This then causes the melancholic to confuse himself with the disappointing love-object, a confusion which represents a psychotic symptom.

Abraham, Rado, Gero and Fenichel have progressively elucidated different aspects of the role of *orality* in depression. The latter three writers' formulations of the psychological implications of this term added conceptual depth to Abraham's original semivisceral usage of this concept. The meaning of this term has gradually expanded to include the need for warmth, love, approval and recognition, the external narcissistic supplies that seem to be so necessary for the depressive's self-esteem.

It was Bibring's contribution to point out that the frustration of *aspirations* other than the oral also play a role in some depressives' psychopathology. It was he who helped us understand that some depressives feel helpless and experience loss of self-esteem because of frustrations having to do with other aspirations such as the wish to be good and worthy or adequate and effective. Both he and Jacobson emphasized the special role that *self-esteem* plays in depression. It was Sandler and Joffe who pointed to an even more basic need, namely, for a *sense of well-being*, the loss of which produces psychic pain. It was, they argued, when defensive operations designed to reduce this pain were not effective that helplessness and depression ensued. They saw the significance of the loss of the object, which was remarked on so early in the literature, as deriving its significance from the loss of the sense of well-being which then ensued and which then could be followed by depression.

The concept of *aggression* has been central to psychoanalytic concepts about depression from the very beginning, although writers such as Cohen et al. and Bibring regarded it as secondary to other factors. When the emotion that Abraham referred to as "an attitude of hate" later became transmuted in other analysts' writings into a form of psychic energy which cathected the self-image, the whole concept of aggression in depression became removed to a more abstract theoretical metapsychological realm at an infinitely greater distance from clinical data. This subject with the linguistic and conceptual confusion to which it is so particularly vulnerable has been extensively discussed in Chapter VII.

Bibring's conception of depression as an *ego phenomenon* seems to have been formulated to indicate that, since depression, like anxiety, is an affect, it must, like anxiety, have the ego as its "seat." Depression as an ego phenomenon also implies that depression should not be thought of as an intersystemic conflict and therefore does not involve guilt, except perhaps secondarily as a result of the individual's failure to live up to his moral aspirations.

Although Jacobson went a considerable distance to agree with Bibring that many depressions were indeed intrasystemic, she still maintained that intersystemic conflicts also occurred in depression. She disagreed, however, with authors such as Rochlin and Beres who maintained that depressions were characterized solely by that intersystemic conflict between the superego and the ego that is experienced as guilt.

In all of this we have observed that different writers perceived partial aspects of the whole phenomenon. One writer would emphasize orality; another, chiefly guilt; still another, hostility or aggression. There is a recurring trend in psychoanalytic writing to label depressed states that do not happen to fit some arbitrary definition by some term other than depression, so that the purity of definitions might be preserved despite the intrusion of unacceptable observations. We thus find authors resorting to terms such as "loss complex," "object deficiency," "apathy," etc., in order that their cherished formulations not be tarnished.

I believe that Jacobson went furthest in perceiving depression in a formulation broad enough to include many of the partial insights of previous writers. Yet even she became wedded to concepts and definitions that depended too much on deductive metapsychological reasoning and that strayed too far from clinical and empirical observations. But it was she more than any other writer who perceived that depressive disorders consisted of more than the psychological elements that she visualized so clearly— that they contained, in addition, psychosomatic features that called for different explanations.

There has been a recurring theme from the days of Abraham through Klein to Jacobson, expressed in different theoretical frameworks, that adult depressive illnesses recapitulate early infantile parathymias or disappointments, a view that in my opinion Zetzel (1960) very properly criticized.

To repeat, the danger lying in wait for every psychoanalytic writer on depression is to be restricted to the partial visions of his predecessors, to pass on received doctrine and definitions and to become conceptually constricted within the parameters of their definitions and concepts. It was the great contribution of the writers I have chosen to review that they were each able to break through the formulations of their predecessors and to establish areas of broader understanding of the psychopathology of depression, even while still remaining enmeshed in other uncritically accepted assumptions that were left for later writers to view more critically and more realistically.

[4]

Careful observers have long cautioned that, in depressions, improvement with psychotherapy should not be confused with validation of specific psychodynamics or theories. Clark (1923), for example, made no secret of his chagrin concerning the results of psychoanalytic treatment of manic-depressives. He states: "It is interesting and at the same time discomforting to the analyst to review what the members of this group indicate afterward what really helped them most as the result of treatment. They all state it was the transference and none are able to give any accurate or precise statement of the main faults disclosed in the analysis."

Kaufman (1937), reporting on the improvement after psycho-analysis in two patients with late-life depressions, emphasized that "probably the most important factor in the improvement of these patients was the transference relationships, and one might put them down as 'transference cures.' "

Jacobson (1954b) makes similar observations about her patients and supplies a more complete theoretical explanation of the situation. She notes that treatment may begin with a marked positive transference in which the patient attributes magical therapeutic qualities to his idealized physician. In this mood of renewed—but unrealistic—optimism, the patient's depression may lift and he may enter a phase of well-being colored by hope and confidence. It is the improvement in this phase that Jacobson categorizes as spurious. No genuine change has occurred in the patient's personality structure and improvement has taken place purely for transference reasons.

These writers were very clear that symptomatic improvements could and did occur primarily as a result of the relationship between the patient and his therapist and that they were curiously unrelated to the resolution of any of the patient's real problems. Symptomatic improvements of this kind are not to be dismissed as unimportant. To the patient they are very important. But they are not necessarily due to any significant modification of the patient's personality structure.

[5]

The writer has from time to time indicated that the literature on depression has not grown and flourished independently of the development of general analytic theory. Instead, it represents the application to the depressed states of insights and conceptualizations derived from advances in the general body of analytic theory. Each step forward in psychoanalytic theory has been followed by a renewed consideration of depression with a further gain in understanding.

Abraham started off by seeing depression in the light of Freud's insights into psychosexual development. Freud was able to apply his grasp of the vicissitudes of aggression to the symptomatology of the melancholic. Rado recast analytic thinking on depression in the framework of Freud's new structural concepts. And Gero took advantage of Reich's contribution on the subject of character analysis to discuss depression from this point of view.

Melanie Klein focused attention on the importance of object relationships in depression. Fairbairn and Cohen, disparate as they are in their theoretical allegiances, have nevertheless expanded our understanding of the interpersonal and object relationships of depressed individuals. And Jacobson has worked out most comprehensively of all the implications for depression that she felt were inherent in the advances in structural theory and ego psychology. But, as we saw in Chapter VII, it was only when Rapaport, Sandler et al., Schafer and others critically examined various confusing aspects of the structural theory that it became apparent that some of the theoretical issues that Bibring and Jacobson were concerned with were, in fact, pseudo-issues. Problems of classifying clinical data had come to be mistaken for substantive issues about reified structures and energies.

The increasing sophistication of analytic concepts has added to our understanding of the depressive reactions. But it has done more than that. It has focused attention on gaps in our knowledge and theory, gaps which were harder to discern when the theoretical framework was more primitive.

Bibring and Jacobson attempted to comprehend the psychodynamics of depression within more sophisticated versions of structural and economic theory. Ultimately, as I have indicated, their actual contributions were preeminently clinical. They introduced a broader understanding of the determinants of self-esteem and thus of depressive illness itself.

Beck and Sandler and his colleagues examined the cognitive and affective components of self-esteem, respectively, thus demonstrating that this seemingly basic psychological state could be broken down and considered in its more elementary components. And in a previous chapter I have examined certain psychoanalytic concepts of depression in the light of recent developments in general psychoanalytic theory and demonstrated that the debates that have been waged about them in the literature were generated by semantic and conceptual unclarity.

[6]

As early as 1951, Rado was calling for an investigational inquiry into depression that would "include the *physiologic* and *genetic* aspects of this emotional overreaction" since psychodynamics still left many aspects of this illness poorly understood. Psychodynamics had, for example, "so far . . . offered no clues to explain why some depressed patients are subject also to spells of elation and others are not."

Jacobson (1971, Chapter 6) also contends that a psychodynamic approach to the understanding of depressive psychosis is insufficient. She takes issue with writers such as Bibring (1953) who reduce the diagnostic lines between the various types of depression to matters of "content." As we have seen, she, in contrast to the earlier Rado (1928) and Fenichel (1945), also argues for a qualitative rather than a quantitative difference between psychotic and neurotic depressions. She expresses her belief that depressive psychoses probably involve "an as yet undiscovered psychosomatic process." She calls for what Bellak (1958, p. 5) refers to as a "multiple-factor psychosomatic approach" to the affective disorders. Insofar as such an approach deals with the psychological aspects of neurotic or psychotic depression, she takes it for granted that it will use psychoanalytic theory. She believes that progress in the understanding of the psychology of the depressive psychoses can only be made by studying the specific psychogenetic factors, the nature and structure of psychotic conflicts and the specific psychotic defense and restitutive mechanisms.

Since it became clear that reserpine reduced the CNS level of neurotransmitters, and since the introduction of the monoamine oxidase inhibitors and the tricyclic antidepressants and the growing understanding of their mechanisms, many of the factors in "the multiple-factor psychosomatic approach" that Bellak and Jacobson refer to are beginning to be better understood. Some progress has been made in the genetics of manic-depressive disorders (see Rosenthal, 1970; Gershon et al., 1971; Mendels, 1974). Winokur (1973) and his colleagues have demonstrated that the first-degree relatives of patients with primary affective disorders are at risk with respect to varying patterns of morbidity.

Schildkraut (1965) has contributed his catecholamine hypothesis of depression which has generated an immense amount of fruitful work. Endocrine studies (Carroll, 1972, 1973; Sachar, 1967a, 1967b, 1973) have added to our understanding of neurophysiologic variables in various kinds of depression. Goodwin and Bunney (1973), however, in a valuable review of the biologic studies of depression, have emphasized the incompleteness of the work that has so far been done. Despite the tantalizing findings of a number of gifted investigators, we still do not completely understand the neurobiological substructure of depression. We do know, nevertheless, that in what Winokur refers to as the manic-depressive and the pure depressive disorders genetic factors endow the individual with an inherited neurophysiological predisposition to react to a number of variables with depressive illness. In this book we have been reviewing different concepts about one of these variables, namely the psychological one.

But there are other variables that we do not as yet understand. The patient who has periodic cycles of approximately twenty-four hours of mania and twenty-four hours of depression, year in and year out, is not responding to psychological variables, although psychological stress may actually produce slight variations in the length of these cycles according to one interesting report (Fryer, 1974).

In a most provocative and thoughtful paper, Blumenthal (1971) has discussed, among other matters, the heterogeneity of etiological variables in depression. Almost as though in answer to Rado's (1951) hope for the disclosure of a "causative chain of events . . . drawn from genetics, pathologic anatomy, physiology, biophysics, biochemistry and psychodynamics" which might elucidate the etiology of depression, Blumenthal has provided a simplified version of "a hypothetical model of [a] causally linked etiologic sequence leading to depression." She proposes the following sequential chain: psychic event $\longrightarrow$ hormone imbalance $\longrightarrow$ electrolyte disturbance $\longrightarrow$ neurotransmitter imbalance $\longrightarrow$ depression. She emphasizes the hypothetical nature of this sequence. Actually, we know more about some of the links in this chain, e.g., psychic events and the imbalance of transmitter substances in the central nervous system, than we know about others, although there is no doubt that the other links may play a role in the etiological sequence in particular instances. Actually Blumenthal suggests more probable but more complicated hypothetical sequential chains which I will, for the sake of simplicity, not review.

With respect to the sequential chain that I have reproduced above, Blumenthal states that "such a schema is consistent with the biological facts that are available nowadays though it is not the only schema consistent with the facts." She points out that "such a sequence of events could begin at any point in the chain. It might be possible to arrive at the end state of depression by beginning with a psychic event, or at the stage of hormone imbalance, or the stage of hormone imbalance might be circumvented and the initiating disturbance might be one of electrolyte imbalance, a mechanism which might account for some depressions occurring postoperatively. Similarly, the electrolyte imbalance step might be bypassed and the chain entered directly at the level of transmitter imbalance, as in the reserpine-induced depressions."

Speaking of treatment, she suggests that if the patients were suffering from some continuing psychic stress no amount of treatment directed at transmitter substances (i.e., antidepressants) would be effective "since the strain repeatedly renews the imbalance." In fact, this continuing strain, as she puts it, could be counteracted by the continued administration of antidepressants, but for didactic purposes the point is well made. As was well-known before the days of specific treatments, when an identifiable psychic event precipitated a melancholia, the depression might persist autonomously and indefinitely despite the ending or even the reversal of the precipitating event. The early analysts, aware of this, would speculate about why such a melancholia would eventually come to a spontaneous end. As late as 1951, Rado stated: "Treated or untreated, after a period of time the depressive spell spends its fury and subsides; we do not know why or how." The modern reader might be reminded that such a spell may last for years and even for decades before it spontaneously subsided.

In a very imaginative attempt to conceptualize a unified hypothesis of depressive disorders with the data currently available, Akiskal and McKinney (1973) suggest that melancholic or endogenous depressions constitute a final common pathway of a variety of interpersonal, intrapsychic and neurophysiological processes. As they view it: "(i) no matter what interpersonal factors elicit or maintain depressive behaviors, once these behaviors assume severe proportions they become biologically autonomous"—the stage of endogenous or melancholic depression—"and, consequently, require somatic therapies; (ii) severe depressions have underlying biochemical predispositions and, therefore, would not respond to any appreciable degree to verbal therapy."

To illustrate the autonomous nature of depressions once they are precipitated, I might mention a fifty-year-old female patient who had never had a psychiatric illness before in her life, who responded with depression one week after being started on reserpine. Her internist recognized the role of reserpine in her depression and immediately discontinued this medication. When I first saw her one year later, the patient was still profoundly depressed. The neurotransmitter imbalance caused by the reserpine apparently remained unchanged for that whole period of time.

Looking at the situation from the reverse point of view, I have seen depressions precipitated by psychological events years before, still persisting, resistant to years of psychotherapy or psychoanalysis, and responding promptly to antidepressant medications—and not recurring when the medication was finally discontinued.

There is by now ample evidence for a number of physiological variables in the causation of depression. It seems increasingly likely that the final link in the etiological chain in primary affective disorders (endogenous or psychobiological or psychotic depressions), whatever the precipitant, is the imbalance in neurotransmitter substances. These substances are believed by most workers to be the biogenic amines and by others, more specifically, to be a catecholamine, namely norepinephrine. How the depression manifests itself clinically, psychodynamically and phenomenologically will be a consequence among other factors of the patient's individual life history, the stage of development of his intrapsychic structures and the nature of his conflicts.

Relevant to this is Lehmann's (1972) recent reminder of certain basic factors useful in conceptualizing the determinants of psychopathology. These factors might be characterized as (1) the pathogenic, (2) the personality characteristics, (3) the predisposing factors, (4) the precipitating factors and, finally, (5) the cultural factors. "As an illustration, the pathogenic factor of a depression might be the hypothesized disturbance of the biogenic-amine balance in the CNS; [then] the personality make-up that determines the choice of specific symptoms; the precipitating factors, the traumatic life stresses that determine the point in time at which the depression manifests itself; the predisposing factors, the hereditary potential; and [finally] the cultural environment that plays an important role in the shaping of symptoms."

With reference to the cultural factors, I am reminded of the findings of many cross-cultural psychiatrists who quite generally report that guilt tends to be a symptom of depressive illness only in Westernized populations or in individuals affected by the Christian tradition. Compared to these findings, Rochlin's (1953) and Beres' (1966) view of the impossibility of depressions without guilt appears parochial. I am also reminded of Bazzoui's (1970) findings among Iraqi tribesmen that they experience their depressions primarily somatically rather than psychologically. They experience a dysphoria that they refer to their bodies and they appear to have little access to their feelings or affects. I noted previously that I have observed the same unawareness of depressed feelings in middle-class white Americans and even in a university-based scientist who had been in analysis for five years.

Thus that psychobiological condition which we call depressive illness or endogenous depression produces a dysphoria that is experienced in ways that are to a considerable extent determined by one's cultural and life circumstances and experiences. Phrased differently, that disorder, apparently correlated with functional levels of certain neurotransmitters and which we call depressive disease, manifests itself in very different ways. A native of Iraq will experience his dysphoria in a way different from that of a Bryn Mawr college girl. And the latter will experience and manifest her depression differently than will a young child. And young children will experience their depressive dysphoria in ways that correspond to their age.

Is depression therefore a consequence only of intersystemic conflicts or, for that matter, intrasystemic conflicts? Speaking meta-psychoneurophysiologically, must a depression of neurotransmitters be dependent on object constancy? What basis is there for denying that a depletion of biogenic amines can exist in an infant or in a small child? True, at these ages the dysphoria may be experienced and manifested differently from the depressive dysphoria in a Nigerian tribesman or Japanese business executive.

Karno and Mandell (1972), in a paper that has some relevance to this theme, speculate about the effect on the neurochemical systems of infants and children when there is a defect or withdrawal of mothering. They point out that Fries and Woolf (1953) have described different congenital activity types in newborn infants. In other words, infants respond to the stimuli of their environment with a wide range of responsiveness. They argue, referring to the work of Spitz and others, that "the withdrawal of a mothering companion apparently precipitates a *decline* in responsivity which would presumably be correlated with the neurochemical events which our model predicts should be regularly present in the depressed states. . . ." (the details of which it is unnecessary to go into in this book). They go on to propose that "the anaclitically depressed infant . . . is in a state of [maternal] stimulus deprivation" and altered biochemical equilibrium "leading to depressive or dysphoric affect." On the basis of some animal research, they go on to speculate that some infants may similarly be born with congenitally different CNS levels of important biochemical substances. "If this is so, we might predict that such infants would be 'genetically prone' to the depressive experience. Thus, these might be the children with potentially depressive ego structures." Speculatively, they go on to wonder whether the depression-prone whom Rado (1928) long ago described as "addicted to love" may be "the individual who is constitutionally suffering from a very thin buffer-zone between normal baseline and clinically depressed levels of biosynthetic enzymatic activity. Thus, such individuals might be those who respond quickly and profoundly to object loss."

All this is very speculative indeed! Whether their particular biochemical model is valid or not is beside the point. What is to the point is that early deprivation produces affective and behavioral changes in infants and small children. These changes must be mediated by neurobiochemical changes. Animal studies have amply demonstrated that early deprivation or isolation bring about changes in the brain levels of neurotransmitters. This presumably occurs in infants and children, too. Furthermore, certain children must be genetically more liable to suffer such changes, and probably to suffer such changes to levels of deprivation that would not affect other children so adversely. We frequently read about children who survive early deprivation without marked psychopathology.

From a different perspective, I must mention certain patients with an acute endogenous psychobiological depression who have recovered from their depression after the administration of an antidepressant but who then report not only that are they no longer depressed but that they feel better than they ever have. In going over their histories with them, I have been impressed with what appears to be almost lifelong subclinical depressions for which they never sought treatment. How can one conceptualize such chronic lifelong subclinical depressions which improved markedly with antidepressants except with speculations about lifelong decreased levels of vital CNS neurotransmitters? Again meta-neurophysiology! The case is not proven. But one wonders.

To return to my point, the argument is that genetically or environmentally induced disturbances of biochemical equilibria will produce dysphoria in children. The fact that object constancy or adequate levels of superego formation may not have been reached would seem to determine how these children experienced their dysphoria or depression, rather than make it impossible for them to be depressed. In simpler words, they may not manifest low self-esteem or experience or express feelings of guilt—but they will be depressed. They will presumably experience dysphoria, or, to use Sandler and Joffe's admirable concept, a lack of a sense of well-being, a descriptive phrase that can be thought of as independent of any particular level of psychological or cognitive development. It is only after such development has occurred that the lack of a sense of well-being may be experienced as a lack of self-esteem or as guilt, or, as in the Iraqi patients, a dysphoria experienced as somatic.

What I have been attempting to do is indicate that what psychoanalytic theory and observations have accomplished is to bring a fuller understanding of what Jacobson refers to as the psychological factors in a multiple-factor psychosomatic disorder. When the psychological aspects of this syndrome are conceptualized as representing the whole of this clinical picture, this can only lead to the conceptual errors that Jacobson deplores and that are exemplified in the papers of writers such as Rochlin (1953) and Beres (1966).

I must remind the reader, however, that not all depressive illnesses are primary or endogenous or psychotic depressive disorders. Although neurotic depressions must ultimately be correlated with neurophysiological substrata, just as are all affects and cognitions, we have no more information about them than we have about the biochemical correlates of normal thoughts and feelings. The biological understanding of neurotic depressions is light years removed from our still very imperfect but developing grasp of the biochemical events accompanying endogenous depressions.

Therefore, in our thinking of neurotic depression, we remain almost entirely in the realm of the psychological. Not only are the themes of oral needs, low self-esteem and negative self-concepts supremely relevant to the understanding of the origins and contents of the factors and conflicts that predispose to and constitute neurotic depressions, but they provide us with the conceptual tools to cope therapeutically with them. To understand the aspirations, needs, frustrations and the determinants of self-esteem and to comprehend the cognitive distortions that undermine the self-esteem and sense of well-being of the neurotically depressed individual is of supreme importance in the treatment of such a patient. And as yet we have no other fully developed understanding of such a patient except the experiential and the psychodynamic. One must point out, however, that there is some beginning interest in the behavioral modification of depressive illness in addition to the cognitive therapy that Beck has described.

[7]

Durell (1973), deploring old-fashioned factionalism as represented by psychological versus biological alternatives, suggests—correctly, I believe—that "an intellectual atmosphere appears to be developing that allows for the importance of multiple physical and psychological factors in the etiology and pathogenesis of the psychological disorders. . . ." Let us therefore look more closely at the interactions of the psychological, psychoanalytic and biological perspectives in depression.

One of the major focuses of interest in the psychoanalytic study of depressive disorders is the role that psychological stresses and conflicts play in precipitating this illness. A great deal of psychoanalytic attention has been paid to the predisposition to depression, to the effect of early loss on depression, to the role of lowered self-esteem, or a lowered sense of well-being or negative self-concepts in the precipitation of depression. Yet, when one reviews the most sophisticated psychiatric studies of endogenous depression, e.g., the studies of Kiloh and Garside, Kendell and Winokur and his collaborators, a persistently uniform theme is the absence of psychological precipitants in the onset of these depressions, or at most the presence of such precipitants in the first episode of illness and their absence in subsequent episodes. This is an incongruous and paradoxical situation indeed. What one group of workers regards as of utmost importance is, by another group of workers, considered to be almost incompatible with the diagnosis of psychotic or primary depression. What are we to make of this incongruity?

Goodwin and Bunney (1973) suggest that this finding, namely, that there is an absence of precipitating events in endogenously depressed patients, might well be an artifact of the data-gathering method. Psychiatric investigators usually obtain their information concerning precipitating events in one or two interviews early in the hospitalization when the patient is still badly depressed. "Considering the disturbance in thought processes and in psychomotor state so characteristic of severely depressed patients, it is certainly no surprise that the various groups of investigators were unable to uncover precipitating events in the endogenous group."

In a study of their own, conducted on forty consecutively admitted depressed patients throughout the period of their hospitalization, Leff, Roatch and Bunney (1970) discovered that early data collected from the endogenous group during the first week of hospitalization provided little information concerning environmental stress. It was only after four to six weeks of hospitalization that events such as a stillbirth or the recent death of a family member were elicited. They grant that this kind of information, obtained without a control group, cannot answer the question about whether environmental events precipitate depressive illness. But one is reminded of Sir Aubrey Lewis' (1934b) observation that the better one knows a patient the harder it becomes to decide whether or not some event or accumulation of events had precipitated the depression. The debate still goes on. The psychiatric literature is not totally agreed on this topic but certainly leans heavily in the direction of seeing no correlation between precipitating events and endogenous depressions. At the other extreme, the psychosomatic literature is filled with papers attempting to establish that losses precipitate not only depressions but also infections and disorders as grave as leukemia and cancer.

Heron (1965) notes that Kraepelin (1921, pp. 180–81) commented that one of his patients fell ill after the death of her husband, once after the death of her dog and on the latest occasion after the death of her dove. This was no doubt reported derisively as illustrating the unimportance of precipitating events. In fact, Kraepelin concluded shortly after commenting on this patient that manic-depressive illness was "to an astonishing degree independent of external influences" (pp. 180–81). What this indicates, of course, was that Kraepelin was to an astonishing degree unaware of the symbolic and psychological implications of these losses.

Freud (1917) noted that melancholia as well as mourning "is regularly the reaction to the loss of a loved person, or to the loss of some abstraction which takes the place of one, such as one's country, liberty, an ideal, and so on." The understanding of the loss involved in depression has gradually evolved in the psychoanalytic literature. Rado and Fenichel understood it as the loss of external narcissistic supplies. Bibring and Jacobson saw the loss of self-esteem as the critical loss in depressions. And Sandler and Joffe view the critical loss as the loss of a previous state of well-being, of which the lost object might be the "vehicle," but which might equally consist of a loss of a previous developmental or life phase. They see adolescence, marriage, parenthood, removals to new surroundings or to new jobs, retirement, etc., as potentially producing a loss of well-being and causing psychic pain and perhaps a depressive reaction or illness.

The depressed patient may not even be aware of the nature, or even of the existence of such a loss. I have seen a depression, in a patient who denied any precipitating event, clearly precipitated by a move from one role in a company to another involving no loss of income, status or prestige. Still, there was a loss of a sense of well-being (though not a loss of self-esteem) which could only be identified as treatment went on.

And yet—I have seen profound depressions occur suddenly within five minutes in the middle of a sunny afternoon without any identifiable prior change of any kind, and I have seen depressions abruptly cease, just as Jacobson (1971) describes, also within five minutes and for no apparent reason. It would seem that while the psychiatric investigators to whom I have referred undoubtedly miss many subtle losses as well as losses of the more obvious kind that Goodwin and Bunney (1973) refer to, there are, nevertheless, many depressive episodes that do seem to occur without identifiable environmental precipitants.

To make the situation more complex, I have seen patients become depressed over circumstances no different than those which on previous and subsequent occasions did not precipitate depressions. And, of course, there are the brief daily cycles of mania and depression that seem to have no psychological meaning whatsoever.

The subject of loss brings up the subject of vulnerability to loss, sometimes called narcissistic vulnerability, a vulnerability to loss of self-esteem or to a loss of the sense of well-being. The tendency is to relate this vulnerability to early experience as authors as diverse as Abraham, Jacobson and Bowlby do. We have all seen insecure patients with an insatiable need for reassurance and a constant need for external narcissistic supplies to maintain their sense of self-esteem. They are certainly vulnerable to loss.

Do manic-depressive patients represent this kind of insecure person? Abraham emphasized the obsessive-compulsive pre-morbid personality of manic-depressives. Rosenthal and Gude-man (1967) look at these same characteristics from a different, perhaps American perspective, and refer to these patients as effec-tive, well-adjusted and well-integrated. The various psychiatric writers on endogenous depression also tend to emphasize a nor-mal premorbid personality and a nonneurotic personality struc-ture between episodes of illness. Jacobson (1971, p. 231) as well notes that "we are also surprised to see that as long as they are not ill, they may be delightful companions or marital partners. . . . In their sexual life they may show full sexual responsiveness, and emotionally . . . a touching warmth." However, she discerningly observes that "although they do not manifest a lack of inner re-sources, they seem to suffer from a specific ego weakness which shows in their remarkable vulnerability, their intolerance of frus-tration, hurt, and disappointment." She (1973) also agrees that "they are mostly compulsive people."

As I have noted, Karno and Mandell (1972) speculate about ge-netic contributions to this vulnerability. That there is a genetic predisposition to manic-depressive illness is beyond doubt. Is it too speculative to hypothesize that there is a genetic predisposition to the kind of personality structure, to the specific ego weakness that Jacobson describes. I have often been impressed by the experi-ence of seeing able, effective, successful, seemingly well-balanced manic-depressive individuals, during their well phases, fill their treatment hours, time after time, with endless reports of accom-plishments, successes and compliments received. They do not fail to mention being greeted or recognized by important people. They almost display their narcissistic needs on their sleeves in their seemingly casual accounts of successes and compliments. If one were unkind, one could describe their recitations as boasting and name-dropping. Jacobson (1973), too, refers to the insatiable " 'narcissistic' involvement of manic-depressives with them-selves" in terms that are not too different from mine. She stresses as I do that these characteristics which "may greatly vary in these patients according to their special qualities and quantities" are noticeable even during their so-called healthy periods.

The specific ego weakness that Jacobson refers to is certainly there, a continuing need to bolster their self-esteem by impressing themselves and their therapists with their effectiveness. I must repeat that the patients I refer to—and by no means are all manic-depressives like that—realistically have no need to impress others with their success. They are successful and effective and are known to be so. To what extent, then, is this continuous exaggerated need for a sense of effectiveness and self-esteem and for external narcissistic supplies—as well as the corresponding vulnerability to frustration, disappointment and hurt—experiential or genetic? In treating any one patient one cannot tell. But, when I see many manic-depressive patients successfully treated for their illness with lithium carbonate with no recurrences and with their vulnerability to narcissistic injuries apparently greatly reduced or even perhaps eliminated, and yet continuing to recite their accomplishments, one begins to wonder. Especially after I have seen in other patients the astonishing effectiveness of lithium carbonate on the modification not only of mood swings but of lifelong personality structures, I wonder more about the effect of neurophysiology on character. I refer, for example, to the sudden, dramatic transformation of an acting-out, promiscuous, unfeeling, "hysterical" personality into a stable, disciplined individual with a capacity for warmth and for lasting relationships following dramatically upon the administration of lithium carbonate, with relapses occurring in the early stages when the patient, unconvinced of the role of lithium in what was happening to her, would discontinue her medication, only to change once more when she began to take her lithium regularly.

Under these circumstances, one cannot help wonder about the effect of neurobiochemistry (genetics?) on the temperament and personality structure of individuals and on the specific ego weaknesses to which Jacobson refers, and, of course, about the vulnerability to depressive illness.

I have tried in a rambling, discursive, speculative way to attempt some rapprochement between neuropharmacology, neurophysiology and psychoanalysis. The literature on these subjects seems to exist in different universes from one another. Of the analysts reviewed in this book, only Beck, who has perhaps strayed furthest from classical formulations, gives any space to the remarkable effectiveness of the antidepressants. He devotes a section of a recent book (1973) to a straightforward account of psychopharmacology, although Ostow (1962) has created a strange amalgam of pharmacology and psychic energy in his lengthy volume dedicated to the subject.

In these last two sections I have speculated in a necessarily sketchy way about the sequential chain leading to depression and to the narcissistic vulnerability that predisposes to depression. I have touched on genetic aspects of depressive illness which, of course, do not operate in a vacuum but only by producing a neurophysiologic vulnerability which is then, in turn, affected by imbalances in the endocrine system, electrolyte imbalances and modifications in the neurotransmitter equilibrium, as well as by psychic events which must operate via the neurophysiological substratum to produce a depression.

To illustrate what I mean in a specific instance, let us imagine an individual who, because of a genetic predisposition, has an unstable CNS level of critical neurotransmitters. If he experiences early deprivation, he may furthermore experience a permanently somewhat depressed level of these transmitters and may suffer from a lifelong subclinical (or occasionally clinical) depression, perhaps characterized by apathy, pessimism and lack of vitality. Even without this early deprivation, this genetic predisposition may affect his development in that it is conducive to a specific ego weakness which makes him, despite his possible effectiveness and charm, narcissistically vulnerable to disappointment and hurt. He compensates for this, if he has the innate ability to do so, by conducting his life in an effective, successful, well-adjusted way but nevertheless has to shore up his self-esteem by the narcissistic boastful behavior that I have referred to or by a variety of other defense mechanisms, the nature of which may be determined by the patient's own individual endowments.* I may add that if the person has a cyclothymic personality he may have unusual levels of energy, which suggests a specific biological contribution to his personality and temperament and which makes it possible for him to be unusually hard-working, successful and capable. Such a person might be described as obsessive-compulsive or as oral, depending on which aspect of his make-up is more prominent.

Such a patient on the occasion of a disappointment, hurt or loss, or perhaps for no reason that can be discovered, may gradually or suddenly wake up depressed with the particular qualitatively specific type of depression that Jacobson has described so well. He may or may not be delusional. He may or may not experience low

---

*In an interesting paper on the significance of individual differences at birth for later development, Korner (1964) refers to Hartmann's (1950) linkage of early individual differences to later choice of defense mechanisms.

self-esteem. Usually he does, but when he does it may be secondary to his decreased effectiveness, which in turn is a consequence of his psychomotor retardation and his difficulty in concentration. He will typically experience his depression as an illness befalling him from the outside.

This depressed state, untreated, may last for days, months or years. In psychoanalytic treatment he may display the family constellation that Cohen et al. described—or, more probably, he will not. He may or may not have problems with his ego boundaries (i.e., overlapping of self- and object-representations). He may or may not exhibit self-directed aggression in the form of self-reproaches. Beres (1966) believes that the form that this aggression assumes is more characteristically that of an intersystemic conflict between the superego and the ego, namely, guilt. However, he may or may not experience guilt.

A depression like this responds to ECT or to antidepressants which appear to operate by raising the functional levels of the biogenic amines or other essential neurotransmitters.

I have speculated about the dysphoria, the final common pathway of imbalances in the biogenic amine or neurotransmitter systems, and have discussed the manner in which the depressive dysphoria may manifest itself in adult Western and non-Western populations. In doing so, I have touched upon the parochialism of some of the formulations of depression found in the psychoanalytic literature. I have also wondered about how this depressive dysphoria manifests itself in children and infants—for who is to say that the neurobiochemical events that I refer to do not occur in children. After all, English workers (e.g., Frommer, 1968) do describe depressions in children and, moreover, treat them successfully with antidepressants, a circumstance that must reflect underlying biochemical changes.

All of this causes me not only to see psychoanalytic formulations as providing insight into the factors and conflicts predisposing to depression but simultaneously to see them, in a circular kind of process, as the epiphenomena, the manifestations of underlying physiological changes. And no doubt the relative importance of the psychological and experiential as opposed to the neurophysiological contributions differ from patient to patient. Perhaps one can think of two extremes as represented by a neurotic depressive reaction precipitated by a negative self-concept of the kind that Beck describes or by a disappointment in studies or in love and a manic-depressive illness with bipolar cycles of twenty-four hours each that go on endlessly year after year.

And, finally, I have philosophized about the interaction of neurophysiology and personality structure, about neurotransmitters and narcissistic vulnerability, about lithium and warmth and object constancy. Speculations indeed—but grounded on research findings and on clinical observation.

[8]

After having reviewed this extensive body of literature with its many theoretical disagreements, it should be emphasized that an impressive consensus nevertheless exists.

There is no basic disagreement, for example, about how a child acquires the blissful certainty of being loved and wanted, with its accompanying sense of security and self-esteem. It is now clear that this desirable outcome is mainly the result of fortunate relationships with the first love-objects. Furthermore, there is wide agreement that until this happy state of affairs is reached the infant is recurringly overwhelmed by what can best be described in adultomorphic terms as feelings of abandonment, loss, loneliness, depression and anxiety.

The importance of parental and in particular maternal attitudes for the development of emotional security in the child is now taken for granted. It is also becoming clearer that maternal attitudes can be influenced in turn by the behavior of the infant, which depends, among other things, on its inherited or acquired activity patterns, disabilities and rudimentary temperament. This results in a relationship which is much more complex than was originally postulated.

It is now clear that severe early deprivation results in very pathological personality development. However, no correlation between such early experiences and any particular kind of adult depressive reaction has as yet been established.

Most writers feel that the predisposition to some types of depressive illness includes more than psychological factors. There is, in particular, conclusive evidence for a hereditary predisposition to the manic-depressive disorders; far less evidence exists for hereditary factors in neurotic depressive states.

There is, nevertheless, a psychoanalytic consensus that in even the most "endogenous" of depressions emotional factors play a highly significant role. The onset of the illness can frequently be correlated with situations of loss or disappointment or with circumstances that have these meanings for the patient.

These situations of loss or disappointment producing severe mood disturbances in predisposed individuals as well as less pronounced fluctuations of mood in other people are now generally considered to represent fluctuations in self-esteem or well-being.

However, it has become clear in recent years that a psychotic depression consists of more than simply a fall in self-esteem and represents more than a regression to an infantile mode of behavior. Somatic manifestations are usually found as well as frequent alterations in reality testing and ego identifications. To describe these changes as regressive is to emphasize their resemblance to infantile states. But to describe them so simply is to overlook the profound difference that exists between a psychotic condition and the modes of functioning of infants and children.

Finally, there is a consensus that the term "depression" is applied to a variety of affective states. These states differ not only objectively but subjectively. People are depressed in different ways. They experience and manifest and describe their depressions differently. The subjective affective state of the guilty, self-reproachful, agitated involutional patient is clearly different from that of the hopeless, futile, retarded schizoid adolescent, although both of these refer to themselves as "depressed."

[9]

As I indicated previously, the first edition of this volume represented the summary of an era of broadly conceived theoretical and clinical observations about the psychodynamics of depression. The decade and a half since that edition was published has seen, in the general psychoanalytic literature, a sustained critical analysis and refutation of certain structural and economic constructs— a critique which I used to examine several key elements in the psychoanalytic concepts of depression. In the child psychoanalytic literature, there has appeared, it seems to me, an overconfident series of publications based on a much too narrow empirical base and which largely neglects very important related data. The psychiatric field is characterized by an impressively successful an-

tidepressive armamentarium and by a skillfully mounted inves-
tigative attack on the neurophysiological correlates of depressive
illness, an attack which has not yet met with final success but
which cannot be far away from achieving its goals.

As we gradually understand more and more about the biology
of depression, and as we gain access to better and more effective
antidepressants together with improved techniques for predicting
the effects of specific medications for individual patients, what role
will our painfully acquired psychoanalytic understanding of
depression play? Even now, many psychoanalysts and most psychiatrists, aware of the genetic and biochemical components of
primary affective disorders, prefer to treat these illnesses with
medications. They reserve psychoanalysis or psychotherapy either
for the treatment of the no longer depressed patient or, abandoning altogether the psychotherapeutic treatment of the more
severe endogenous depressions, use such treatment only for the
neurotic depressive patient or for the less seriously ill endogenously depressed patient. Sometimes as Jacobson (1971, p. 173)
notes, the latter is mistaken for a neurotic depressive and is
treated as such.

Every clinician knows how often spontaneous remissions are
mistaken for successful analyses. I remember especially one patient, with recurrent depressive episodes, discharged from an apparently successful analysis, only to become, six months later,
more severely and stuporously depressed than she had ever been.
This same confusion between spontaneous remissions and the apparently successful use of medications can also occur.

As more effective medications and predictive methods become
available, it seems clear that the tide will turn away from a purely
psychoanalytic to a mainly pharmacological treatment approach
to primary depressive *illness,* although many a *patient* who is
prone to depression will still need and receive psychoanalytic or
psychoanalytically oriented treatment. And in the treatment of
such patients (rather than in the treatment of the depressive illness itself) the understanding of depression provided by Abraham,
Freud, Rado, Gero, Bibring, Jacobson, Sandler et al., Beck, as well
as the other contributors to the psychoanalytic understanding of
depression, will remain of supreme importance.

A similar phenomenon has taken place in the field of psychosomatic medicine (in which there is increasing evidence that endogenous depression belongs), where at one time high hopes were

held out for the psychoanalytic treatment of illnesses such as peptic ulcer, bronchial asthma and ulcerative colitis. These hopes were not sustained by clinical experience. The illnesses continue to be treated by medical means, although the patients with such illnesses are often greatly helped by psychoanalysis or by analytically oriented treatment. The vulnerability to these illnesses usually remains, although the conflicts and the stresses which may trigger them off may be relieved or resolved by treatment. This also seems to occur with patients with endogenous depressions.

As for the future progress in the understanding of depression, I believe that a very heartening sign is the increasing number of sophisticated and broadly trained psychoanalytic investigators and clinicians who, in their respective areas of research and treatment, have approached their subjects from a number of viewpoints with equal dexterity, erudition, originality and competence. I need only refer to workers such as Roy Grinker, Sr., George Engel, Aaron T. Beck, Daniel X. Freedman, Gerald Klerman and many others.

I believe that the psychoanalytic task of understanding depression has been largely completed, although there will undoubtedly continue to be revisions and refinements of theory. Writers such as Sandler and Joffe, Beck and Bowlby will ensure this. But it seems to me that the significant focus of new work on depression will continue to shift in a neurophysiological and psychopharmacological direction. It will be when that enterprise achieves some definitive success that the important task of coordinating the psychoanalytic and biological understanding of depression can finally be undertaken in earnest.

BIBLIOGRAPHY

Abraham, Karl (1911). Notes on the psycho-analytic investigation and treatment of manic-depressive insanity and allied conditions. In *Selected Papers on Psycho-analysis*. London: Hogarth Press and The Institute of Psycho-analysis, 1927, pp. 137–56.

———— (1916). The first pregenital stage of the libido. In *Selected Papers on Psycho-analysis*. London: Hogarth Press and The Institute of Psycho-analysis, 1927, pp. 248–79.

———— (1924). A short study of the development of the libido, viewed in the light of mental disorders. In *Selected Papers on Psycho-analysis*. London: Hogarth Press and The Institute of Psycho-analysis, 1927, pp. 418–502.

Ackner, B., and Pampiglione, G. (1959). An evaluation of the sedation threshold test. *J. Psychosom. Res.* 3:271–81.

Akiskal, Hagop S., and McKinney, William T., Jr. (1973). Depressive disorders: toward a unified hypothesis. *Science* 182:20–29.

Alexander, Franz (1950). *Psychosomatic Medicine: Its Principles and Applications.* New York: Norton.

Angst, J. (1966). *Zür Ätiologie und Nosologie endogener depressiven Psychosen.* Berlin.

Anthony, James, and Scott, Peter (1960). Manic-depressive psychosis in childhood. *Child Psychol. Psychiat.* 1:53–72.

Apfelbaum, Bernard (1965). Ego psychology, psychic energy and the hazards of quantitative explanation in psychoanalytic theory. *Int. J. Psycho-anal.* 46:168–82.

Applegarth, Adrienne (1971). Comments on aspects of the theory of psychic energy. *J. Am. Psychoanal. Assn.* 19:379–416.

Arieti, Silvano (1962). The psychotherapeutic approach to depression. *Amer. J. Psychother.* 16:397–406.

Arlow, Jacob A. (1955). Reporter on Panel on Sublimation. *J. Am. Psychoanal. Assn.* 3:515–27.

———— (1970). Some problems in current psychoanalytic thought. In Silvano Arieti, ed., *The World Biennial of Psychiatry and Psychotherapy*, I. New York: Basic Books.

———, and Brenner, Charles (1964). *Psychoanalytic Concepts and the Structural Theory.* New York: International Universities Press.

Arthur, Bette, and Kemme, Mary L. (1964). Bereavement in childhood. *J. Child Psychol. Psychiat.* 5:37–49.

Asch, Stuart S. (1966). Depression: Three clinical variations. *Psychoanal. Study Child* 21:150–71.

Ascher, Edouard (1952). A criticism of the concept of neurotic depression. *Amer. J. Psychiat.* 108:901–08.

Astrup, C., Fossum, A., and Holmboe, R. (1959). A follow-up study of 270 patients with acute affective psychoses. *Acta Psychiat. Neurol. Scand.* 34 (Suppl.) 135: 1–65.

Baker, Max, Dorzab, Joe, Winokur, George, and Cadoret, Remi J. (1971). Depressive disease: classification and clinical characteristics. *Comp. Psychiat.* 12:354–65.

——— (1972). Depressive disease: evidence favoring polygenic inheritance based on an analysis of ancestral cases. *Arch. Gen. Psychiat.* 27:320–27.

Balint, Michael (1949). Early development states of the ego. Primary object love. *Int. J. Psycho-anal.* 30:265–73.

——— (1952). New beginning and the paranoid and the depressive syndromes. *Int. J. Psycho-anal.* 33:214–24.

——— (1953). *Primary Love and Psycho-Analytic Technique.* London: Hogarth Press.

Ball, J. R., and Kiloh, L. G. (1959). A controlled trial of imipramine in treatment of depressive states. *Brit. Med. J.* ii:1052–55.

Barkas, M. P. (1925). Treatment of psychotic patients in institutions in the light of psychoanalysis. *Jour. Neurol. and Psychopath.* 5:333–40.

Barrett, A. M. (1931). Manic depressive psychosis in childhood. *Int. Clin.* 3:205.

Bazzoui, Widad (1970). Affective disorders in Iraq. *Brit. J. Psychiat.* 117:195–203.

Beck, Aaron T. (1961). A systematic investigation of depression. *Comp. Psychiat.* 2:162–70.

——— (1963). Thinking and depression: 1. Idiosyncratic content and cognitive distortions. *Arch. Gen. Psychiat.* 9:324–33.

——— (1967). *Depression: Clinical, Experimental and Theoretical Aspects.* New York: Paul B. Hoeber.

——— (1970). The core problem in depression: the cognitive triad. *Science and Psychoanalysis* 17:47–55.

——— (1971). Cognition, affect and psychopathology. *Arch. Gen. Psychiat.* 24: 495–500.

——— (1972). The phenomena of depression: a synthesis. In Daniel Offer and Daniel X. Freedman, eds., *Modern Psychiatry and Clinical Research: Essays in Honor of Roy R. Grinker, Sr.* New York: Basic Books.

——— (1973). *The Diagnosis and Management of Depression.* Philadelphia: University of Pennsylvania Press.

——— (1974). Depressive neurosis. In *American Handbook of Psychiatry,* 3, revised and expanded 2nd ed. New York: Basic Books, pp. 61–98.

——— and Hurvich, Marvin, S. (1959). Psychological correlates of depression. *Psychosom. Med.* 21:50–55.

———, Sethi, Brij B., and Tuthill, Robert W. (1963). Childhood bereavement and adult depression. *Arch. Gen. Psychiat.* 19:295–302.

———, Ward, Clyde H., Mendelson, Myer, Mock, John, and Erbaugh, John (1961).

R. M. Mowbray, eds., *Depressive Illness*. Springfield: Charles C. Thomas, pp. 69–86.

———— (1973). Psychoendocrinology of depression versus schizophrenia. Presented to American Psychosomatic Society, Annual Meeting, Denver, Colorado, April 8, 1973.

Carver, Alfred (1921). Notes on the analysis of a case of melancholia. *J. Neurol. and Psychopathol.* 1:320–24.

Cassirer, Ernst (1961). *The Logic of the Humanities*. New Haven: Yale University Press.

Chodoff, Paul (1972). The depressive personality. *Arch. Gen. Psychiat.* 27:666–77.

Clark, L. Pierce (1914). The mechanism of periodic mental depressions as shown in two cases, and the therapeutic advantages of such studies. *Rev. Neurol. and Psychiat.* 12:433–48.

———— (1919). The psychologic treatment of retarded depressions. *Am. J. Insan.* 75:407–10.

———— (1923). In a symposium on manic-depressive psychosis. *J. Nerv. and Ment. Dis.* 57:162–65.

Cohen, Mabel Blake, Baker, Grace, Cohen, Robert A., Fromm-Reichmann, Frieda, and Weigert, Edith V. (1954). An intensive study of twelve cases of manic-depressive psychosis. *Psychiatry* 17:103–38.

Court, J. H. (1968). Manic-depressive psychosis: an alternative conceptual model. *Brit. J. Psychiat.* 114:1523–30.

———— (1972). The continuum model as a resolution of paradoxes in manic-depressive psychosis. *Brit. J. Psychiat.* 120:133–41.

Cronick, C. H. (1941). A manic-depressive reaction in an eight-year-old child. *Quart. Bull. Indiana Univ. M. Center* 3:11–13.

Cytryn, Leon, and McKnew, J. (1972). Proposed classification of childhood depression. *Amer. J. Psychiat.* 129:149–55.

Dennehy, Constance M. (1966). Childhood bereavement and psychiatric illness. *Brit. J. Psychiat.* 112:1049–69.

Despert, J. Louise (1952). Suicide and depression in children. *Nerv. Child* 9:378–89.

Detre, T., Himmelhoch, J., Swartzburg, M., Anderson, C. M., Byck, R., and Kupfer, D. J. (1972). Hypersomnia and manic-depressive disease. *Amer. J. Psychiat.* 128:1303–05.

Deutsch, Helene (1932). *Psychoanalysis of the Neuroses*, Chapter XI. London: Hogarth Press and The Institute of Psychoanalysis.

————(1937). Absence of grief. *Psychoanal. Quart.* 6:12–22; also in Helene Deutsch, *Neuroses and Character Types*. New York: International Universities Press, 1965, pp. 226–36.

Diagnostic and Statistical Manual: Mental Disorders. Washington: American Psychiatric Association, 1952.

Dreyfus (1907). Referred to in Hoch and MacCurdy (1922).

Durell, Jack (1973). Introduction. In J. Mendels, ed., *Biological Psychiatry*. New York: John Wiley and Sons, pp. 1–7.

Eissler, Kurt R. (1971). Death drive, ambivalence and narcissism. *Psychoanal. Study Child* 26:25–78.

Engel, George L. (1954). Studies of ulcerative colitis: II. The nature of the somatic processes and the adequacy of psychosomatic hypotheses. *Am. J. Med.* 16:416–33.

———— (1955a). Studies of ulcerative colitis: III. The nature of the psychologic processes. *Am. J. Med.* 19:231–56.

——— (1955b). Paper read at Psychosomatic Meeting, Atlantic City, N.J.

——— (1961). Is grief a disease? *Psychosom. Med.* 23:18–22.

——— (1962). Anxiety and depression-withdrawal: the primary affects of unpleasure. *Int. J. Psycho-anal.*, 43:89–97.

——— (1971). Attachment behavior, object relations and the dynamic-economic points of view. *Int. J. Psycho-anal.* 52:183–96.

——— and Reichsman, Franz (1956). Spontaneous and experimentally induced depression in an infant with a gastric fistula. *J. Am. Psychoanal. Assn.* 4:428–52.

English, O. Spurgeon, and Finch, Stuart M. (1964). *Introduction to Psychiatry*, 3rd ed. New York: Norton.

Erikson, Erik H. (1950). *Childhood and Society*. New York: Norton.

Everett, B. S., Gourlay, A. J., and Kendell, R. E. (1971). An attempt at validation of traditional psychiatric syndromes by cluster analysis. *Brit. J. Psychiat.* 119:399–412.

Ewalt, Jack R., and Farnsworth, Dana L. (1963). *Textbook of Psychiatry*. New York: McGraw-Hill.

Eysenck, H. J. (1970). The classification of depressive illness. *Brit. J. Psychiat.* 117:241–50.

Fairbairn, W. Ronald D. (1952). *Psychoanalytic Studies of the Personality*. London: Tavistock Publications.

——— (1955). Observations in defense of the object-relations theory of the personality. *Brit. J. M. Psychol.* 28:144–56.

Feigenbaum, Dorian (1926). A case of hysterical depression. *Psychoanalyt. Rev.* 13:404–23.

Fenichel, Otto (1931). Ueber respiratorische Introjektion. *Internat. Ztschr. f. Psychoanal.* 17:234–55.

——— (1935). A critique of the death instinct. *Imago* 21:458–66. Also in Hanna Fenichel and David Rapaport, eds., *Collected Papers of Otto Fenichel: First Series*. New York: Norton, 1953, pp. 363–72.

——— (1937). The scoptophilic instinct and identification. *Int. J. Psycho-anal.* 18:6–34. Quoted in Lewin (1950).

——— (1945). *The Psychoanalytic Theory of Neurosis*. New York: Norton.

Field, M. J. (1958). Mental disorder in rural Ghana. *J. Ment. Sci.* 104:1043–51.

Fish, Frank (1964). A guide to the Leonhard classification of chronic schizophrenia. *Psychiat. Quart.* 38:438–50.

Fleming, Joan, and Altschul, Sol (1963). Activation of mourning and growth by psychoanalysis. *Int. J. Psycho-anal.*, 44:419–31.

Fox, Ruth (1967). Alcoholism and reliance upon drugs as depressive equivalents. *Amer. J. Psychother.* 21:585–96.

Frank, Richard L. (1954). The organized adaptive aspect of the depression-elation response. In Hoch and Zubin, eds., *Depression*. New York: Grune and Stratton, pp. 51–65.

Freud, Anna (1952). The mutual influences in the development of ego and id: introduction to the discussion. *Psychoanal. Study Child* 7:42–50.

Fries, Margaret E., and Woolf, Paul J. (1953). Some hypotheses on the role of the congenital activity type in personality development. *Psychoanal. Study Child* 8:48–62.

——— (1953). Some remarks on infant observation. *Psychoanal. Study Child* 8:9–19.

_____ (1954). Psychoanalysis and education. *Psychoanal. Study Child* 9:9–15.

_____ (1958). Adolescence. *Psychoanal. Study Child* 13:255–78.

_____ (1960). Discussion of Dr. John Bowlby's paper, "Grief and mourning in infancy and early childhood." *Psychoanal. Study Child* 15:53–62.

_____ (1972). Comments on aggression. *Int. J. Psycho-anal.* 53:163–71.

_____ and Dann, Sophie (1951). An experiment in group upbringing. *Psychoanal. Study Child* 6:127–68.

Freud, Sigmund (1895). Project for a scientific psychology. *Standard Edition* 1: 295–397. London: Hogarth Press, 1966.

_____ (1896). Further remarks on the neuro-psychoses of defense. *Standard Edition* 3:167–89. London: Hogarth Press, 1962.

_____ (1905). *Three Essays on the Theory of Sexuality. Standard Edition* 7:130–243. London: Hogarth Press, 1953.

_____ (1909). Notes upon a case of obsessional neurosis. *Standard Edition* 10: 155–318. London: Hogarth Press, 1955.

_____ (1911). Psycho-analytic notes on an autobiographical account of a case of paranoia. *Standard Edition,* 12:9–82. London: Hogarth Press, 1958.

_____ (1914). On narcissism: an introduction. *Standard Edition* 14:73–102. London: Hogarth Press, 1957.

_____ (1915). Instincts and their vicissitudes. *Standard Edition* 14:117–40. London: Hogarth Press, 1957.

_____ (1915–1917). *Introductory Lectures on Psycho-analysis. Standard Edition* 15, 16. London: Hogarth Press, 1963.

_____ (1917). Mourning and melancholia. *Standard Edition* 14:243–58. London: Hogarth Press, 1957.

_____ (1920). *Beyond the Pleasure Principle. Standard Edition* 18:7–64. London: Hogarth Press, 1955.

_____ (1921). *Group Psychology and the Analysis of the Ego. Standard Edition* 18:69–143. London: Hogarth Press, 1955.

_____ (1922). Psychoanalysis and telepathy. *Standard Edition* 18:117–93. London: Hogarth Press, 1955.

_____ (1923). *The Ego and the Id. Standard Edition* 19:12–66. London: Hogarth Press, 1961.

_____ (1924). The economic problem in masochism. *Standard Edition* 19:159–70. London: Hogarth Press, 1961.

_____(1926). *Inhibitions, Symptoms and Anxiety. Standard Edition* 20:77–175. London: Hogarth Press, 1959.

_____ (1927). Fetishism. *Standard Edition* 20:77–175. London: Hogarth Press, 1959.

_____ (1929). Letter to Binswanger. In E. L. Freud, ed., *Letters of Sigmund Freud.* New York: Basic Books, 1960.

_____ (1931). Female sexuality. *Standard Edition* 21:225–43. London: Hogarth Press, 1961.

_____ (1933). *New Introductory Lectures on Psycho-analysis. Standard Edition* 22:7–182. London: Hogarth Press, 1964.

_____(1940). *An Outline of Psycho-Analysis. Standard Edition* 23:141–207. London: Hogarth Press, 1964.

Friedman, Abraham S., Cowitz, Bernard, Cohen, Harry W., and Granick, Samuel C. (1963). Syndromes and themes of psychotic depression. *Arch. Gen. Psychiat.* 9:504–09.

Fries, Margaret E., and Woolf, Paul J. (1953). Some hypotheses on the role of the congenital activity type in personality development. *Psychoanal. Study Child* 8:48–62.

Frommer, Eva A. (1968). Depressive illness in childhood. In Coppen and Walk, eds., *Recent Developments in Affective Disorders: A Symposium.* Ashford: Headley Brothers.

Fryer, John E. (1974). Diurnal cyclothymia—a subjective report. Paper given at APA Annual Meeting, Detroit, Mich. May 1974.

Fuchs, S. H. (1937). On introjection. *Int. J. Psycho-anal.* 18:269–93.

Furman, Robert A. (1964a). Death and the young child. *Psychoanal. Study Child* 19:321–33.

———— (1964b). Death of a six-year-old's mother during his analysis. *Psychoanal. Study Child* 19:377–97.

Garside, R. F., and Kay, D. W. K. (1968). A communication. *Brit. J. Psychiat.* 114:121–22.

Gay, M. J., and Tonge, W. L. (1967). The late effects of loss of parents on childhood. *Brit. J. Psychiat.* 113:753–59.

Gaylin, Willard (1968). Ed., *The Meaning of Despair.* New York: Science House.

Geleerd, Elisabeth R. (1949). The psychoanalysis of a psychotic child. *Psychoanal. Study Child*, 3/4:311–32.

Gero, George (1936). The construction of depression. *Int. J. Psycho-anal.* 17:423–61.

———— (1953). An equivalent of depression: anorexia. In Phyllis Greenacre, ed., *Affective Disorders.* New York: International Universities Press.

Gershon, Elliot S., Dunner, David L, and Goodwin, Frederick K. (1971). Toward a biology of affective disorders. *Arch. Gen. Psychiat.* 25:1–15.

Gibson, Robert W. (1963). Psychotherapy of manic-depressive states. *Psychiat. Res. Rep. Amer. Psychiat. Assn.* 17:91–102.

Gill, MertonM. (1963). *Topography and Systems in Psychoanalytic Theory.* Psychological Issues, No. 10. New York: International Universities Press.

Gillespie, R. D. (1930). The clinical differentiation of types of depression. *Guy's Hosp. Reports* 79:306–44.

Gillespie, W. H. (1971). Aggression and instinct theory. *Int. J. Psycho-anal.* 52: 155–60.

Gitelson, Maxwell (1952). Re-evaluation of the role of the oedipus complex. *Int. J. Psycho-anal.* 33:351–54.

Glover, Edward (1931). Sublimation, substitution and social anxiety. *Int. J. Psychoanal.* 12:263–97.

———— (1945). Examination of the Klein system of child psychology. *Psychoanal. Study Child* 1:75–118.

———— (1955). *The Technique of Psycho-Analysis.* New York: International Universities Press.

———— (1966). Metapsychology or metaphysics. *Psychoanal. Quart.* 35:173–90.

Glueck, S., and Glueck, E. (1950). *Unraveling Juvenile Delinquency.* Cambridge, Mass.: Harvard University Press, pp. 88–91, 122–25. Cited in Gregory (1966b).

Goertzel, V., and Goertzel, M. G. (1962). *Cradles of Eminence.* Boston: Little, Brown, pp. 149–52, 214–16, 272. Cited in Gregory (1966a).

Goldfarb, Alvin I. (1967). Masked depression in the old. *Amer. J. Psychother.* 21: 791–96.

Goldfarb, William (1945). Effects of psychological deprivation in infancy and subsequent stimulation. *Amer. J. Psychiat.* 102:18–33.

Good, R. (1946). Depression. *Brit. J. M. Psychol.* 20:344–75.

Goodwin, Frederick K., and Bunney, William E., Jr. (1973). A psychobiological approach to affective illness. *Psychiat. Annals* 3:19–53.

Gorer, Geoffrey (1965). *Death, Grief and Mourning*. New York: Doubleday. Also in Anchor Book ed. New York: Doubleday, 1967.

Greenacre, Phyllis (1951). Respiratory incorporation and the phallic phase. *Psychoanal. Study Child* 6:180–205.

Gregory, Ian (1965a). Anterospective data concerning childhood loss of a parent: I. Delinquency and high school dropouts. *Arch. Gen. Psychiat.* 13:99–109.

———— (1965b). Anterospective data concerning childhood loss of a parent: II. Pathology, performance and potential among college students. *Arch. Gen. Psychiat.* 13:110–20.

———— (1966a). Retrospective data concerning loss of a parent: I. Actuarial estimates vs. recorded frequencies of orphanhood. *Arch. Gen. Psychiat.* 15:354–61.

———— (1966b). Retrospective data concerning childhood loss of a parent: II. Category of parental loss by decade of birth, diagnosis, and MMPI. *Arch. Gen. Psychiat.* 15:362–67.

———— (1968). *Fundamentals of Psychiatry*. Philadelphia: W. B. Saunders.

Grinker, Roy R., Sr., Miller, Julian, Sabshin, Melvin, and Nunn, Robert (1961). *The Phenomena of Depression*. New York: Paul B. Hoeber.

Gross, George E., and Rubin, Isaiah A. (1972). Sublimation. *Psychoanal. Study Child* 27:334–59.

Grossman, William J., and Simon, Bennet (1969). Anthropomorphism: motive, meaning and causality in psychoanalytic theory. *Psychoanal. Study Child* 24:79–111.

Guntrip, H. (1952). A study of Fairbairn's theory of schizoid reactions. *Brit. J. Med. Psychol.* 25:86–103.

Hall, Muriel B. (1952). Our present knowledge about manic-depressive states in childhood. *Nerv. Child* 9:319–25.

Hamilton, Max (1960). A rating scale for depression. *J. Neurol. Neurosurg. Psychiat.* 23:56–62.

———— and White, J. M. (1959). Clinical syndromes in depressive states. *J. Ment. Sci.* 105:985–98.

Hammerman, Steven (1963). Ego defect and depression. *Psychoanal. Quart.*, 32:155–64.

Harms, Ernest (1952a). The problem of depressive and manic sickness in childhood. An editorial. *Nerv. Child* 9:310–15.

———— (1952b). Differential pattern of manic-depressive disease in childhood. *Nerv. Child* 9:326–55.

Harrington, Molly, and Hassan, Janet W. M. (1958). Depression in girls during latency. *Brit. J. Med. Psychol.* 31:43–50.

Hartmann, Heinz (1939). *Ego Psychology and the Problem of Adaptation*. New York: International Universities Press, 1958.

———— (1948). Comments on the psychoanalytic theory of instinctual drives. *Psychoanal. Quart.* 18:368–88. Also in Hartmann (1964), pp. 69–89.

———— (1950). Comments on the psychoanalytic theory of the ego. *Psychoanal. Study Child* 5:74–96. Also in Hartmann (1964), pp. 113–41.

———— (1955). Notes on the theory of sublimation. *Psychoanal. Study Child* 10:9–29. Also in Hartmann (1964), pp. 215–40.

———— (1956). The development of the ego concept in Freud's work. *Int. J. Psycho-*

anal. 37:425–38. Also in Hartmann (1964), pp. 268–94.

———— (1964). *Essays on Ego Psychology.* New York: International Universities Press.

———— Kris, Ernst, and Loewenstein, Rudolph M. (1946). Comments on the formation of psychic structure. *Psychoanal. Study Child* 2:11–38. Also in Hartmann et al. (1964), pp. 27–55.

————, Kris, Ernst, and Loewenstein, Rudolph M. (1949). Notes on the theory of aggression. *Psychoanal. Study Child* 3/4:9–36. Also in Hartmann et al. (1964), pp. 56–85.

————, Kris, Ernst, and Loewenstein, Rudolph, M. (1964). *Papers on Psychoanalytic Psychology.* Psychological Issues, No. 14. New York: International Universities Press.

———— and Loewenstein, Rudolph M. (1962). Notes on the superego. *Psychoanal. Study Child,* 17:42–81. Also in Hartmann et al. (1964), pp. 144–82.

Heimann, Paula, and Valenstein, Arthur F. (1972). The psychoanalytic concept of aggression: an integrated summary. *Int. J. Psycho-anal.* 53:31–35.

Henderson, D., and Batchelor, I. R. C. (1962). *Henderson and Gillespie's Textbook of Psychiatry,* 9th ed. London: Oxford University Press.

Henderson, Sir David, and Gillespie, R. D. (1950). *A Text-Book of Psychiatry,* 7th ed. London: Oxford University Press.

Hendrick, Ives (1943). Work and the pleasure principle. *Psychoanal. Quart.* 12: 311–29.

Herold, Carl M. (1941). Critical analysis of the elements of psychic functions, Part 1. *Psychoanal. Quart.* 10:513–44.

Heron, M. J. (1965). A note on the concept endogenous-exogenous. *Brit. J. Med. Psychol.* 38:241–45.

Hill, Sir Denis (1968). Depression: disease, reaction or posture. *Amer. J. Psychiat.* 125:445–57.

Hill, O. W., and Price, J. S. (1967). Childhood bereavement and adult depression. *Brit. J. Psychiat.* 113:743–51.

Hoch, August (1921). *Benign Stupors.* New York: MacMillan.

———— and Kirby, George H. (1919). A clinical study of psychoses characterized by distressed perplexity. *Arch. Neurol. and Psychiat.* 1:415–58.

———— and MacCurdy, John T. (1922). The prognosis of involutional melancholia. *Arch. Neurol. and Psychiat.* 7:1–37.

Hoch, Paul, and Polatin, Philip (1949). Pseudoneurotic forms of schizopohrenia. *Psychiat. Quart.* 28:248–76.

———— and Rachlin, H. L. (1941). An evaluation of manic-depressive psychosis in the light of follow-up studies. *Amer. J. Psychiat.* 97:831–43.

Hoche, A. (1910). Quoted in Lewis, Aubrey (1934a).

Hollister, Leo E. (1973). *Clinical Use of Psychotherapeutic Drugs.* Springfield: Charles C. Thomas.

Holt, Robert R. (1965). A review of some of Freud's biological assumptions and their influence on his theories. In N. S. Greenfield and W. C. Lewis, eds., *Psychoanalysis and Current Biological Thought* Madison: University of Wisconsin Press, pp. 93–124.

———— (1967a). Beyond vitalism and mechanism: Freud's concept of psychic energy. In J. H. Masserman, ed., *Science and Psychoanalysis,* 11. New York: Grune and Stratton, pp. 1–41.

_____ (1967b). Ed., *Motives and Thought: Psychoanalytic Essays in Honor of David Rapaport.* Psychological Issues, Nos. 18/19. New York: International Universities Press.

Home H. J. (1966). The concept of mind. *Int. J. Psycho-anal.* 47:42–49.

Hope, K. (1969). Book review of Kendell, R. E. (1968). In *Brit. J. Psychiat.*, 115: 731–741.

Hopkinson, Geoffrey (1964). A genetic study of affective illness in patients over 50. *Brit. J. Psychiat.* 110:244–54.

_____and Reed, G. F. (1966). Bereavement in childhood and depressive psychosis. *Brit. J. Psychiat.* 112:459–63.

Horney, Karen (1936). *The Neurotic Personality of Our Time.* New York: Norton.

Hudgens, Richard W., Morrison, James R., and Barchha, Ramnik G. (1967). Life events and onset of primary affective disorders. *Arch. Gen. Psychiat.* 16:134–45.

Jacobson, Edith (1946). The effect of disappointment on ego and superego formation in normal and depressive development. *Psychoanalyt. Rev.* 33:129–47.

_____(1953). Contribution to the metapsychology of cyclothymic depression. In Phyllis Greenacre, ed., *Affective Disorders.* New York: International Universities Press.

_____ (1954a). Transference problems in the psychoanalytic treatment of severely depressed patients. *J. Am. Psychoanal. Assn.* 2:595–606.

_____ (1954b). The self and the object world: vicissitudes of their infantile cathexes and their influences on ideational and affective development. *Psychoanal. Study Child* 9:75–127.

_____ (1954c). Contributions to the metapsychology of psychotic identifications. *J. Am. Psychoanal. Assn.* 2:239–62.

_____ (1957a). On normal and pathological moods. *Psychoanal. Study Child* 12: 73–113.

_____ (1957b). Denial and repression. *J. Am. Psychoanal. Assn.* 5:61–92. Also in Jacobson (1971), pp. 107–36.

_____ (1964). *The Self and the Object World.* New York: International Universities Press.

_____ (1971). *Depression.* New York: International Universities Press.

_____ (1973). The depressive personality. *Int. J. Psychiat.* 11:218–21.

Joffe, Walter G., and Sandler, Joseph (1965). Notes on pain, depression and individuation. *Psychoanal. Study Child* 20:394–424.

_____ (1967a). Some conceptual problems involved in the consideration of disorders of narcissism. *J. Child Psychother.* 2:56–66.

_____(1967b). On the concept of pain, with special reference to depression and psychogenic pain. *J. Psychosom. Res.* 11:69–75.

_____(1968). Comments on the psychoanalytic psychology of adaptation, with special reference to the role of affects and the representational world. *Int. J. Psycho-anal.* 49:445–54.

Jones, Ernest (1957). *Sigmund Freud: Life and Work, III.* London: Hogarth Press.

Jones, Robert O. (1949). Depressive reactions: their importance in clinical medicine. *Canad. M. A. J.* 60:44–48.

Joseph, Edward J. (1973). Aggression redefined—its adaptational aspects. *Psychoanal. Quart.* 42:197–213.

Kalinowsky, Lothar B. (1959). Convulsive shock treatment. In S. Arieti, ed., *American Handbook of Psychiatry*, II. New York:Basic Books, pp. 1499–520.

Kallman, Franz J. (1948). Genetics in relation to mental disorders. *J. Ment. Sc.* 94:250–57.

―――― (1953). *Heredity in Health and Mental Disorder.* New York: Norton.

Kardiner, Abram, Karush, Aaron, and Ovesey, Lionel (1959). A methodological study of Freudian theory: II. The libido theory. *J. Nerv. Ment. Dis.* 129:133–43.

Karno, Marvin, and Mandell, Arnold J. (1972). Autism and anaclitic depression: clinical loci for a counterintuitive neurochemical hypothesis. In J. H. Masserman, ed., *Science and Psychoanalysis: XXI. Research and Relevance* New York: Grune and Stratton, pp. 3–11.

Kaufman, Irving (1955). Three basic sources for pre-delinquent character. *Nerv. Child* 11:12–15.

―――― (1958). Relationship between therapy of children and superego development. In panel report on superego development and pathology in childhood. *J. Am. Psychoanal. Assn.* 6:540–51.

―――― and Heims, Lora (1958). The body image of the juvenile delinquent. *Am. J. Orthopsychiat.* 28:146–59.

―――― and Makkay, Elizabeth (1955). Paper read at annual meeting of American Orthopsychiatric Association.

Kaufman, M. Ralph (1937). Psychoanalysis in late life depressions. *Psychoanal. Quart.* 6:308–35.

Kay, D. W., Garside, J. R., Roy, J. R., and Beamish, Pamela (1969). "Endogenous" and "neurotic" syndromes of depression: a 5- to 7-year follow-up of 104 cases. *Brit. J. Psychiat.* 115:389–99.

Kaywin, Louis (1960). An epigenetic approach to the psychoanalytic theory of instincts and affects. *J. Am. Psychoanal. Assn.* 8:613–58.

Keeler, W. R. (1954). Children's reactions to the death of a parent. In Paul H. Hoch and Joseph Zubin, eds., *Depression.* New York: Grune and Stratton, pp. 109–20.

Kendell, R. E. (1968). *The Classification of Depressive Illness.* Maudsley Monograph No. 18. London: Oxford University Press.

―――― and Gourlay, Jane (1970a). The clinical distinction between psychotic and neurotic depressions. *Brit. J. Psychiat.* 117:257–60.

―――― and Gourlay, Jane (1970b). The clinical distinction between the affective psychoses and schizophrenia. *Brit. J. Psychiat.* 117:261–66.

Kennedy, F. (1944). The neuroses: related to the manic-depressive constitution. *Med. Clin. of N.A.* 28:452–66.

Kiloh, L. G., Andrews, G.,Neilson, M., and Bianchi, G. N. (1972). The relationship of the syndromes called endogenous and neurotic depression. *Brit. J. Psychiat.* 121:183–96.

Kiloh, L.G., and Ball, J. R. B. (1961). Depression treated with imipramine: a follow-up study. *Brit. Med. J.* ii:168–71.

Kiloh, L. G., Ball, J. R. B., and Garside, R. F. (1962). Prognostic factors in treatment of depressive states with imipramine. *Brit. Med. J.* i:1225–27.

Kiloh, L. G., and Garside, R. F. (1963). The independence of neurotic depression and endogenous depression. *Brit. J. Psychiat.* 109:451–63.

Kirby, G. H. *State Hosp. Bull.* 1:459, 1908–09. Quoted in Titley (1936).

Klein, Melanie (1932). *The Psychoanalysis of Children.* London: Hogarth Press and The Institute of Psychoanalysis.

―――― (1934). A contribution to the psychogenesis of manic-depressive states. In Klein (1948).

_____ (1940). Mourning and its relation to manic-depressive states. In Klein (1948).

_____ (1948). *Contributions to Psycho-Analysis, 1921–1945*. London: Hogarth Press and The Institute of Psycho-analysis.

_____, Heimann, Paula; Isaacs, Susan, and Riviere, Joan (1952). *Developments in Psycho-Analysis*. London: Hogarth Press.

Klerman, Gerald L. (1971). Clinical research in depression. *Arch. Gen. Psychiat.* 24:305–19.

Knight, Robert P. (1940). Introjection, projection and identification. *Psychoanal. Quart.* 9:334–41.

_____ (1953). Borderline states. *Bull. Menninger Clin.* 17:1–12.

Kohn, M. S., and Clausen, J. A. (1955). Social isolation and schizophrenia. *Am. Sociological Rev.* 20:265–73.

Korner, Anneliese F. (1964). Some hypotheses regarding the significance of individual differences at birth for later development. *Psychoanal. Study Child* 19:58–72.

Kraepelin, Emil (1894). Quoted in Meyer (1904b).

_____ (1902). *Clinical Psychiatry*. New York: Macmillan.

_____ (1913). *Psychiatrie: Ein Lehrbuch für Studiende und Artze: II. Klinische Psychiatrie*. Leipzig: Barth.

_____ (1921). *Manic-depressive Insanity and Paranoia*, transl. Mary Barclay. Edinburgh: E. and G. Livingstone.

_____ (1920). Quoted in Lewis, Aubrey (1934b).

Kraines, Samuel H. (1957). *Mental Depressions and Their Treatment*. New York: Macmillan Company.

Kretschmer, E. (1931). *Physique and Character*. New York: Harcourt, Brace.

Krupp, George R. (1962). The bereavement reaction. *Psychoanal. Study Society* 2:42–74.

Kubie, L. S. (1947). The fallacious use of quantitative concepts in dynamic psychology. *Psychoanal. Quart.* 16:507–18.

Kubie, Lawrence S. (1952). Problems and techniques of psychoanalytic validation and progress. In E. Pumpian-Mindlin, ed., *Psychoanalysis as Science*. Stanford: Stanford University Press.

_____ and Lewin, Bertram D. (1936). Footnotes to "An endocrine approach to psychodynamics" by R. G. Hoskins. *Psychoanal. Quart.* 5:87–107.

Kuhn, Roland (1958). The treatment of depressive states with G–22355 (imipramine hydrochloride). *Amer. J. Psychiat.* 115:459–64.

Kupfer, David J., Himmelhoch, Jonathan M., Swartzburg, Marshall, Anderson, Carol, Byck, Robert, and Detre, Thomas P. (1972). Hypersomnia in manic-depressive disease. *Dis. Nerv. System* 33:720–24.

Lambo, T. Adeoye (1956). Neuropsychiatric observations in the western region of Nigeria. *Br. Med. J.* ii:1388–94.

Lampl-De Groot, Jeanne (1953). Depression and aggression. In Rudolph M. Loewenstein, ed., *Drives, Affects, Behavior*. New York: International Universities Press.

_____ (1960). On adolescence. *Psychoanal. Study Child* 15:95–103.

_____ (1962). Ego ideal and the superego. *Psychoanal. Study Child* 17:94–106.

Lange, J. (1928). The endogenous and reactive affective disorders and the manic-depressive constitution. In Bumke, ed., *Handbook of Mental Diseases*, 6. Berlin.

Laufer, Moses (1966). Object loss and mourning during adolescence. *Psychoanal. Study Child* 21:269–93.

Lazare, Aaron, and Klerman, Gerald L. (1968). Hysteria and depression: the frequency and significance of hysterical personality features in hospitalized depressed women. *Amer. J. Psychiat.* 124(Suppl):48–56.

Leff, Melitta J., Roatch, John F., and Bunney, William E., Jr. (1970). Environmental factors preceding the onset of severe depressions. *Psychiatry* 33:293–311.

Lehmann, Heinz E. (1959). Psychiatric concepts of depression: nomenclature and classification. *Canad. Psychiat. Ass. J.* 4(Suppl.):1–12.

—— (1972). Discussion of Dr. Robin's paper. In Joseph Zubin and Fritz A. freyhan, eds., *Disorders of Mood*. Baltimore: The Johns Hopkins Press, pp. 46–49.

Leonhard, K. (1957). *Aufteilung der Endogenen Psychosen*, 1st ed. Berlin.

—— (1966). *Aufteilung der Endogenen Psychosen*, 3rd ed. Berlin.

Lesse, Stanley (1967). Hypochondriasis and psychosomatic disorders masking depression. *Amer. J. Psychother.* 21:607–20.

Levin, Sidney (1965). Some suggestions for treating the depressed patient. *Psychoanal. Quart.* 34:37–65.

—— (1966). Report, panel on depression and object loss. *J. Am. Psychoanal. Assn.* 14:142–53.

Lewin, Bertram D. (1930). Kotschmieren, Menses and Weibliches Ueberich. *Int. Ztschr. f. Psa.*, 16. Quoted in Lewin (1950).

—— (1950). *The Psychoanalysis of Elation*. New York: Norton.

Lewis, Aubrey (1934a). Melancholia: a historical review. *J. Ment. Sc.* 80:1–42.

—— (1934b). Melancholia: a clinical survey of depressive states. *J. Ment. Sc.* 80:277–378.

Lewis, Nolan D. C., and Hubbard, Lois D. (1931). The mechanisms and prognostic aspects of the manic-depressive-schizophrenic combinations. *Assn. for Research in Nervous and Mental Diseases* 11:471–538.

Lewis, Nolan D. C., and Piotrowski, Zygmunt (1954). Clinical diagnosis of manic-depressive psychosis. In Paul H. Hoch and Joseph Zubin, eds., *Depression*. New York: Grune and Stratton.

Lewis, William C. (1974). Hysteria: the consultant's dilemma. *Arch. Gen. Psychiat.* 30:145–51.

Lichtenstein, Heinz (1965). Towards a metapsychological definition of the concept of self. *Int. J. Psycho-anal.* 46:117–28.

Lindemann, Erich (1944). Symptomatology and management of acute grief. *Amer. J. Psychiat.* 101:141–48.

Lipkin, K. Michael, Dyrrud, Jarl, and Meyer, George G. (1970). The many faces of mania. *Arch. Gen. Psychiat.* 22:262–67.

Lipson, Channing T. (1963). Denial and mourning. *Int. J. Psycho-anal.*, 44:104–07.

Loevinger, J. (1959). A theory of test response. In *Invitational Conference on Testing Problems*. Princeton: Educational Testing Service.

Loewald, Hans W. (1971). On motivation and instinct theory. *Psychoanal. Study Child* 26:91–128.

Löfgren, L. Borje (1968). Report, panel on psychoanalytic theory of affects. *J. Am. Psychoanal. Assn.* 16:638–50.

Lorand, Sandor (1946). *Technique of Psychoanalytic Therapy*. New York: International Universities Press.

Lorand, Sandor (1967). Adolescent depression. *Int. J. Psycho-anal.* 48:53–60.

Lorenz, Konrad (1955). Discussion, in *Group Processes: Transactions of the First Conference*. New York: Josiah Macy, Jr., Foundation, p. 18.

Lowrey, Lawson (1940). Personality distortion and early institutional care. *Am. J. Orthopsychiat.* 10:576–85.

Lurie, Louise A., Tietz, Esther B., and Hertzmann, Jack (1936). Functional psychoses in children. *Amer. J. Psychiat.* 92:1169–84.

Lussier, André (1972). Report, panel on aggression. *Int. J. Psycho-anal.* 53:13–19.

McClary, Allen R., Meyer, Eugene, and Weitzman, Elliot L. (1955). Observations on the role of the mechanism of depression in some patients with disseminated lupus erythematosus. *Psychosom. Med.* 17:311–21.

McConaghy, N., Joffe, W. D., and Murphy, B. (1967). The independence of neurotic and endogenous depression. *Brit. J. Psychiat.* 113:479–84.

MacCurdy, John T. (1921). In editor's preface to Hoch (1921).

McHarg, James F. (1954). Mania in childhood. *A.M.A. Arch. Neurol. Psychiat.* 72: 531-39.

Mahler, Margaret G. (1952). On child psychosis and schizophrenia. *Psychoanal. Study Child* 8:286–306.

——— (1961). Sadness and grief in childhood. *Psychoanal. Study Child* 16:332–51.

——— (1966). Notes on the development of basic moods: the depressive affect. In R. M. Loewenstein, L. M. Newman, M. Schur and A. J. Solnit, eds., *Psychoanalysis—A General Psychology.* New York: International Universities Press, pp. 152–68.

Malamud, M., Sands, G. L., and Malamud, I. (1941): The involutional psychoses: A socio-psychiatric study. *Psychosom. Med.*, 3:410–426.

Mapother, E. (1926). Manic-depressive psychosis. *Brit. M. J.* 2:872–79.

Marris, P. (1958). *Widows and Their Families.* London: Routledge and Kegan Paul.

——— (in press). *Loss and Change.* London: Routledge

Martin, I., and Davies, B. M. (1962). Sleep thresholds in depression. *J. Ment. Sc.* 108:466–73.

Maudsley, Henry (1895). *The Pathology of Mind,* 3rd ed. Referred to in Lewis (1934a).

Mayer-Gross, W., Slater, Eliot, and Roth, Martin (1960). *Clinical Psychiatry,* 2nd ed. Baltimore: Williams and Wilkins.

Mendels, Joe (1965a). Electro-convulsive therapy and depression: I. The prognostic significance of clinical factors. *Brit. J. Psychiat.* 111:675–81.

——— (1965b). Electro-convulsive therapy and depression: II. Significance of endogenous and reactive syndromes. *Brit. J. Psychiat.* 111:682–86.

——— (1965c). Electro-convulsive therapy and depression: III. A method for prognosis. *Brit. J. Psychiat.* 111:687–90.

——— (1974). Biological aspects of affective illness. In *American Handbook of Psychiatry,* revised and expanded ed., 3:491–523.

——— and Cochrane, Carl (1968). The nosology of depression: the endogenous-reactive concept. *Amer. J. Psychiat.* 124(Suppl):1–11.

Mendelson, Myer (1964). Psychological aspects of obesity. *M. Clin. N.A.* 48:1373–85.

——— (1967). Neurotic depressive reaction. In Alfred M. Freedman and Harold I. Kaplan, eds., *Comprehensive Textbook of Psychiatry.* Baltimore: William and Wilkins, pp. 928–36.

——— and Stunkard, Albert J. (1964). Obesity and the body image. *Psychosom. Med.* (abstract) 26:638.

Mendlewicz, J., Fieve, R. R., Rainer, J. D., and Fleiss, J. L. (1972). Manic-depressive illness: a comparative study of patients with and without a family history. *Brit. J. Psychiat.* 120:523–30.

Meyer, Adolf (1895). A Review of the signs of degeneration and of methods of registration. In *The Collected Papers of Adolf Meyer*, II. Baltimore: The Johns Hopkins Press, 1951.

———— (1904a). A few trends in modern psychiatry. In *The Collected Papers of Adolf Meyer*, II. Baltimore: The Johns Hopkins Press, 1951.

———— (1904b): A review of recent problems of psychiatry. In *The Collected Papers of Adolf Meyer*, II. Baltimore: The Johns Hopkins Press, 1951.

———— (1908). The problems of mental reaction types. In *The Collected Papers of Adolf Meyer*, II. Baltimore: The Johns Hopkins Press, 1951.

———— (1916). Pathology of mental diseases. In *The Collected Papers of Adolf Meyer*, II. Baltimore: The Johns Hopkins Press, 1951.

———— (1921). Constructive formulation of schizophrenia. In *The Collected Papers of Adolf Meyer*, II. Baltimore: The Johns Hopkins Press, 1951.

Miller, Jill B. M. (1971). Children's reactions to the death of a parent: a review of the psychoanalytic literature. *J. Am. Psychoanal. Assn.* 19:697–719.

Modell, Arnold H. (1963). Report, panel discussion on the concept of psychic energy. *J. Am. Psychoanal. Assn.* 11:605–18.

Moebius, P. J. (1894). *Diagnostik der Nervenkrankheiten*. Leipzig: V. Vogel.

Morel, B. A. (1857). *Traité de Degenerescences Physiques, Intellectuelles et Morales de l'Espèce Humaine*. Paris: J. B. Bailliere.

Mowbray, Robert M. (1969). Classification of depressive illness. Correspondence. *Brit. J. Psychiat.* 115:1344–45.

———— (1973). The classification of depression. In Brian Davies, Bernard J. Carroll and Robert M. Mowbray, eds., *Depressive Illness: Some Research Studies*, Chapter 11. Springfield: Charles C. Thomas, pp. 261–77.

Munro, Alistair (1966). Parental deprivation in depressive patients. *Brit. J. Psychiat.* 112:443–57.

———— and Griffiths, A. B. (1969). Some psychiatric non-sequelae of childhood bereavement. *Brit. J. Psychiat.* 115:305–11.

Nacht, G., and Racamier, P. C. (1960). Symposium on depressive illness. II. Depressive states. *Int. J. Psycho-anal.* 41:481–96.

Nagera, Humberto (1970). Children's reactions to the death of important objects. *Psychoanal. Study Child* 25:360–400.

Nash, Harvey (1963). The role of metaphor in psychological theory. *Behavioral Science*, 8:336–45.

Nelson, Marie (1967). On the therapeutic redirection of energy and affects. *Int. J. Psycho-anal.* 48:1–15.

Nissl, F. (1902). Quoted in Meyer (1904a).

Novey, Samuel (1955). The role of the superego and ego ideal in character formation. *Int. J. Psycho-anal.*, 36:254–59.

Noyes, Arthur P. (1948). *Modern Clinical Psychiatry*, 3rd ed. Philadelphia: W. B. Saunders.

———— and Kolb, Lawrence C. (1963). *Modern Clinical Psychiatry*, 6th ed. Philadelphia: W. B. Saunders.

Nymgaard, Kirsten (1959). Studies on the sedation threshold. *Arch. Gen. Psychiat.* 1:530–36.

Oltman, Jane E., McGarry, John J., and Friedman, Samuel (1951). Parental deprivation and the "broken home" in dementia praecox and other mental disorders. *Amer. J. Psychiat.* 108:685–94.

Ostow, Mortimer (1962). *Drugs in Psychoanalysis and Psychotherapy.* New York: Basic Books.

Overall, John E. (1963). Dimensions of manifest depression. *J. Psychiat. Res.* 1:239–45.

Palmer, Harold D., and Sherman, Stephen H. (1938). The involutional melancholia process. *Arch. Neurol. and Psychiat.* 40:762–88.

Parens, Henri (1973). Aggression: a reconsideration. *J. Am. Psychoanal. Assn.* 21: 34–60.

Parkes, C. Murray (1964a). Recent bereavement as a cause of mental illness. *Brit. J. Psychiat.* 110:198–204.

———— (1964b). The effects of bereavement on physical and mental health: a study of the case records of widows. *Brit. Med. J.* 2:274–79.

———— (1971). The first year of bereavement: a longitudinal study of the reaction of London widows to the death of their husbands. *Psychiatry* 33:444–67.

———— (1972). *Bereavement.* New York: International Universities Press.

———— and Brown, R. J. (1972). Health after bereavement: a controlled study of young Boston widows and widowers. *Psychosom. Med.* 34:449–61.

Paykel, E. S. (1971). Classification of depressed patients: a cluster analysis derived grouping. *Brit. J. Psychiat.* 118:275–88.

Peck, Martin W. (1939). Notes on identification in a case of depression: reaction to the death of a love object. *Psychoanal. Quart.* 8:1–17.

Penrose, L. S. (1945). *Digest Neurol. Psychiat.* Quoted by Eliot Slater in G. W. T. H. Fleming, ed., *Recent Progress in Psychiatry.* London: J. & A. Churchill, 1950, pp. 1–28.

Perris, Carlo (1966). *A Study of Bipolar (Manic-Depressive) and Unipolar Recurrent Depressive Psychoses.* Acta Psychiat. Scand. (Suppl), 194.

Peterfreund, Emanuel (1971). *Information, Systems and Psychoanalysis.* Psychological Issues, Nos. 25/26. New York: International Universities Press.

Peto, Andrew (1972). Body image and depression. *Int. J. Psycho-anal.* 53:259–63.

Pilowsky, I., Levine, S.; and Boulton, D. M. (1969). The classification of depression by numerical taxomy. *Brit. J. Psychiat.* 115:937–45.

Pitts, Ferris, N., Jr., Meyer, Jay, Brooks, Michael, and Winokur, George (1965). Adult psychiatric illness assessed for childhood parental loss, and psychiatric illness in family members—a study of 748 patients and 250 controls. *Amer. J. Psychiat.* 121(Suppl.):i–x.

Poznanski, Elva, and Zrull, Joel P. (1970). Childhood depression. *Arch. Gen. Psychiat.* 23:8–15.

Pulver, Sydney E. (1970). Narcissism: the term and the concept. *J. Am. Psychoanal. Assn.* 18:319–41.

Rachlin, H. L. (1935). A follow-up of Hoch's benign stupor cases. *Amer. J. Psychiat.* 92:531–58.

———— (1937). A statistical study of benign stupor in five New York state hospitals. *Psychiat. Quart.* 11:436–44.

Rado, Sandor (1928). The problem of melancholia. *Int. J. Psycho-anal.* 9:420–38.

———— (1951). Psychodynamics of depression from the etiologic point of view. *Psychosom. Med.* 13:51–55.

Rank, Beata (1949). Aggression. *Psychoanal. Study Child* 3/4:43–48.

Rapaport, David (1957). A theoretical analysis of the superego concept. In Merton M. Gill, ed., *The Collected Papers of David Rapaport.* New York: Basic Books, 1967, pp. 685–709.

_____ (1059). Edward Bibring's theory of depression. In Merton M. Gill, ed., *The Collected Papers of David Rapaport*. New York: Basic Books, 1967, pp. 758–73.

_____ (1960). *The Structure of Psychoanalytic Theory. Psychol. Issues*, 6. New York: International Universities Press.

_____ (1967). In Merton M. Gill, ed., *The Collected Papers of David Rapaport* New York: Basic Books.

Redlich, Frederick C., and Freedman, Daniel X. (1966). *The Theory and Practice of Psychiatry*. New York: Basic Books.

Rees, W. D. (1970). *The Hallucinatory and Paranormal Reactions of Bereavement*. M.D. thesis.

Reich, Annie (1953). Narcissistic object choice in women. *J. Am. Psychoanal. Assn.* 1:22–44.

_____ (1954). Early identifications as archaic elements in the superego. *J. Am. Psychoanal. Assn.* 2:218–38.

_____ (1960). Pathologic forms of self-esteem regulation. *Psychoanal. Study Child* 15:215–32.

Reich, Wilhelm (1945). *Character-Analysis: Principles and Techniques for Psychoanalysts in Practise and in Training*, 2nd ed., transl. by Theodore P. Wolfe. New York: Orgone Institute Press.

Rennie, T. A. C. (1942). Prognosis in manic-depressive psychosis. *Amer. J. Psychiat.* 98:801–14.

Reynell, W. R. (1930). *Proc. Roy. Soc. Med.* 23:889–90.

Ribble, Margaret A. (1943). *The Rights of Infants: Early Psychological Needs and Their Satisfactions*. New York: Columbia University Press.

Rice, Katherine K. (1944). Regular 40- to 50-day cycle of psychotic behavior in a 14-year-old boy. *Arch. Neurol and Psychiat.* 51:478–80.

Rickman, John (1951). Methodology and research in psychopathology. *Br. J. M. Psychol.* 24:1–7.

Riddoch, G. (1930). Discussion on the diagnosis and treatment of the milder forms of the manic-depressive psychosis. *Proc. Roy. Soc. Med.* 23:886–87.

Rie, Herbert E. (1966). Depression in childhood: a survey of some pertinent contributions. *J. Amer. Acad. Child Psychiat.* 5:653–85.

Riviere, Joan (1936). A contribution to the analysis of negative therapeutic reaction. *Int. J. Psycho-anal.* 17:304–20.

Roberts, Julian M. (1959). Prognostic factors in the electro-shock treatment of depressive states. II. The application of specific tests. *J. Ment. Sc.* 105:703–13.

Robertson, James (1952). Film, *A Two-Year-Old Goes to Hospital*. London: Tavistock Child Development Research Unit. New York: New York University Film Library.

_____ (1953). Some responses of young children to the loss of maternal care. *Nurs. Times* 49:382–86.

_____ (1958a). Film, *Going to Hospital with Mother*. London: Tavistock Child Development Research Unit. New York: New York University Film Library.

_____ (1958b). *Young Children in Hospital*, 2nd ed. London: Tavistock, 1970.

_____ (1962). *Hospitals and Children: A Parent's-Eye View*. London: Gollancz.

_____ and Robertson, Joyce (1967–1973). Series of 5 films, *Young Children in Brief Separation*. London: Tavistock Institute of Human Relations. New York: New York University Film Library.

_____ and Robertson, Joyce (1971). Young children in brief separation: a fresh look. *Psychoanal. Study Child* 26:264–315.

Robins, Eli, Munoz, Rodrigo A., Martin, Sue, and Gentry, Kathye A. (1972). Primary and secondary affective disorders. In Joseph Zubin and Fritz A. Freyhan, eds., *Disorders of Mood* Baltimore: The Johns Hopkins Press, pp. 33–45.

Rochlin, Gregory (1953a). The disorder of depression and elation. *J. Am. Psychoanal. Assn.* 1:438–57.

———— (1953b). Loss and restitution. *Psychoanal. Study Child* 8:288–309.

———— (1959). The loss complex. *J. Am. Psychoanal. Assn.* 7:299–316.

Rogers, J. (1956). The menopause. *New Eng. J. Med.* 254:697–703, 750–56.

Rogerson, D. H. (1940). The differentiation of neuroses and psychoses with special reference to states of depression and anxiety. *J. Ment. Sc.* 86:632–44.

Root, Nathan N. (1957). A neurosis in adolescence. *Psychoanal. Study Child* 12: 320–34.

Rose, J. T. (1963). Reactive and endogenous depressions—response to E.C.T. *Brit. J. Psychiat.* 109:213–17.

Rosenblatt, Allan D., and Thickstun, James T. (1970). A study of the concept of psychic energy. *Int. J. Psycho-anal.* 5:265–78.

Rosenthal, David (1970). *Genetic Theory and Abnormal Behavior*. New York: McGraw-Hill.

Rosenthal, Saul H. (1968). The involutional depressive syndrome. *Amer. J. Psychiat.* 124(Suppl.):21–35.

———— and Gudeman, Jon E. (1967). The endogenous depressive pattern. *Arch. Gen. Psychiat.* 16:241–49.

———— and Klerman, Gerald L. (1966). Content and consistency in the endogenous depressive pattern. *Brit. J. Psychiat.* 112:471–84.

Roth, Martin (1959). The phenomenology of depressive states. *Canad. Psychiat. Assn. J.* (Special supplement on depressive and allied states) 4:32–52.

Rubinfine, David L. (1968). Notes on a theory of depression. *Psychoanal. Quart.* 37:400–17.

Rubinstein, Benjamin B. (1965). Psychoanalytic theory and the mind-body problem. In N.S. Greenfield and W.C. Lewis, eds., *Psychoanalysis and Current Biological Thought*. Madison: University of Wisconsin Press, pp. 35–56.

———— (1967). Explanation and mere description: a metascientific explanation of certain aspects of the psychoanalytic theory of motivation. In Holt (1967b).

Ryle, Gilbert (1949). *The Concept of Mind.* New York: Barnes and Noble.

Sachar, E. J. (1967a). Corticosteroids in depressive illness: a re-evaluation of control issues and the literature. *Arch. Gen. Psychiat.* 17:544–53.

———— (1967b). Corticosteroids in depressive illness: a longitudinal psychoendocrine study. *Arch. Gen. Psychiat.* 17:554–67.

———— (1973). Endocrine factors in psychopathological states. In J. Mendels, ed., *Biological Psychiatry.* New York: John Wiley and Sons, pp. 175–97.

Sandifer, Myron G., Wilson, Ian C., and Green, Linda (1966). The two-type thesis of depressive disorders. *Amer. J. Psychiat.* 123:93–97.

Sandler, Joseph (1960a). The background of safety. *Int. J. Psycho-anal.* 41:352–56.

———— (1960b). On the concept of superego. *Psychoanal. Study Child* 15:128–62.

————, Holder, Alex, and Meers, Dale (1963). The ego ideal and the ideal self. *Psychoanal. Study Child* 18:139–58.

———— and Joffe, Walter G. (1965). Notes on childhood depression. *Int. J. Psychoanal.* 46:88–96.

———— and Joffe, Walter G. (1969). Towards a basic psychoanalytic model. *Int. J. Psycho-anal.* 50:79–90.

———— and Rosenblatt, Joseph (1962). The concept of the representational world. *Psychoanal. Study Child* 18:128–45.

Sarwer-Foner, Gerald J. (1966). A psychoanalytic note on a specific delusion of time in psychotic depression. *Canad. Psychiat. Assoc. J.* 11(Suppl.):221–28.

Schafer, Roy (1967). Ideals, the ego ideal, and the ideal self. In Holt (1967b).

———— (1968). *Aspects of Internalization.* New York: International Universities Press.

———— (1970). An overview of Heinz Hartmann's contributions to psychoanalysis. *Int. J. Psycho-anal.* 51:425–46.

———— (1972). Internalization: process or fantasy. *Psychoanal. Study Child* 27:411–36.

———— (1973). Action: its place in psychoanalytic interpretation and theory. *The Annual of Psychoanalysis*, 1 (in press).

Scharl, Adele E. (1961). Regression and restitution in object loss: clinical observations. *Psychoanal. Study Child* 16:471–80.

Schildkraut, Joseph J. (1965). The catecholamine hypothesis of affective disorders: a review of supporting evidence. *Amer. J. Psychiat.* 122:509–21.

Schmale, Arthur H., Jr. (1958). Relationship of separation and depression to disease. *Psychosom. Med.* 20:259–77A.

———— (1964) genetic view of affects: with special reference to the genesis of helplessness and hopelessness. *Psychoanal. Study Child* 19:287–310.

Schur, Max (1960). Discussion of Dr. John Bowlby's paper, "Grief and mourning in infancy and early childhood." *Psychoanal. Study Child* 15:63–84.

———— (1966). *The Id and the Regulatory Principles of Mental Functioning.* New York: International Universities Press.

Searles, Harold F. (1965). Review of Edith Jacobson's *The Self and the Object World* (1964). *Int. J. Psycho-anal.* 46:529–32.

Shagass, Charles, and Jones, Arthur L. (1958a). A neurophysiological test for psychiatric diagnosis: results in 750 patients. *Amer. J. Psychiat.* 114:1002–10.

———— and Kerenyi, Albert (1958b). The "sleep" threshold, a simple form of the sedation threshold for clinical use. *Can. Psychiat. Assn. J.* 3:101–09.

————, Naiman, James, and Milalik, Joseph (1956). An objective test which differentiates between neurotic and psychotic depression. *Arch. Neurol. & Psychiat.* 75:461–71.

Shambaugh, Benjamin (1961). A study of loss reactions in a seven-year-old. *Psychoanal. Study Child* 16:510–22.

Siggins, Lorraine D. (1966). Mourning: a critical review of the literature. *Int. J. Psycho-anal.*, 47:14–25.

Silverberg, William V. (1952). *Childhood Experience and Personal Destiny.* New York: Springer.

Smith, Joseph H. (1960). The metaphor of the manic-depressive. *Psychiatry*, 23:375–83.

———— (1971). Identificatory styles in depression and grief. *Int. J. Psycho-anal.* 52:259–66.

Solnit, Albert J. (1970). A study of object loss in infancy. *Psychoanal. Study Child* 25:257–72.

———— (1972). Aggression: a view of theory building in psychoanalysis. *J. Am. Psychoanal. Assn.* 6:435–50.

Sperling, Melitta (1959). Equivalents of depression in children. *J. Hillside Hosp.* 8:138–48.

Spiegel, Leo A. (1959). The self, the sense of self, and perception. *Psychoanal. Study Child* 14:81–109.

———— (1966). Affects in relation to self and object. *Psychoanal. Study Child* 21: 69–92.

Spitz, René A. (1946). Anaclitic depression. *Psychoanal. Study Child* 2:313–41.

———— (1953). Aggression: its role in the establishment of object relations. In Rudolph M. Loewenstein, ed., *Drives, Affects, Behavior.* New York: International Universities Press.

———— (1960). Discussion of Dr. John Bowlby's paper, "Grief and mourning in infancy and early childhood." *Psychoanal. Study Child* 15:85–94.

Stenback, A. (1963). On involutional and middle age depressions. *Acta Psychiat. Scand.* 39(Suppl.) 169:14–32.

Stengel, E. (1945). A study on some clinical aspects of the relationship between obsessional neurosis and psychotic reaction types. *J. Ment. Sc.* 91:166–87.

———— (1948). Some clinical observations on psychodynamic relationship between depression and obsessive-compulsive symptoms. *J. Ment Sc.* 94:650–52.

Stenstedt, Ake (1952). A study in manic-depressive psychoses. *Acta Psychiat. Neurol. Scand.* 79(Suppl.).

Stone, Leo (1971). Reflections on the psychoanalytic concept of aggression. *Psychoanal. Quart.* 40:195–244.

Strachey, James. Ed., Standard Edition of Sigmund Freud's Works. London: Hogarth Press.

Strauss, E. B. (1930). *Proc. Roy. Soc. Med.* 23:894–95.

Strongin, E. L., and Hinsie, L. E. (1939). A method for differentiating manic-depressive depressions from other depressions by means of parotid secretions. *Psychiat. Quart.* 13:697–704.

Stunkard, Albert J. (1957). The "dieting depression." *Am. J. Med.* 23:77–86.

Stunkard, A. J., and Mendelson, Myer (1961). Disturbances in the body image of some obese persons. *J. Am. Dietet. Assn.* 38:328–31.

Sullivan, Harry Stack (1947). *Conceptions of Modern Psychiatry.* Washington: The William Alanson White Psychatric Foundation.

———— (1953). *The Interpersonal Theory of Psychiatry.* New York: Norton.

Taft, Jessie (1958). *Otto Rank.* New York: Julian Press.

Taylor, Michael A., and Abrams, Richard (1973). The phenomenology of mania. *Arch. Gen. Psychiat.* 29:520–22.

Teja, J. G., Narang, R. L., and Aggarwal, A. K. (1971). Depression across cultures. *Brit. J. Psychiat.* 119:253–60.

Thomson, Kay C., and Hendrie, Hugh C. (1972). Environmental stress in primary depressive illness. *Arch. Gen. Psychiat.* 26:130–32.

Titley, W. B. (1936). Prepsychotic personality of patients with involutional melancholia. *Arch. Neurol. and Psychiat.* 36:19–33.

Toolan, James M. (1962). Depression in children and adolescents. *Amer. J. Orthopsychiat.* 32:404–15.

Tredgold, R. F. (1941). Depressive states in the soldier. *Brit. M. J.* 2:109–12.

Van Ophuijsen, J. H. W. (1920). On the origin of the feeling of persecution. *Int. J. Psycho-anal.* 1. Quoted in Lewin (1950).

Venkoba, Rao A. (1966). Depression—a psychiatric analysis of thirty cases. *Indian J. Psychiat.* 8:143–54.

Waelder, Robert (1936). The principle of multiple function. *Psychoanal. Quart.* 5:45–62.

———— (1956). Critical discussion of the concept of an instinct of destruction. *Bull. Phil. Assn. Psychoanal.* 6:97–109.

———— (1960). *Basic Theory of Psychoanalysis.* New York: International Universities Press.

———— (1966). Adaptional view ignores "drive." *Int. J. Psychiat.* 2:569–75.

Watts, C. A. H. (1947). Endogenous depression in general practice. *Brit. M. J.,* 1:11–14.

Werner, Heinz (1940). *Comparative Psychology of Mental Development.* New York: Folett.

Wetmore, Robert J. (1963). The role of grief in psycho-analysis. *Int. J. Psychoanal.* 44:97–103.

White, Robert W. (1963). *Ego and Reality in Psychoanalytic Theory.* Psychological Issues, No. 11. New York: International Universities Press.

Whitehorn, John C. (1939). Physiological changes in emotional states. *Assn. for Research in Nervous and Mental Diseases,* 19:256–70.

———— (1952). Psychodynamic approach to the study of psychoses. In Franz Alexander and Helen Ross, eds., *Dynamic Psychiatry,* Chapter IX. Chicago: University of Chicago Press.

———— (1953). Chairman, Editorial Board, 1952 Conference on Psychiatry Education. *The Psychiatrist, His Training and Development.* Washington: American Psychiatric Association.

———— (1955): *Psychiatric Education and Progress.* Salmon Lecture. Unpublished.

Whybrow, P. C., and Mendels, J. (1969). Toward a biology of depression: some suggestions from neurophysiology. *Amer. J. Psychiat.* 125:1491–500.

Wilson, Ian C., Alltop, Lascoe B., and Buffaloe, W. J. (1967). Parental bereavement in childhood: MMPI profiles in a depressed population. *Brit. J. Psychiat.* 113:761–64.

Winnicott, Donald W. (1954). The depressive position in normal emotional development. In Winnicott (1958), pp. 262–77.

———— (1958). *Collected Papers.* London: Hogarth Press.

Winokur, George (1972). Depression spectrum disease: description and family study. *Comp. Psychiat.* 13:3–8.

———— (1973). Diagnostic and genetic aspects of affective illness. *Psychiat. Annals* 3:6–15.

————, Cadoret, Remi, Dorzab, Joe, and Baker, Max (1971). Depressive disease: a genetic study. *Arch. Gen. Psychiat.* 24:135–44.

———— and Clayton, Paula (1967). Family history studies: I. Two types of affective disorders separated according to genetic and clinical factors. In Joseph Wortis, ed., *Recent Advances in Biological Psychiatry,* IX. New York: Plenum Press.

————, Clayton, Paula J., and Reich, Theodore (1969). *Manic Depressive Illness.* Saint Louis: C. V. Mosby.

———— and Pitts, Ferris N., Jr. (1964). Affective disorder: I. Is reactive depression an entity? *J. Nerv. Ment. Dis.* 138:541–47.

———— and Pitts, Ferris N., Jr. (1965). Affective disorder: V. The diagnostic validity of depressive reactions. *Psychiat. Quart.* 39:727–28.

————, Reich, Theodore, Rimmer, John, and Pitts, Ferris N., Jr. (1970). Alcoholism: III. Diagnosis and familial psychiatric illness in 259 alcoholic probands. *Arch. Gen. Psychiat.* 23:104–11.

Wolfenstein, Martha (1966). How is mourning possible? *Psychoanal. Study Child* 21:93–123.

_____ (1969). Loss, rage and repetition. *Psychoanal. Study Child* 24:432–60.

Woodruff, Robert A., Jr., Murphy, George E., and Herjanic, Marijan (1967). The natural history of affective disorders. I. Symptoms of 72 patients at the time of index hospital admission. *J. Psychiat. Res.* 5:255–63.

Yap, P. M. (1965). Phenomenology of affective disorder in Chinese and other cultures. In de Reuck and Porter, eds., *Ciba Foundation Symposium on Transcultural Psychiatry.* Boston: Little, Brown.

Zetzel, Elizabeth R. (1953). The depressive position. In Phyllis Greenacre, ed., *Affective Disorders.* New York: International Universities Press.

_____ (1956). An approach to the reaction between concept and content in psychoanalytic theory. *Psychoanal. Study Child* 11:99–121. Reprinted in Zetzel (1970b).

_____ (1960). Introduction to symposium on depressive illness. *Int. J. Psycho-anal.* 41:476–80.

_____ (1970a). Concluding remarks of the moderator of "Discussion of 'Towards a basic psychoanalytic model.' " *Int. J. Psycho-anal.* 51:188–89.

_____ (1970b). *The Capacity for Emotional Growth.* New York: International Universities Press.

Zilboorg, Gregory (1933). Manic-depressive psychoses. In Sandor Lorand, ed., *Psycho-Analysis Today.* New York: Covici-Friede.

_____ (1941a). Ambulatory schizophrenia. *Psychiatry* 4:149–55.

_____ (1941b). *History of Medical Psychology.* New York: Norton.

Index